UNMAKING RUSSIA'S ABORTION CULTURE

POLICY T🌐 PRACTICE
Ethnographic Perspectives on Global Health Systems

SERIES EDITORS: Svea Closser, Emily Mendenhall, Judith Justice, & Peter J. Brown

Policy to Practice: Ethnographic Perspectives on Global Health Systems illustrates and provides critical perspectives on how global health policy becomes practice, and how critical scholarship can itself inform global public health policy. Policy to Practice provides a venue for relevant work from a variety of disciplines, including anthropology, sociology, history, political science, and critical public health.

For the Public Good: Women, Health, and Equity in Rural India, Patricia Antoniello
Delivering Health: Midwifery and Development in Mexico, Lydia Z. Dixon

Unmaking Russia's Abortion Culture

Family Planning and the Struggle for a Liberal Biopolitics

MICHELE RIVKIN-FISH

VANDERBILT UNIVERSITY PRESS
Nashville, Tennessee

Library of Congress Cataloging-in-Publication Data

Names: Rivkin-Fish, Michele R., author.
Title: Unmaking Russia's abortion culture : family planning and the
  struggle for a liberal biopolitics / Michele Rivkin-Fish.
Description: Nashville, Tennessee : Vanderbilt University Press, [2024] |
  Series: Policy to practice ; book 3 | Includes bibliographical
  references and index.
Identifiers: LCCN 2024011387 (print) | LCCN 2024011388 (ebook) | ISBN
  9780826506962 (paperback) | ISBN 9780826506979 (hardcover) | ISBN
  9780826506986 (epub) | ISBN 9780826506993 (pdf)
Subjects: LCSH: Family planning--Russia (Federation) | Birth
  control--Social aspects--Russia (Federation) | Abortion--Political
  aspects--Russia (Federation)
Classification: LCC HQ766.5.R9 R58 2024 (print) | LCC HQ766.5.R9
    (ebook)
  | DDC 344.04/1920947--dc23/eng/20240315
LC record available at https://lccn.loc.gov/2024011387
LC ebook record available at https://lccn.loc.gov/2024011388

Dedicated to the memory of Andrej A. Popov (1957–1995) and Henry P. David (1923–2009) and to all who struggle for reproductive health and justice

The poster says, "After the Ban on Abortion in the Soviet Union, Thousands of Women Were Killed by Criminal Abortions, but Fertility Did Not Rise. Will We Do This Again?" (*Povtorim?*)

Left-Fem protest, St. Petersburg, 2015.
Photo by Maria Rakhmaninova.

CONTENTS

ILLUSTRATIONS

Every child has the right to be wanted and loved.

—THE RUSSIAN ASSOCIATION OF FAMILY PLANNING

ACKNOWLEDGMENTS

In 1991, Andrej Popov introduced me to the issues discussed in this book and invited me to collaborate with him. He included support for me in a grant he won from the MacArthur Foundation and also introduced me to Henry David, whose work on abortion worldwide became a touchstone for this project. This book aims to honor their legacies and those of the many other reproductive health activists dedicated to rights, justice, and the importance of addressing history and culture in public health strategies.

It was from friends in Russia, and Russian-speaking friends around the world, that I grew attuned to the many ways of expressing care. I am indebted to them for these valuable gifts, which made this book—and much more in my life—possible. From the first time I undertook research in Russia in 1993, Lenya Shtutin has welcomed me to Saint Petersburg with great warmth. Sasha Tolkacheva gave me a home away from home and patiently put up with my workaholism. Natasha and Liuba have been family to me since 1993, and I'm immensely grateful for all their love and support. Viktor Samokhvalov taught me so much about the themes in this book and much more; he holds a very special place in my heart. Anna Temkina, Zhanna Chernova, Maya Rusakova, Larisa Shpakovskaya, Oksana Karpenko, Veronika Odinokova, and Elena Zdravomyslova have been wonderful colleagues and friends in Piter; their work has profoundly impacted both the intellectual development of this project and my personal growth.

In Moscow, Andrej Popov led me to Sergei Zakharov, Galya Rakhmaninova, and Lena Zakharova, whose contributions to this project and my life are immeasurable. Sergei introduced me to the world of demographic expertise and introduced me to people and research that became foundational for this study. Galya and Lena provided the warm and loving connections that are especially meaningful when so far from home. I am immensely grateful to Viktoria Sakevich and Boris Denisov for their great help locating difficult-to-find research materials and answering all my questions, and for their friendship. I thank Misha Denisenko for his insights about abortion, population processes, and Odesa—as well as his hospitality and kindness. I am extremely grateful to Lyubov Erofeeva for her steadfast commitment to reproductive rights and her openness to all my questions.

The ability to travel to Russia for archival and ethnographic research was made possible by the generous support of a 2013 IREX short-term travel grant and a UNC University Research Council Grant. Karen Petrone taught me how to do archival work and gave me the confidence to try it out.

Additional research and writing was supported by a 2013 UNC Institute for Arts and Humanities Fellowship, a 2016–17 Carolina Women's Center Faculty Scholar award, a Schwab Excellence Award, and a 2019 Lady Davis Visiting Fellowship at the Hebrew University of Jerusalem. I am so grateful to Michal Frenkel, Gili Hammer, Areej Sabbagh, and Nurit Stadler for welcoming me to the department of sociology and anthropology and to Otni Dror, Arie Kacowitz, and Timna Seligman for their hospitality in Israel. I have boundless appreciation for Michal Frenkel, Julia Lerner, Inna Leykin, Galia Plotkin Amrami, Guy Ravid, Guy Shalev, and their families for the many wonderful discussions in Tel Aviv and for teaching me all about the city's culture and politics.

A large part of the research for this book took place online, and I am highly fortunate to have had the extraordinary assistance of Kirill Tolpygo, who has been the most diligent and committed reference librarian one could ever hope for. I am forever grateful to Kirill, Boris Denisov, and Viktoria Sakevich for assisting me in obtaining the Soviet Minzdrav Prikaz No. 620-DSP of June 6, 1979. Being able to study Henry David's papers was the equivalent of discovering a treasure chest, and I wholeheartedly thank Tema David for her gracious welcome and information, and Julia Cleaver, librarian at Ipas, and Jessica Murphey, reference archivist at Harvard's Countway Library, for their enormous help. My thanks also go to my wonderful colleagues at UNC—Kobi Ariel, Karen Auerbach, Amy Bryant, Chad Bryant, Mara Buchbinder, Jocelyn Chua, Emily Curtin, Sian Curtis, Martha King, Radik Lapushin, Lauren Leve, Louise McReynolds, Don Raleigh, Graeme Robertson, Patricia Rosenmeyer, Aaliya Sadruddin, Barry Saunders, Stas Shvabrin, Mark Sorensen, Amanda Thompson, Jane Thrailkill, Eren Tsar, Ruth von Bernuth, and Rebecca Walker—for all they do to make UNC a fabulous community.

I am extremely grateful to the numerous colleagues who invited me to present my work in progress and provided feedback: the University of Bern; the University of Western Bohemia; the Havighurst Center of Russian Studies at Miami University; the Departments of Gender Studies and Sociology and Anthropology at Ben Gurion University; the John J. Reilly Center for Science, Technology, and Values at Notre Dame University; Ural Federal University; the Higher School of Economics in Moscow and Saint Petersburg; the European University of Saint Petersburg; the MIT-Russia program; the Hebrew University of Jerusalem; the Kennan Institute; Centre d'Études des Mondes Russe, Caucasien et Centre Européen (CERCEC), École des Hautes Études en Sciences Sociales; the Inter-University Consortium for Russian Studies at Tel Aviv University; and the Summer Research Laboratory, University of Illinois, Urbana-Champaign; at various meetings of the Association for Slavic, East European, and Eurasian Studies, and at UNC's Slavic, Eurasian, and East European Center's colloquium. I thank Alexandra Konovalova and Pavel Vasilyev from the Higher School of Economics for sharing their work on oral contraceptives research in the Soviet era with me and for collaborating on presentations at SciencePo, Paris, and the Higher School of Economics, Moscow.

For their very helpful feedback on my presentations and questions over the years, I kindly thank Maria Alexandrova, Zhanna Chernova, Boris Denisov, Michal Frenkel, Anna Geltzer, Igal Halfin, Emma Hrešanová, Anu Kumar, Ernie Light, Julia Lerner, Inna Leykin, Daria Litvina, Tomas Matza, Louise McReynolds, Paula Michaels, Joanna Mishtal, Dina Moyal, Anastasia Novkunskaya, Victoria Pardini, Karen Petrone, Sarah Phillips, Luisa Piart, Eugene Raikhel, Don Raleigh, Larissa Remennick, Natalia Roudakova, Rochelle Ruthchild, Viktoria Sakevich, Larisa Shpakovskaya, Veronika Siegl, Sabine Strasser, Alexandre Sumpf, Anna Temkina, Kirill Tolpygo, Silvia Tomášková, Elena Trubina, Sergei Zakharov, and Elena Zdravomyslova.

Yulia Gradskova, Anu Kumar, Julia Lerner, Inna Leykin, Liubochka, Anastasia Novkunskaya, Natalia Roudakova, and Anna Temkina kindly sent me materials related to this study, for which I'm extremely grateful.

For their awesome administrative support and friendship, I thank Irina Olenicheva, Katie Poor, Melanie Whisnant, and Megan McCall. My heartfelt gratitude goes to my superb research assistants, Katie Danis, Patience Daur, Sasha Deyneka, Jessica Glushkina, Sofya Olenicheva, Everette Oxrider, and Anastasia Zeegers, and to my editor Anne Menkens. For their heroic fortitude and support with a massive bibliographic reformatting adventure, I thank Iman Amadou and Madison Holt. I am very grateful to Zachary Gresham and Emily Mendenhall for believing in this project and helping usher it through the long process of getting it into print.

For their help improving my translations, I thank Gleb Finkelstein, Stella Finkelstein, Radik Lapushin, Irina Olenicheva, Galia Plotkin Amrami, Stanislav Shvabrin, and Kirill Tolpygo.

Several friends read one or more chapters, and I thank them greatly for their time, support, and astute feedback: Nancy Berkman, Ekaterina Borozdina, Maxine Eichner, Anna Geltzer, Shai Ginsburg, Ellen Harnick, Julie Hemment, Olga Kuminova, Julia Lerner, Inna Leykin, Daria Litvina, Tomas Matza, Galia Plotkin Amrami, Eugene Raikhel, Ziggy Rivkin-Fish, Anna Temkina, Jane Thrailkill, and Sergei Zakharov. Olga Shevchenko and two anonymous reviewers read the entire manuscript and gave extraordinarily helpful, detailed feedback which significantly improved this book.

Ongoing conversations with Michal Frenkel, Julie Hemment, Anu Kumar, Julia Lerner, Elena Trubina, and Sergei Zakharov about the themes in this book have been profoundly important in inspiring me, helping lift my confusion, and coming to a semblance of clarity.

Debbie Barrett, Jon Farber, Jehanne Gheith, Elyza Halev, Michele Lynn, Irina Olenicheva, Jeff Spinner HaLev, and Jonathan Weiler provided much-appreciated support and friendship. Debbey Altman-Diamant, Bonnie Chernin, Jen Feldman, Galia Plotkin Amrami, Anu Kumar, Lew Margolis, and Mina Silberberg stuck it out with me during difficult moments and celebrated with me at hopeful ones. I thank my parents, Betty and Neil Noble and Jerry and Barbara Miller, and my brother and sister-in-law, Jason and Lita Miller, for all their wonderful support. To Ziggy, I am full of the deepest gratitude for his enduring love and understanding, fantastic computer skills, and research support extraordinaire. I also thank Sophie, Itai and Janae, and Dexter for their love, patience, encouragement, and firm belief that one day, this project would truly be finished.

Note on Transliterations

In general, this book follows the Library of Congress transliteration system from Cyrillic. If an alternative transliteration has been used in a publication, I cite the published version. I also use the conventional spelling of terms Russian commonly used in English (e.g., Glasnost instead of Glasnost').

Abbreviations

IPPF: International Planned Parenthood Federation
PS: *Planirovanie sem'i*, Family Planning: International Medical Journal
MINZDRAV: Ministerstvo Zdravookhraneniia, Ministry of Health
OCs: Oral Contraceptives
RAFP: Russian Association of Family Planning
RAPD: Russian Association of Population and Development

PREFACE

Russia's full-scale invasion of Ukraine on February 24, 2022, which expanded the aggressive war it had been fighting in the Donbas since 2014, shocked the world in its imperialism and brutality. While this book does not examine Russian-Ukrainian relations, the war is a symptom of broader struggles that Russian elites have been waging since the end of the Soviet Union and that my book does address: the desire to re-establish the country's geopolitical power and contest Western hegemony. Russian elites have long viewed fertility decline as symbolic of national and moral weakness, making policies and cultural discourses about population a major political preoccupation. In particular, conservatives and nationalists have emphasized the need for higher fertility as an urgent state interest. At the same time, public health efforts to decrease abortions and promote contraceptives involved liberalizing changes to state policy and expertise, to gender relations and family. In the 1990s, Western organizations supported these changes, along with related transitions away from Soviet governance. This book traces the rise of Russia's first family-planning institutions, revealing the specific kinds of liberal values contraceptive proponents endorsed. It also traces these organizations' demise, as Russian nationalists discredited, de-funded, and dismantled them in the name of demographic and sexual sovereignty. Exploring Russian reproductive health politics helps us understand a key domestic terrain where the country's illiberal seedlings ripened into belligerence and violence.[1]

Just months after Russia's invasion of Ukraine, in June 2022, the US Supreme Court overturned *Roe v. Wade*, the decision that had established abortion as a private matter for women to make decisions about in consultation with their doctor. While this disturbing change had been a long time coming, it surprised many because the right to privacy from state interference in intimate matters and related advocacy for abortion as matters of "choice," bodily autonomy, and women's equality reflect deeply held American values. I had long conceptualized this project as a study of what happens when legal abortion is not justifiable through these liberal concepts: in the Soviet Union, abortion had been the most accessible form of birth control available and was used routinely. But women described it as symbolizing their pervasive "lack of choice."[2] Given the deficit of effective contraceptive devices, they were unable to effectively prevent unwanted pregnancies; provided with abysmal housing conditions, they felt unable to raise a(nother) child. The routine use of abortion in conditions marked by deprivation shaped the debates surrounding this practice in the late Soviet and post-Soviet eras, even when its use fell dramatically. A key argument inspiring me to write this book was the need for "pro-choice" and reproductive rights frameworks to be amended in order to resonate with Russian, and presumably other, global contexts. With the dismantling of *Roe* and resulting bans on abortion in numerous states, questions about the erosion of liberal values and growing illiberal modes of governance in the US itself have gained urgency. In dialogue with progressive critics of the pro-choice movement who embrace the reproductive justice framework, *Unmaking Russia's Abortion Culture* explores what a global view can teach us about the significance of incorporating cultural diversity and attention to care in campaigns for reproductive rights.

A Few Words about Origins

The seeds of this project were sown amid another set of historical thresholds—the hopeful reconciliation between Soviet and American societies inaugurated by Gorbachev's Glasnost. In September 1991, during my first month of graduate training for a PhD in anthropology, I learned that in the Soviet context, politically progressive reproductive politics treated abortion as a moral problem for society. In contrast to my own understanding of abortion as a woman's right under attack in the name of moral absolutism, abortion in the Soviet Union had been the most widely available form of fertility control since its (re)legalization in 1955. Given the deficit of effective contraceptives, many women relied on abortion and experienced it as a routine, loathsome procedure. Even when effective contraceptives became available in the early 1990s, many Russian professionals, political actors, and lay persons were wary of contraceptives due to questions about safety and their impact on fertility rates. This counterintuitive situation inspired me to explore the meanings abortion and contraceptives had acquired in Soviet society. Committed to cultural anthropology's project of uncovering the limits of Western (American) assumptions for understanding others' lives, I sought to explain how and why a quest to promote family planning as a means of "fighting abortion" had become a highly controversial, politicized project.

Over the following two decades, I continued observing Russia's politics of abortion and reproduction with an eye toward historical and cultural differences between post-socialist and Western societies. With abortion increasingly stigmatized as a "Soviet throwback" by conservative and progressive Russian advocates alike, I saw how the Western defense of abortion as a liberating "choice" made little sense in this context. With Russian Orthodox Church leaders pushing for criminalization, and political leaders aiming to raise Russia's fertility, it seemed crucial to understand the particular logics that Russians who were concerned with keeping abortion legal and accessible were devising. I framed my research as explaining the specific cultural strategies that resonated for defending abortion access and promoting contraceptive use in this unfamiliar and increasingly hostile conflict. In short, I argued that, to be persuasive, feminist strategies needed to address specific concerns of local political culture—characterized in Russia by pervasive demographic and nationalist anxieties.

In 2012 I decided to write a book-length monograph historicizing the Soviet and post-Soviet "fight against abortion" through the promotion of contraceptive habits. By that time, Russian conservatives had succeeded in establishing the first restrictions on abortion since the Stalin era—virtually eliminating access to second trimester abortions—and were now pushing hard for limiting access in the first trimester. The most pressing question, it seemed, was how to successfully legitimize liberal concepts of women's bodily autonomy when the nation's future was deemed in jeopardy due in part to low fertility? Concurrently, tens of thousands of urban Russians had been taking to the streets to protest fraudulent elections, met in response by violent state repression. In both these protests and the campaign for family planning I saw Russians striving to apply and improvise with aspects of liberal political thought in their increasingly nationalist and repressive context. In the US, too, activists were critiquing the failures of classic liberal political ideas such as individual autonomy and the private sphere to adequately foster gender equality and reproductive justice. What might learning about the Russian experience offer global reproductive rights activists? Worried that Russia would ban abortion, I did not expect that it would happen first in the US. My interest in tracing the eroding sway of liberal values in Russia, unfortunately, has thus gained global relevance.

The war, the Western sanctions against Russia that followed, and Putin's repression of protests brought the "post-Soviet era" to a violent, horrifying end. Although I conceived of this project as a genealogy of the present through abortion and contraceptive politics, the abrupt changes of 2022 make it more appropriate to describe this as a study of Russian eras past. The atrocities committed by Russia's military—grave events that continue to unfold as of this writing—are destroying Ukrainian lives and infrastructures. The Russian military's bombing of apartment buildings with unarmed residents and civilian infrastructures including maternity hospitals, and widespread raping of women and girls—many of whom are native Russian speakers—all expose Putin's biopolitics of pronatalism as a cynical campaign to control women's bodies. Perpetrated partly in response to nationalist concerns about increasing Russia's population, this war presents a painful irony: tens of thousands of Russian soldiers have been killed and even more highly educated young Russian professionals have emigrated. Among those who remain, political and economic uncertainty may lead women to rethink bringing new life into this world. The reckless drive to forcibly colonize Ukraine and incorporate its people into the Russian Federation cannot strengthen Russia's demographic trends or societal well-being.

Amid an unprovoked war of aggression, this book's critical exploration of Russian hopes to rejoin the global scientific community, rationalize family formation, cultivate respect for persons, and re-enchant interpersonal relations can no longer be read as a call for present and near-future action. Instead, sadly, it presents an account of fragile opportunities that currently appear lost. I hope that understanding the particular kinds of humanistic approaches to reproductive health that Russian liberals envisioned and promoted—and the severe and shifting obstacles they sought to overcome—may provide observers and participants with the historically and culturally informed awareness necessary for successful collaborations when renewing global ties becomes possible.

Through the Looking Glass

"I hate a state that has the death penalty, I hate a world in which abortions are convenient. It's a difficult, stupid male world in which for stealing a wallet you get a sentence of ten years, and for an abortion—three days off work in the hospital. This world is organized in such a way that it's simpler to kill than to raise a person. I hate this world, but today it is stronger than me, it is even inside me. . . . And I sit and I wait, in compliance with this world's hierarchy . . . and the instinct of self-preservation will triumph in me over the maternal instinct."[1]

Maria Arbatova, one of the few Russian public figures who has persistently drawn attention to women's issues, included these reflections in her 1997 memoir, *Menia zovut zhenshchina* (My name is woman). Recalling her younger self awaiting an abortion, Arbatova decried the social conditions motivating her decision while admitting that the harsh reality in which she lived overpowered her ideals. This reality was that state socialism had promised but failed to establish the conditions for human well-being and care.

Abortion was the most common method of fertility control in the Soviet Union. On average, Soviet women had approximately four abortions over their reproductive lifetime, although stories abound of women who had many, many more.[2] From 1955 and through the 1980s, Russia had more than twice the number of abortions as live births. Arbatova's account captures the melancholy but resigned conclusion of many women facing unwanted pregnancies: abortion provided an unpleasant solution in a world full of unsatisfying compromises. For Arbatova, talking publicly about women's experiences of routine abortions was an important step in changing post-Soviet Russia for the better. Proudly calling herself a "feminist" when most Russians consider that label an obscenity, Arbatova tried to channel her values about women and care into creating social change. She became a democratic political activist and a TV talk show host for the program *Ya sama* (I myself) during the Yeltsin era, introducing discourses celebrating women's individual agency.

Yet from a liberal, Euro-American perspective on abortion, Arbatova's feminism is unfamiliar. Whereas a typical US feminist might align abortion with empowerment, Arbatova laments her society's "convenient" (that is, opportunistic and apathetic) approach to abortion. While pro-choice women in the US might agonize over terminating a pregnancy, Arbatova does not; instead of considering it a personal moral dilemma, she recognizes her decision as a symptom of society's failures to support the lifelong work of nurturance. Arbatova condemns the social order that makes ending a pregnancy—which she equates here with committing violence—easier than providing care for children and women's health. In short, she is promoting a liberal culture of societal nurture rather than an individualist, American-style liberal ethos.

In this respect, Arbatova's women-centered critique resembles the US reproductive justice movement established by women of color in the 1990s. Both emphasize that an individual right to abortion is secondary to the core project of establishing broad socioeconomic conditions for enabling reproduction, childrearing, and human flourishing.[3] Yet Arbatova's perspectives were inspired by very different circumstances. Unlike in the US, abortion had been legalized by the Bolsheviks in 1920, just after the establishment of the Union of Soviet Socialist Republics. Stalin criminalized abortion in 1936, hoping thereby to raise fertility. In 1955 it was made legal again—not on the basis of liberal values such as autonomy or "choice," but pure pragmatics: to stem the disastrous mortality caused by illegal abortions. But the centrally controlled Soviet economy did not provide adequate contraceptive supplies (and neither did it acknowledge its failure and encourage nontechnological modes of preventing unwanted pregnancy). In the absence of effective alternatives, abortion remained a dreadful procedure that women routinely endured. Conceiving unwanted pregnancies because of unreliable or inaccessible birth control, terminating pregnancies because of unreliable husbands or immiserating living conditions, Soviet women described abortion as a symptom of (and not a solution to) their pervasive "lack of choice."[4]

The apparent paradox of Arbatova's Russian feminism—that a critique of the normalization of abortion can co-exist with unquestioning support for the procedure's legality and accessibility—animates this study. Understanding this paradox requires entering a "looking-glass" world that challenges many basic Western assumptions about both reproductive politics and the sensibilities of self-defined Russian liberals.[5] Centering on Russian professionals' efforts to replace routine abortion with contraceptive use, this book reveals their struggle to establish liberal changes in public policies, health care institutions, and civic discourses from the late Soviet 1950s until Russia's invasion of Ukraine in February 2022. We will explore the specific way I conceptualize liberalism in this study shortly; for now, it is notable that Russian debates over how to reduce abortion have reflected an enduring tension between prioritizing state-centered concerns with increasing fertility on the one hand, and prioritizing women's health and individual goals as a means of strengthening population dynamics on the other. This lens thus challenges Euro-American expectations of what it means to fight for reproductive rights, and what women's empowerment looks like, by bringing into focus Soviet and post-Soviet biopolitical goals and their differences from Western-style liberal biopolitics.[6] Russia's politics of reproduction, in terms of the governance of both individual bodies and population dynamics, embodies the broader contest between statist, nationalist, and liberal orientations shaping the first three post-Soviet decades.

To begin to understand these dynamics, it is necessary to understand some basics about contraception and abortion in Russia's twentieth and twenty-first centuries. The terms *pro-choice* and *pro-life* were not salient in the Soviet or first post-Soviet decades. Citizens did not lobby for changes to abortion's legality and wide availability. For the staunchly atheistic Soviet regime there were no moral qualms over an embryo/fetus as a "soul" or abortion as "murder." State planners and health providers were both officially "against" the use of abortion because they wanted women to give birth to more babies. During the Soviet era, many interpreted abortion as representing concerns with personal comforts over collective interests, a trend they believed would weaken the state and society. Soviet reproductive health experts continually engaged in ineffective campaigns to "fight abortion," even as they took for granted abortion's routine use for limiting childbearing. Where experts differed among themselves was in their specific tactics. While the predominant approach urged women seeking abortions to continue their pregnancy and give birth, some experts encouraged contraceptive use. Although their strategies developed over time, contraceptive supporters consistently valued women's health over state pronatalism. I thus characterize their efforts as promoting a liberalizing mode of governing reproductive health.

With the introduction of market reforms, Western pharmaceutical companies flooded former socialist economies with all manner of contraceptives.

Russian family planning proponents mobilized to educate clinicians and the public about modern, safe, and effective technologies for preventing unwanted pregnancy. Although until 2007 the number of abortions consistently surpassed the numbers of births, the use of abortions steadily declined as contraceptives grew in popularity.[7] In 1992 there were 89 abortions per 1,000 women aged 15 to 49; by 2018 this rate was down to 12, a decrease of approximately 7.4 times.[8] While 2021 still saw a ratio of approximately 37 abortions for every 100 live births (meaning that about 27 percent of all pregnancies were terminated), this ratio was dramatically lower than it had ever been since abortion trends were recorded following the procedure's re-legalization in 1955. Still, over the same decades campaigns to restrict abortion access became vociferous.[9]

This book calls on global health and reproductive rights activists to reflect on the case of Soviet and post-Soviet Russia. Typically, global reproductive health work focuses on developing world contexts where high fertility is accompanied by high levels of infant and maternal mortality and women's subordination under patriarchy. Less work has focused on contraceptives and reproductive health in the socialist contexts of Eastern Europe and the former Soviet Union, where literacy is universal, health infrastructure is developed, and fertility is very low.[10] Yet family planning and gender politics in this region hold lessons relevant for understanding global health and social politics worldwide.[11] *Unmaking Russia's Abortion Culture* presents historical, cultural, and political evidence to demonstrate this argument.

Let's start with a few facts. Fertility rates of fewer than two children per woman create imbalanced dependency ratios (the proportion of working-age population to those who need care). They are symptoms of broad socioeconomic problems, including women's continually disproportionate responsibility for domestic labor and childrearing, even when they enjoy equality in the workplace, and cultural expectations for marriage and family formation that are often unachievable, leading to childbearing at older ages, often by single mothers.[12] Older women are more likely to struggle with infertility and use ARTs, which pose health risks. The global market for oocytes and surrogate mothers, which enables wealthier would-be parents to export the health risks of infertility to people in poorer communities, reveals that very low fertility has implications for maternal and child health globally.[13]

Very low fertility and the demographic changes it portends have also been recruited by illiberal activists to stoke racialized anxieties and violent populism.[14] If the backlash against women's equality in the late twentieth century planted one seed of illiberalism in both Euro-American and former Soviet contexts, disdain for brown and black migrants in the twenty-first century has further sowed this political trend. Understanding how and why such broad-ranging illiberal trends arose is an urgent problem. Scholars focusing on the former Soviet bloc, where the 1989 dawn of liberal democracy was eclipsed merely thirty years later, have several explanations. Some compare how the actual liberal processes undertaken diverged from the hoped-for changes liberals expected.[15] Others blame liberals themselves for being elitist and "failing" to persuade their larger publics.[16] Still others contend that Russian leaders never sincerely adopted a liberal worldview, but merely "imitated" it to gain access to global networks and resources.[17] While all of these insights have merit, a more holistic examination of historical, cultural, and institutional processes surrounding the rise and fall of liberalism is needed.

Unmaking Russia's Abortion Culture contributes to these debates by examining Russian reproductive health care as a site of liberal ideas and reforms from the late 1950s to the eve of the 2022 invasion of Ukraine. I build on work by Jerzy Szacki and Maureen Laruelle, respectively, to view liberalism not as a definitive platform but as a multifaceted worldview and cultural sensibility.[18] Liberalism may feature a political approach to governance based on checks and balances, free elections, individual rights, and/or representatives' honesty and accountability to the electorate; it may prioritize economic systems based on markets, private property, self-sufficiency, and/or consumption. At the level of everyday values, liberal sensibilities may prize individual empowerment, consumer subjectivities, a tolerance for pluralism and the non-violent reconciliation of conflict, or even the importance of national identity.[19] Additionally, liberalism can manifest in geopolitical institutions that enforce liberal political and economic dynamics, such as the UN, IMF, and WHO; and a liberal worldview can be a form of ideological colonialism, such that populations are required to demonstrate their adoption of liberal political-economic relations and cultural values to be recognized as "modern."[20] The forms of liberalism that political actors choose to emphasize are related to the specific struggles they are waging; in Central and Eastern Europe, for example, liberals have historically valued the family and nation over the individual and ascribed women a gendered duty to sacrifice to these collectivities.[21] This background helps explain why Soviet and Russian contraceptive advocates— experts who formulated liberal sensibilities in the name of public health—treated global initiatives to advance women's reproductive *autonomy* with ambivalence.

Indeed, it is important to recognize that contraceptive technologies in-and-of-themselves are not necessarily empowering; their effects depend on the broader socio-political and cultural systems in which they are taken up and the purposes to which they are put.[22] From the mid-twentieth-century population-control movement targeting developing countries, to the 1990s' dissemination of family planning techniques in post-socialist nations, efforts to promote contraceptive use have involved a range of political agendas.[23] Reproductive health policy and practices can be a terrain for expanding liberalizing agendas, from the value of individual choice and sexual liberation, to the reach of global pharmaceutical markets, to the self-determination of women in particular. On the other hand, contraceptive technologies can be tools to strengthen patriarchal control and heteronormative families, as well as to suppress individuals and communities by limiting their reproduction.[24] The concept of biopolitics illuminates how contraceptives may be used simultaneously as a tool to "liberate" people (say, from "tradition"), and control them (for example, according to rationalities of "modernity").[25] Restrictions on abortion and related conservative family politics are central to the spread of illiberal movements in the US, Poland, Hungary, and Russia; and global Christian and conservative organizations agitate for their reproductive politics worldwide.[26] Yet much global health research does not adequately consider how such politics impact efforts to intervene in local communities. Studies of former Soviet contexts, for example, examine how shifting laws and policies impact abortion, contraception, and fertility rates—an important task—but the cultural and political causes of liberalizing or illiberal health policies cannot be understood through global health and demographic methods.[27] Pronatalist campaigns are underway in much of Europe and lauded by nationalists; they link support for child-bearing and patriarchal families with saving the precarious nation.[28] It is thus imperative to understand how efforts to promote reproductive health and contraceptive use become politically and culturally entangled with such demographic and nationalist politics. No less importantly, studying conflicts over reproduction in health experts' strategies and in community organizing can reveal major insights about the social and political conditions of (il)liberalism.[29]

My approach brings an ethnographer's sensibility to uncover the cultural history of efforts to replace abortion with contraceptives from the late 1950s until Russia's 2022 invasion of Ukraine. Drawing on fieldwork that I began in

1993 and expanded over the decades to include relationships with clinicians, demographic researchers, and feminist activists, this study goes beyond statistics, laws, and policies to highlight the social processes enabling these tremendous historical transformations. The shift to preventing, rather than terminating, unwanted pregnancies was not an automatic consequence of Russia's entering the global market and gaining access to contraceptives. It involved multifaceted, institutional changes—from the establishment of nongovernmental organizations (NGOs) that created new channels of communication to the restructuring of state health services, which legitimated new ideas about clinical practices. Global collaborations were key to many of these changes. In addition, the neoliberal economy incentivized people to become economically self-sufficient before becoming parents and led to a new consciousness about the need to plan, and often postpone, pregnancy. Through all these processes, family-planning advocates provided practical alternatives to abortion, justified these alternatives scientifically and ethically, and created institutional changes to ensure their continuity. This book focuses on the professional work and advocacy of a select group of particularly creative Russian reformers as a lens onto these liberalizing transformations. These were experts and in some cases visionaries who strove to strengthen both women's health and Russian society more generally through a commitment to individual over narrow state priorities. They worked at once with hope and caution, treating contraceptives as a means for enhancing heteronormative families and practices of care; and many of them faced troubling political backlashes for their daring.

Abortion as a Problem for Liberal and Pronatalist Demographic Politics

When the Soviet Union collapsed, intensified political anxiety over demographic trends pushed abortion to the forefront of public policy debates. In 1991, the fertility rate was 1.73 children per woman; the severe economic and social upheaval that followed led births to plummet even further, hitting a low of 1.16 in 1999.[30] These trends prompted nationalists to protest vehemently that Russia was "dying out," and to demand urgent political-economic resources to raise fertility. Proposals ranged from providing economic incentives for women to bear children to restricting abortion access; some proposed creative tactics such as matching pregnant single women with unmarried men willing to become fathers if they gave birth.[31] The resurgent Russian Orthodox Church, with assistance from global antiabortion organizations, lobbied for restrictions in abortion access.[32] Their efforts built on public antipathy toward abortion as a symbol of Soviet-era harms and the broader resentment of socialist-era gender equality. Over time, campaigns to restrict abortion channeled objections to the chaos unleashed by neoliberal reforms. Conservatives framed contraception and family planning as harmful to the demographic and spiritual interests of the Russian nation, while promoting their own policies of supporting a neotraditional model of a patriarchal family with many children.

Thus, rather than debating women's rights or fetal rights, proposals to restrict abortion cited the urgency of raising fertility. The medical and demographic experts who defended abortion and contraceptive access, in turn, argued the irrelevance of these technologies to declining birth rates. Struggles to establish the authority of the scientific analysis of population thus lay at the heart of Russian liberal reproductive politics.[33] A maverick school of Russian demography founded by Professor Anatoly Vishnevsky took the lead in this debate, debunking ideas about population dynamics in the media and political platforms. For example, when the Minister of Health and Social Development stated in 2012 that "fertility can be increased by 20 to 30 percent merely through reducing the number of abortions," Vishnevsky, in his online journal *Demoscope*, took on the implication that "reducing abortions" through restricting access would meaningfully increase population growth.[34] He pointed out that although "between 1988–2008 the number of abortions in Russia decreased by 70 [percent] . . . the fertility rate not only didn't rise by 70 percent, on the contrary, it decreased by 27 percent."[35] He goes on, "We don't know what happened with Russians during these years, but they apparently began to conceive less. *Demoscope* has already written about how, according to some medical-philosophical experts, something befell their (Russians, not the experts') sperm. According to another explanation, they began, finally, to use contraceptives."[36]

Vishnevsky had been the country's leading liberal voice on demographic issues since the 1970s.[37] Here, he insisted that Russia's two-decade long decrease in abortions occurred through new practices of preventing unwanted pregnancy—and that such contraceptive use had no effect on the birth rate. His obvious sarcasm stems from having explained these simple demographic dynamics to policymakers and the public repeatedly over the same two decades, to no avail. Fertility trends receive widespread coverage in the Russian media, but neither journalists nor politicians strive to analyze them in accordance with global demographic knowledge. The common assumption that introducing contraception reduces birth rates holds true in developing world contexts with high average rates of fertility, but is not relevant for Russia, where the birth rate has been lower than the population replacement level of an average 2.1 children per woman since at least the 1980s.[38] Contraceptive use in Russia does not affect *levels* of fertility but replaces abortion as the *means* of fertility control.[39] At stake in Vishnevsky's and his colleagues' project is the need to convince the public that limitations on fertility are inevitable; the issue is *how* control will take place—whether in relative safety and in a manner affording women and men maximum personal control over their lives (i.e., through contraception), or brutally, through the use of routine and/or even criminal abortion.[40]

Vishnevsky's argument is hardly surprising for feminists concerned with women's equality, self-determination, and health, but understanding the intensity and ferociousness of anxieties about population is necessary for grasping the ways contraceptives became politicized in Russia.[41] The notion that "reducing abortion" will increase fertility has long been a form of cultural "common sense" based in the assumption that pregnancies are routinely unexpected and can be "saved" by persuading women against termination.[42] The deliberate prevention of pregnancy, in this view, appears as a selfish rejection of family values and national interests. And arguments to the contrary are dangerous: nationalists publicly accused the liberal scholars and social activists who made such statements of political treachery.[43] Such denunciations of demographers foreshadowed the surging aggression against "enemies" underway in 2021 and '22.

Arbatova and Vishnevsky express the key concerns that Russian contraceptive supporters brought to Russian struggles over reproductive health: facilitating care and prioritizing science. The latter will be familiar to a Western audience: accepting science is a liberal value that Euro-American pro-choice advocates embrace. Essentially, professionals sought to legitimize routine contraceptive use in place of routine abortion as a rational and healthy life strategy. The focus on facilitating care is less familiar. Russians who endorsed contraceptive habits saw these as a new way for men to care for their women partners, and a new way that potential parents would prioritize the birth of children who are wanted and loved. Rather than emphasizing individual "rights," they advocated for socioeconomic circumstances that enabled well-being for children, women, and (heteronormative) families.[44] Inspired by the humanistic spirit prevalent in late

Soviet society, liberals' longing to revive a culture of care remained unconcerned about the specter of paternalism. It expressed an exhaustion with the political alienation, material deprivation, and state indifference shaping everyday life, and it enacted a rejection of the Soviet gender regime that, despite its language of "women's emancipation," produced gross inequalities and punitive reproductive health care. Underlying support for family planning was the liberal effort to rationalize policy making and health behavior and what I call a hope to re-enchant social relationships around care and nurturance. Rather than a preoccupation with establishing individual rights, I argue that hopes for rationalizing and re-enchanting society, reviving science and realizing humanism, were central to liberals' visions of a post-Soviet Russia.

In the chapters that follow, I trace how Soviet and post-Soviet discussions of abortion indexed a wide swath of problems related to gender, social welfare, professionalism, and the state. Promoting contraceptives to reduce abortion was an alternative to the more common strategy in the state's enduring "fight against abortion"—that of pushing pregnant women to give birth. Contraceptive advocates valued the insights of global science and joined them with a humanistic sensibility. Indeed, the cultural knowledge of physicians, scientists, public intellectuals, and political actors who advocated contraceptives tracks broader commitments to Russian liberal sensibilities manifest since the post-Stalin era. As an arena where liberal experts established new institutions, achieved measurable social improvements, but also faced stiff nationalist reprisals, reproductive politics illuminates important but largely unrecognized struggles for liberalizing social change preceding Russia's 2022 descent into war, repression, and global marginalization.

The Politics of Reproduction in Socialist Ideology and History

A historical glimpse of population politics in socialist ideology and history will help set the stage for understanding the Soviet governance of reproduction and the kinds of liberalizing reforms contraceptive advocates endorsed. From the onset of Soviet socialism, the state addressed reproduction as relevant to the biopolitical project of increasing population size. We will examine the theory of biopolitics expounded by Foucault, including its application to socialist regimes, but essentially it describes governance related to fostering life. The Soviet model of public health, known as "social hygiene," drew on Marxist principles to address "the influences of economic and social factors on the health of the population."[45] As a biopolitical technology, social hygiene fit conceptually in the broader socialist welfare framework of guaranteed, universal health care, employment, housing, and access to food, and highlighted prevention of illness. Additionally, social hygiene involved the sanitary "enlightenment" of the population about how to properly behave to optimize health.[46]

In 1920 the Soviet Union became the first country to legalize abortion, symbolizing women's emancipation and enabling their mass participation in the labor force.[47] Yet Soviet leaders were more concerned with managing the relationship between ideology, reproduction, and population dynamics than with preventing iatrogenic injuries from abortions. Terminations occurred in poor conditions, not infrequently harming women's health. At the same time, concerns about a possible decreasing birthrate loomed, making some elites reluctant to promote contraceptives.[48] Socialist ideology rejected Malthusian arguments that resource limitations made population growth a danger; Lenin asserted that with socialism's guarantees of basic material needs, people would have no objective reason to reject childbearing. Not foreseeing that cultural changes might lead people to wish for smaller families, he and all subsequent leaders considered a moderately growing population as necessary for producing workers and demonstrating the country's geopolitical strength.

Actual population dynamics, however, moved in the opposite direction, with continual population losses from World War I, the Revolutionary period, Civil War, and famines. In 1936, Stalin took aggressive measures to raise fertility by criminalizing abortion, applying a coercive biopolitics to governance promoting life and population.[49] Women resorted to unsafe, illegal abortions to avoid giving birth to a(nother) child amid war and severe postwar hardships, and maternal mortality skyrocketed, with approximately four thousand maternal deaths annually from unsafe abortions.[50] Deaths from World War II further resulted in population losses of approximately twenty-seven million people, with grossly imbalanced male-female ratios.[51] In an attempt to maximize the reproductive productivity of the remaining men, the regime expanded its pronatalist strategies with the Family Law of 1944, which relieved men from any responsibility for children they fathered out of wedlock. And despite state promises to support the resulting single mothers and their children, these families fell into deep poverty and suffered stigma for being "fatherless."[52] After Stalin's death in 1953, calls to reform the Law were thwarted by state functionaries who celebrated it as a pronatalist achievement.[53] In 1955, the Soviet Minister of Health, Mariia Kovrigina, proposed decriminalizing abortion as a means of improving women's health and increasing fertility.[54] As Nakachi details, Kovrigina's strategy highlighted not women's rights but social necessity, particularly addressing "the creation of thousands of orphans after fatally unsuccessful abortions."[55] Although conceding the need for safely provided abortions, the state still fervently desired higher fertility. Essentially, it provided safe abortions not in order to respect people's reproductive self-determination, but to prevent the injuries that might prevent future births.

In line with the social hygiene framework, some health experts called for contraceptives to be produced as a material component of prevention. Several socialist states supplied effective contraceptives to the population, including the German Democratic Republic (GDR), Yugoslavia, Hungary, and Poland, where IUDs, diaphragms, and the pill were relatively accessible.[56] On the other hand, central economic planners did very little to produce or import contraceptives in Romania, Cuba, and the Soviet Union.[57] The pill was practically unavailable (a situation we will examine in Chapter 2). Describing problems with contraceptive supplies in the Soviet 1970s, the renowned abortion researcher Henry P. David observed, "the diaphragm was produced in only one size and is believed to be less reliable than the condom. One form of IUD, a modified Lippes loop, was available in five sizes, although supplies were always inadequate to meet demand."[58] IUDs, moreover, would mainly be available for married women. Soviet-made condoms were colloquially known as "galoshes," for their thick, unlubricated latex; they were "erratic in dimension and unpopular. . . . There are strict legal prohibitions against vasectomy and female sterilization."[59]

In addition to material shortages, contraceptives were difficult to access due to the shame associated with acknowledging sexuality in public spheres. The challenge of obtaining condoms was captured by a male psychologist I interviewed in 1994 who vividly invited me to imagine the ordeal necessary to procure them: "You'd have to muster the courage to announce to the middle-aged female clerk behind the pharmacy counter what you want and then face her piercing glare of judgment and maybe even explicit retort of 'SHAMEFUL.' Very few people could withstand that—and of course no teenagers [would]."

Rather than contraceptives, couples typically used withdrawal, the calendar method, or douching in attempts to prevent pregnancy. Most experts themselves had little knowledge about effective contraceptives and Soviet health education literature provided little information about preventing pregnancy. Brochures that harped against abortion generally discussed contraception as a hypothetical possibility while providing few details about how to use specific methods or their respective risks, benefits, and availability. Many authors' tones belied any expectation that people would deliberately, habitually, and devotedly strive to prevent pregnancy. Instead, "sanitary enlightenment" efforts largely involved detailing the harms to women's health and fertility that would befall a woman from abortion; since Soviet abortions involved dilation and curettage in poor (even if legal) conditions, they could cause scarring and/or a perforated uterus.[60] State planners presumed the alternative to abortion was to give birth, and experts often pressured women seeking abortions to reconsider.

Shortages, shame, and the absence of cultural expectations to prevent unwanted pregnancy, all resulted in a norm of post-conception decision making.[61] For example, in Leningrad oblast' between 1961 and 1967, the total number of pregnancies that resulted in a live birth fell from 29 percent to 19 percent, with 70 percent of pregnancies aborted in 1961 and 80 percent in 1967.[62] The vast majority of women obtaining abortions were already mothers.[63] The social hygiene paradigm contributed to this norm by focusing on the "enlightenment" and sometimes repression of women seeking abortions without providing useful and realistic advice about prevention. Andrej Popov, the leading researcher of abortions in the Soviet Union, described this as the formation of a Soviet "abortion culture," defined as "the adaptation of society to the widespread use of abortion as the main or even only method of regulating the number of children in a family; a society-wide psychology in which the unrestricted use of abortion was normalized by women and doctors." This system involved an "abortion industry structurally embedded in the public health system through the allocation of personnel, equipment, clinically designated abortion beds, resources and budgets, and in the production of scholarly research, dissertations, and specialists."[64]

These were some of the contextual conditions shaping "convenient" abortions that Arbatova decried.[65]

Family Planning and Critiques of Liberalism after Socialism

This book builds on critical insights that debunk Western conceits about the main problems of Soviet society and the right path to democratic redemption after socialism. Writers familiar with late Soviet culture and everyday life challenged Western cold war assumptions that the society was mired in estrangement and deception. Ethnographers and memoirists detailed the many forms of solidarity arising during socialism and the value placed on friendship.[66] The extensive strata of Soviet engineer-technical workers (ITRs) sustained a vibrant unofficial culture of musicians and artists; their tremendous creativity generated a rich oral tradition of jokes and poetry and personal writings they never expected to publish. Whether through cultivating erudition or irony, they developed complex understandings of state power and treated freedom of conscience as a sacred value. Detailing the reciprocity that partially compensated for socialism's deficits—and that sometimes made illegal and corrupt actions feel legitimate—scholars revealed the moral economies surrounding everyday exchange relationships.

Western advisors were blind to these complex dynamics when major reforms and global collaborations became possible. The architects of structural adjustment policies argued for "freeing" prices, creating markets, and teaching democratic values; they proceeded to measure post-socialist "success" or "lag" vis-à-vis this hegemonic standard of modernity. Ethnographers who studied state socialism's unravelling, however, described the mass dislocations and losses in social solidarity that occurred alongside the enrichment of elites. Millions were plunged into desperation as inflation eroded the remnants of socialism's safety net. The economic reforms known as "shock therapy" rendered the life skills people honed during socialism largely obsolete; educated professionals, such as teachers and doctors, felt betrayed as their living standards fell dramatically and poorly educated but well-connected groups accumulated wealth.[67] Explaining the failures of liberal policy makers to predict or explain what was needed, these critiques highlighted the inability of ongoing reforms to produce expected and socially benevolent outcomes.[68]

In the first post-Soviet years, the cultural homogeneity that had characterized educated Soviet people rapidly unraveled. Gessen demonstrates how the search for a new identity led people to become mystics and nationalists, entrepreneurs and entertainers, embracing drastically different visions for a new Russia.[69] Some held on to ideals of humanism embedded in both socialist values and unofficial, intelligentsia culture, and joined these to newly accessible ideas, from feminism to religion, to new age spirituality and social justice.[70] Many yearning for Western-style liberalism held pragmatic orientations to social and personal change. Rejecting the idealistic habits of moral suffering that long characterized Russia's intelligentsia, liberals transformed themselves into productive professionals.[71] The arrival of liberal market reforms was their opportunity to build and run functioning institutions. Anthropologists have detailed how some adopted neoliberal subjectivities, contributing to a cultural zeitgeist where competition and entrepreneurship reigned. A consumer-driven model catering to individual persons (rather than the collective) emerged—and met with contestation—in fields such as medicine, psychology, and education, with palpable inequalities between public and private services.[72]

Inspiring much of this research is the haunting question of how actual neoliberal societies compare with the aspirations of liberal democratic promises.

Roudakova's examination of journalists provides insight into this issue by recognizing specific Soviet-era forms of liberalism that market economics dismantled.[73] Highlighting the long-form essay (*ocherk*), she shows how liberal journalists investigated problems that bureaucracy caused citizens, found solutions, and presented moral lessons. Without challenging the taboo on criticizing the Party, many journalists considered it their mission to pursue justice for ordinary people. Yet with the end of censorship and advent of market economics, journalists faced entirely new constraints: they needed to sell their stories. Violent and cynical accounts of society now pervaded the media.[74] Roudakova challenges Western assumptions that the Soviet press simply spouted ideology and the end of censorship meant the triumph of "free speech." Her findings that unregulated neoliberalism dislodged the pursuit of liberal humanistic ideals provides us a starting point for understanding the fate of liberal doctors and demographers.

Unmaking Russia's Abortion Culture expands our knowledge about liberalizing aspirations in the decades before, during, and after Glasnost. In addition to looking beyond the specific concerns presupposed by dominant Western discourses on liberalism—the prioritization of markets, elections, and individual "freedom"—this project is complicated by another challenge. Many Russian liberal hopes clashed with the sensibilities of Euro-American thinkers who were critical of the long-established liberalism in their own societies. Misunderstandings and conflicts abound. Critics have pointed out how Russian liberalism is trapped in binary thinking and supportive of social inequalities around class, race, gender, and sexuality. In addition to highlighting the biases and prejudices of Russian liberals, some scholars have tried to grasp how and why Russian liberal thought "failed" to persuade Russia's public and effectively counter Putin's revival of authoritarianism.[75]

Yet there is much we do not know about the nuanced visions of liberalizing thought that developed during state socialism and its aftermath, or the fate of these various ideas. This book delves into the strategies of family-planning supporters in medicine and demography, experts who challenged Russian pronatalists and nationalists for decades. I retain an abiding focus on the limits of the liberal vision family planners developed, but ultimately, my goal is to move beyond a critique of these ideas; I am interested in demonstrating the scope of liberalizing arguments that could be leveraged to contest (post-)Soviet pronatalism and tracing these strategies' impacts. Unearthing these shifting historical dynamics is especially important given the fact that, by 2016, Russia's key family planning institutions were dismantled. This does not imply that their message of planning pregnancies has or will wane. Indeed, family planners' success challenges arguments that blame Russian liberals for "failing" to speak to the masses. But as we will see, in contrast to popular attitudes, illiberal activists made family planning a bête noire of their anti-Western campaigns through moral policing and nationalist agitation. And in the face of severe hardships, neoliberal disarray, and pervasive deception and corruption, liberal promises of rationalization and re-enchantment were tough to defend. The rise and fall of family-planning institutions offers an illuminating case study for understanding the fate of liberal visions and transformations in late Soviet and post-Soviet society.

Analyzing Gender and Reproductive Politics under Socialism: Through the Looking Glass

For many observers, understanding Russian reproductive politics involves a trip "through the looking glass" to a space that challenges our basic assumptions and expectations. Aspirations for gender relations that emerged in the late socialist era are counterintuitive for Euro-American progressives, as Western feminists who met with Eastern European women scholars in the late 1980s and 1990s powerfully described.[76] Western feminists assumed that pursuing women's interests meant fighting patriarchal dominance, while Eastern European women intellectuals insisted that both they and men were subordinated to a common adversary, the socialist state. The shortage economy made support from family and friends a necessity for basic survival; people did not seek "freedom from" their families or intimate communities. And although an instrumental logic can be found in this, Soviet and post-Soviet Russians consistently downplayed utilitarianism and spoke of valuing intimate relations for both affective experiences and disinterested reciprocal care. Turns of phrase such as "being needed" (or conversely, "needed by nobody") signified a cultural understanding that self-esteem and personal dignity were determined by one's relationships: supporting others was a metric for assessing the value of one's life.[77] Being needed and fulfilling others' needs shaped people's sense of self in a way unfamiliar to those who prize the ideal of autonomous individualism.

In short, intellectuals from socialist societies and feminists from market democracies had very different understandings and social experiences. Western feminists marveled at how the socialist welfare state guaranteed women full-time employment, childcare, paid maternity leave, and protection from sex discrimination, establishing a degree of economic equality between women and men far beyond what Western, particularly US, women enjoyed.[78] They cautioned that the demise of socialist regimes would likely dismantle these gains and urged women to fight for their rights. But the region's women intellectuals resisted feminist politics, explaining that the socialist state had deeply discredited the language of "women's emancipation" when it mobilized women into the labor force without also collectivizing housework, as early socialist thinkers had envisioned.[79] Women's "equality" was an experience of being saddled with the double burden of work and domestic responsibilities, in harsh material conditions and cramped living spaces. The state's rhetoric of "emancipation," which touted its achievements for women while ignoring their continuing hardships, appeared cynical. Politically engaging with this hypocritical state hardly seemed a path toward progress. The debates between Eastern European women intellectuals and Western feminists were intense and ultimately productive, transforming both sides' perspectives in powerful ways by revealing the deterministic roles of history and socioeconomic organization in knowledge.[80]

These debates also led many feminist scholars to theorize the limits of Western assumptions about gender politics for explaining socialist contexts.[81] Comparing dynamics of gender inequality under socialism and capitalism, scholars illuminated how liberal assumptions about the public and private spheres, the individual, the family, and the state did not hold up for state socialist contexts.[82] For example, whereas under liberal, capitalist

regimes, the home is idealized as a private sphere protected from state intervention, the socialist state claimed the right to reshape people's personal
lives as well as public spaces. In turn, people living under socialism tried
to carve out spheres for personal, apolitical experiences and relationships
within public spaces as well as in domestic settings. Given these struggles,
Western feminist critiques such as "the personal is political"—which aimed
to show how intimate relationships and actions held political implications—
irritated people raised under state socialism. They longed for a private and
apolitical sphere unreachable by the surveillance state.[83] Similarly, whereas
in American society middle-class (white) women's association with the family and caregiving determined their exclusion from the public sphere and
economic autonomy, under Soviet socialism, women's full-time labor was
a condition of their full citizenship. Consequently, many Russian women
prized family as a refuge from the state, a site of authenticity and heartfelt
commitment, in contrast to state-run institutions where their participation
was officially mandated. For another example, the Western assumption
that every (adult) citizen is an autonomous agent and "dependency" is a
wound to human dignity did not exist in socialist Russia. Later American
feminist efforts to destigmatize dependency and naturalize the human need
for social relations would not have proven newsworthy in Eastern Europe;
in that context, as Funk argued, a feminist, liberatory task would be to
cultivate women's independence from the state and other persons (even
if full independence is not humanly achievable).[84] These insights help us
realize that understanding gender in the socialist and post-socialist contexts requires a entering a looking-glass world that challenges many basic
Western assumptions.

Given these experiences, activism for women's interests in post-socialist
contexts emerged only gradually. Much of the organizing women undertook in the 1990s aimed to help themselves, as mothers, cope with their economic desperation.[85] Still, some highly educated Eastern European women
(particularly those who read English) began organizing feminist-inspired
NGOs. Western organizations eager to support gender equality provided
them funding and support.[86] Mostly their activities focused on academic
goals and the creation of crisis centers modeled on domestic violence assistance but addressing the many kinds of crises women were experiencing.[87]
Notably, progressive foreign donors rejected supporting groups that highlighted maternal identities, seeking explicitly feminist-oriented organizations.[88] These processes were fraught. Competition for foreign resources and

the need to pass feminist litmus tests generated resentment among local activists, while global observers raised concerns about the elite character of the organizations being supported. Critiquing the process of creating "feminism-by-design," Ghodsee questioned both the global and local power inequalities at stake and these organizations' ability to affect broad social change.[89] Still, transnational friendships and collaborations emerged from these projects, enhancing the lives of participants and laying the groundwork for numerous additional progressive activities.[90] Poland was the only place in the 1990s where women activists fought explicitly for reproductive rights; threats to abortion access in the early 1990s and the 1993 ban on most abortions spurred this activism.[91] In Russia, a major awakening and organizing at the grassroots level by feminist and queer activists was spurred during the 2011–12 protests against rigged elections, when they faced discrimination from their male peers.[92] In short, feminist and queer consciousness in post-socialist contexts emerged from the material and symbolic conditions shaping everyday life, not from abstract ideas about equality. Recognizing this history is crucial for making sense of abortion and contraceptive politics as a liberalizing project—but not necessarily a feminist one—in Soviet and post-Soviet Russia.

Comparing Biopolitics in Liberal and Soviet Political Rationalities

Studying efforts to control reproduction and manage fertility dynamics raises questions about biopolitical forces in diverse political regimes. Michel Foucault described the emergence of biopolitics in the eighteenth century as a new form of political rationality: unlike the longer-standing sovereign form of governance that prioritized the interests of the ruler, biopolitical governance claimed to serve the interests of the population—by promoting its health and welfare. Biopolitics makes life itself the purpose and focus of government.[93] Moreover, whereas sovereign rule emanates in a top down manner from the sovereign or state to the people, biopolitics governs more diffusely. Experts and the institutions they are embedded in, such as educational and health care systems, are among the main instruments of biopolitics, promoting ideas and behaviors that serve to extend or enhance life. Interestingly, the state's and experts' claims to promote population welfare simultaneously serves to legitimize their governing power and to obscure it. Foucault showed that when people accept expert authority and institutional claims to benevolence, governance involves little coercion; people come to discipline themselves. They value the norm of health and comply with rules of well-being, without recognizing the webs of power and mechanisms of control inherent in the governance of bodies, persons, and communities.[94] Foucault identified the emergence of biopolitical rationality as marking the advent of modernity.

This initial work on biopolitics developed in myriad directions. Foucault's analysis of racism exposed the fact that biopolitics is a *selective* valuing of life that often exacerbates social inequalities. Moreover, his well-known statement that biopolitical governance manifests in both the forces that "make live" (productively promote life) and those that "let die" (neglect, withhold, or ignore the necessities for life) revealed how biopolitics takes place on a continuum with thanatopolitics, the political forces that shape groups' vulnerability to dying and causes of death.[95] Biopolitics does not necessarily empower the subjects it targets; feminists demonstrate how biopolitical governance of the family and human reproduction involves efforts to control women's bodies. By governing sexuality, birth, and childrearing, experts, community leaders, and political elites compete to reshape society and establish certain kinds of collective futures. To analyze the specific channels through which such reproductive governance occurs, Morgan and Roberts direct attention to such varied techniques as "legislative controls, economic inducements, moral injunctions, direct coercion, and ethical incitements."[96] For example, in the US, the reproductive governance of adolescents induces postponing pregnancy and childbearing until becoming economically independent or married. This occurs through moral injunctions to practice "abstinence" in fundamentalist religious discourses on female virtue but also in secular moral injunctions to practice "safe sex" in the name of health and responsibility; it occurs through state economic disincentives such as minimal welfare, so that young, single mothers and their children likely face poverty; and it occurs in clinical and consumer opportunities to purchase contraceptive methods. The US Supreme Court's 2022 overturning of *Roe v. Wade* enables more coercive modes of reproductive governance, criminalizing abortion and forcing births regardless of whether they are wanted. Feminist NGOs that lobby to preserve legal abortion and that provide access to terminations regardless of abortion's legality deploy their own biopolitical techniques in the name of reproductive freedom.[97] The concepts of biopolitics and reproductive governance are thus valuable for exposing numerous techniques of power exerted by the state,

experts, community leaders, and political contenders.[98] Studying biopolitics opens up questions about how such forms of power shape people's
actions, knowledge, and consciousness, or, in Foucault's framework, create
people as subjects (of governing technologies and political rationalities)
with varying degrees of agency.

A major legacy of Foucault's work is the critique of liberal democracy's claim to have replaced governance via tyranny with human freedom.[99]
Contrary to this conceit, Foucault argued that governance in the name of
population welfare did not eliminate power over people but deployed it in
new ways. The embrace of life and pursuit of health became coextensive
with "rationality" and "wellness." These concepts serve as tools for arbi-
trating definitions of normality, morality, and deviance in people's bodies
and thoughts. Under neoliberal consumer society, the moral imperative
of healthy living and the cultural value placed on individual responsibility
spawn all manner of techniques for disciplining the self, from diet, exercise, and sex to emotion management.[100] A key to the success of biopolitical
regimes is that, with the legitimation of scientific and state authority, people do not experience the power that constrains them as emanating from
coercive forces inhibiting their "freedom." Rather, they discipline their own
bodies, and make personal decisions that conform to expert and state ideals,
while understanding themselves as "free" to make their own "choices."[101]

Foucault's overwhelming focus on the West, and his preoccupation with
dismantling the conceits of democratic regimes, raise questions about how
to apply a biopolitical lens to the governance of life in non-Western or nonliberal regimes.[102] Important work has deployed Foucault's methods and
mode of inquiry to characterize diverse political rationalities and biopolitical techniques without wholly adopting his political or normative agenda.
For while in a general sense biopolitics involves harnessing, promoting,
and administering life, state- and community-level politics determine the
specific kinds of biopolitical goals pursued and the ways biopolitical technologies get deployed.[103] For one example, some Muslim communities have
drawn on religious legal justifications to encourage family planning in what
has been called a form of Islamic biopolitics.[104]

Soviet and socialist cases illuminate the profound importance of examining how nonliberal political rationalities make life an object of intervention, or in Foucault's words, "problematize" life. Stephen Collier and Sergei
Prozorov, respectively, have compared the liberal and socialist approaches
to population in order to explain the differences between these political

rationalities.[105] Liberal political understandings treat population as an entity whose dynamics arise autonomously; population processes such as births, deaths, disease, and migration patterns are assumed to be a "quasi-natural reality."[106] This means that liberal forms of governance will track vital statistics and intervene to decrease disease or increase longevity, but they also assume there are natural limits as to what can be changed.[107] Collier observes that under liberal governance, the study of population processes aims to discern regularities and shifts within a sphere of life perceived as independent of government.[108]

By contrast, Soviet political rationality treated population as an object that needed to be made anew to conform to socialist ideals. Norms were not derived from statistical findings but from ideological assumptions about how society and population *should* be.[109] Expressed in a popular 1920s song acclaiming "we were born to turn the fairy tale into life," Soviet governance sought to create the new Soviet man and woman who would physically and mentally embody this new world.[110] Bringing socialism into being also required the destruction of all other forms of social existence. Prozorov captures how this socialist political rationality blurred boundaries between biopolitics and thanatopolitics, such that "eradicating epidemics and organising famines, support to families and their forced separation, fixing one's teeth and kicking them out, are not to be opposed as a salutary effect and its unfortunate 'cost,' but rather viewed as two aspects of the same process of forcing in the new by forcing out the old, in which cost and effect become indistinct."[111]

Given that this political rationality persisted throughout the Soviet era, Prozorov refers to all of Soviet biopolitics as "Stalinist."[112] For although Soviet governance after Stalin applied less repressive and coercive biopolitical techniques, later Soviet leaders never renounced the political rationality of forcing life to conform to the socialist idea. Thus, while Stalinism banned abortion and Khrushchev's regime decriminalized it, continuing the fight against abortion through propaganda campaigns, the underlying political rationality of transforming the population by engineering higher fertility remained. Engineering the population to serve industrial production was central to Soviet statecraft. The universal social welfare system, including family support, health care, and abortion provision, became the technical apparatus through which a socialist population was manufactured. The enduring problem for socialism was that the grandeur of its promises never materialized, leaving citizens dismayed and often disaffected.

FIGURE 0.1. Billboard, "To the Idea of Increasing! Only 6.6 percent of Russian families have three or more children." Photo by the author.

Socialist Biopolitical Regimes and Cultural Legitimacy

Ethnographies of reproduction demonstrate how biopower works through particular cultural logics that differ globally. Socialist regimes all treated the human body as the property of the state, a resource to be used for its benefit. They did so through a range of biopolitical techniques. As Greenhalgh and Winkler describe, in the 1970s, China developed an elaborate birth planning bureaucracy to dramatically reduce population growth. Births needed to be authorized by the state. Through surveillance and the use of both medical technologies and social welfare institutions, the birth planning cadres worked to ensure that unauthorized (female) fetuses and babies were eliminated. Women's bodies became sites of mandated longterm contraceptive use or sterilization, and society was taught to value child "quality" over quantity. Through this combination of coercion, incentives, penalties, changing cultural understandings, and shifting socioeconomic conditions, the state succeeded in reducing fertility from six children per woman in 1949 to fewer than two by the mid-1990s.[113]

Eastern European regimes, by contrast, deployed biopolitical techniques to raise fertility. Because socialism prescribed women's political

and economic equality, the goal of increasing births was to happen alongside women's participation in the labor force and communist struggle. The
state urged people to make reproductive decisions in accordance with the
society's needs, not "egotistical" calculations.[114] As noted earlier, these states
differed in their supplies of contraceptives, but the combination of pronatalist state agendas, patriarchal cultures, and little education about preventing pregnancy resulted in widespread abortion use throughout the region.
The most extreme case was Romania, which banned abortion in 1966 and
made no contraceptives available. Despite severe material deprivation, the
state expected that every woman would bear and raise four or five children.[115]
Attempting to legitimize this coercion, official rhetoric fused people's interests with those of the state, cynically asserting "We are building socialism
with and for the people."[116] The socialist state established formal economic
guarantees, but people's everyday experiences severely belied those fantasies. Kligman details how pursuing these biopolitical objectives involved
the instrumentalization of the human body, the politicization of statistics and science, the coercion of health professionals, and the co-optation
of expertise for state goals.[117] Mandatory gynecological exams to discover
pregnancies illustrate such processes; doctors were charged with discern-
ing, monitoring, and protecting pregnancies as their professional duty to
the state.[118] Women feared sexual intimacy and gynecological medicine as
channels for the state to intrude in their most intimate spheres of life.[119]

Juxtaposing the mid-twentieth-century population policies of China
and Romania highlights the value of studying biopolitical techniques in
socialist regimes and comparing them with liberal regimes. Although China's leaders strove to reduce fertility, and Romania's dictator aimed to
increase it, they used similar biopolitical techniques: the enunciation of
a clear population agenda, state surveillance of human bodies and populations to monitor progress toward state goals, and coercion and persuasion to achieve them. Medical practitioners, state bureaucrats, and ordinary
citizens were to implement state agendas. Yet the two countries experienced very different outcomes. In China, a discourse that wed the goals
of modernity and national welfare justified limiting births as a means of
engineering higher "quality" children.[120] Culturally, many Chinese came to
accept these ideas and disciplined their own practices to fulfill state agendas
(while the state itself decreased coercion over time).[121] By contrast, Roma-
nians rejected the coercion of childbearing, undertaking unsafe abortions
and abandoning unwanted babies in orphanages. Their dictator, Nicolae

Ceausescu, was murdered by a mob in 1989. Access to legal abortion was immediately restored.

These contrasting cases demonstrate that when socialist biopolitics appears to serve well-being, it functions similarly to liberal cases: rendered as benevolence, state power becomes internalized if not invisible. When deployed through techniques of coercion or punishment, efforts to engineer reproduction can result in the state being discredited.[122]

Thus, although family planning presents itself as a scientifically rooted, universally relevant model for achieving health, it takes shape around local cultural circumstances and messaging. Rationally planning sexual activity and childbearing, and the interpersonal techniques and material technologies that make doing so possible, are social inventions that become valued in specific contexts.[123] Yet because family planning habits seem so natural to those who practice them, the question of what makes family planning valued or problematic for others rarely gets posed. As a result, Westerners who disseminated ideas about family planning to the Soviet and Russian contexts were usually unaware of the complex social terrain their ideas were encountering, or the political challenges Russian supporters were confronting. Exploring such differences is a key goal of this book.

CLASHING FORMS OF (BIOPOLITICAL) COMMON SENSE

A revealing example of the misunderstandings between Soviet and American understandings of reproductive practices took place in 1987, when American talk show host Phil Donahue went to Moscow and invited an audience of Soviet citizens to discuss problems of everyday life in the two countries. Raising the issue of teen pregnancy, a topic Donahue assumed was a shared concern to the two societies, Donahue asked a young Soviet man if he had used contraceptives when having sex at age eighteen. This elicited an awkward laugh and ambiguous reply: "Yes, I knew about it," the man said.

Donahue characterized this response as revealing the speaker's "reluctance" to discuss the topic, seemingly interpreting the exchange as yet "more evidence for a 'closed society,' people unable, perhaps even constrained by the state, to speak their mind."[124] Yet Donahue's focus on teen pregnancy was an erroneous starting point for exploring shared concerns, for Soviet public discourse treated this phenomenon quite differently than American discourses did. In the US context, having children before completing one's education and attaining economic self-sufficiency places the family at great risk of poverty, leading policy makers and experts to fervently inveigh against teen pregnancy and parenthood. Beginning in the 1970s, American teenagers were disciplined to either refrain from premarital sex or use contraception, and also to calculatedly plan reproduction to coincide with their personal economic independence. For Donahue, reproductive discipline and habits of rational planning were aligned. In the late Soviet era, by contrast, teenage sex was highly stigmatized as promiscuous, but the economic consequences of adolescent childbearing were not a major concern for Russian leaders. Soviet socialism provided a universal welfare system, including higher education, childcare, and employment. For young women, early childbearing would add challenges to completing higher education, but it did not create the severe hurdles to social mobility seen in the US. The main problem surrounding teen pregnancy was the possibility that dilation and curettage for abortion could result in iatrogenic sterility, leaving a young woman childless. Health experts thus warned women of all ages not to abort their first pregnancy.

Beyond the different starting assumptions about teen pregnancy, sociolinguist Donal Carbaugh reveals the dramatically different speech conventions that underlay this exchange. Donahue and his Soviet interlocutors held different assumptions about how to undertake public discussions in general, and how to talk about physical intimacy in particular. Donahue was undertaking problem-solving—introducing an issue for public discussion, collaboratively exploring the problem through participants' disclosing their personal experiences and opinions, and arriving at potential solutions to undertake. Calling this "a ritualized way of being American together," Carbaugh contrasts it with Soviet conventions, where discussion with outsiders was sharply distinct from discussion with insiders (trusted, personal intimates).[125] With outsiders, Soviets were socialized to reiterate collective morals and virtues, not dissect problems; culturally, people recognized such interactions as "shallow" and expected reticence.[126] Expressing personal views and experiences happened in intimate contexts, where speech could be structured through pouring out one's soul, bonding through toasts, or lamenting, for example.[127] There, expressing emotions was considered "deep" and people appreciated volubility.[128] Russians took these ritualized speech genres for granted, just as Americans did their collaborative-based problem solving.

Moreover, when Soviets discussed topics related to physical intimacy, they used an emotional vocabulary of love, passion, and soul.[129] Yet when

Donahue posed the questions "When you had sex . . . did you use a con-traceptive?" and "Who took initiative?," the register he used presented a culturally alien idiom of physiology and technology.[130] Shorn of emotional expression, this language was perceived as mechanistic and inappropriate for discussing human physical intimacy. Indeed, Soviets associated the con-ceptual field of "sex" with animals.[131]

Donahue's cultural faux pas and flawed assumptions provide an entry into the challenges that would arise a few years later as global family plan-ning consultants and Russian experts began collaborating. Working from distinct biopolitical contexts, they held dramatically different understand-ings about the meanings of contraceptive and abortion. While those social-ized under liberal biopolitical regimes assume the prevention of unwanted pregnancy through contraceptives is an obvious alternative to abortion, this view was neither presumed nor universally embraced in Soviet Russia. We shall now examine how that society's socialist welfare state and enduring pronatalism shaped its particular approach to biopolitics.

Social Hygiene and Sanitary Enlightenment: Technologies of Socialist Biopolitics

With the Bolshevik revolution and establishment of a socialist biopolitics, the sovereign governance of tsardom was replaced not with the illusion of personal freedom, but with the promise of equality and freedom from material want. The state appointed itself the arbiter of truth and forcibly restructured society to reflect its ideology of a classless, scientific-atheistic, industrialized, and politically equal utopia. Wealth was expropriated from property owners, and economic inequalities were minimized. Russian crit-ics of the regime called it an "equality in poverty," but a universal social wel-fare system was established. Health care services were available as a right of citizenship, and physicians became employees of the state, paid minimal wages to end medicine's class structure. Alongside these transformations was the creation of the new Soviet man and woman: the state, through its educated expert cadres, would enlighten the population about how to live properly, including how to behave virtuously and maximize health.[132]

All this is to show that Soviet biopolitics governed not through individ-ual freedom, but through state sovereignty, a socialist approach to popu-lation and subjectivity.[133] In the realm of population health, Soviet biopol-itics was organized through the specific techniques of social hygiene and sanitary enlightenment.[134] The deployment of these techniques and their consequences varied over time, along with the political-economic dynamics of the regime. Reproductive politics are exemplary.

During Stalin's reign, the ban on abortion and efforts to coerce childbearing resulted in illegal and unsafe abortions, maternal mortality, and abandoned children.[135] After Stalinism, overt coercion decreased, but "enlightenment" expanded: citizens were bombarded with reminders about the state's expectations for their reproductive behaviors. Since the late 1950s, pronatalist biopolitics, or the state's push for childbearing and childrearing, involved three overarching institutional components: First, pronatalism was manifest in a socialist ideological agenda that shaped the expected use of people's energy and bodily capacities for socially valuable purposes, rather than for individual choices and responsibilities. This agenda sanctioned sexuality solely for procreation purposes (though by the late 1970s, also for strengthening marriages), and the state titrated available information about sexuality to support only these minimal goals. Second, pronatalist biopolitics informed central economic planning by determining production and imports based on a view of societal needs conceptualized mainly through mass infrastructure. Thus, the state ensured the provision of housing and heat but not intimate toiletry products (body soap, deodorant, toilet paper, menstrual supplies for women, contraceptives).[136] Sometimes, enlightenment programs to raise citizens' level of "sanitary hygiene" implicitly acknowledged the need for practical solutions amid material deficits. Thus, educational pamphlets explicating the "harms of abortion" for example, also included instructions for homemade tampons and spermicides. Third, despite these occasional, tacit recognitions of material want, state population plans favored fertility increases, specifically among Slavic ethnicities.[137] Soviet social hygiene thus treated pregnancies as opportunities for birth, rather than as necessarily wanted events; health authorities minimized women's personal concerns in comparison with state-defined goals for fertility. The state consistently related to women as potential mothers.

To prevent maternal mortality from unsafe abortions, access to legal, free terminations was guaranteed on a woman's request through the first trimester, and with demonstrable social or economic problems through relatively late gestational periods. With medical problems, abortion would be provided at any time. Yet material shortages severely compromised care; even anesthesia was not guaranteed. There was no privacy, either within the hospital, as several women underwent procedures together, or in terms of medical records: the required documentation for explaining a work absence noted when a woman had had an abortion. With Soviet biopolitical rationality defining women as necessarily (potential) mothers, the governance of abortion aimed to prevent negative consequences (death or sterility) that would impede future maternity. It was not oriented toward liberal humanistic goals such as individual autonomy, privacy, or comfort.

These features of Soviet biopolitical goals and techniques, and their differences from liberal biopolitics, help explain the changes that followed the end of socialism. Soviet deficits, ideological incitements, and regulatory techniques made the state a formidable, visible presence in people's lives. Health professionals were charged with promoting the state's priorities, not determining healthy practices according to their scientific expertise alone.[138] Faced with the state's unfulfilled promises of material well-being and heavy-handed efforts to engineer intimate life, Soviet people reacted with irony, resentment, and a conviction that decisions about family and reproduction were a sphere where one had to figure out her own interests.[139] Unlike the subjects of liberal biopolitics who considered themselves "free" to make autonomous decisions about their bodies and lives because the power working on them remained largely invisible, late Soviet subjects held no illusions of freedom. They longed for access to scientifically competent and benevolent medical expertise so their sphere of personal decision making—however narrow or broad—could avoid damage and pain.

Imagining Liberalizing Alternatives to Soviet Biopolitics

Professionals educated during the Soviet era deployed liberal ideas using strategies that changed over time. Contraceptive advocates sometimes aimed to liberalize Soviet biopolitics while preserving pronatalism, and sometimes rejected pronatalism in favor of individual autonomy.[140] Contraceptive advocacy presents a valuable example for understanding liberal thought as a cultural or "situational" sensibility, rather than a specific political platform, as Jerzy Szacki suggested.[141] Liberal thought takes different shapes depending on the historical and social context.[142] As liberalizing reforms came under attack during Russia's post-Soviet decades, family planning experts' changing strategies offer a window onto the conceptual possibilities for defending liberal ideas about family and reproduction amid an illiberal, nationalist resurgence.

The first aim of this book, then, is to illustrate the various ideas and institutions that Russian writers, bureaucrats, clinicians, and scientists pursued for a liberalized biopolitics. Literary scholars and historians of the post-Stalin era have detailed the unique liberal sensibilities among what Mark Lipovetsky calls the "technical intelligentsia," whose worldview was characterized by a faith in scientific rationality and progress, a skeptical attitude toward Soviet ideology and politicized speech, and a commitment to humanistic values.[143] Alongside their work in scientific professions (often chosen to avoid the more explicitly politicized work in humanities), these white-collar employees read and composed poetry, engaged in amateur comedy and music troupes, and avidly discussed underground literature. They spoke of the need for a feedback system between social policy and ordinary people's needs.[144] Prior to the mid-1980s, their relationship to the Soviet government remained "a rebellion in a minor key," as Svetlana Boym describes; with Glasnost, they gained a euphoric sense of possibility and sought to realize their ideals in institutions and daily practices.[145]

Vishnevsky's and Arbatova's critiques, introduced earlier in this chapter, illustrate two aspects of the liberal political rationality inspiring Russian contraceptive advocacy. Vishnevsky's correction of the notion that reducing abortions would increase fertility exemplifies one liberal prong—the struggle to prioritize science and recognition of the limits of governance. He rejected the socialist approach of engineering population dynamics to fit state interests.[146] Working with demographic transition theory, Vishnevsky observed that as societies become industrialized and urbanized and their public health systems improve, mortality rates decline; fertility rates follow suit as the household economy no longer benefits from childbearing. Parenting gradually becomes a personal decision rather than a cultural requirement. Low fertility, he continually explained, is an inevitable—"natural"—component of modernization, irreversible by state policy. He recommended that the state end its pronatalist campaigns and enhance people's reproductive autonomy by providing contraceptives.[147] Yet as Russia's 1990s witnessed unprecedented declines in births, conservatives repudiated arguments against striving to increase fertility as traitorous. Vishnevsky countered by juxtaposing science-based truth-telling with Soviet ideology and nationalist delusions.[148]

Arbatova's memoir reflects other features of the liberal political rationality in late- and post-Soviet Russia. In casting her unplanned pregnancy as an internal dilemma between the competing "maternal instinct" and the "instinct of self-preservation," Arbatova accepts the Soviet notion that motherhood was central to women's "nature," even as she holds fast to her individual agency in reproduction.[149] She describes the "triumph" of self-preservation as a pyrrhic victory, manifesting her subordination to a world that enables violence, not care. This inclination to prioritize nurturance stemmed from the late 1950s, when society's exhaustion from the horrors of war and repressions, and Khrushchev's political relaxation away from revolutionary zealotry, allowed the cultural expression of new longings. Post-Stalin society turned to recognizing personal concerns and contradictory emotions.[150] Arbatova's melancholic acceptance of her abortion echoes longings to prioritize care and love over necessity.

The search for liberalizing social change thus proceeded from historical and experiential problems based in socialism; it was not oriented around abstract concepts that residents of liberal societies themselves held dear, whether "freedom," "individualism," or "markets."[151] Vishnevsky sought to instill the rationality of demographic science in population policy; Arbatova longed for a re-enchantment of relations based on care. These ideals—of prioritizing science and humanism over ideology, of rationalization and re-enchantment—were key cultural sensibilities of the late Soviet technical intelligentsia.[152] Their visions and pragmatic techniques channeled hope through liberalizing biopolitical aspirations without fully accepting Western feminist or family planning models.

Liberal Openings

During Glasnost and after 1991, developments in reproductive politics initially appeared to be moving toward the promises that liberals longed for. For example, in comparison with the Soviet law legalizing abortion in 1955, the newly independent Russian Federation's law appeared to take a rational, pragmatic approach to women's health. The Decree of the Presidium of the Supreme Soviet of the USSR of November 23, 1955, entitled "On the Cancellation of the Prohibition of Abortion," stated:

> The measures undertaken by the Soviet state for encouraging motherhood and protecting childhood, and women's continual growth of consciousness and culturedness as they actively participate in all areas of the country's economy, makes it possible to now rescind the legal prohibition against abortion. The reduction of abortions can henceforth be realized by continually expanding

state measures for encouraging motherhood and undertaking moral education and informational work. Cancelling the abortion ban also allows for reducing the significant harm to women's health caused by abortions performed
outside of hospitals and by untrained persons.[153]

This decree inaugurated the post-Stalin approach to reproductive governance, overturning the eighteen-year ban on abortion that had resulted
in thousands of women's deaths. Yet while cancelling the abortion ban
effectively legalized abortion, this decree underscored state benevolence,
not a principled respect for autonomy.[154] It boasted that the changes being
implemented reflected state achievements (rather than its fatal mistakes,
such as outlawing abortion in the first place) and highlighted the continuing agenda of "encouraging motherhood."[155] This law exemplified a political
rationality key to late Soviet biopolitics—government of bodily capacities
in the name of state interests and population vitality.

In 1993, by contrast, legislation addressing abortion guaranteed women
"the right to independently decide the question of motherhood. The artificial
termination of pregnancy will be done on the basis of a woman's desire until
twelve weeks gestation, on the basis of social indicators, until twenty-two
weeks gestation, and under conditions of medical indicators and with the
woman's agreement, without regard to the period of gestation."[156] Notable
here is the absence of any rhetoric celebrating state benevolence. The new
law appears to be a straightforward statement of rights. Moreover, the policy of granting second trimester abortions for women facing certain social
problems aimed to recognize and address a practical reality—the overall
decline of socioeconomic stability in the country.[157]

Other changes were similarly hopeful. By 1990, candid discussions
about sexuality and the general need for routinely preventing pregnancy
had become possible, as will be examined in Chapter 3. Opportunities for
uncensored, global collaborations and the establishment of nongovernmental organizations also emerged. In 1993, contraceptive advocates founded
the Russian Association of Family Planning (RAFP), the first such NGO in
the country. With financial and technical assistance from the International
Planned Parenthood Federation, the RAFP established a professional journal and physician training programs in contraceptive consultations. Chapter 4 explores these developments. State support was also forthcoming in
the early 1990s. To promote contraceptives, abortion clinics around the
country were transformed into centers for reproductive health and family planning; a new center for teenage reproductive health was founded in

St. Petersburg to train physicians in this specialty nationwide. These clinics also had access to all modern contraceptive supplies for their clients. Their efforts succeeded: contraceptive use increased and abortions consistently declined.

Detailing such processes, this book describes the specific liberal sensibilities that shaped discussions about reproductive health in post-Stalin and post-Soviet Russia. Women writers exposed widespread cruelty—in men's indifference about abortion, the punitive behaviors of gynecologists, and the moral judgments women made of each other. Experts took up this charge by transforming the tone and content of health education and clinical consultations. In contrast to sanitary enlightenment's approach of explicitly dictating correct behavior, family planning education communicated expert knowledge through recommendations, presenting fact-based and sometimes even humorous intonations.[158] Accepting individuals' right to make decisions about their own lives, and with a new openness to the possibility that there were multiple reasonable ways to live, family planning promoted contraceptives without pushing childbearing. Importantly, however, such support for individual autonomy did not mean experts should be "value-free," which Russian doctors and patients interpreted as meaning indifferent to what decisions a patient made.[159] Seeking to revive the medical profession's authority, family planners saw themselves as responsible not to the state's agenda of communist ideology, but to their patients' well-being. With varying degrees of self-reflection, they navigated between providing directed recommendations and tolerating patients' individual agency. Liberal condemnations of routine abortion and support for contraceptives drew selectively on Soviet social hygiene and family planning models; they expressed culturally resonant aspirations for humanistic and rationalized change.

Alongside these struggles for a liberal biopolitics, a fervent religious revival and demographic panic was also underway. In 1993, the Russian Orthodox priest Maksim Obukhov opened the "Life" clinic in Moscow, starting a movement to combat abortion through moral transformation (and not contraceptives). Both Russian state representatives and Church activists expressed anguish over declining fertility, linking it to the economic collapse accompanying market reforms, society's accompanying moral dissolution, and abortions. In August 2003, the state eliminated the majority of social criteria for second-trimester abortions, leaving only rape, imprisonment, the death or severe disability of one's husband, and the loss of parental rights.[160] Interestingly, the director of the Russian Family Planning Association, Inga

Grebesheva, did not object to this policy change, arguing that it "would not greatly affect a woman's access to abortion."[161] Grebesheva did not realize that this was just the first of many obstacles to abortion access that would be established as conservatives intensified their campaigns to delegitimize family planning and restrict abortion. Neither Russian advocates for liberal reproductive reforms nor their global supporters anticipated the barrage of well-funded and internationally connected illiberal religious nationalism that would sweep Russia to oppose their goals.

The second goal of this book is to analyze the strategies Russian experts deployed to defend their liberal institutions and biopolitical techniques. As we will see, the majority of Russian family-planning advocates presented themselves as supporting (heterosexual) families and fertility; they did not emphasize women's autonomy. They drew on select ideas from Western liberal family planning and remained ambivalent toward others. Contraceptive habits and deliberate pregnancy planning, they argued, would strengthen children's welfare, improve fertility, and benefit the nation. Predominantly, they sought inclusion in global scientific practices, social policies that met people's actual needs (not ideological platforms), humanistic orientations toward social relationships, and the embrace of tolerance, pluralism, and respect for individuals. Many hoped for robust state support for families, such that couples who wanted to have more children would have the economic means to do so. Indeed, with abortion widely accessible but the conditions for parenting abysmal, their visions differed significantly from the Western liberal mantra of individual choice. Russian advocates prefigured what we currently know as "reproductive justice," or the "human right to maintain personal bodily autonomy, have children, not have children, and parent the children we have in safe and sustainable communities."[162] Yet attacks against family planning began quite soon after its institutions were established. Chapters 4, 5, and 6 explore how family planners revised their strategies and re-envisioned their liberal commitments in confronting Russia's nationalist hostility.

Liberal Aspirations, Neoliberal Realities

The actual reforms Russians endured as the Soviet system disintegrated sorely belied liberal hopes. Hyperinflation began during Gorbachev's perestroika, with consumer prices 160 percent greater in 1991 than the prior year; then, Russia's 1992 debut as a "free" society saw inflation rise by an astounding 2,510 percent.[163] The economic policies Yeltsin undertook (guided by the IMF, World Bank, and Harvard development specialists), resulted in further crises—high unemployment rates and long wage arrears for those still employed.[164] Simultaneously, post-Soviet leaders sold off state assets for a pittance, enriching a miniscule number of well-connected Russians at the expense of the citizenry.[165] While prioritizing markets, the state ended many Soviet-era social entitlements, deepening people's immiseration. The stated goal was to launch the market in one fell swoop, rather than proceed gradually and risk a return to communist controls. But abruptly unleashing "shock therapy" was enormously destabilizing. In 1998, the government defaulted on its foreign debt, the ruble was devalued by an estimated 63 percent, and people's savings were wiped out for the second time.[166] Terms that sprung up such as *catastroika* and *prikhvatizatsia*—a play on the word privatization that means "a grab"—hint at the profound loss, fear, and anger that Russians experienced. Being in crisis seemed a permanent condition.[167]

Cultural transformations of the era also shocked. While Soviet people initially greeted the end of censorship in 1985 euphorically, ugly revelations about past terror and contemporary violence were bitter.[168] Moreover, the media environment was now wholly unregulated: television served a continual diet of violence, sex, and violent sex.[169] Many denounced "freedom of speech" as moral chaos, the absence of limits (*bezpredel'*). Reversals to standard historical narratives, such that Soviet heroes were recast as villains, left many with the aching sense that their and their parents' sacrifices had been in vain. Young adults faced the daunting challenges of meeting unprecedented requirements for basic economic stability, and with existing criteria for social competence entirely upended, they had to forge new paths that their elders could neither help with nor grasp.[170] With the public sphere becoming filled with alluring images of glamour, the ultra-rich became at once a sign of corruption and a new measure of privilege. Discourses claiming adolescent girls aspired to become prostitutes in order to access this lifestyle indexed a widespread panic that market reforms had eroded basic morality.

The destruction of economic stability and a pervasive sense of moral dissolution led many to characterize Russia's turn toward the liberal West as a fatal error.[171] They pointed to demographic trends as proof: since 1992, deaths exceeded births.[172] Indeed, in 1998, Russia's population had 6.1 million fewer people than the US Census had previously forecasted. Adjusting for emigration, demographers estimated that this loss resulted from 2.7

million fewer births and 3.4 million excess deaths.[173] Similar indicators were continuously cited in Russian media, contributing to a pervasive sense of national vulnerability. Although objective measures were rarely discussed, medical experts lamented that women's and children's health was poor and births were frequently complicated, contributing to visions of a bleak future. Conservatives insisted that the Russian nation was literally "dying out" and demanded social policies to raise fertility, revive the traditional family, and ensure the nation's future.[174]

But, as we have seen, low fertility was not new. By the late 1960s Soviet demographers recognized that no postwar baby boom had taken place and advocated policies to increase fertility. Some promoted social policies to lessen women's double burden of full-time work and childrearing; others blamed the weakening of family values, for which they blamed socialism's push for women's "emancipation." A common sense belief held that the Bolsheviks empowered women at the expense of men, with cases of wives using Party organs to punish profligate, drunk, or philandering husbands cited as evidence. By the 1970s, public discourse and popular culture spoke of a crisis of masculinity.[175] While liberal commentators identified the need for men to become more responsible fathers and husbands, conservatives pushed for the reinvigoration of patriarchal authority and revival of women's maternal instinct as necessary for raising fertility.[176] As fertility plummeted in the 1990s, these long-standing debates took center stage.[177] Political contenders saturated the media with continual waves of moral panic that the Russian nation was "dying out."[178] Some argued that market reforms were making it too difficult to raise children, while others insisted that moral dissolution based on Western influences made people uninterested in doing so. Nationalist activists cast family planning itself as a Western ploy to convince Russians to reject childbearing.[179] They advocated combatting abortion as a demographic threat to fertility and—authorizing Orthodox theology—as a sin.

Many Russian liberal supporters of family planning had consistently endorsed strengthening the (heterosexual) family and increasing fertility, but nationalist discourses put them on the defensive. In the 2000s, Russian nationalism became ever more preoccupied with achieving control over demographic and sexual practices as a means of establishing national sovereignty.[180] In 2009 the Russian Association of Family Planning renamed itself the Russian Association of Population and Development (RAPD) to de-emphasize the term *family planning*, which had become associated with the cynical and permanent rejection of childbearing.[181] Nonetheless, the attacks continued. Antiabortion groups undertook street protests in front of clinics providing abortion and proposed legislation modeled on antiabortion laws in the US. The St. Petersburg teenage reproductive health clinic, Yuventa, which pioneered contraceptive education for adolescents and trained physicians nationwide in family planning, was particularly targeted.[182] The first public defense of legal abortion took place in 2011, organized by RAPD and a coalition of grassroots feminists; they defended abortion again in 2015 to stave off another round of legislative attacks. Their campaigns are the subject of Chapter 6. In 2015 RAPD was labeled a foreign agent; with no funding and an official stigma, the organization soon ceased functioning. In 2016 the St. Petersburg model clinic for teenage reproductive health was transformed beyond recognition by a new, conservative director who established a permanent presence of Orthodox priests in the clinic.

The rise and fall of family planning institutions illustrates the challenges of promoting and defending liberal humanistic changes in Russian society following 1991. I argue that prior to market reforms, Russian family planners had been guided by assumptions that, with liberalizing political-economic change, global scientific knowledge would prove socially authoritative, and health policy would rationally prioritize individual health over ideological goals. New access to the array of market-developed contraceptive devices would enable experts to guide the population to effective prevention. Instead, neoliberal reforms filled public discourse with sexually explicit and cynical, manipulative rhetoric. Conservative critics accused family planners of contributing to the obscenity, inasmuch as they addressed sex instead of only chastity and love. And when family planners strove to defend themselves by reference to global science, they were charged with aligning themselves with foreign rather than Russian interests. The brutal economic collapse and gross levels of inequality, lawlessness, and injustice made liberal promises for a good society seem hollow.[183] They fueled wide-ranging resentment against Western influences tout court, such that family planning—the habitual, safe prevention of unwanted pregnancy—became framed as a hostile demographic politics.[184] Liberal claims of rationalizing policy and re-enchanting relations were drowned out by the din of neoliberal-generated moral panics.

Russian Reproductive Politics in Global Perspective

In its conservative embrace of family values and antiabortion politics, Russia is not unique. As socialist regimes throughout Eastern Europe unraveled in 1989, re-establishing patriarchal control over gender and reproduction became central to the elite's reconsolidation of political power.[185] Poland presented the starkest example, banning abortion immediately upon democratization, but challenges to women's reproductive autonomy spanned the region.[186] New governments established policies to shore up fertility rates, reinvigorate the patriarchal family, and revive masculinity to compensate for what was branded socialism's egregious experiment with women's "emancipation."[187] Gal and Kligman demonstrated why elites found such topics politically opportune: in the face of regime collapse and reconstruction, claiming to revive families enabled political contenders to claim they were fighting on behalf of the nation, not their own personal interests.[188]

Antiabortion and family-values campaigns have of course also been a major force in the US for decades. These specific movements are worth briefly examining; inasmuch as this book focuses on the diversity of liberal approaches in reproductive politics, understanding the commonalities and differences in the global conservative movements that liberals contend with is also important.

Ethnographies of American abortion debates have unearthed the cultural logics shaping activists' concerns and tactics over time. During the 1980s in the US Midwest, Ginsburg found that moderate abortion opponents shared some concerns with abortion rights supporters (and, I would add, with Russian arguments)—namely, anxiety about the encroachment of market logics into everyday life and marginalization of nurturance in society.[189] Tracing the roots of this dilemma historically, Ginsburg observes that as white women increasingly joined the workforce, anxieties arose about how to accomplish caregiving labor. Feminists called for expanding opportunities for public childcare and encouraging men to share domestic tasks—to recognize collective responsibilities for nurturance. Conservatives, by contrast, sought to revive nurturing by promoting traditional gender roles and marriage. They supported an abortion ban as a means of re-establishing the value of motherhood and family and forcing men to take responsibility for the outcomes of sexual activity.[190]

While all antiabortion activists consider themselves protecting society's most innocent members, "unborn children," against an instrumentalist attitude toward human life, antiabortion tactics have evolved and diverged. On sidewalks outside abortion clinics, some activists silently pray while others verbally harass people and display photos of bloody fetuses.[191] Antiabortion activists have established Christian summer camps where memorializing rituals and political protests become a collective youth experience.[192] A common opposition narrative portrays abortion providers as exploiting women's vulnerability for profit; though undercover operatives have tried to expose corruption, antiabortionists themselves ended up charged with felonies.[193] The most extreme activists used violence—bombing clinics and murdering abortion providers. A different strategy is to attract women, often through deceptive advertising, to so-called crisis pregnancy centers; these both communicate false information about abortion and often provide material assistance for those who continue the pregnancy.[194] Some support single mothers.

Other antiabortion activists reject providing economic support to single mothers as a tactic for preventing abortions, arguing that doing so justifies a pragmatic approach to life and detracts from moral absolutism.[195] They focus on the fetus and tend to envision a restored patriarchal order in which women are submissive to their husbands and God's laws.[196] Contested relationships between women and men and the uncertain significance of marriage in contemporary society are thus at the heart of US antiabortion perspectives. Long before the rise of transgender rights, cultural shifts for women's empowerment and LGBTQ rights raised vexing questions about what it means to be a man; economic disruptions associated with neoliberalism, from the loss of the male breadwinner model to the disenfranchisement of workers and middle class precarity, have furthered a sense of disorientation and loss.[197] Against this background, antiabortion activists' heroic self-designation as "rescuers" of "babies" offers a means of restoring traditional masculine and feminine roles.[198] Through antiabortion activism, men experience themselves as respected authorities protecting the weak, and women reaffirm their idyll of selfless nurturers; a sense of firm moral order is revived.[199]

The motivations of Russian conservatives and nationalists are strikingly similar.[200] They lamented low fertility as a symptom of women's waning maternal instinct, itself perceived as caused by early Bolshevik experiments to make women equal to men. More liberal commentators suggested that women were overburdened with work and family responsibilities, and that better housing and more part-time work options would promote increased births. But even among liberals, a widespread view held that masculinity was in crisis, symbolized by men's high rates of alcoholism and alienation from their families. Again, some blamed women's equality and the strong state for usurping men's role as head of the household; others saw men's irresponsibility as the cause. In the 1980s, pedagogical efforts began to revive femininity among girls and masculinity among boys as a means of re-establishing moral order and promoting marriage and higher fertility as values.[201]

So the perception that the family and gender relations were in crisis has pervaded Russian society since the 1960s. And families suffered more intense challenges when the Soviet Union ended, challenges that affected the abortion argument in ways it did not in the US. The shocks of unemployment, wage arrears, and out-of-control inflation were economically and emotionally traumatic. Research documents that women developed a range of strategies to ensure their children's well-being; many men, however, had a harder time doing so.[202] Beginning in 1992, mortality among working-age men spiked dramatically and their life expectancy—already significantly lower than women's—fell to fifty-eight years in 1994, with the main causes including alcohol, accidents, and violence.[203] Yet Russia's post-Soviet biopolitical regime harped on low births, not the working-age mortality of men.[204] They defined the crises facing the family as a threat to national continuity and portrayed abortion as a key cause of population decline.

For Russians who interpreted the Soviet collapse as a national humiliation, the need to reformulate an identity and establish collective pride was urgent. In 2000, Vladimir Putin assumed power and replaced a visibly alcoholic Boris Yeltsin with a new image of male leadership—sober, physically fit, and self-assured. Moreover, through his tough rhetoric and cultivated public persona, Putin used masculinity as a political tool; he portrayed his regime as an aggressive alternative to the feminized, socialist past.[205] Increasingly, he also leveraged discourses juxtaposing "patriots" with "traitors," "enemies," and the (collective) West.

Even before Putin's arrival, conservatives were routinely attacking fledgling family planning and sex education as threats to national security. They joined forces with the Russian Orthodox Church to insist on promoting births, not "pregnancy prevention"; they claimed that resurrecting patriarchal family values would produce a more populous, powerful nation. Putin's regime and the Orthodox Church seized on these rather marginal ideas, expanded on them, and created an illiberal political stance formulated as the revival of traditional values.[206] As Sergei Medvedev has described, this occurred through numerous policies, including "punitive hygiene"—rhetoric and actions of "cleansing" public space of any types of persons or things that did not fit what Putin considered the nation's interests, including queer identities, non-white bodies, the homeless, and stray dogs.[207]

Moreover, through pronatalist policies and increasing restrictions on abortion, the "protection" of children from information about "nontraditional" sexualities, a partial decriminalization of domestic violence, and elimination of "child rights" (juvenile justice), nationalists sought to re-establish Russia's patriarchal order at home.[208] Rejecting Western ideologies of gender equality and strengthening the traditional family was to strengthen the state geopolitically.[209] Drawing on Makarychev and Medvedev, I see the pursuit of demographic and sexual sovereignty as the core goal of Russia's illiberal-nationalist vision.[210]

Thus, conservatives in both the US and Russia have confronted the precarity of neoliberalism and broader uncertainty regarding gender relations by mobilizing a revitalized patriarchal order, in part through opposing abortion. US campaigns have largely focused on saving the fetus; Russian campaigns have sought to save the Russian nation—perceived by conservatives as the most vulnerable, and valuable, cultural entity. While the Russian struggle for revitalizing the nation involves tools not prominent in the US, such as demographic surveillance and stimuli for increasing fertility, Russian antiabortion activists have also adopted numerous tactics from their Western peers to obstruct women's access to abortion, discredit abortion providers, and stigmatize the procedure.[211] The claim to be resurrecting family values became central to Putin's alliance with the Orthodox Church, a longtime symbol of Russian nationalism; similarly, Trump's antiabortion promises secured the fundamentalist religious base for his antiglobalist agenda. Both subverted their society's normative behavior for head of state by performing aggressive masculinity, sexual prowess, and vulgarity in the service of white nationalism.[212]

At the same time, Russian contraceptive supporters differed from feminist family planning supporters in notable ways. Russian experts expressed "opposition" to abortion due to the dangers that repeat dilation and curettage posed to women's health. Their antagonism emerged in educational rhetoric and reprimands of women; they did not support criminalization or restrictions because they knew those would only push abortion underground and make it unsafe. Initially, Russian family planning proponents collaborated with global advocates from both pro-choice and pro-life camps. In 2000, one clinic I visited in a St. Petersburg neighborhood was showing the antiabortion film *The Silent Scream*, which they had received, along with the VCR and resources needed to refurbish a teen lounge with plush bean bags and attractive décor, from a foreign antiabortion organization.

As Russian antiabortion activism adopted global tactics of protest, family-planning supporters reassessed their strategies, shifting their defenses of contraception and abortion through socialist-inspired arguments about economic and social well-being and liberal arguments based on "choice." Justifications for abortion access provide a key site for understanding Russians' ambivalent embrace of liberal ideas of autonomous personhood.

Finally, I show how the inherent tensions between Russia's neoliberal and nationalist politics seemed to be, at least before the Russian invasion of Ukraine, shaping a new stage of reproductive politics—the emergence of grassroots, feminist arguments for reproductive rights. Between 2011 and prior to the 2022 invasion, feminist activists protested against both neo-traditionalism and neoliberalism. When a legislative proposal to severely ban abortions was being considered in 2015, they undertook creative performance art underscoring the state and Church's hypocrisy in trying to restrict abortion while supporting the vicious war in Eastern Ukraine. Moreover, a grassroots initiative included an internet video campaign in which women and men submitted over 150 short, self-made videos explaining why they believed that abortion should remain legal and accessible. While some argued that the state doesn't provide sufficient economic support for families and therefore should not compel reproduction (an argument evoking socialist obligations for the state to guarantee citizens' basic needs), younger women proclaimed liberal political arguments about individual privacy: "my body—my business" (*moe telo—moe delo*). Such resistance to patriarchal revival illustrates the growth of liberal political reactions and explicit articulations of a right to privacy—something barely ever seen in earlier Russian eras.

The demise of family-planning organizations—training for providers and advocacy and education for the public—threatens to dislodge the knowledge and practices necessary for successful prevention, and the loss of family planning services may increase unwanted pregnancies and unhealthy forms of controlling reproduction. Yet culturally, Russians have already undergone the significant shift in social consciousness required by neoliberal economics: people expect to rationally manage their reproduction in accordance with their personal goals. Russians are fully ensconced in the opportunities and demands of consumer society. They live with the awareness that they are responsible for themselves and can design their lives with a deliberative, reflexive concern regarding what they personally want and need in life, not based on social expectations or state interests.[213]

Their consumer subjectivities will continue to shape their sexual and reproductive lives; they will continue to postpone childbearing to suit their own desires, and some will purposefully remain "child free." Repression will not succeed in governing the realm of private life that has emerged with neoliberalism, nor will a fundamentalist pursuit of moral purity achieve national demographic sovereignty. The costs of seeking control through a Church-state regime of ignorance remain to be examined.

Outline of the Book

Chapter 1, "Birthing a Voice through Narratives of Abortion," examines Russian women authors' fictional and memoir scenes of unplanned pregnancy in the late Soviet and early post-Soviet era. Depicting conflicts in intimate relations and health care relations, authors captured the silences of the Soviet era, and, during Glasnost, women's gradual coming into consciousness about the social and ethical problems routine abortion reflected. These accounts of deprivation, betrayal, humiliation, and injustice—and the challenges of making sense of these experiences—introduce readers to the experiential world of the Soviet abortion culture. Chapter 2, "Fighting Abortion with Soviet Biopolitics" traces expert strategies from the late 1950s until the start of Glasnost to reduce abortions by increasing contraceptive use. The chapter also places Soviet health politics into global context, as these decades saw the birth control pill transform women's lives in the US and Western Europe, but not in Soviet spaces. The state's failures to procure contraceptives despite its claims to "fight abortion" expose the existence of a specifically Soviet form of biopolitics. In Chapter 3, we explore how Glasnost made it possible by 1990 to promote contraceptive use as a means of managing sexuality for individual health and pleasure, not fertility. "Conceptualizing Liberal Reproductive Governance" traces the origins of this new perspective to a specifically late-Soviet, liberal worldview. Blending humanism with experts' longing for global scientific knowledge and networks, the liberalism of contraceptive supporters aimed to renew society's commitments to science and care, to rationalize public health practices, and re-enchant intimate relations. Western models of women's empowerment and freedom were not inspirations.

The emergence of Russia's first family planning institutions in the early 1990s is the focus of Chapter 4, "Adopting Global Family Planning with Neoliberalism." Russian experts saw in family planning a means of renewing their professional authority and improving women's health. Family planning involved new clinical approaches and the transformation of expert knowledge. It became the subject of political advocacy and social change as well as medical practice. The use of abortion significantly declined. Still, an illiberal-nationalist opposition cast the idea of rationally preventing pregnancy as a threat to national security, launching an enduring campaign to control Russia's population and geopolitical status by pursuing demographic and sexual sovereignty.

We home in on the careers of two Russian family-planning experts in Chapter 5, "Creating and Defending Liberal Health Professionals." Dr. Viktor Samokhvalov, a psychotherapist and sex educator, worked to transform physicians' interactions with their teenage clients by training them in safe sex promotion. Dr. Liubov Erofeeva, the second director of the Russian Association of Family Planning (RAFP), disseminated new knowledge and models of care inspired by her relationships with global NGOs and pharmaceutical firms. A key feature of both leaders' liberalizing approach was the need for clinicians to respect clients' individuality. Through their careers, and the repression they and their organizations faced, we see the central role of reproductive politics in liberalizing reforms and the Russian backlash against them.

Until viable proposals to restrict abortion were debated in Russia's legislature, family planning experts largely emphasized their contributions to strengthening fertility and family. Chapter 6, "Defending Legal Abortion through New Civic Activism," details innovative, feminist campaigns to preserve abortion access against unprecedented threats in 2011 and 2015. The moral claims of these activists drew on the values of both individual autonomy and care for self and others. As Russia's neoliberal conditions made the concepts of privacy and choice increasingly relevant, activists claimed "my body, my business" (*moe telo- moe delo*), while retaining a humanist view of mothering as an interpersonal obligation. They also insisted on collective investments in well-being, urging the state to "Fight Abortion, Not Women" (*borot'sia s abortami, ne s zhenshchinami*).

The conclusion brings together the book's findings and highlights the lessons that struggles for a liberal biopolitics hold regarding the disturbing illiberal backlash underway worldwide. Given the fact that late Soviet and post-Soviet Russian family planners did not advocate Western ideals of individual freedom or feminism but spoke to mainstream Russian concerns for stronger families and higher fertility, the enduring nationalist attacks against these institutions are telling.

These campaigns reflect the vitriolic, anti-liberal backlash to neoliberalism and the physical and psychological degradation it brought to Russia. Efforts to establish neotraditional family politics, including opposition to family planning, have become a major vehicle of nationalists' response. The illiberal agenda aims to establish demographic and sexual sovereignty. My book suggests that this backlash has been successful in part because neoliberalism lacks a shared moral economy establishing obligations for care and well-being between the state and its residents. Certainly, the visions of Russian liberal family planners had notable limits. But the main goals that they and their feminist supporters emphasized—to renew belief in the trustworthiness of science and promote care, preserve abortion access, and support families—offer starting points for reversing illiberalism globally.

Despite the illiberal success in shuttering Russia's family planning institutions, the ideals of rationally planning pregnancy persist. The neoliberal subjectivity that has formed over the past three decades is irreversible, even if key technologies such as birth control methods once again become deficit items.[214] Although the Russian state is obsessed with achieving demographic and sexual sovereignty, Russian people understand reproductive and sexual autonomy as personal goals, not obligations to the nation. The question, once again, is how they will achieve their interests—through safe or brutal actions, rational or desperate measures.

CHAPTER 1

Birthing a Voice through Narratives of Abortion

"Women getting abortions, don't take the burgers!" So begins a novella published in 1989 by Elena Makarova, with a hospital orderly calling patients to the dining hall.[1] Soviet health services roomed abortion patients alongside women being treated for infertility and potential miscarriage, while implicitly communicating their inferior status: aborting women were not rewarded with meat. This vignette captures an enduring paradox of Soviet approaches to abortion: the procedure was simultaneously normalized and shadowed with disapproval.

Literature and film from the last Soviet decades (the 1950s through 1991) note the frequent use of abortion. Natalya Baranskaya's 1967 novella "A Week Like Any Other Week" includes unplanned pregnancies and abortions among the daily banalities women scientists in a Moscow lab casually shared with each other.[2] Everyone knew, for example, that "Dark Lusya" kept her serial abortions secret from her husband to resist his pressure to abandon her career, give birth, and stay home with the children. In Baranskaya's story and Soviet society in general, a tacit assumption reigned that pregnancies happened and decision making took place afterwards; terminations were consequently a routine, if loathsome, event—similar to toothaches and dental visits.

Yet abortion's normalization was partly attenuated by the state's opposition to it, manifest in its persistent efforts to convince women against terminating and its punitive treatment of those who nonetheless did so. As I learned during fieldwork in 1995, women often rejected official state interpretations about what their abortion decisions meant. While visiting a woman who had recently given birth, I asked why Russian women have so many abortions. Taking for granted the fact that controlling fertility is a basic necessity, I expected an answer regarding contraceptive shortages. But before Irina could answer, her mother burst into the conversation, bellowing, "Do you know what a *komunal'ka* (communal apartment) is?[3] We don't reject having children!" The mother was offended, I later realized, because my phrasing seemed to echo Soviet state accusations that abortions indexed women's disinterest in family life; by contrast, she insisted, women would have more children but for their abysmal living conditions. In fervently rejecting the state's problematization of abortion, Irina's mother reminded me that abortion was a symbol that could evoke a range of ideas. In many Soviet state discourses, abortion symptomized women's flagging "maternal instinct"; for Irina's mother, it symbolized the state's own failure to provide decent housing for families; and for Baranskaya's Dark Lusya, it presented a reliable solution to a marital conflict.

This chapter traces the meanings associated with abortion in women writers' fictional and autobiographical narratives about the late Soviet era. Methodologically, my turn to literary texts as an anthropologist deserves comment. In the course of ethnographic fieldwork during the 1990s, I often observed how clinicians normalized abortion, by taking for granted that women made reproductive decisions after conception and casually recommending terminations to women based on medical concerns without inquiring whether they desired the pregnancy.[4] In my long-term relationships with Russian women, I learned how they retrospectively reflected on past abortions and how they related to contemporary political debates over the procedure. Yet it was in literary texts that I found richly textured portraits of the social and cultural worlds in which women faced unintended pregnancies and deliberated on their next steps in the historically distant Soviet era.[5] These accounts depict the affective and moral valence of experiences, some of which remain outside of speech or entail ambivalence. Through narrative techniques of incorporating multiple and discordant voices, writers portray numerous social dynamics: the judgmental sting of social norms, the bewildered encounter between people from different social backgrounds, the confusion felt when experiencing problems for which there is no established discourse. Methodologically, I approach these texts as I do other ethnographic material—with an anthropologist's eye to the social positionings and inequalities they reveal, and the implicit cultural assumptions, ways of challenging dominant scripts, and moral debates that are possible in a given social context.[6]

Before exploring these questions, a glimpse into the historical and cultural ideas underlying abortion debates in the late-twentieth-century US will help clarify why late Soviet texts did not echo the pro-choice/pro-life divisions familiar to readers. The contemporary, globalized abortion debate reflects a series of particularly American cultural values and, in particular, American notions of personhood and autonomy. The conceptual seeds for the problematization of abortion law were planted in 1963, with Betty Friedan's *The Feminine Mystique.* Addressing the widespread malaise many white middle-class women were experiencing in postwar America, despite their seemingly comfortable lives as homemakers in the affluent suburbs, Friedan identified the problem as gender norms, captured in the concept of "the feminine mystique." She argued that norms defining genuine womanhood through marriage and motherhood alone were harmfully limiting women's self-realization. The unstated cultural assumption was that dignified adulthood involved individual self-determination, which (white) men were achieving; (white) women, by contrast, were suffering because they were limited to the roles of dependent or caregiver, stunted from achieving independent selfhood. New social norms and the reorganization of gender relations were necessary to enable women's full human flourishing—which would happen through self-realization outside the home. As the civil rights movement and cultural revolutions of the late 1960s and 1970s got underway, the broader zeitgeist challenged numerous political inequalities and social hierarchies; it celebrated notions of individual self-determination, bodily and sexual autonomy, and personal freedom. Women's rights became a rallying cry, and the reproductive rights movement pressed for sexual freedom and legal abortion. The 1973 Supreme Court decision in *Roe v. Wade* only partly fulfilled this vision when it granted access to first trimester abortions as a matter of women's right to privacy. What is notable, from the perspective of Soviet cultural assumptions, is that the ability to realize oneself as a self-determining individual free from state intervention was taken as a norm in the US. Soviet women, by contrast, were required to work full time. Although they thereby enjoyed a degree of economic independence from men, Soviet state rhetoric framed this as a citizen's duty, not a personal choice.

Friedan and the *Roe* decision made way for new kinds of gendered subjectivity, and the concomitant changes in the availability of contraceptives and abortion ushered in a new system of (neo)liberal reproductive governance. Women and men were expected to discipline themselves to prevent unwanted pregnancy and, especially with the AIDS epidemic in the mid-1980s, sexually transmitted illnesses (STIs). These were new norms of respectability that mobilized people to optimally manage their life economically and socially. These norms both idealized sexual autonomy and compelled people to take personal responsibility for timing conceptions. The notion of personal choice in marriage and childbearing—as in other life spheres—became paramount, and defenders of legal abortion called their position "pro-choice."

Opponents of *Roe* argued for (re)criminalization by also invoking individual selfhood, extending "the right to life" to embryos from conception. Thus, grounding both the pro-choice and pro-life positions is the cultural value of individualism; the debate focuses on whether a woman's or a fetus's individualism should be considered sovereign.[7] Additional differences are that pro-lifers argue that abortion is equivalent to "murder" and therefore must be illegal; pro-choicers tend to evade publicly defining the morality of abortion, allowing it to remain a personal matter for each woman to decide. Finally, American abortion debates are subsumed within anxieties over the work of nurturance, spurred by the social acceptance of middle-class mothers working outside the home.[8] Along with banning abortion, pro-life activists seek to re-value the work of motherhood and endow it with the aura of valiant social accomplishment. Pro-choice advocates aim to ensure that nurturance is voluntary by ensuring access to abortion while also seeking to make caregiving a wider, collective responsibility by expanding daycares and normalizing men's equal participation in family caregiving.[9] Despite these different visions of an ideal society, the major organizations campaigning on abortion emphasize the moral issue of individual rights (to choice or life).

In Soviet contexts, entirely different political-economic conditions shaped the conflicts surrounding reproduction. The fact that abortion was the most readily available and widely used form of fertility control in the state-dominated economy—while state authorities politically condemned the practice and disparaged its users—illustrates a contradiction frequent in Soviet life. Socialism had promised to end material need and establish the conditions for people—both workers and women as a class—to make life decisions on the basis of genuine freedom, but socialism's severe economic realities made a mockery of such promises. Women's experiences of reproductive governance, consequently, were laden with contradictions. They manifested in a dissonance between the socialist state's celebrated support for mothers, on the one hand, and the atrocious material conditions facing families, on the other. Women gained the right to abortion in 1955, but not the right to contraceptives. And women came to understand that accessible, legal abortions did not imply their provision with pain relief, material comfort, or moral support. It was unthinkable to demand better conditions, because, as recipients of entitlements from the paternalistic state, Soviet workers were expected to accept its provisions with patriotic loyalty. To emphasize the subordination of individuals to the state, bureaucrats and experts communicated in authoritarian attitudes, diminishing recipients into voiceless supplicants. The kind of subjectivity known as "consumer empowerment," in which seekers of goods and services feel entitled to influence the conditions of exchange, would only emerge with conditions of late capitalism.

Women also perceived a dissonance between the state's harangues against abortion and its disregard for their need to limit childbearing. Discussions about the dangers of abortion were often framed as if a woman was already pregnant and deciding what to do; health experts urged giving birth. Soviet health education, in other words, did not assume that either preventing or planning pregnancies was normal. For their part, women saw life as a perpetual confrontation with risk and were not especially persuaded by state scare mongering. With the state highlighting only the risks of abortion and eliding some of the most pressing reasons that women used abortion, official discourses contradicted people's sense of their own interests.[10]

Soviet state-approved literary narratives generally cast abortion as problematic in two ways: as a health risk, leading to infertility or death, especially in the case of illegal abortions, and emotionally, as a cause for women's later regret at "rejecting" motherhood.[11] The threat of remaining childless posed grave consequences as motherhood was culturally prescribed as a necessity for a woman's social identity and virtue. An idyllic attitude toward the maternal as sacred shaped both Russian folk culture, where the maternal was symbolized through the fertile, nourishing icon of damp mother earth (*syraia zemlia*), and Russian Orthodoxy, which venerated Mary as the Mother of God (*Bogomateri*), rather than as virgin.[12] This sentimental imagery became reworked in the Soviet era and sometimes afforded mothers a degree of authority to make public demands on behalf of their children; but any power women accrued through leveraging the maternal identity was always tenuous at best.[13] Classic Russian literature further elaborated these tropes by projecting onto women expectations of selflessness; any mother who failed to demonstrate a self-sacrificing nature was a devastating threat.[14] Some pronatalist advocates drew on these associations to define abortion as the rejection of motherhood and a source of women's spiritual and social demise.

How did Russian women writers characterize the contradictory world in which abortion was at once officially denounced and yet routine? What do their narratives about women's experiences of unintended pregnancies and abortions reveal about these writers' relationships to dominant ideologies of gender, maternity, and the state? To explore these questions, textual interpretations must be accompanied by attention to the historical contexts in which the narratives were written and published. The sections below examine Soviet-era scenarios from five fictional accounts and two memoirs; one story was published in 1967 (Baranskaya), and one memoir was never published (Makarova's 1983 "Ulitka v kosmose" [A Snail in the Cosmos]). Five were published after censorship had ended (Palei, 1988; Petrushevskaia, 1988; Arbatova, 1999; Ulitskaya's *Kazus Kukotskogo*, 2001, and her "Orlovy-Sokolovy," 2002).[15] I note some of the ways these shifting political contexts of publication, and the broader literary trends characterizing different eras, impacted writers' representations.

In the following sections, I highlight three themes common in Soviet abortion stories: the tensions women faced between prioritizing love and making utilitarian calculations, the effects of societal and interpersonal indifference to women's suffering, and the personal struggles of living ethically in relationship to ideals and other persons. Through such themes, these texts evoked both classic Russian framings of ethical struggles and the Glasnost-era outpouring of pent-up indignation at Soviet state power. Without pronouncing a feminist agenda, and in a variety of more or less explicit ways, they disrupt ideological visions of women as necessarily mothers and of mothers as necessarily self-sacrificing.[16] Their narratives echoed Russian historical and cultural anxieties regarding the value of love, care, and allegiance to humanistic ethics, while rejecting state efforts to co-opt the cultural value of nurturance for pronatalism.[17]

We begin with Natalia Baranskaya's 1967 story "A Week Like Any Other Week" and Elena Makarova's unpublished memoir, "Ulitka v kosmose" [A Snail in the Cosmos] (written in 1983), which both portray women struggling in the face of an unintended pregnancy to value love over utility. As Baranskaya's title implies, her story aims to capture experiences readers will recognize; her protagonist, Olga, is struggling to combine career aspirations with the burden of domestic labor and caregiving that Soviet society placed squarely on women's shoulders. Abortion per se plays a minor role in this text, but Olga's retrospective reflections about her unexpected pregnancy and fraught decision to give birth structure the plot; they vividly demonstrate some of the reasons abortion was so common among married, professional women by exposing the limits of state ideology and support. Makarova's memoir, by contrast, is an account of her anguish over terminating an unexpected pregnancy at the insistence of her husband and parents. While on many levels presenting an atypical perspective—from how she weighs abortion in terms of collective memory and historical consciousness to her profound grief over the procedure—Makarova's valuing love over utilitarian calculations is highly culturally salient. Indeed, it echoes the same logic that Baranskaya's Olga invoked, even as it reveals that prioritizing "love" can result in varying outcomes, not necessarily only in continuing a pregnancy. No less importantly, both stories reveal that this longing to prioritize love over utility was perceived as divorced from politics and only made more difficult by the state.

The second section examines two fictional narratives published during Glasnost: Marina Palei's "The Loser's Division" (1988) and Liudmila Petrushevskaia's "Bednoe serdtse Pani" (1990; Pani's Poor Heart), stories that seize the new possibilities afforded by Glasnost to expose the mundane horrors of Soviet society and its medical institutions. Through juxtapositions between the narrator's voice and other women's inarticulateness or silence, these stories highlight the sadistic physicians, negligent clinics, and cruel social norms that demeaned poor and rural women. Portraying abortion as a common site of women's victimization, these authors, more directly than the others I examine, used abortion scenarios to expose the hypocrisies of Soviet ideology and state institutions.

In the chapter's third section, we see how writers used abortion to catalyze women's realizations that their intimates—husbands, lovers, or mothers—did not care for them as needed. In Maria Arbatova's 1991 memoir *My Name Is Woman* and Ludmila Ulitskaya's 2002 short story "OrlovySokolovy" (abbreviated in this text as OS), abortions became markers of others' failure to provide care by remaining silent about relationships, sexuality, and health. Additionally, in Ulitskaya's 2001 novel *Kazus Kukotskogo* (abbreviated KK; published in English as *The Kukotsky Enigma* in 2015), abortion becomes a site of intimate betrayal through an ethical disagreement between spouses. Through a variety of narrative techniques—retrospective reframing in Arbatova and Ulitskaya, OS, and conflict in Ulitskaya, KK—these authors reject dominant ideologies defining womanhood through the self-sacrificing maternal image. Abortion emerges in these narratives as a symptom of the failure of men, mothers, and the state, to care.

The final section of this chapter, "Abortion, Relational Ethics, and the Search for Selfhood," explores additional selections from Ulitskaya's KK and Arbatova's memoir, both of which depict how abortion stimulates questions about personal ethics. In Ulitskaya's narrative, a budding scientist realizes that her commitment to "progress" has made her numb toward the sacredness of human life. Arbatova remembers the relief she experienced in having her abortion decision justified by a man she cares for, who told her she has the right to prioritize her own life over that of a future child. In both narratives, protagonists search for a selfhood understood not as "autonomous," but committed to other persons and ideals, without allowing those relationships to subsume the self.

Abortion and the Struggle between Love and Utility

Natalya Baranskaya's "A Week Like Any Other Week" (*Nedelia kak nedelia*) is notable among publications before Glasnost for delving into the social conditions of women's lives in the 1960s. Socialist ideology demanded that women embody both the worker and mother roles, and Baranskaya's account exposes the tensions this presented for women from Moscow's scientific intelligentsia. As a twenty-six-year-old married mother of two, Olga's life is a frantic swim against the tide of thankless domestic chores and out-of-reach career goals. Neither her husband nor her male boss recognize the burdens she bears. When the women in her lab are required to complete a state survey explaining their reasons for limiting childbearing, they erupt with anxiety over what new (re)production plan the state may push them to fulfill. The argument of one colleague—"Comrades, what are you so excited about? After all, each one of you chose her own lot"—particularly gives Olga pause. "Do we really make free choices?" she asks herself.[18]

This question leads Olga to revisit her decision to have a second child. Olga was at the clinic waiting to be called for an abortion when she began allowing herself to indulge the pleasurable images of having a daughter to love and nurture. She decides to have the baby, arousing her husband's anger and her own ethical realization in defense: "I can't kill my daughter just because it won't be easy for us."[19] Baranskaya brings us inside Olga's memories and then returns us to her present day and her internal retort to her colleague's statement: "Did I 'choose' this? No, of course not. Do I regret it? No, never. It's not even a question that can be asked. I love them so much, our silly little fools."[20] "Choice," in the sense of an empowering expression of agency, does not match Olga's experience: she simply felt she could not go ahead with the abortion. She saw herself undertaking an act that was both irrational and necessary, embracing the possibilities of love instead of capitulating to the despair of practicality.

Olga also reflects on her co-workers' reproductive fates; all of their pregnancies were unplanned. Routinely facing the need to decide about a pregnancy already conceived reminded women that they did not fully control their lives. In seeking abortions, they expected a disagreeable if not hostile and painful process would follow. Far from an empowering choice, abortions represented a means of escape from yet another systemic-rooted aggravation.

And Olga's next reflection to herself, "Do I regret it? No, never. It's not even a question that can be asked," embodies the contradiction at the heart of this story about Soviet women's lives. We know that Olga did not proactively seek to have the second child, and we also know her life is significantly more difficult because she receives no support at home or at work. What Baranskaya shows is that Olga had no language for conceptualizing this problem of systemic gender inequality. Olga's reflections lead her to an awareness that she has not chosen her lot, and she has a troubling ambivalence about her life. But her dilemmas are not socially legitimated. The impossibility of either regretting her daughter's birth or expecting more supportive conditions for combining family and career leaves Olga confused. She realizes her good fortune relative to her co-workers: she is married, her husband is not an alcoholic, and he is not pressuring her to quit work and become a homemaker. Olga's family lives in a new, thirty-four-square-meter apartment, a genuine privilege in Soviet society. Her children are healthy and sleep peacefully. "Then what is disturbing me?" Olga asks herself. "I don't know."

"A Week Like Any Other Week" highlighted the absence of a culturally legitimate framework through which Soviet women could grasp their own gendered suffering. Soviet women had full-time jobs and representation in politics; they had the right to abortion. But these political and economic rights did nothing to solve the hardships of the deficit economy or the gendered inequalities at home and the workplace. Baranskaya's fictionalized account thus presented a Soviet-era version of Betty Friedan's the "problem that has no name."[21] Baranskaya's plot structure of a neverending cycle of daily burdens and exhaustion reveals the social production of women's malaise, even as Olga herself remains at a loss as to why she is frustrated and discontented.

The publication of Baranskaya's story reveals the social changes underway in the Soviet 1960s, the post-Stalin years of flourishing creativity and aesthetic debates known as the Thaw. Pomerantsev's essay "On Sincerity," which aroused calls for acknowledging the morass of social life, had been published in the respected literary journal *Novyi mir* in December 1953. It opened up the possibility of rejecting the hackneyed portrayal of heroism and progress characterizing socialist realism, and invited critiques of the chains of bureaucratization that held back creativity. Yet a more holistic examination and public critique of women's systematic, *gendered* suffering would not arise at the center of Russian public debate for many decades— arguably not until the Russian version of the me-too campaign (*ianeboius*) exploded in 2016.

If Baranskaya's Olga ultimately adheres to ideological demands when she keeps her unintended pregnancy, she did so because she embraced the value of love, not because she felt a duty to the state. Indeed, Olga gently mocked the idea of bearing children to help fulfill population goals. Whether they gave birth or aborted a pregnancy, Soviet women tended to ignore state ideology in their decision making, deeming it irrelevant to their personal interests.[22]

An unpublished account by Elena Makarova tragically echoes Baranskaya's Olga's statement "I can't kill my daughter just because it won't be easy for us," even as she goes ahead with the abortion.[23] A writer, historian, artist, and art therapist, Makarova was born in 1951 in Baku to the poet Inna L'vovna Lisnianskaia, a contributor to the 1979 samizdat (underground) literary collection, *Metropol'*. After growing up in Moscow from the age of nine, Makarova immigrated to Israel in 1990. I contacted Makarova to learn more about her short story "Na sokhranenie," (On Bedrest; quoted in the beginning of this chapter), and she generously sent me another piece of her writing, entitled "Ulitka v kosmose" [A Snail in the Cosmos].[24] This essay was written in 1983 to recount and lament an abortion she had after her two children were born. It has not been published.

"A Snail in the Cosmos" takes place in the vortex of her anguish over the decision to terminate her pregnancy. A mother of two, Elena construes abortion as the sacrifice of one of her children for the others, and of the child she now awaits, for her husband. Merging temporalities, she appraises her own devotion toward childbearing and family in light of her community's collective history of brutality. Mothers in her Belorussian town during the Holocaust were forced to wager on their loved ones. Their horrific, irreconcilable fate haunts Elena: "Which of your two children will you send to the slaughter [*zaklanie*]? That woman who I'm talking about chose the younger, her daughter. And clutching a doll, the girl went into the gas oven. Her son died in her arms later, in the ghetto. And she lost her mind. She lived to an old age, crazy Nioba . . ."[25]

For Elena, these witnesses to the murderous Nazi bloodbath present a cautionary sign: life without loved ones leaves a person to roam incomprehensibly in a ghost-like existence.[26] Such searing memories of genocide—the murder of children, the destruction of family, and the unending grief among those who physically remain in this world—provide the ethical backdrop for Elena's howl against an abortion. Her pregnancy was not conceived amid starvation or genocidal violence; she is married, she and her husband are fortunate to have their own apartment—a Soviet era index of a decent standard of life. But her husband and her parents insist on an abortion; the economic burden, the physical hardship make it too hard to raise a third child. "Everything is stressing us, we have no breathing room, the pressure is everywhere" her husband implores.[27] Elena does not disagree. But she prizes love, and her maternal love for her children, over utilitarian concerns. The spirits of murdered masses present her with an ethical charge for seizing the opportunity to give life. Challenging the use of utilitarian rationality, she recoils in anger at the notion that "murdering her child" in the name of convenience could be a willful choice.

Indicting herself, then opposing this act, Elena calls up Dostoevsky's rejection of utilitarian logics, captured in his utopian statement, "The whole world is not worth the tears of a tortured child."[28] She recalls her husband's rational arguments, including the concern for her that he also conveys. He says to her, "Tell me—what do you need? You wanted to be an artist—you became one. You wanted a studio, you got one. You wanted children, you gave birth . . . By the way, you haven't gone to the studio for a whole month. With a third one you'll forget how to even get there."

But Elena rejects the calculus that her creativity comes at a price, that it can be preserved through limiting her commitment to nurturing her children: "These down-to-earth, practical arguments—my husband wants things to be good for me. He jealously protects my talent. But now—it's all over. After THIS I'll not be able to do anything."[29] Envisioning a loss of her creativity as an existential punishment for her action, Makarova is not invoking any religious doctrine. She is expressing what Mikhail Epstein describes as a post-atheistic spirituality, a sense that personal morality and social harmony will result from reviving human awe toward the sublime and ineffable.[30] Makarova senses that violating her conscience will leave her creative spirit in tatters. "It is motherhood that is my self-expression," she avers. "Abortion is not an exit but a dead end; The murderer—the murdered." Within the whirl of unbearable emotions, competing arguments crash through her thoughts. The case for pragmatism echoes in her mother-in-law's admission: "I, by the way, had two abortions. When they were prohibited. Because I was facing the practical realities—we had to rebuild after the destruction of the war, strengthen the reconstruction efforts. I worked night and day."[31] And she hears a contemporary version of this pragmatism from another woman in the clinic: "In general, I love kids. It's just not the time. Each time, when the deadline for an abortion gets close, I think—I'll keep it. But then it gets scary. And I think, next time."

Then, reflecting on what this utilitarian rationality offers in light of the world's anguish, Makarova interrogates, "From which bowels of the earth has this kind of consciousness arisen? What will it bring the world? Perdition? Or the opposite—will there no longer be starving people in India? Will mothers who can only give their child an empty breast become a thing of the past? Women feeding their children their own saliva, sleeping together with corpses—what is all this [reasoning good] for?"[32] In response, she sarcastically recalls Soviet rhetoric celebrating the ongoing march of progress: "It's tempting. You've already contributed your part to the creation of a sterilized existence. Glory to you, Architect of the New World!"[33] But in the next breath she refutes this logic, likening her experience of exploring it to that of a desperate, trapped animal: "Enough. I need to run away like a cat escaping so fast it doesn't care that the friction rips out the claws from its paws."[34]

Makarova cries out for valuing human life against its instrumentalization and destruction. She refuses utilitarian explanations, grounding herself in the embrace of love as the ultimate purpose of life, her love for her children as surpassing and overcoming economic needs and practical convenience. But in addition to this moral vision, Makarova also protests the idea of aborting a pregnancy in the wake of the Nazis' brutal violence just a few decades previously—"they shot our children in front of the pits of Babi Yar; . . . a mother had to choose which of her two children to send to the gas, which to keep, . . . she lost her mind forever. . . . How, in the aftermath of that cruelty and horror, can I kill my own child?"—she cries.

Intimately attuned to the reverberations of war-era mass violence and brutality, Elena sees the apparent indifference toward routine abortion in Soviet society as profoundly disturbing. She associates both phenomena with the rationalizing mentality labeled "progress," which, she recognizes, included instrumentalizing and destroying human life in the name of some other good or desire.[35] Embracing love over rationality and convenience, Makarova's rejection of abortion expresses her rejection of the dehumanizing social logic characterizing history and contemporary Soviet society. She terminated this pregnancy for the sake of her marriage, at once subordinating her will to her love for her husband and refusing to erase herself by accepting the decision. "Everything in me is against it, everything is opposed to it, everything. 'It's not my choice.' . . . And so what, then, is in MY control? To live, submitting to my harsh fate."

When I presented an earlier version of this analysis, a Russian colleague strongly cautioned me against implying that such grief over abortion was common; she herself had had four abortions and each was a source of great relief, she asserted. Indeed, one Russian sociologist has investigated a discourse among some Soviet women that positively celebrated abortion as a sign of femininity and proof of fertility.[36] And so I underscore—abortion in Soviet society was open to a range of meanings, and generally not considered a moral dilemma. For Makarova, having cast her termination as a betrayal of existential obligations in the aftermath of war and genocide and in the name of convenience, it was unusually anguished. Yet her struggle presents a mode of ethical reasoning that extends far beyond reproductive matters in Russia, illustrating a Dostoevsky-inspired conscience recognizable among Russia's intelligentsia as the tragic longing to take the path affirming love and life, even where doing so requires extreme sacrifice. Collapsing pragmatism with indifference, Makarova rejected her husband's reasoning but terminated the pregnancy to affirm that her love for him was supreme. The questions of where pragmatism turns into indifference, and what kinds of sacrifice can be offered without compromising the virtue being pursued, were common to Soviet-era humanism. As with Baranskaya, other authors grapple with this too, as examined in the next section.

Abortion as a Lens onto Institutional Indifference and Cruelty

Texts published during Glasnost and the early post-Soviet era problematized abortions in ways newly possible—highlighting the institutional indifference, and at times cruelty, state services perpetrated on women obtaining them. Notably, Arbatova's memoir was the only text I found that indicted political decisions or the deficit in contraceptives. She does so by characterizing her hospital roommate as a twenty-year-old woman with a luxurious braid, make-up on her eyes and cheeks, a cute shirt, and her nails neatly polished—awaiting her fifth abortion. Arbatova finds this situation "frightening. Not for me, personally. It's frightening in general. Such a meaningless emblem of a meaningless civilization. . . . [It makes] you want to call up the Supreme Soviet and say, 'You old he-goats, either come here and look at her, or finally procure contraceptives!'"[37]

In the contradictory image of a young woman who makes obvious efforts to have a pretty appearance, but who has no healthy options for birth control, Arbatova sees the horror of political indifference. This "meaningless civilization" leads to the desecration (*k narugatel'stvu*) of a young woman's body.

In Marina Palei's harrowing fictional story "The Losers' Division," published in 1988, the rural women undergoing abortions appear confused and inarticulate.[38] The third-person narrative offers only oblique glimpses of their experiences on the receiving end of the senior male doctor's angry desperation and the young male doctor's crass and careless egoism. Palei exposes the senior doctor's language games for degrading his women supplicants, from his rude insinuations to his boorish hand gestures, rhetorical outbursts and overt refusals to provide care. She details the junior doctor's violence against women—both the abortion patients and his medical trainees, whom he sexually assaults. Speech and silence reflect both unequal verbal capacities and unequal access to the right to talk. Those with a relative degree of power wield language creatively and flexibly as a brutal weapon.

In Palei's vivid descriptions, the rural women patients seem to subsist in a fog, either not understanding the insults or, due to their vulnerability and intimidation, simply unable to respond. They certainly have no grasp of their health providers' concerns or calculations about their treatment. The women are kept ignorant of birth control methods, deprived of contraceptive devices, and mocked by the clinicians on whom they depend. When one local woman returns for a yet another abortion only two months following her previous one, the sadistic doctor confronts her, demanding an explanation: "What do you have to say for yourself?" It is the narrator, not the character, who provides a response: "to out-talk him is impossible, but she can out-silence him."[39] Indeed, Palei's rural women have learned the rules—they dare not irritate the doctors. When they do express dissatisfaction with their treatment, it is in "timid whispers" and "stilted written complaints" that the "scraping" (slang for the curettage) has left them bleeding and in pain. Women's routine reliance on abortion is the embodied outcome of their deprivation at the hands of state medicine, which dispenses humiliation but neither care nor information.

Another picture of voicelessness emerges in Petrushevskaia's 1990 short story "Bednoe serdtse Pani" (Pani's poor heart), in which the tribulations of the eponymous Pani become the object of societal judgments. We never hear directly from Pani herself.[40] Narrating the story is an unnamed woman in the same maternity hospital ward as Pani. The narrator's opening portrait of Pani as "already a really old woman of about forty-seven," "an almost illiterate, unskilled worker, wrinkled," "with her pendulous, drooping stomach," and "cunning narrow eyes" frames Pani as intrinsically and irredeemably Other.[41] By presenting her account as the collective voice of the maternity hospital inmates—"Everyone called her Granny Pani," and "she's made of totally different dough than the rest of us"—the narrator's curious, casual disdain for Pani assumes the normative voice of society.[42]

Unlike the women hospitalized on bedrest awaiting childbirth, Pani is at this clinical-scientific-research center for a late-term abortion. Her husband, injured at work, was unemployed, they had three children, and Pani herself had had a heart attack a year previously, resulting in her acquiring an official disability status.[43] Petrushevskaia's narrator exposes the communal construction of Pani's story through the gossip mill:

> We'd have all exclaimed, "What'd you wait so long for?" but nobody did so, because we all knew that they first diagnosed her with a tumor, and the tumor grew and grew until it started to move and jerk its feet. And then Pani wandered for some time around her local and regional public health committees, was sent with a folder full of papers to seek her truth [*iskat' pravdu*] in the Ministry of Health in Moscow, and she won, the stubborn soul, because really with that heart of hers she could die from giving birth and leave three children orphans.[44]

Having endured medical negligence, Pani faced an unwanted, dangerous pregnancy, and was left to navigate the labyrinthine public health bureaucracy alone; but the narrator treats Pani's hellish misfortunes as a curiosity tale. And although a hint of compassion emerges when the narrator observes that after her arrival at the hospital, "everyone targeted a mix of confusion and hatred toward the guilty-of-nothing Pani," this tone shifts to moral judgment following Pani's surgery.[45] She now refers to Pani as "the murderer."[46] Pani ends up in the infection ward with a temperature, and barely recovered, leaves the hospital to face the twelve-kilometer walk from the station to the construction site where she lived and worked.[47]

While the reader's voyeuristic glimpse of Pani concludes here, the narrator continues with her own story. She enters the nursery to feed her own son and notices another small baby in an incubator. The narrator surmises that Pani's late term surgery resulted in a viable child rather than an aborted fetus and shares the nurse's delight that the premature baby is "already drinking from a pipette." She closes by commenting on how this creature "touched everyone's heart, except for the poor heart of Granny Pani, who worked as a guard and was an invalid." Through this strikingly romanticized gaze on the outcome of Pani's tribulations, readers become aware of one more arena of medical failure: the institution's lack of honesty with Pani, and by implication, with all patients. Given the immiserating and lonely life awaiting children abandoned in Soviet orphanages, the narrator's readiness to feel joy at the baby's survival appears a naively irresponsible conclusion.

Through Pani's story, Petrushevskaia indicts Soviet medicine's and society's devastating numbness to women's pain. It was the medical system that caused Pani's need for a late term abortion, forced her to fight obstinately to obtain it, traded her for it with a severe post-surgical infection, abruptly discharged her from its responsibility with no concern for her condition, and gave her no information about the actual procedure. Pani is treated like refuse by the system and as a freakish curiosity by others on the ward. Petrushevskaia's story exposes Soviet society's cruel indifference to both the hardships that led Pani to the hospital and those the hospital experience cause her. Exemplifying the critical realist style erupting with Glasnost, Palei and Petrushevskaia both depicted state medical institutions as sites of horror and the grotesque. Although these grim narratives provided no glimpse of societal redemption, they arouse pathos in the reader, conjuring a humanist protest.

Abortion as a Barometer of Intimate Betrayal

Another prevalent theme developed through abortion narratives is that of betrayal by intimates. In an essay from Maria Arbatova's 1991 memoir, *Menia zovut zhenshchina* (My Name Is Woman), and in a short story by Ludmila Ulitskaya, abortions are the outcomes of mothers and lovers' failures to act with appropriate care. Women's personal growth comes from their learning, in the aftermath of this betrayal, to discern the requirements of a loving and nurturing relationship.

Arbatova's titular story, "Menia zovut zhenshchina," recalls her eighteen-year-old self sitting in the health clinic office having just found out she is pregnant. She hones in on an exchange between her mother and the doctor, whom she refers to as "Auntie" as a sign that they are acquainted. After interrogating them about what work Arbatova and her fiancée do, the doctor erupts at the absurdity of their status as students majoring in opera and philosophy, respectively, and says she'll write a referral for an abortion.

> "Of course for an abortion," Mom chimed in. "What would they do with children?"
>
> "That's exactly right," said Auntie, who, having barely rinsed her hands, gets sucked into the conversational back-and-forth.
>
> "You have to first finish university and then get pregnant," Mom announces with importance, as if someone at some time had asked her what to do after what, and as if she had at some time shown even a tiny bit of concern about my education in the area of pregnancy prevention.
>
> "Yes, they have wind in their heads—what do they understand about life?" sighed Auntie.
>
> "It's strange that she didn't try to convince me to give birth," I said as we were outside the door.
>
> "Well, she's had fifteen abortions herself," Mom replies.[48]

The retrospective structuring of this scene, in which Arbatova the memoirist recalls her younger self first hearing about information that supposedly "everyone knows," but which neither her mother nor any other adult had ever told her, newly marks her earlier upbringing as a failure: her mother had not educated her about sexuality, reproduction, and the expected chronology of life course stages, and she should have done so.[49] This discussion delivers Arbatova a double sense of betrayal: first, at hearing her mother's formulaic chronology of the expected life course for the first time at age eighteen, and second, in her mother's judgment that she acted irresponsibly and recklessly when none of the adults in her life ever helped her understand how to handle herself in this supposedly "responsible" manner.[50] In this way, the scene captures an exemplary moment of coming-into-new-awareness so characteristic of Soviet people's experiences during Glasnost—the past became reconceptualized as a time of problematic discursive absence. Indeed, not only the revelations themselves, but also the new realization that knowledge had been withheld, raised profound resentment.[51]

Arbatova's narrative identifies multiple layers of indifference structured into routinized abortion and on this basis, depicts it as a phenomenon to question, lament, critique. While Baranskaya's Olga remains confused and lacks a coherent explanation for her discontent, Arbatova, writing over two decades later, traces her vulnerability to her mother's, teachers', and doctors' failure to communicate about the body, sex, and family formation.

In Ulitskaya's fiction, indifference and neglect stem from other sources. In her 2002 short story "Orlovy-Sokolovy," we follow the relationship of promising young lovers from Moscow's educated class from the charmed beginnings of their love through the tolls they experience as gendered inequalities gradually divide them.[52] Although Tanya and Andrei are exceptionally intelligent, energetic, and self-confident, they do not talk about avoiding pregnancy, preventing abortions, whether and when they want a child, or how they would manage their careers and domestic responsibilities if they had one. Tanya gets pregnant again and again and has abortion after abortion. They live with the pretense that "they share everything," with the differences in their reproductive biology and resulting social expectations ignored. While registering untimely pregnancies as "inconvenient," they seem to have no vocabulary for discussing pregnancy prevention or childbearing, or any template for conceptualizing how these issues differently affect each of them and their goals for the future. Yet what they do not talk about intermittently surfaces, if only through tensions and inarticulate allusions.

The narrator simultaneously presents us with Tanya's nonmoralized approach to abortion—a practical means to take care of a problem—and the official medical perspective on abortion—that it represents a serious risk to women's health and fertility that increases each time the procedure is undertaken. Both Tanya's and Andrei's mothers were doctors, both disapproved of the repeated resort to termination, yet both also respected the couple's right to make their own decisions and provided support; Andrei's mother arranged Tanya's second abortion through her contacts. In this way, we see abortion as a normalized, if regrettably risky, act.

It would be Tanya's mother, Galina, who first problematized Tanya's abortions beyond the risk to her health. As Tanya prepared to deal with what had become her "annual autumn abortion," Galina informed her daughter that

Andrei was "a real asshole": implicit in her critique is that after witnessing Tanya deal with two mistimed pregnancies, Andrei had still not made the effort to care for her health by doing all he could to prevent another pregnancy.[53] Repeat abortions, Galina was implying, index a man's indifference to his partner.

Andrei's selfishness became further evident when he and Tanya come into direct competition over a single scientific research position that they both wanted. They face the situation with tension and avoidance. Again, they had no language to discuss their career ambitions or how, together, they might attempt to make both of their dreams possible. Eventually, Andrei articulates the patriarchal vision he expected would shape their relationship: "You're being silly, Tanya. I am the man, for heaven's sake. Rely on me. Don't feel bad about it. I love you. We share everything. We have everything in common." Tanya discloses that she is pregnant yet again. Andrei then suggests what he has heretofore always avoided: "It's time to go for it, I reckon. Have the baby this time . . ." It is at this moment that Tanya wakes up to Andrei's indifference. "Oh, I get it. You go for the postgraduate place and I go for a baby and changing diapers."

The situation finally becomes clear to Tanya: Andrei puts his own ambitions, his own needs, and his own dreams over hers. He determines the appropriate timing for starting a family, or more precisely, for keeping a pregnancy, on the basis of his, not their, career needs; he assumes she will back down and minimize her own scientific ambitions, allowing his career to flourish. Tanya's new consciousness about Andrei's selfishness motivates her to end the relationship.

While the plot readily suggests a critique of unequal gender norms, it is notable that the couple's relationship is cast as intertwined selves, not autonomous ones. Andrei says to her, "Rely on me. I love you. We share everything. We have everything in common." Tanya's new realization, consequently, could be interpreted as his failure to care about and nurture her career aspirations, rather than his failure to respect her individuality and equality. The conflict, in other words, may be read as a transgression of relational connections—Andrei's selfish indifference to Tanya's needs and well-being, like his failure to prevent her pregnancies and abortions.

Ulitskaya's 2001 novel *Kazus Kukotskogo* (*The Kukotsky Enigma*) explores abortion as a matter of relational ethics between the state and women; it also enmeshes political disagreements about abortion in intimate betrayals.[54] Set during the Stalin era and the first post-Stalin decades, the novel

centers on Pavel Kukotskii, a gifted obstetrician-gynecologist and a generous, nurturing, wise, and courageous man; his wife, Elena, whose parents
raised her with Tolstoy's Christian pacifism and whom Pavel met when he
saved her life with an emergency hysterectomy; and Tania, Elena's daughter
by her first husband, whom Pavel adopts and raises with great love. Their
arguments over the ethics of abortion become an important terrain through
which Ulitskaya portrays her characters' construction of themselves and
their varying approaches to relational ethics; indeed, these disagreements
propel the plot forward in important directions.

Ulitskaya establishes Kukotskii as a man of outstanding moral strength,
expressed through his intelligence, competence, and sober pragmatism.
Unlike many of his peers who were devoted to the abstract ideal of "progress" and, in its name, the pursuit of state interests, Kukotskii recognizes
the dangerous cant in this rhetoric.[55] He is committed to the truths of science and its practical use for the population's social welfare; he uses Soviet
ideological language strategically only to pursue his humanitarian goals.
One of Kukotskii's focused efforts is to convince the Ministry of Health
and Soviet leadership to legalize abortion, to stem the country's enormous
maternal and infant mortality caused by unsafe, illegal abortions.

And this issue motivates the major conflict of the novel: Kukotskii's
conflict and rupture with his wife Elena over their opposing views about
the correct state abortion policy. The caretaker of their apartment building, Lizaveta Polosukhina, a poor single mother of three children, dies a
bloody, painful death from a botched, illegal abortion. Helping out in the
first hours after the death, Kukotskii and Elena bring the children to their
home and put them to sleep. Kukotskii then says to his wife, "Now do you
understand why I've spent so many years trying to legalize this?"[56]

Elena refuses to even consider his point, calling it "legalized infanticide,"
"a crime worse than murdering an adult." She then addresses the case at
hand: "If abortions were legal, [Lizaveta's existing children] too would have
been murdered. Lizaveta didn't have much need for them."[57]

Kukotskii, disdainful of ideologies that romanticize lofty ideals without
regard to practical realities, retorts, "Are you feeble minded, Elena? Perhaps
they wouldn't exist. Then there wouldn't be three unfortunate orphans
doomed to poverty, hunger, and prison . . ."

When Elena digs in and labels women who abort "criminals, they kill their
own children," Kukotskii deploys the pivotal moral argument, asserting that
only those vulnerable to pregnancy have the right to define its legitimacy: "You

don't have the right to vote. You don't have that organ. You're not a woman. If you can't get pregnant, then you can't judge," he said to her morosely.

As a novel published in 2001, this scene can certainly be viewed as making a contemporary political statement, for Russians were already vigorously debating the moral and legal status of abortion. With Lizabeta's death, we see the tragic consequences of abortion's criminalization inscribed in a family. But Ulitskaya avoids straightforward political intervention. She complicates the plot with Kukotskii's denial of Elena's femininity. From that moment, the couple's relationship is permanently scarred.[58]

Abortion, Relational Ethics, and the Search for Selfhood

Ulitskaya does not leave the topic of abortion at Kukotskii's insistence on legal accessibility. She delves further into questions about abortion's moral status, noting that Kukotskii himself viewed the termination of pregnancy as the "gravest of operations in moral terms both for the woman and for the doctor." Still, he also recognized it as a moral option, embodying "the essential divide between humans and animals . . . the ability and right to step beyond the limits of biological law, to breed not at the will of natural rhythms, but of one's own desire. Was this not where human choice, the right to freedom, ultimately was realized?"[59] Access to abortion, in other words, provided the means of ensuring that reproduction is an individual's conscious choice, not a form of enslavement to nature. Here, ensuring women's right to reproductive self-determination is an affirmation of the human need for freedom.

But Ulitskaya also suggests that the morality of abortion becomes newly problematic when the termination of life becomes routine, as abortion was in the post-Stalin Soviet era. She does so not by depicting an abortion decision, but another routinized context of killing, in the research lab where Tania, Elena and Pavel Alekseevich's daughter, works to gain experience for her promising scientific career. It is 1960 and Tania is enthralled with her day job as a lab assistant, where she sterilizes equipment and undertakes procedures such as injecting rat embryos with dye for analysis. One day, her lab partner requests instruments for injecting a human embryo. Unmoved by this new situation, Tanya proceeds to retrieve the metal instruments and matter-of-factly inquires, "alive or dead?" The embryo was dead, but the realization that shook Tania to her core was her own act of posing that very question. She realized she had just accepted the possibility of experimenting on a living human embryo, even stood ready to do so. Out-wardly, Tania remained calm, but we learn that a life-altering realization, a profoundly disturbing coming-into-consciousness has just been put in motion, as she "put the key to the operating room in its place, took off her white lab coat and hung it on a hanger, and left the laboratory. She would never return there. Nor would she return to the university. Her romance with science had ended at that very moment, forever."[60]

Shocked at herself and at the path her devotion to science had led her down, Tania does not immediately figure out in words how she landed in this ethical quagmire. The narrator captures Tania's new awareness and horror as inchoate pangs of conscience: "deep inside her dwelt a thought that turned itself this way and that," and an honest recognition that, even had the answer been that the fetus was alive, "she would have given Raya the instruments necessary to inject dye into its veins, killing in the process not a baby rat or kitten or little rabbit, but a live child."[61]

Soon thereafter, unlike Petrushevskaia's Pani or the nameless rural women in Palei's story, Tania gains the ability to articulate her predica-ment. In a confession to her father-doctor, she explains, "What have I been doing these two years? Murdering rats. I've slashed a whole mountain of rats. It seemed really easy. Snip, snip. . . . As a result . . . some barrier just sort of broke down."

Kukotskii, the moral pragmatist, rejects her allusion to holding ideal-ized moral absolutes:

No, no, no. That's for your mother. I know nothing and don't want to know anything about those barriers. There is a certain hierarchy of values, and hu-man life is at the top. And if in order to save the life of a single person, to learn how to treat only one human disease, hundreds of thousands—whatever num-ber—of animals need to be destroyed, there is no question.

Tania tries again to clarify what is at stake for her:

Dad . . . I'm talking about something else. Lord take the rats. I'm talking about me. What's happened to me? . . . Don't you understand? I'm cutting heads off of rats, piling up whole baskets of little corpses, in order to achieve some result. In order to discover something, to cure something and along the way something happens to me that makes me lose my fundamental values: I lose sight of the difference between the life of a human being and a rat.[62]

Considered in light of Ulitskaya's short story "Orlovy-Sokolovy," I argue that Ulitskaya is suggesting that the routinization of abortion reflected a society-wide indifference to the value of human life. In two of her three plots about abortion we examined, the characters of Tanya Orlova and Tania Kukotskaya come to realize that the dominance of utilitarian norms—embracing technological control over life as "progress"—can blind us to violence against living beings. Ulitskaya certainly does not endorse restrictive policies; motivating her plot in *Kazus Kukotskogo* with the tragic death of a desperately poor mother of three from an illegal abortion leaves that clear. But Ulitskaya asks us to contemplate a more existential dilemma about the governing values that shape our society. Do they enable care and promote nurturance, or do they make us numb to killing? What kind of relationships, and what kinds of selves, are we creating?

Finally, in Arbatova's memoir, abortion experiences also provide an entry point for defining her sense of self vis-à-vis the broader society and its apathy. Recalling her first unwanted pregnancy at age eighteen when she was looking forward to starting college, Arbatova asserts, "It didn't occur to me that the outcome of the pregnancy . . . could be the birth of a child. . . . Lofty philosophical thinking beckoned me stronger than the shitty Soviet daily grind that accompanies college-age motherhood."[63] Prizing self-realization even before being introduced to feminist thought, Arbatova also felt troubled by abortion's routinization as she experienced it in the clinic's waiting room:

> An industrialized work-place drudgery; women waiting, glancing in a business-like way at their watches, thinking about what other household responsibilities they'll be able to fit in today besides an abortion. The tired, angry nurses, the screech from behind the closed door . . . it's evident on the people's faces that everything is proceeding correctly, adults are properly undertaking their adult business, and only I, an infantile fool, feel the events around me in the genre of tragedy.[64]

In depicting herself as out-of-sync with the apparent normalcy of the clinic's mechanistic grind, with its heartless nurses and painful shrieks, Arbatova suggests an alternative to apathy is possible.

Yet her memoir also inspires a question: what kind of self gets constructed through literary reflections on abortion? In her chapter "Abortion from an Unbeloved," Arbatova explores the ethics of abortion by combining Soviet-era humanism with an incipient feminism. Pregnant from a one-night stand with someone she was not interested in, Arbatova has met someone else, a French man with whom she hopes to get involved. As she narrates for the reader the interaction that ensues when she tells him about her plan to get an abortion, Arbatova identifies both her ideal type of intimate relationship and the ethical basis for women's reproductive autonomy:

> Without any prologue, I say: "I'm going to be getting an abortion."
>
> He is silent for some time, precisely the amount of time necessary so nobody would regret what they had said. Because what he would say would determine not only our future relationship, but each of our individual human integrity, because Actions are not only undertaken on Red Square.[65] He takes my hand and says:
>
> "You're suffering because you don't want to sacrifice yourself . . . for a future person who doesn't exist yet. . . . You're suffering because you aren't certain whether you have the right to decide to be an individual [*lichnost'*] or only a physiological apparatus for reproduction of the species.
>
> "But you have the right, once you've decided. And besides all of this, I hope you're having an abortion from someone you don't love. There's something of communist morality in the idea of undertaking an outrage against oneself for an abstract future."
>
> And I then received the kind of look for which it becomes possible to follow a person to [exile in] Siberia.[66]

By commenting that he hesitated "for exactly the amount of time necessary so nobody would regret what they had said," Arbatova emphasizes what she sees at stake—his demonstrating care for her humanity and integrity. The abortion, by contrast, seems rather insignificant to her, a temporary exigency; mentioning it to this man allows Arbatova to figure out something about his character.

Arbatova then details the many aspects of his argument she finds appealing—his reassurance that she should not suffer pain, his ambivalence over the procedure's existential character—he reveals his sensitivity to the sacred aspects of life and still recognizes that a woman has the right to decide on reproduction for herself. Finally, by asserting that devotion to an abstract idea (or "future person") over the concrete interests of a particular individual smacks of communist morality, he casts the idea of continuing an unwanted pregnancy as an obsolete and unacceptable stance.

Arbatova closes this scene acknowledging she has been seduced: his affirmation that she has the right not to sacrifice herself and endorsing her decision to prioritize her own life over a possible, future child communicate his support for her self-determination. And yet, in her enthusiasm, Arbatova imagines herself through the historical Russian trope of the loyal Decembrist wife, following her man to Siberian exile.[67] Committed to being a self-in-relation, Arbatova's embrace of reproductive autonomy remains distinct from a Western feminist celebration of individualism.

In Place of a Conclusion

Certainly, treating literary texts as evidence of historical and cultural dynamics requires caution. There is no single authoritative interpretation of a text; a reader's assumptions and interests co-create its meanings. Moreover, understanding a text's aesthetics requires contextualizing it historically—writers' use of Aesopian symbols during Soviet censorship exemplifies this.[68] Still, literary texts hold significant affordances for capturing subtleties of everyday life: they can depict situations that characters feel but don't articulate, providing textured insights into cultural logics that would likely be inaccessible through retrospective interviews. Indeed, in the cases where the language and discursive frame to talk about an issue are absent, literary texts can uniquely illuminate social dynamics around the unspoken, as seen with Baranskaya's portrayal of Olga's searching confusion and Arbatova's resentment of her mother's reaction to her abortion at age eighteen.

In contrast to the issues of personal autonomy or fetal life raised in American public debates over abortion, a very different set of concerns troubled Soviet women as they confronted unexpected pregnancies.[69] There, legal abortion was embedded in ethical dilemmas inspired by Russian cultural longings to prioritize love even when inconvenient or costly or irrational to do so. Writing about abortion enabled authors to explore the painful contradictions emerging from embracing nurturance but conceding to pragmatism. It also afforded authors the opportunity to highlight the contradictions of state socialism, as they exposed how routinized abortion symbolized the state's medical services with their rampant malpractice, mean-spirited cynicism, and gendered-forms of punishment. Women's Soviet and post-Soviet writing on abortion, moreover, reveals that the values of love, nurturance, and selflessness were anchored in an understanding of selfhood as relational, not individualized. Human integrity and a meaningful life were tied to caring for and nurturing intimate others; notably, in the texts we examined, this is expected of men as well as women. Abortion was problematized as a sign of the failure to care, and its routine, normalized use for fertility control was an index of society's numbness to human pain.

With Glasnost, writers depicted Soviet medical institutions as warehouses of neglect and abuse; in this, they underscored a key contradiction of Soviet reproductive governance. Though numerous other Russian texts (not examined here) depict women dying from illegal abortions, Ulitskaya's *Kazus* uniquely indicts the state's ban for the horrors that ensue from unsafe procedures. Moreover, while there are depictions of women inducing illegal abortions (from the gruesome practice of inserting an onion into the uterus so the fibrous roots would grow to enmesh the fetus in *Kazus Kukotskogo* to pouring scalding water on a woman's stomach in *Children of the Arbat*), my review of Soviet fiction and memoir found almost no discussions of contraception or efforts to proactively prevent unwanted pregnancy.[70] Arbatova's realization that no one had taught her the need to deliberately postpone pregnancy or methods for doing so suggests that such discussions were rare. Her new awareness of having been deprived of knowledge is echoed in Glasnost-era texts on many other topics—most notably, about discoveries of truths about Soviet history.

Authors who criticized abortion as an ethical transgression did not endorse a politics of repression or criminalization in the name of establishing a more ethical social order; they considered abortion as a stimulus to reflect on the moral character of their society and their own personal actions. As in much Soviet literature, these texts offer a humanism sobered by confrontations with layers of tragedy, from the hypocrisies of governance to the violations of individual persons and communities.[71] This is a humanism that problematizes the acceptance of violence as a necessary cost of progress, and it doubts the ready combination of virtue and convenience. Instead, Soviet-era humanists deployed the moral imagination to determine how to act in a world of human-made brutality and hypocrisy, to figure out the least-bad alternatives; they idealized prioritizing care and love for one's intimates over self-determination.[72] Often despairing of finding neat solutions to complex socioeconomic dilemmas, many Soviet humanists concluded that living with integrity required an abiding disquiet. They struggled amid violence and hypocrisy with a conscience that remained disturbed: in Elena Makarova's words, "to live, submitting to my harsh fate."

CHAPTER 2

Fighting Abortion
with Soviet Biopolitics

For Soviet-era health experts, reducing both out-of-hospital abortions and the overall use of abortion were enduring strategic challenges.[1] Researchers debated the most effective approaches in scientific journals, and authors tried out diverse tactics in health education texts. A 1991 article, for example, suggested drawing on literary texts to fight both antiabortion battles at once, since stories communicated three relevant messages: that out-of-hospital abortions cause women to die brutal deaths, that childlessness ruins marriages, and that "true love" can overcome all challenges.[2] Their concern to prevent illegal abortions is paradoxical, since the procedure had been readily available in hospitals for over three decades. Moreover, as we saw in Chapter 1, Soviet women generally saw abortions as a miserable experience conducted in poor conditions by disrespectful providers. Those seeking abortions were doing so despite the punishing experience it involved. So why did antiabortion strategies assume clinicians would be convincing pregnant women against termination, instead of instilling effective habits of preventing unwanted pregnancy?

To explain these paradoxes, this chapter explores the evolving efforts of Soviet researchers, health administrators, and sanitary enlightenment workers to reduce abortion use after the procedure was legalized in 1955 and through the start of Glasnost.[3] The place of contraceptives in the late Soviet "fight against abortion" brings into particular relief characteristic features of Soviet biopolitics, or how the Soviet system governed population production. Specifically, reproductive health matters were addressed through the socialist frameworks of social hygiene and women's emancipation. Social hygiene was the socialist ideological framework that conceptualized health as a collective and social concern, not a narrow individual matter.[4] This involved state provisions of the material conditions to support population health, including access to health services. Importantly, conceptualizing what was needed for health was a top-down process determined by the state and implemented by experts. Yet ideologically, the state could not be criticized. The persistence of poor health was thus defined as the result of citizens refusing to change improper behavior in spite of expert-led "sanitary enlightenment" instructing people how to live a healthy life.[5] By examining educational manuals teaching Soviet citizens proper "marital hygiene" and the prevention of abortion, this chapter provides a lens onto the limits of sanitary enlightenment as a key technique of socialist biopolitics.

The second socialist policy shaping reproductive health was the principle of women's emancipation. After the re-legalization of abortion in 1955, this ideological position meant that under socialism, women had the legal right to decide whether to continue or terminate a pregnancy. This right, however, was not conceptualized as a recognition of individual privacy or autonomy. Experts knew that women experienced pressures from their partners and mothers about how to deal with a pregnancy, and they themselves assumed the right to pressure women on behalf of the state and medical interests. Nevertheless, legal access to abortion remained unquestioned, as did the fact that women would be largely responsible for the children they bore.

While social hygiene and women's emancipation shaped the fight against abortion as an ideological process, the deficit economy and state censorship had immense impacts on these efforts. The shortage of both contraceptives and accurate information about preventing pregnancy contributed to women's need for abortion. They sought black market terminations due to several reasons, including long waiting times for appointments, poor quality anesthesia, and the lack of privacy in hospital abortions. Indeed, Soviet medical referral slips (which were necessary to be excused from work) communicated the request for an abortion to employers, which some researchers recognized as motivating women to seek alternatives to official institutions.[6] Experts designing the "fight against abortion" thus recommended a range of tactics: one suggested that clinicians "change the diagnosis on the referral" as a means of protecting women's privacy and preventing them from seeking illegal procedures,[7] while many others encouraged the use of sentimentalism or fear tactics to try persuading women to keep a pregnancy. By exploring the strategies that Soviet era researchers, Health Ministry experts, and sanitary enlightenment authors created to "fight against abortion," we will grasp the possibilities and limitations of socialist biopolitics for changing reproductive health.

This chapter begins by examining the ways health researchers studied contraception and abortion as they drew on social hygiene and sanitary enlightenment paradigms to make policy recommendations. After outlining research efforts, we examine Ministry of Health (Minzdrav) administrators' plans and official decrees on abortion and contraception. Internal reports demonstrate that bureaucrats trying to reduce abortions sought the development of contraceptives and their widespread distribution, and planners repeatedly issued orders for research into new contraceptive methods and increases in contraceptive availability. However, material deficits, demographic politics, and medical concerns for control all sabotaged these orders.

With regard to hormonal contraceptives, the state's preoccupation with increasing fertility undermined Minzdrav's claims to be motivated solely by safety concerns. Although research and policy statements in the 1970s and early 1980s highlight a focus on safety and contraceptive effectiveness, the policies that bureaucrats actually established ignored evidence about the relative safety of low dose pills. In 1974, the Ministry prohibited hormonal contraceptives for routine birth control, ignoring the fact that women were facing greater health risks from having frequent dilation and curettage abortions in poor conditions. The chapter demonstrates the significance of this policy by contrasting it to the ways hormonal contraceptives were introduced, politically contested, and ultimately regulated in two liberal biopolitical contexts, Great Britain and the US. These contrasting political and social approaches to the pill bring into relief the specific mode of reproductive governance established by Soviet biopolitics.

While Minzdrav continually directed clinicians and health bureaucrats to fight against abortion and improve women's health care services, the lack of financing impeded success.[8] Alongside Minzdrav's opposition to mainstreaming hormonal contraceptives, the perennial shortage of barrier methods largely reduced the fight against abortion to a persuasion campaign for women to continue unwanted pregnancies. The chapter's third section details specific tactics used by writers to "enlighten" the public about abortion and contraception. Public outreach involved the one-way expert transmission of a limited body of knowledge to supposedly ignorant laypeople. Information was rationed: experts determined what people needed to know and often relied on scare tactics to conjure up negative consequences awaiting those who ignored instructions. Tactics of persuading pregnant women against abortion reflected the feeble solution experts devised in light of the constant shortages of barrier contraceptives and bureaucrats' worries that hormonal contraceptives were unsafe and would reduce fertility.[9]

These three prongs in the fight against abortion—scientific research, Ministry policies, and public outreach—demonstrate the shifting ways that Soviet socialism governed reproductive health. While in the 1950s and '60s experts advocated for contraceptive supplies as helping fulfill the socioeconomic conditions for health, by the late 1970s they largely resorted to persuading pregnant women against abortions. The 1991 recommendation to share melodramatic messages from literature indexed not only a growing conservative approach to gender, but also experts' tacit recognition that socialism's socioeconomic guarantees were hollow. Changes in experts' fight against abortion track broader shifts in the governance of late Soviet society.

Fighting Abortion in the Wake of Legalization: Researchers

In the post-Stalin decades, Soviet researchers published work recognizing that contraceptive methods would provide a safe alternative to abortion and should be promoted.[10] In 1971, the prominent scholar I. P. Katkova approvingly recalled a 1926 Soviet publication on the rationality of preventing unwanted pregnancy: "why should a woman get pregnant and go through an operation to free herself from a child she cannot have at this time, when there exist methods to prevent its conception?"[11] Yet contraceptives, like so many personal hygiene items, were in deficit. From the time abortion was re-legalized, researchers decried the dearth of scientific studies of "new, effective, and convenient contraceptive devices" and the shortages of existing ones.[12] For these researchers, contraceptives were a logical technical fix the state should make available. Katkova invoked social hygiene to argue that the common use of abortion was "not compatible with the country's dominant preventative orientation to medicine."[13]

Beginning in the early 1960s, contraceptive advocates lamented the gross underdevelopment of contraceptive methods, availability, and knowledge. They noted that a few of the country's research institutes were working on developing new forms of contraception.[14] Gramicidin paste was being tested as a spermicide by the All-Union Scientific-Research Chemical-Pharmaceutical Institute.[15] But despite these seemingly promising beginnings, researchers complained that the huge demand was not being seriously addressed, and they admonished those who "are called upon to solve problems connected to the protection of women's health, [not to] stand on the side and [instead to become] involved with questions of contraception."[16] Such researchers advocated that contraceptives should be conveniently available for purchase, not only at pharmacies but at women's neighborhood and workplace clinics and rural health posts, and that medical personnel should be trained in contraceptive use and education.[17] One author placed the responsibility specifically on ob-gyns, calling on them to become educated about contraceptives and to recognize that providing contraceptive services was their professional priority.[18]

Some researchers empirically investigated women's efforts to prevent pregnancy. A study on birth control use in seven cities between 1961 and 1962 found that as many as 80 percent of women who terminated pregnancies had tried preventing pregnancy, often using methods with low efficacy.[19] Authors identified a range of problems: "Often, it is a consequence of contraceptives' unreliability, their difficulty of use, discomfort, and the decrease of sexual feeling they cause, their non-aesthetic appearance and ways of working."[20] Clearly, these researchers saw contraceptives as ideologically compatible with Soviet biopolitics. They also recognized that people's ignorance about preventing unwanted pregnancy or about the "harms of abortion" was not the sole reason for frequent terminations; contraceptives were in deficit and the few available methods were undesirable and/or of poor quality.

But amid the staunch pronatalism of the post-War era, researchers saw the need to do more than advocate greater and higher quality contraceptive supplies; they felt compelled to legitimize these technologies in terms of Soviet population ideology. In the following section, we will examine Soviet researchers' strategies for disassociating pregnancy prevention from fertility decline while supporting the need for increased births. The challenges they faced bring into relief the affordances and limitations of social biopolitical methods for governing reproduction.

LEGITIMATING CONTRACEPTIVES UNDER SOCIALISM

The most important Soviet study endorsing contraceptives as acceptable for socialism was Elizaveta Alikhanovna Sadvokasova's 1969 monograph *Social-Hygienic Aspects of the Regulation of the Size of Families*.[21] Key to Sadvokasova's justification is her rejection of neo-Malthusianism, which employed contraceptives as a technical solution to poverty by reducing poor people's childbearing.[22] In contrast, Sadvokasova framed the provisioning of contraception as part of the socialist guarantee of people's material needs and women's equality through the knowledge availed by science.[23] She makes this argument through two extensive analyses: first, a global comparison of legislation and policy approaches to abortion and contraception that traces their effects on fertility; and second, an analysis of the reasons that women sought abortions in Soviet Russia over the past decades. To understand how Sadvokasova establishes a socialist biopolitical approach to "fighting abortion," we will briefly examine each of these analyses.

In a sweeping examination, Sadvokasova pairs changes in abortion and contraceptive laws in Europe, North America, and Asia from the eighteenth century through the time of her writing, with analyses of these countries' changing rates of abortion and fertility. She cites comparative cases under socialism to exemplify the positive effects of legal abortion and contraceptive services. In Bulgaria, expanded access to abortion drastically reduced the number of terminations undertaken outside medical facilities and, consequently, the number of complications women suffered.[24] In Czechoslovakia, public health authorities both disseminated contraceptives and supported women in a way compatible with socialist ideology, by "providing free medical care for mothers and children up to age fifteen, increasing slots in day care and preschools, increasing material assistance for families with three children, hastening housing construction, and improving salaries."[25] All of these, she argues, helped stem abortion use. Moreover, women often used the Czechoslovak contraceptive services without telling their husbands, implying that institutional confidentiality was another key element in achieving success.

In discussing the West, she observes that under capitalism the poor inevitably face worse conditions and greater exploitation than wealthier groups.[26] Still, Sadvokasova describes American family planning services empirically and without political prejudice:

> in the USA, fertility regulation is undertaken by private, state, and municipal institutions... on a woman's return visit to the clinic, the doctor asks her if she is satisfied with the results of the method... On the basis of 140,000 married couples who went to the Margaret Sanger Bureau at the start of their marriage, and who had fewer abortions than those who didn't use the clinic, the researchers came to the correct conclusion that there is a high inverse correlation between the amount of abortions and the use of contraceptives.[27]

She further details the multiple ways the U.S. system distributed contraceptives to meet the population's demand:

> In 1966 in 39 states of the United States the local public health authorities had special institutions for contraceptive consultations with the goal of planning the number of children.... The USA is a country of business – the production of contraceptives has become a line of industry. To acquire them, the population had already spent by the 1950s approximately $250 million per year. There were already about 300,000 locations selling contraceptives, of which 60,000 were pharmacies and 240,000 were vending machines.[28]

While for some Soviet authors in the mid-1960s, the characterization of a society as "a country of business" would resonate as criticism, Sadvokasova clearly hoped that Soviet officials would learn from the US's approach to making contraceptive supplies accessible and ensuring patients' satisfaction with their chosen method.

Ultimately, Sadvokasova aims for this comparative analysis to show that abortion and contraceptive use are inversely correlated, while abortion and fertility are not necessarily so. She lacks sufficient data to unquestionably prove this—in Western societies, abortion was largely illegal and so accurate data were not readily available, and in socialist societies, contraceptives were hard to come by—but she makes a clearly reasoned argument based on what is known. She also points to Romania's ban on abortion in 1966, which—like the Soviet ban under Stalin—was intended but failed to raise fertility.[29] Throughout this study, Sadvokasova shows that prohibitions against abortion do not reduce its use, while increased contraceptive use results in fewer abortions and lower maternal mortality rates, without negatively impacting fertility.

The book's second set of arguments stems from detailed analyses of hospital records and survey data on women's stated reasons for terminating pregnancies. Sadvokasova attempts to determine systematically which causes of abortion may be eliminated through economic development and policy making.[30] Here we see a foundational premise of socialist biopolitics that shaped scientific knowledge. Observing that 35% of all abortions among city residents and 26.3% of abortions among rural residents were explained as due to inadequate housing, lack of childcare, and general material lack, Sadvokasova classifies these as "definitely avoidable"; her assumption is that the improved material conditions accompanying developing communism will incline people to have more children.[31] She recognizes that reasons such as "inadequate living conditions" and "lack of resources" are based on subjective judgments that would require different kinds of inputs to satisfy different people; still, she expects many abortions occurring due to these reasons will disappear as living conditions improve.[32]

While holding fast to the idea that policy can channel people's behavior toward decisions that fulfill the state's interests, some issues that Sadvokasova uncovers trouble this basic premise. These are the facts that people with higher incomes are less likely than those with lower incomes to have more children; women with higher education were more likely to terminate pregnancies; and women's involvement in society—their work and engagement in building socialism— challenges their ability to raise children.[33] Sadvokasova responds to these revelations by reiterating the need to provide better information about contraceptives and the "harms of abortion."[34] She thus invokes other principles of socialist biopolitics even as these data cast doubt on the feasibility of engineering higher fertility itself.

Along with bringing attention to the material obstacles impeding fertility increases and pushing for policy changes to increase childbearing—"To raise the level of fertility, it is necessary to create the conditions in which parents want not one, but two to three children,"[35] Sadvokasova works unrelentingly to justify contraceptives. She argues: "the necessity of replacing abortion with other methods of preventing births is absolutely correct, but we can hardly agree . . . that the reduction in births [is caused by] the number of abortions. Women's life conditions lead them to limit the size of their families. Abortion is only a means for realizing this necessity, a barbaric method that should be replaced with more cultured contraceptive methods."[36]

Moreover, socialist principles of women's emancipation temper her pronatalist impulse. Sadvokasova insists that women must be allowed to decide on reproduction for themselves: "In a situation when there is no desire for a child, women and men must have the necessary knowledge and means to prevent pregnancy. If an unwanted pregnancy nonetheless arises, a woman should have the right to resort to abortion."[37] Her research thus affirms that the state should facilitate people's ability to fulfill their own reproductive goals in the healthiest ways possible, regardless of whether their goals coincide with state population interests. Unlike other demographers who prioritized increasing births, Sadvokasova does not suggest that in a socialist society birth rates should continually rise and/or fertility limitation should gradually become unnecessary. When she notes that the term invented to measure the effects of contraceptive use was *"unfortunately* named [the] . . . demographic effect" of contraception, she implicitly faults the term for reinforcing the false assumption that contraceptive use decreases fertility.[38]

Sadvokasova repeatedly argues the need to improve Soviet abortion research by using science as the basis for policy. She faults the Ministry for not doing enough to reduce abortions and urges committing resources to the prevention goals of social hygiene.[39] Notably, her critique is firmly within the boundaries of Soviet ideology on sex: she upholds Soviet puritanism, ignoring that sex occurs for pleasure and warrants decades of pregnancy prevention. She minimizes the many subjective reasons that people would not want children.[40] She trusts that supplying contraceptives and improved material circumstances will solve both the problem of abortion and the birth rate. With her commitment to socialist transformations, women's equality, and social hygiene, and her blind spots regarding non-procreative sexuality, the subjective dimensions of childbearing desires, and the failures possible with even high quality contraceptives, Sadvokasova's work represents the most capacious form of post-Stalinist Soviet biopolitics.

PRIORITIZING STATE FERTILITY GOALS

But not all researchers aligned their recommendations specifically with women's interests when these seemed to differ from state goals. Many argued the need for medical personnel to convince women seeking abortions to continue their pregnancies.[41] Moreover, when calls for the state to develop and supply effective contraceptives went unheeded, they explored ways to use surveillance and persuasion to change women's mind against abortions. The priority for these researchers was increasing births.

Katkova's 1971 book *Fertility in Young Families* exemplifies this approach to Soviet biopolitics. This expansive study draws on a survey of four hundred couples who married in 1960 for the first time.[42] Katkova reviews the women's medical files, recording all pregnancies and their outcomes, and the use of contraceptives in relation to women's level of education, income, and housing conditions. Katkova supports expanding pregnancy prevention efforts.[43] But the core of her conceptual work focuses on how newlyweds control their childbearing and which social factors made it more or less likely for a woman to give birth or terminate a pregnancy. This focus conceptually foregrounds a biopolitics aimed at engineering a higher birth-rate, rather than replacing abortion with contraceptive use as a health measure on its own merits.

She found that among women with equivalent levels of higher education, lower income significantly impacts the number of abortions, but among women with equivalent income levels, the higher the education, the lower the abortion rate.[44] Other important reasons cited for terminating pregnancy included difficulties arranging childcare (21.35 percent of respondents); the difficulties of raising a child while working or studying (34.6 percent); inadequate housing, (24.8 percent), and material difficulties (11.3 percent).[45] Similarly to Sadvokasova, Katkova optimistically asserts that, as material conditions improve, abortion use will decrease.[46] In the meantime, she advocates economic incentives for first-time pregnant women to continue the pregnancy.[47] Without also calling for addressing specific material problems women faced, Katkova prioritizes raising fertility over achieving broader conditions of well-being.

Yet Katkova's own text provides several indications that there were no grounds to expect such an automatic and unmediated change in reproductive practices. She notes that only 27 percent of women surveyed sought medical advice about contraceptives, and of those who did, 40 percent did not follow the advice they received, largely because their life conditions did not allow for it.[48] It is unclear whether "life conditions" refers exclusively to material deprivations (e.g., the inability to use contraceptive techniques such as home-made tampons or douching given the lack of privacy in communal apartments), or whether it also refers to entirely non-material issues, such as men's (un)willingness to cooperate with contraception. Given that 22.1 percent of women she interviewed attributed their abortions to their husbands' excessive drinking, such issues were likely relevant, yet this finding is not addressed in the book's recommendations.[49] Moreover, Katkova cites a 1963 article that found obstetrician-gynecologists themselves frequently did not use contraceptives and periodically obtained abortions. Katkova reiterates those authors' conclusion—that such medical providers were unlikely to successfully reduce abortion usage among their patients—but she does not consider how this problem of lack of knowledge troubled her notion that improved material conditions would go far, in and of themselves, to lower abortion rates. Nor does her study consider how knowledge about contraceptives, among laypersons or professionals, could be improved. Instead, Katkova argues that "Sanitary-enlightenment work in preventing pregnancy should be oriented toward creating a negative public opinion toward abortion," and sexual moral education among youth should promote "the joy of motherhood."[50] This approach—treating contraceptives as ideologically acceptable but focusing research and outreach on persuading people against abortion and for childbearing-- became the most prominent biopolitical technique of Soviet reproductive governance.

Researchers were doing little to explore innovative methods of communicating information about abortion and contraception. Katkova cites a range of Soviet authors who argued for girls' comprehensive "sexual moral education" between thirteen and fifteen years of age, "to prepare them for future motherhood."[51] Their main approach highlighted the importance of emphasizing medical expertise, for the family has "nothing to give" in this regard: a girl may gain superstitions and bad habits from her family that she will have to unlearn. One A. Iu. Lur'e, moreover, argued that all aspects of sexual hygiene should be given a scientific basis so that children did not gain their information from the street.[52] Researchers sometimes mentioned the explicit need to explain how to use contraceptives effectively, but they did not explore strategies of teaching or consulting on this topic; presumably, these were self-evident.[53]

Some attention was paid to tactics of persuading women against abortion, although again, few were detailed. One researcher, for example, criticized antiabortion work for being undertaken as a formality, as if doctors did not believe they could change a woman's mind about termination.[54] Another author claimed to draw on the "data of psychiatrists and neuropathologists," to argue that considering women's psychological state could improve the quality of antiabortion outreach: "pregnant women have a higher degree of emotionality and suggestibility, and an unstable psyche. This is why the conception of a pregnancy, as a rule, arouses wavering and contradictory feelings, especially in the first months. Even when she goes to the doctor, a woman is, not infrequently, undecided, and looks to the doctor for the final word."[55] Such discussions demonstrate how efforts to improve clinicians' work with patients targeted the process of persuading women against abortion, rather than instructing them on preventing unwanted pregnancy.

This same study, moreover, finds that the "subjective, psychological factors" women cited for seeking abortions included the following arguments: "a more responsible attitude toward maternal obligations; the desire to gain independence at work before having a baby; the desire for equality in the family, including attempting to secure more of her husband's help with domestic tasks, childcare, etc."[56] Although the author does not explicitly connect such "subjective factors" with the "emotionality" and "unstable psyche" they've already described, the implication is that medical personnel should strive to convince women to keep the pregnancy, even when these are the reasons a woman seeks an abortion. The article advises that antiabortion efforts should specifically enumerate the complications that abortion causes, from "inflammatory illnesses that require long-term treatment, often preventing future childbearing, complications with processes of future pregnancies and births."[57] In other words, the strategy for responding to women's "subjective" reasons for seeking abortion were the same as those to be taken when women cite poor "material conditions" as their motivation: emphasize the harms of abortion. Innovative ways of educating people about contraceptive use are noticeably absent in these discussions.

Instead, new approaches to the fight against abortion included proposals for comprehensive medical surveillance of women's bodies. Katkova recommends instituting "active forms of observation" beginning with puberty and ending with menopause, in the name of ensuring "all aspects of the childbearing function."[58] One surveillance technology she suggests for achieving this is a medical file on women who have had abortions—what Katkova calls an "obstetric passport."[59] This document would track not only medical visits, previous methods of contraception used, and the method of prevention recommended, but also whether the woman was living with her husband or separately; size of living space in square meters; the reason a pregnancy was not wanted; frequency of sexual intercourse; and libido.[60]

Echoing other demographers of the family, Katkova compares families' actual number of children with the number they said they desired and advised state policy leaders that government measures to improve living standards could help fill the gap between them.[61] Although this seems to be directed at satisfying individual families' desires, it prioritizes population growth. Thus, while sharing Sadvokasova's attention to ways the state could create conditions for higher fertility, Katkova does not reiterate Sadvokasova's emphasis on a women's right to act on her desire not to have a child. Indeed, she presents a competing approach to biopolitics, treating the state as a vehicle for prodding, urging, and incentivizing women to give birth. Thus, while Katkova explicitly endorses the importance of contraception, her work nonetheless contains a revealing ambivalence illustrative of Soviet biopolitics more generally: the fight against abortion was closely entangled with the goal of raising fertility. Katkova's recommendations focus on encouraging women who are pregnant for the first time and seeking abortion to continue the pregnancy and give birth.[62] She recommends this be accomplished through both emphasizing the harms of abortion to women and men and providing state financial entitlements.

The distinct tactics advocated by Sadvokasova and Katkova illustrate Soviet biopolitics' two approaches to reducing abortion. Both reject Malthusian notions of limited resources and endeavor to remake population by increasing fertility. But Sadvokasova emphasizes the state's role in improving social conditions as the main strategy for reducing abortion and advocates abortion accessibility as a woman's right and a means of protecting women's health. Katkova, by contrast, conceives of surveillance measures to follow women and strategies for persuading those who are pregnant against abortion. Beginning in the mid-1970s and throughout the next four decades, Russian scholars studying the family and fertility would be divided along orientations similar to these distinct approaches, with liberals advocating for state policies that improve living conditions so families could have the number of children they desire, and conservatives arguing the need to promote the value of childbearing and family life over "materialistic concerns" and individual interests.[63] And while researchers endorsing contraceptives sometimes collaborated with policy makers, Soviet health bureaucrats did not have sufficient power to enact these changes.[64] It is to their efforts that we now turn.

The Soviet Health Ministry Fights Abortion

Soviet Ministry of Health policy makers had two major goals: preventing unsafe, illegal abortions and reducing abortion use overall. They conceptualized promoting contraceptives as one strategy for reducing abortions, along with enlightening the population about abortion's harms, but did not call for instilling the habitual use of contraceptives as a regular form of discipline. Rather, Ministry bureaucrats envisioned that a reduction in abortion use would result from improvements at numerous societal levels, including material welfare (e.g., better housing and increased preschool slots), public outreach (youth education on postponing sexual activity and general education on the physical damage abortion causes), and clinical interventions (with more persuasive doctor consultations to change the minds of women seeking terminations). An important, early Soviet Ministry of Health statement to this effect was issued in August 1962. *Prikaz* (order) No. 377 noted that since the procedure had been legalized six years earlier, the total number of women dying from abortions decreased by 2.5 times.[65] However, the *prikaz* continued, the number of abortions undertaken had also risen significantly, and out-of-hospital abortions had stayed at almost the same levels, particularly in the Russian Federation regions of Irkutsk, Perm, Rostov, Kemerov, Novosibirsk oblasts and Altai, Krasnoiarsk krai.[66] With this *prikaz*, health bureaucrats in the Ministry outlined necessary actions for reversing these negative trends.

To eliminate out-of-hospital abortions, expanding access to abortion services (more hospital beds) and improving care was imperative. Anesthesia needed to be provided during abortion procedures. Reducing abortions overall was to be addressed by improving living conditions (the *prikaz* specifically notes increasing preschool slots), increasing contraceptive access, and educating women about the harms of abortion.[67] Komsomol youth groups and unions should be recruited in the fight against abortion, teaching men and youth about its harms and methods of preventing unwanted pregnancy.[68] Health bureaucrats call for "all measures to be undertaken to provide the population with existing contraceptive devices [and] arrange for their continual sale in pharmacies and clinics," noting specifically the production of spermicidal agents. Additionally, the *prikaz* recognizes the need for establishing conditions in women's clinics for providers to be able to talk with patients individually about sexual hygiene, by "not allowing more than one doctor to undertake consultations in an office at a time."[69]

These directives would be repeated in future Orders, but they were mostly ignored. Despite issuing Orders, the Soviet Minzdrav did not have the authority to compel institutes to undertake research, or industrial enterprises to produce contraceptive supplies, or clinics to remodel their facilities to ensure individual consultations. Nor did the Ministry have influence over budgeting priorities to allocate funding to fulfill these goals. What the Ministry could do was issue recommendations, require reports, and make prohibitions. These became its major activities in fighting abortion.

THE REFUSAL OF INTERNATIONAL COLLABORATIONS

Despite Minzdrav's limited influence, its officials could have pursued other avenues for reaching their goals, but they chose not to do so. In a Memorandum on a 1970 meeting with top Soviet Health Ministry officials, Henry

P. David, the US-based abortion researcher and women's rights advocate, describes these officials denying their country's high rates of abortion and refusing his invitation to collaborate in reducing abortion use.[70] In Moscow as a researcher and representative of the American Institute for Research's Cooperative Transnational Research Program in Fertility Behavior, David approached Minzdrav bureaucrats as professional colleagues.[71] He had authored the first English-language study of abortion and contraceptive use in Central and Eastern Europe, published by the Population Council, and gave them copies.[72] David's Memorandum recounts his efforts to engage them on these topics. Having thoroughly studied a German translation of Sadvokasova's book, he attempted to discuss its findings and explore potential areas of cooperation to improve women's reproductive health with the Minzdrav specialists. Yet in person and in letters following the meeting, high-ranking researchers and leaders at the institute refuted the existence of an abortion problem. They claimed that Sadvokasova's monograph was outdated, and argued that data from "certain regions of the U.S.S.R. cannot be applied to the country as a whole." In an outright lie, they stated, "the extensive campaign to disseminate information on 'the bad effects of abortion' coupled with 'the widespread manufacture of different contraceptive devices' has produced a condition in which contraception has replaced abortion as the primary method of birth planning in the Soviet Union."[73] Although Soviet and American scientists were collaborating on other medical questions, abortion statistics were kept secret.[74] Rejecting the opportunity to collaborate with David—even while they were researching contraceptive development in their WHO-funded centers—suggests that Soviet health bureaucrats prioritized political concerns over women's health.

AN INITIAL ENDORSEMENT OF ORAL CONTRACEPTIVES

In addition to hiding the Soviet abortion paradigm from global observers, Minzdrav's approach to hormonal (oral) contraceptives illustrates some of the key tactics through which Soviet biopolitics developed. Minzdrav experts understood the efficacy and safety of hormonal contraceptives. Soon after holding a Symposium on Hormonal Contraceptives on October 9, 1970, in Moscow, participants issued a statement summarizing the conference's conclusions and their recommendations to the leading Soviet health organs and research institutions. This two-page statement, published— as would be required—through the Soviet Minzdrav (as no independent professional organizations could exist), came specifically from the Main Administration of Treatment-Prevention Assistance to Children and Mothers, and the All Union Scientific-Research Institute for Obstetrics and Gynecology. It noted that international and domestic research demonstrated hormonal contraceptives have almost 100 percent efficacy in preventing pregnancy.[75] The statement refers to precise drugs that had been approved by the Soviet Minzdrav and recommends that these be promoted for contraceptive purposes as well as for medical treatment.[76] The authors note that in both domestic and international scientific studies, side effects are mainly observed in the first two months of use and then decrease significantly, occurring in only 5 to 10 percent of cases with variation based on dosage and extent of use.[77] Moreover, citing research done at the Soviet Academy of Medical Sciences, the authors observed that combining hormonal contraceptives with neurotropic substances "significantly reduced the negative side effects of taking synthetic progesterone."[78] The statement concedes that the most serious complications are thromboembolism but notes that this risk has been decreased in modern formulations.[79]

The Symposium report encourages doctors to recommend the use of IUDs and oral progesterone as contraceptives. They call on scientific research institutes, Soviet and SSR Ministries, and departments of ob-gyn to begin the production of synthetic progesterone, undertake clinical trials, and develop instructions for its clinical use. While expressing caution about safety and asserting the need for continual monitoring and refinement of hormonal contraceptives, these statements cite international and domestic research in support of allowing women to use the pill to prevent pregnancy.

But this was not to happen during the Soviet era. Expert research on hormonal contraceptives continued, both in Minzdrav labs and in WHO-sponsored Soviet research centers on human reproduction.[80] But in their research publications and policy statements, Minzdrav experts consistently depicted hormonal treatment as relevant only for treating illness, not the routine prevention of pregnancy.

ORAL CONTRACEPTIVES IN LIBERAL BIOPOLITICAL CONTEXTS

The early regulatory histories of oral contraceptives in the US and Great Britain highlight the dramatically different approaches characterizing liberal biopolitics—themselves diverse—from Soviet biopolitics. The first oral contraceptive was approved for patient use by the FDA in 1960; it was judged safe because its risks were no higher than those a woman faces in childbirth. Yet by late 1961 in both Britain and the US, there had been reports of serious medical problems and deaths among women taking the pill. By August 1962, twenty-six US women were reported to have suffered blood clots in their veins (thrombophlebitis) and six of them died.[81] The US and British government issued warnings to doctors and funded studies of the problem.[82] Working with data gathered from the centralized health care system of the National Health Service (NHS), British researchers were able to prove the causal relationship between high doses of estrogen pills and thrombosis; these data also enabled the national Committee on Safety of Drugs (CSD) to study the long-term effects of drugs on the market. In December 1969, the British government took the decisive step of only allowing physicians to prescribe oral contraceptives containing less than 50 micrograms (5 mg) of estrogen, which excluded two-thirds of the oral contraceptives then on the market.[83] Very quickly, higher doses of the pill virtually disappeared from the British market.[84]

In the US, where drug safety was regulated by the FDA but implemented in a decentralized system of health care heavily influenced by the pharmaceutical industry, things proceeded differently. Media reports of serious illnesses and deaths by thromboembolism, including journalist Barbara Seaman's 1969 *The Doctor's Case against the Pill*, mobilized feminists and emerging consumer rights groups to call for action. At the same time, Senator Gaylord Nelson was leading Congressional hearings to investigate the pharmaceutical industry for possible abuses in antibiotics, barbiturates, and tranquilizers. Upon reading Seaman's book, Nelson added an investigation of oral contraceptives to the hearings, which were held on January 15, 1970. Sitting in on the hearings were members of the radical feminist group DC Women's Liberation, outraged that not a single woman who had experienced negative side effects from the pill was brought in to testify. They disrupted the hearings with accusations that they were "using women as guinea pigs" and "letting the drug companies murder us for their profit and convenience."[85] The national media widely covered their protests, and many American women stopped taking the pill in response.[86] Nelson's hearings led to a new requirement that all medications include patient information inserts describing the possible risks, seen as a way of empowering patients to make their own decisions and reducing physicians' paternalistic authority by creating the conditions for informed consent.[87] Unlike in

Britain, there was no federal requirement about doctors' prescribing rights, and while many doctors reduced their prescriptions of high-dose estrogen pills, as late as 1986 there were still 400,000 US women taking them. In a telling choice of words, Lara Marks notes, "only in 1988 did the FDA finally *persuade* the last three pharmaceutical companies who were manufacturing high dose estrogen pills to withdraw them from the market."[88]

In both countries, attention to the risks of oral contraceptives aroused intense debates among government regulators, physicians, and the public regarding what constituted decisive evidence that the pill *caused* thrombosis, cancer, metabolic effects, and so on. But as we have seen, in the face of public pressure, government regulators responded differently to the complex, often elusive process of establishing definitive levels of risk: in Britain, physicians' prescribing authority was limited in the name of protecting women's health; in the US, policy makers required industry to provide consumer information and placed the responsibility for navigating risk onto individual patients. In the Soviet Union, there was no public discussion. Contrary to Soviet expert recommendations, Minzdrav took a restrictive approach and banned the use of oral hormones for contraception. This top-down approach to reproductive governance, which excluded and ignored the voices of local professionals and laypersons (not to mention global experiences), exemplifies the specific mode of power deployed in Soviet biopolitics.

SOVIET BIOPOLITICS AND THE FATE OF ORAL CONTRACEPTIVES

The Minzdrav's 1974 "Informational Letter on the Harmful Effects and Complications of Oral Contraceptives" observes that approximately eighteen million women around the world were taking combined synthetic progesterone and estrogen for contraception, "having been attracted by unrestrained advertisements for these drugs."[89] Without citing specific references, the letter states that evidence from fifteen global centers for medicinal safety found that "of all deaths caused by medications, 14.3 percent arose after taking oral contraceptives" and noted that "negative reactions and complications linked to oral contraceptives in Great Britain occurred in 27.1 percent of cases, in Sweden, in 24 percent, and in Denmark 15 percent." The letter suggests "it is possible that when taken in an uncontrolled fashion, the harmful and unaccounted-for consequences of oral contraceptives are even higher."[90]

Minzdrav's stated goals were to prevent pharmacies from selling oral contraceptives without doctors' prescriptions, and to stop doctors from prescribing them without medical indicators. The letter further aims "to familiarize the medical community . . . with the harmful effects of oral contraceptives."[91] To do this, they present statistics showing that the frequency of thromboembolic dysfunctions is nine to ten times higher among oral contraceptive users, and mortality from thromboembolic complications among oral contraceptive users is 1.3–3.4: 100,000 (and higher among thirty-five to forty-four year-olds), while only 0.2–0.5: 100,000 among non-users.[92] A host of other negative side effects are listed, some connected with particular dosages or drugs, including elevated blood pressure, migraines, psychoneurological dysfunctions, thyroid dysfunction, fibroadenomas, secondary infertility due to the morphological changes in the ovaries and endometrium, and steroid-induced diabetes.[93] While distinguishing between complications caused by estrogens and those caused by progesterone, the letter presents the points in highly general terms (mainly without accompanying data on incidence rates or other population characteristics). Although the scientific literature in the West continually emphasized the need for additional studies, the Soviet Minzdrav letter mentions only that the possible carcinogenic effects of oral contraceptives require further research to verify.[94] The letter concludes by listing a variety of contraindications to the use of oral contraceptives.

While presenting the harms of the pill in an avalanche of lists with few details or descriptions of the scientific method, samples, or hormonal doses related to these outcomes, the letter notes three times over its six total pages that the risk of serious complications rises when hormonal contraceptives are taken without medical supervision or when untrustworthy doctors and pharmacists make the pill available according to inappropriate criteria. Clearly, Ministry bureaucrats feared that if they did not stem the availability of the pill, it would continue to circulate unofficially.

Thus, to the extent that health authorities' fight against abortion would be waged through promoting contraceptive use, it would rely on IUDs and condoms, which were always in short supply and of poor quality when available. Douching with supposed spermicides, most of which were ineffective, was also a frequent Minzdrav recommendation. The Ministry's opposition to the pill seems connected to fears that its health risks would be difficult to manage and its effectiveness could lower the birth rate. Since pronatalists' goal in reducing abortion was to increase fertility, they retained hope in the strategy of persuading pregnant women against termination. As will become clear, with these tactics, even modest success would prove elusive.

REGIONAL HEALTH AUTHORITIES FIGHT ABORTION

In 1979, the Soviet Minzdrav issued Order No. 620, "On the Situation and Measures for Reducing Abortions in the Country," which acknowledged tremendous problems in all areas of work. Although between 1970 and 1978 the Soviet abortion rate had fallen by 1.5 percent, and out-of-hospital abortions decreased by 9.2 percent, in a range of republics both indicators had risen.[95] More worrying, "the number of women dying from abortion has not fallen."[96] The cause of death in 90.6 percent of these cases was sepsis, which, the Order explains, hospitals are not equipped to address. Conditions are wanting in less emergent cases as well, as the Order admits that many "departments that provide abortions do not have an operating room; such departments are cramped and crowded, beds are in the hallways; abortions are often provided without anesthesia."[97]

Prevention efforts were described as inadequate. True, the Order notes, new consultation services on "Marriage and Family" had opened in several large cities to teach about "marital hygiene and the family's planning of births," and work with men "to protect women's health."[98] Yet citing "on-site inspections," the Order notes that "sanitary enlightenment work is often undertaken as a formality."[99] Deficits of contraceptives are common.[100] The reasons women still sought out-of-hospital abortions were poorly understood.[101] The Soviet Minister of Health, V. Petrovskii, ordered the Ministries of Health of the Union republics to study abortion dynamics and undertake measures to improve them. Among the many tasks this Order establishes, it alludes to the need for scientific data to inform these changes, calling on bureaucrats to study the "true" (*istinnuiu*) demand for specific types of contraceptive devices and establish future requisitions based on these data.[102] It also requires that clinicians get training in contraceptives and the diagnosis and treatment of sepsis after abortion, and that health authorities study the causes of maternal mortality and out-of-hospital abortions.[103]

Beyond establishing the scientific basis of policy making, the Order calls on other Ministries to make changes in policy. The head of the

Pharmaceutical Administration of the Soviet Minzdrav was to ensure the uninterrupted and full supply of contraceptive types requisitioned and to increase the production and supply of seamless condoms; the Central Institute for Sanitary Enlightenment was to provide large supplies of public informational resources to health care institutions; and the regional Ministries of Health of the Tatar Autonomous Soviet Socialist Republic, of Altai krai, Kaliningrad, Kurgansk, and Ivanov oblasts, and of the cities of Kyiv, Minsk, Alma-Ata, and Kishinev were "to organize experiments in decreasing abortions" through addressing the supply problems and undertaking enlightenment activities.[104] While the Order said nothing about improving the quality of women's experiences in medical institutions to promote their trust, a small nod to women's well-being was included in the order that abortions always be provided with anesthesia. Medical paternalism remained firmly entrenched, as the Order recommended surveillance of and corrective actions with women who have frequent abortions.[105] A report on the outcomes of these experiments was to be presented at the USSR's Collegium of Ministry of Health 1982 meeting.

As an official legal statement, Order 620-DSP of June 1979 compelled action and responses from local ministerial agents.[106] However, some notable language suggests the Ministry was unable to compel implementation of the changes it sought. For one thing, the Order does not mention appropriating funds for local regions to carry out these tasks, nor does it articulate expectations that local health authorities would do so. Indeed, it admits that consultation offices will be established "*within the limits of staffing and salaries*" (emphasis added), implicitly acknowledging expected gaps in coverage.[107] Moreover, it tasks leading administrators with the job of *requesting* that the Soviet Ministry of Medical Industry have its research institutes develop new contraceptive methods and improve existing ones (making specific mention of the need for seamless condoms).[108] This language strongly suggests that the division of labor and authority among Soviet Ministries hindered certain kinds of research and development processes. If the Ministry of Health could merely request, but not order and fund research into new contraceptive technologies, its ability to realize the population's needs for health protection and effective services was limited.

Based on this and similar Orders from the Soviet and Russian Republic's Minzdravs, regional health authorities were required to improve their fight against abortion and continually report back on their progress.[109] Although the regions' reports were not rigidly standardized, they addressed the issues of the Orders they responded to, and so the data they provided was similar, including the numbers of abortions provided in and outside of hospitals (i.e., legal and illegal abortions). Changes in the absolute number of abortions and the rate of abortions per live births were both calculated. Data on abortion mortality was closely tracked. The data on abortion in these documents were categorized as secret and withheld from the public.[110]

Regional health authorities all emphasized their diligence in striving to fight abortion, but time and again note that any improvements were minor in light of the continual high use of legal and illegal abortions. Notably, these reports make no clear conceptual distinction between efforts to reduce abortion use in general and to reduce out-of-hospital abortions in particular, despite the fact that logically, efforts to address the latter would not also reduce the former. Thus, authorities always cite growth in the number of hospital beds specifically devoted to abortions—understood as a positive sign of preventing waiting times and thus out-of-hospital terminations. As one report noted, "Waiting times for abortions do not exceed seven to ten days."[111]

Another indicator of "improvement" included the use of anesthesia during abortions. A Russian Republic Health Ministry reported confidently in 1983 that "the quality of medical assistance to women has been perfected [*sovershenstvovalos'*]: vacuum aspiration methods predominate, with different kinds of anesthesia: local, paracervical Novocain blocker, nitrous-oxygen and neuroleptic analgesia."[112] Yet the report makes no mention of their varying availability, quality, and effects on women. And a statement issued by the same authorities soon thereafter acknowledges that the use of local anesthesia for abortions was sub-optimal: "In the majority of hospitals local anesthesia is used for the surgical termination of pregnancy, [but is] often not effective."[113] If this admission betrays the deceptiveness of the 1983 report, the very next sentence gingerly adds another loaded observation: "Anesthesiologists are interested in providing anesthesia only when abortions are undertaken due to medical criteria."[114] This laconic statement implicitly acknowledges that clinicians treated women seeking abortions for personal reasons punitively, by withholding anesthesia. But it offers no further statement about ending this practice. Similarly, none of the reports I analyzed from the 1980s mentioned taking measures to ensure patient confidentiality or improving the quality of interactions women encountered from staff—these were outside the required parameters of social hygiene. But they were some of the main reasons women sought out-of-hospital terminations.

In their fight against abortion use generally, regional reports note two main tactics: the promotion of contraceptives and education. As IUDs were the main contraceptive medical providers distributed, they often served as a proxy measure for all effective contraceptive use. Reports listed the number of IUDs ordered, supplied, and inserted in women, but usually did not comment on how these numbers related to actual demand. In their 1983 report on initiatives to reduce abortions, the Belarusian Republic's health authorities did so, citing the Soviet Minzdrav's calculations of estimated annual demand for contraceptives in Minsk to be 20 million condoms, 150,000 IUDs, and 70,000 cervical caps.[115] However, the report continues, "the city of Minsk experienced difficulties in providing contraceptives, foremost—IUDs," and the effort to reduce abortions failed "due to the shortage of IUDs and unpersuasive sanitary-enlightenment work."[116] Similarly, after noting that efforts were underway to optimize the distribution and shipment times of IUDs, the deputy minister of the RSFSR concedes that by July 1, 1986, only 25.6 percent of the total amount requisitioned for the year had been fulfilled.[117] Acknowledging the increase in abortion use between 1984 and '85, he concludes, "it is difficult to conclude that the measures undertaken have been effective."[118]

As the Belarusian Republic's report alludes, the second practical tactic in the fight against abortion involved professional training and laypeople's "enlightenment." Some regional health authorities enumerated the number of doctors who raised their qualification levels in reproductive health care. Yet again, they included few substantive details. For example, a report from 1982 covering Altai krai, Tatarskii autonomous republic, Ivanovskoi, Kaliningradskoi, and Kurganskoi oblasts, notes that training courses "included issues of diagnosis, treating sepsis after abortion, and lessons on contraceptives." Medical interns in Kaliningrad oblast' were taught "modern contraceptive methods."[119] The vagueness of this kind of reporting suggests that training was likely intermittent and potentially disassociated from the realities of clinical practice. The reports also depict extensive sanitary-enlightenment work among the public. Minsk health authorities, for example, boast that "in 1982 alone, 806 lectures were given" to convince the public against abortion. A Leningrad report covering 1985 to '86 devotes more than three pages to listing public outreach venues—undertaken in high schools and vocational schools, at marriage bureaus, sanitary-enlightenment centers, and more. But questions about how to increase these courses' effectiveness are not asked.

If Minzdrav could merely request, but not order and fund research into new contraceptive technologies, its ability to improve reproductive health was severely limited. What it could do was urge clinicians to undertake public education and target women who have frequent abortions for surveillance and contraceptive assistance. And while Minzdrav reports note the shortages of contraceptives, they shift attention away from planners to place blame on doctors. As a reform plan concludes, "All of this [continual, high abortion usage] is evidence of the unsatisfactory antiabortion propaganda and inadequate moral educational work [*vospitatel'noi rabote*] in medical workers' collectives."[120] If bureaucrats felt that strong critiques of state planners might be dangerous, simply blaming doctors for poor work provided an ideologically acceptable explanation for the stubborn problems of abortion use and abortion-related mortality.

INCREASING CONTRACEPTIVE USE THROUGH CLINICAL RECOMMENDATIONS

If Minzdrav's Orders generated reams of data and carefully crafted statements of accountability, Ministry officials also produced a more in-depth genre of practical recommendations aimed at other administrators and clinicians. The question of how to increase contraceptive use was the topic of two Ministry booklets published in 1983, one that addressed the dilemma of properly calculating contraceptive demand, and another that explained contraceptive use. In both sets of recommendations, we see reflections of how the Soviet biopolitical context shaped scientific knowledge and the use of science in health policy, themes that would remain central to struggles over reproductive governance for decades to come.

While working in the Medical Demography laboratory of the RSFSR's Minzdrav, Andrej Popov recognized that the process of calculating public demand for contraceptives was under-developed, and that Ministry officials often obscured the problem: their reports included data about whether a requisitioned amount of contraceptives was fully or only partially supplied, but they did not investigate how the requisitions themselves were determined. What Popov learned was that pharmacies based their orders on the amount of contraceptives previously purchased, without exploring the broader potential consumer demand that existed or could be created. He developed mathematical formulas for calculating population demand in an attempt to rationalize contraceptive requisitions, which Minzdrav published as a booklet of clinical recommendations. I have no evidence as to whether they ever led to changes in health authorities' requisitions. But the intellectual effort itself, as an example of Popov's work to rationalize contraceptive supplies in the absence of market mechanisms, reflects an early sign of his aspiration for liberalizing health policy; he aimed to find ways of understanding and incorporating the public's interests in state policy making.[121]

Minzdrav's other recommendations booklet issued in 1983 reflected a very different set of guiding principles. Written by a team headed by Irina Manuilova, the booklet purports to give scientifically updated information about contraceptive methods.[122] It discusses different types of IUDs, including those with hormonal components, and methods of inserting and removing them. The section emphasizes contraindications and potential complications. By contrast, in discussing chemical contraceptives, which, it notes, were produced by the Soviet medical industry, the text ignores both possible complications and rates of effectiveness.[123] The text also provides instructions for women to make their own spermicide for douching by combining milk acid, table vinegar, galascorbin, and permanganate calcium, diluting them in water and applying via syringes or a home douching/enema kit.[124] Minzdrav further contends that these douches could be used for treating vaginitis, cervicitis, and cervical erosion.[125] Given the same text's focus on possible complications of the IUD, it is astonishing that matters of safety and effectiveness for these methods go unmentioned. We cannot know for certain why Manuilova's characterization of different contraceptive methods was so imbalanced and scientifically problematic, but a likely motivation could be the relative unavailability of IUDs (especially imported ones of high quality) in comparison with the domestically produced chemical spermicides. The text does not, however, discuss supply, demand, or user convenience.

MINZDRAV'S UNDERSTATED SHIFT IN ORAL CONTRACEPTIVE POLICY

Significantly, this booklet's discussion of hormonal contraceptives differs from that in Minzdrav's 1974 recommendations. Although reiterating that hormonal contraceptives should be prescribed only in limited cases of medical necessity, the text acknowledges that "With correct usage, the medication provides practically 100 percent contraceptive effect."[126] It provides detailed discussion of several distinct types of hormonal contraceptives.[127] Yet strangely, Postinor, a postcoital hormonal medication that aggressively causes menstruation, is listed along with other hormonal contraceptives and not distinguished from them.[128] In the most favorable statement on oral contraceptives, the text distinguishes their contraindications into absolute and relative, and suggests that a gynecologist may prescribe a microdose of progesterone based on individual patient's situation.[129]

Thus, while continuing to emphasize the negative side effects of oral contraceptives, Minzdrav's attitude toward them in 1983 is less rigid than in 1974, when their harmful attributes alone were enumerated. The 1983 publication explains to physicians the contraceptives' recommended use and reminds them that women should use them for no more than one year.[130] The pro-natalist position has not changed. The text endorses contraceptives explicitly in order to increase childbearing: "to preserve women's normal reproductive function . . .[and ultimately] enable an increase in fertility due to the higher number of fertile women."[131]

By 1985, a wholly new attitude toward oral contraceptives emerges from the Russian Republic's Minzdrav, this time from the Ministry's chief ob-gyn, Vladimir Serov. As part of an order titled "On the Unsatisfactory Work in Preventing and Lowering Abortions in the RSFSR and Raising Its Efficacy,"[132] Serov calls hormonal contraceptives a "necessity" (*neobkhodimost'*) because IUDs cannot be used by everyone. In this respect, he specifically mentions "women who have just become sexually active and don't want to get pregnant" and who may not be "psychologically ready" for IUDs. Serov further states that the low-dose estrogen and progesterone combination pills, when used by young women "properly and under medical supervision . . . are unlikely to cause complications."[133]

If these 1983 and 1985 documents reveal a dramatic reversal in Minzdrav's rejection of oral contraceptives, neither discusses the public health dimensions of changing attitudes and behaviors to promote oral contraceptives and reduce abortion use. There are no comments about the need to publicize these recommendations among physicians, to teach them prescribing practices, or to import or domestically produce oral contraceptives. Given the widespread belief among both medical experts and laypersons that "hormones" were dangerous and not to be used for routine fertility control, these internal Ministry memos—the 1985 policy was even "secret"—can hardly be considered a revolutionary policy change.[134] Minzdrav formally acknowledged that scientific data on the pill had found high levels of safety and reliability, but it did nothing to change professional prejudices and reduce ignorance of oral contraceptives. For Soviet women, very little changed in terms of their opportunities to effectively prevent pregnancy. Small quantities of oral contraceptives trickled into some Soviet regions. A report from the city of Leningrad covering 1983 through 1987, for example, notes that "the requisition for hormonal medications biksekurin, non-ovlon, ovidon, was fulfilled completely since 1983 . . . for postinor in 1985, 5,000 packages were requisitioned and 5,000 were received."[135] Although we cannot know how these requisitions were calculated, or whether they were distributed for contraceptive or medical purposes, the same report later asserts that improving gynecological care and reducing abortions will involve increasing the use of hormonal contraceptives.[136] But again, Minzdrav experts were ignored, and supplies remained grossly insufficient.

Popular Literature Targeted to Reducing Abortions

The contradictions in socialist contraceptive policy we have seen thus far—the prioritization of fertility increases over contraceptive effects, the effort to maintain state control rather than empowering lay people—played out visibly in educational campaigns against abortion. Whereas researchers in the 1950s and 1960s emphasized that socialist commitments ensure socioeconomic well-being, the sanitary enlightenment campaigns in the 1960s and 1970s abandoned such advocacy. Amy Randall's study of the post-Stalin antiabortion campaign demonstrates that two modes of persuasion became central: First, scare tactics, in which educators threatened women that having an abortion could ruin their lives by causing secondary sterility and thereby causing marriages to fail or by leaving women permanently single. Second, campaigns pursued a new strategy of enlisting men in reproductive decision making.[137] Randall sees this as a reaction against the 1944 family law, which distanced men from family responsibilities and made the state central to child support.[138] By the mid-1950s, she argues, Soviet leaders aimed to "domesticate" men, to bring them into reproductive decision making and the family orbit more generally. The campaign against abortion thus became an arena for reconstituting patriarchal gender norms, as the state now called on men to oppose abortion and thereby become more protective husbands and fathers.[139]

So how did socialist biopolitics shape sanitary enlightenment efforts to persuade readers against abortion and for contraception? Two exemplary texts, brochures published in the genre of popular-science education, illustrate this impact. Dobrovol'skaia's 1964 *The Harm of Abortion* is a typical Soviet social hygiene text aimed at women; Khodakov's 1979 *To Young Couples* addresses abortion and contraceptives within the broader topic of sexual disharmony, which was then becoming problematized as contributing to failed marriages and consequently to decreasing fertility rates.[140] The similarities and differences between these texts, published fifteen years apart, reveal how persuasion strategies evolved in the absence of significant changes in the availability of contraceptives or improvement in living conditions. As we will see, Soviet sanitary enlightenment work combined a selective use of socialist ideology with gender essentialism, such that concerns with women's equality were limited to the public sphere while a patriarchal bias informed intimate relations.

The 1964 *The Harm of Abortion* booklet celebrates the Soviet state's interests in people's reproduction and welfare, detailing the "constant care, honor and respect that surrounds women in our country as active builders of communism, and the even greater degree of care and attention to women-mothers, who give most of their strength to raising children."[141] It declares that "no other state has such a huge and extensive network of institutions for providing assistance to mother and child . . . even in the most difficult years [World War 2] the party and government paid great attention to the protection of motherhood and improvement of women-mothers' position."[142] The text elaborates on specific laws that protect women-mothers both during pregnancy and after giving birth, including the provision of daycare and preschools. Its ideological position on what matters in a person's life is also made explicit: "We don't at all want to suggest . . . that raising a child is easy or does not require care and labor. But there is no greater joy for women then the joy of motherhood. It is an inexhaustible source of energy and great human happiness."[143] Socialist attention to material well-being gets expressed in the emphasis on state benevolence in providing for women's equal rights, while reaffirming a gendered essentialism about women's maternal nature.

This text assumes the reader considers abortion a routine practice and perhaps is even already pregnant and deciding how to proceed: "Therefore, before deciding on an abortion, each woman should again carefully reconsider [*eshche raz vse khorosho produmat'*]."[144] It asserts that "every woman must know the minimal information about anatomy and physiology of women's sex organs to be better able to understand what an abortion is and the often harsh consequences resulting from it."[145] The next several pages provide written details and diagrams of women's reproductive system. These details were not taught in Soviet schools and were rare in print media intended for the lay public. Thus, this booklet provides information not otherwise easily accessible to readers. However, the text itself acknowledges that the information to be conveyed is "minimal" and presented only to facilitate women's avoidance of abortion. Matters of pleasure are completely absent.

The title, *The Harm of Abortion*, captures the bulk of this text's intent. It details types of abortion (miscarriage, induced abortion, and criminal abortion) and their specific physical complications and supposed risks— even when provided by physicians—including a weakened immune system, infertility, and ectopic pregnancy.[146] Interestingly, this section of the booklet also devotes over a full page to gonorrhea, explained as usually caused by casual sex that occurs outside of marriage, not the abortion procedure.[147] The booklet thus aims to arouse the reader's fear of consequences, lest she make what is clearly portrayed as the "wrong" decision.

Contraception is finally addressed in the final five pages, introduced with the statement, "If for some reason a woman doesn't want to have children, she needs to know how to prevent pregnancy."[148] With this phrase, the text defines any fertility control as equivalent to a general rejection of childbearing, rather than as a routine part of most heterosexual women's lives, including mothers. The text then asserts the essential need for medical surveillance:

"Contraceptive methods cannot be chosen by oneself. It's absolutely necessary to consult with a doctor, who, after examining the internal sex organs and undertaking a detailed inquiry, will recommend one or another method. However, no matter how good a contraceptive method is, one can't use it for long; from time to time the doctor will replace it with another method."[149]

This explicit medicalization of contraception is followed by a brief discussion of the main types of mechanical and chemical contraceptive devices available at the time of the publication: male condoms, metal and rubber cervical caps, and chemical spermicides.[150] Dobrovol'skaia does not comment on the advantages or disadvantages of the methods; she merely lists them and their proper use. For example, she explains that chemical contraceptives are spermicides, notes that a common one is called kontratseptin-T, which is used together with a homemade douching solution consisting of vinegar, boric acid, and boiled water (for which she gives the recipe). She also explains how to make homemade vaginal tampons to soak in contraceptive spermicides, followed by douching, as another contraceptive method. Leaving aside the fact that douching is not effective and that introducing vinegar and boric acid into the vagina would likely be harmful, the text does not acknowledge that the living conditions of many Soviet women would make preparing douches difficult. The millions of people who shared a kitchen, toilet, and bath in a communal apartment, for example, would be subject to the surveillance of their apartment "neighbors" and may not find douching possible.[151]

Dobrovol'skaia concludes with a brief mention of coitus interruptus, which she roundly rejects for contraception: "It has a negative effect on the husband's and wife's nervous system."[152] Strikingly, this comment is the first mention of anything regarding the effects of contraceptive methods on partners' psychological well-being. One could imagine that the extensive labor necessary for using chemical contraceptives—mixing the solution, using it immediately after sex, or making home-made tampons, acquiring the spermicide, soaking them ahead of intercourse, then making the douching compound and using it afterwards, would also negatively affect women's "nervous system," but this possibility goes unmentioned. While socialist biopolitical improvements of material conditions were limited by state economic constraints, sanitary enlightenment expressed a concern with men's comfort over and above women's needs.

To Young Couples differs significantly from *The Harm of Abortion*. Written for young people planning to marry and for couples encountering sexual problems, this book was in its third edition in 1979. It is structured around answers to common questions from readers, devoting minimal attention to socialist ideology. Notably, the text does not instill fear as a form of behavioral control. Rather, it affirms the importance of harmonious sexual relations for a successful marriage, because "breakdowns in the sexual aspect of life cause people more sad times, disappointment, and suffering, than even life-threatening illness."[153] The author's only nod to ideology aims to clarify socialist morality on sexuality:

In the 1920s the theory of "the glass of water" was extremely widespread. According to this, sexual attraction is not regulated by any societal norms, and therefore sexual needs should be fulfilled as easily as quenching thirst with a glass of water. V. I. Lenin was against this theory, which caused many young men and women misfortune [*stala zlym rokom*], he said, emphasizing that "the relationship between the sexes is not simply the expression of games between societal economy and physical need. . . . Of course, a thirst needs to be satisfied. But would a normal person, in normal conditions, lie down in the street in the dirt and drink from a puddle?" V. I. Lenin categorically affirmed that his criticism of the theory of the glass of water did not mean advocating asceticism.[154]

After decades of official communist attitudes toward sex as an antisocial activity necessary for procreation but otherwise best ignored for more socially productive activities, this statement aims to legitimize sexuality as a healthy part of life.[155] Which norms or moral frameworks should be followed, however, remained vague, and the author's perspective emerges only piecemeal through the ensuing discussion. Having recognized that satisfactory sexual relations are important in marriage, the text acknowledges that preventing pregnancy is frequently necessary due to a range of circumstances:

> Young married couples may not have good living conditions or sufficient material opportunities. Sometimes it's necessary to spend a large proportion of the year away on business trips, or it's necessary to finish one's education or finish up a work contract. There are situations when one's health doesn't allow for having a child, and sometimes you need to wait for the first child to grow up a bit before having a second one. In short, there are a lot of reasons that spouses intend to wait to have a child. In such cases it's necessary to remember that terminating a pregnancy at any stage (abortion) causes harm to the body and can lead to infertility and women's illnesses. Unfortunately, many couples who get married have a very vague perception about contraceptive methods.[156]

While far more detailed and explicit in acknowledging the need for deliberately preventing pregnancy than *The Harm of Abortion*, this text pays virtually no attention to issues that make contraceptive use possible: whether sex was planned or spontaneous (let alone consensual), and the corresponding mindset, habits, and agreements between partners that facilitate making contraceptive practices routine. By ignoring such questions, the text also fails to address the convenience and acceptability of methods such as the barrier and temperature methods, and thus their likeliness of being used. It recommends "the physiological method [based on] safe and unsafe days . . . this method cannot give a full guarantee against pregnancy (and actually no method can give such a guarantee), but many married couples use it successfully."[157] The text presents a table with which readers can figure out a woman's fertile and infertile days based on her ovulation. Still, some of the information presented is scientifically unfounded and wrong, as when it encourages douching: "For preventing pregnancy one can use the extremely simple but effective method of washing the sperm from the vagina immediately after the sex act."[158] It also recommends the use of a lemon slice "inserted into the vagina before intercourse" ("It achieves a good [contraceptive] effect and is entirely harmless for the body"), and the use of petroleum jelly on condoms.[159]

The book's focus on sexual compatibility raises issues not addressed in texts focused on abortion, including the emotional dimensions of sex and the links between emotional and somatic reactions. Still, attention to emotions does not radically transform the proffered advice about contraceptive methods. After describing withdrawal as an "unnatural act," Khodakov explains, it "can lead to serious consequences . . . if used over a long course of time, men can have weakened reactions and premature ejaculation. Women can suffer pseudo-frigidity and, as a result of the stagnated blood in the lower pelvis, genital inflammation."[160]

Although ignoring the severe shortage of IUDs, the text embraces them as an effective and convenient method for preventing pregnancy that also positively impacts sexual enjoyment—"Women no longer think about the possibility of unwanted pregnancy and focus their thoughts on achieving sexual harmony."[161] This mention of women's fear of pregnancy impacting sexual relations is unique in Soviet-era texts. But as the following passage reveals, the concern at stake, again, is men's comfort and pleasure: "The husband should not participate in preparing the woman for intercourse. It's better if he doesn't even know how she contracepts. Tact and a certain intimacy are necessary in such difficult physiological acts as sexual intimacy. When there is sincere love and respect for a wife, a husband will be happy if she avoids abortions and her health is not under threat."[162]

The two texts reviewed here, on abortion and sexual compatibility, typify the ways contraceptives appeared in health education literature after the relegalization of abortion. Explanations of contraceptive methods did not address their availability or convenience. They included inaccuracies and a strong dose of essentialized gender ideology. They offered women minimal information about their bodies but used scare tactics for engineering behavior change. Even though supplies of contraceptive devices remained in deficit, sanitary enlightenment literature did not acknowledge this constraint; nor did it recognize the fact that many women lacked private bathrooms and kitchens to prepare the recommended contraceptive tampons with spermicide. There was no suggestion that both partners should take responsibility for preventing pregnancy. The constant message was that safety required medical control.[163]

Conclusion

The paradoxical treatment of contraception in the state's "fight against abortion" illustrates key tensions at the heart of Soviet biopolitics. There was no ideological prohibition against contraceptives under socialism when embedded in a broader approach to eliminating socioeconomic inequalities. Indeed, states throughout the socialist bloc did a better job of supplying their populations with oral contraceptives, IUDs, and other methods than the Soviet Union. Poland had had family planning collaborations with Great Britain since the 1950s, and urban regions of Poland, Yugoslavia, and Hungary had family planning services beginning in the 1960s and '70s.[164] Soviet researchers recognized that contraceptive use would reduce abortions and emphasized its compatibility with pro-natalism.[165] Public health bureaucrats in Moscow also sought to increase contraceptive use. They instructed regional planners that local campaigns against abortion should involve both increasing contraceptive availability and undertaking public education about contraceptives, ordering them to report back on their progress.

Nonetheless, concerns about maintaining control over women and increasing fertility led Ministry experts to withhold support for hormonal contraceptives. Minzdrav prohibited the pill for contraceptive purposes in 1974 due to safety concerns, including fears that it would circulate illegally, leading to unsupervised and dangerous uses. Even as Soviet-led research showed that low dose OCs were safe and effective in preventing pregnancy, Ministry officials underplayed their endorsement. The 1983 recommendations statement, which formally allowed prescribing oral contraceptives for birth control for up to one year, was not followed up with advocacy to import, produce, or educate the public about them. For at least some Soviet health leaders, hormonal contraceptives posed the threat of lowering fertility and were thus politically unacceptable. Other effective contraceptives, such as the IUD, faced perennial deficits. These contradictions—the promotion of contraceptive use through its medicalization, and the insistence on state control despite the state's failure to provide sufficient resources—characterized the Soviet technology of social hygiene.

Socialist biopolitical technologies were used not only to "foster life," but to remake it. Sanitary enlightenment positioned women as worker-mothers in relationship to the state, which both granted women legal rights and material entitlements and continually reminded them to consider the state's interests when making their reproductive decisions. Sanitary enlightenment involved providing minimal information to lay people and often relied on fear tactics; it did not conceptualize women's equality as a value to be cultivated in behavior change. Social hygiene's concerns with material well-being and women's equality became largely rhetorical affirmations of the state's largesse and did not materialize in adequate supplies of basic items relevant to these values, such as contraceptives.

Consequently, research and practical interventions usually focused on women's decisions to terminate a pregnancy—in other words, why they did not follow state prescriptions—rather than assuming pregnancy prevention is a "natural" part of women's lives and inquiring into why it often failed. The assumption was that women did not know about abortion's harms, and so sanitary enlightenment work focused on teaching them. Knowledge here was not intended to empower, as Foucault described its goal in modern, liberal societies.[166] The aim was to educate women in how to behave to fulfill collective interests. When abortion rates remained high, health planners blamed physicians for their ineffective enlightenment work rather than reflecting on the limitations of this one-way knowledge transfer model.

Soviet biopolitics generated a reproductive habitus that differed dramatically from that in the West, in which women were expected to discipline themselves, manage their sexuality, and plan their reproductive life through efficient contraceptive technologies and according to personal goals.[167] Instead, Soviet women were continually exposed to warnings that abortion was dangerous and reminders about the joys of motherhood. Seeing few other options for prevention, they came to accept routinely undertaking unsafe procedures. Such fatalism was common in other Soviet era contexts, such as those living in the shadow of nuclear accidents and prisoners exposed to tuberculosis in Georgia.[168] As Soviet Russian women resorted to abortion at rates among the highest in the world, many also regarded the state's claims of benevolently protecting its citizens' health with increasing cynicism.

Given Soviet socialism's inability to provide either the governance framework or the practical conditions to allow the routine prevention of unwanted pregnancy, some experts turned to liberal frameworks. The next chapters explore the kinds of liberalism they sought to create and the consequences of these frameworks for both health and social change.

CHAPTER 3

Conceptualizing Liberal Reproductive Governance

I first heard about the Soviet "abortion culture" in the fall of 1991. I had just arrived at Princeton's anthropology department for graduate school, professionally committed to the ethnographer's project of understanding how unfamiliar worldviews and routines make sense to those who practice them. A coup by hardline communists in Gorbachev's Soviet Union had just ended—fortunately, with only minimal bloodshed. Having five years of Russian language study behind me, a flyer posted around campus offering Russian conversation in exchange for English caught my eye. I called the number listed and the friendly voice on the other end introduced himself as Andrej. Suggesting we meet in front of the main library, he assured me I would easily recognize him because of his "typical Russian snout" (*tipichnaia russkaia morda*)—an expression that I found amusing but opaque: I had no idea what it was supposed to tell me. Nonetheless, he was right—I spotted him immediately: wearing a blazer and tie made him seem out of place in the casual American university scene. Andrej was thirty-four years old, with a full head of thick auburn hair, a mustache, and a beard. As we discussed our interests, I learned that he had just arrived from Moscow as a postdoctoral fellow with the Princeton Population Center; he was researching abortion in the Soviet Union. This piqued my curiosity, and I was delighted that our conversations would be substantively interesting as well as useful for language practice.

During our meetings, Andrej explained that abortion was Soviet women's most common form of fertility control and therefore presented numerous problems. He discussed his scholarly goals to statistically model abortion trends and historically detail Soviet reproductive policies. He told me about his social commitment to help replace his country's "abortion culture" with routine contraceptive practices, and his various strategies for trying to do so. To illustrate some of his work, he gave me a copy of a booklet he recently published to educate lay people about preventing pregnancy. But our wide-ranging discussions about Soviet society made me aware that Andrej did not explain routine abortion as a simple consequence of Russian people's ignorance about contraceptives or the fact that supplies were inadequate. Rather, he characterized the reliance on abortion as a symptom of systemic failures of the Soviet regime. When I asked him to explain those failures, he cited Solzhenitsyn's *Gulag Archipelago* to tell me that the Soviet Union had been built on the slave labor of prisoners; human beings were used as instruments for the state's goals. Nor had society transformed sufficiently since the era of de-Stalinization, he argued. Although I didn't write down his words verbatim, I recall him explaining what he saw as a central societal defect: "The Soviet system is fundamentally irrational, in the sense that there's no feedback loop between the state and society. The state does not consider the needs of ordinary people in developing its policies. It doesn't adjust its policies when they result in harmful consequences for the population. It is absurd. The state's planning and activities are disconnected from people's lives." The disdain with which Andrej conveyed these ideas told me they would be crucial to understand. He was characterizing systemic processes by which the Soviet state failed its citizens and worse—treated their bodies and lives instrumentally. It took me years to process the multiple hardships and consequences this involved. But what was clear as soon as I heard about the Soviet abortion culture was that my reproductive-rights worldview was not adequate for understanding such injustices or their implications. In deciding to study routine abortion anthropologically, as a practice created by history, policy, and culture, and as a symbol interpreted at the levels of national politics, expert discourses, and personal experience, Andrej's words echoed in my memory. I came to understand that routine abortion offered an important but under-studied lens onto how the Soviet state embedded its enduring contradictions in institutional practices, personal habits, and intimate relationships.

This chapter explores how Andrej Popov conceptualized family planning in Russia as a means of inaugurating broad, liberalizing transformations. The concepts and techniques of family planning would become characterized in differing ways by the global activists who promoted them, the expert activists and Soviet bureaucrats who supported them, and the Russian skeptics who rejected them. As one of the founders of Russia's family planning movement whose involvement spanned numerous professional and public-facing activities, Popov's vision is significant; it exemplifies the multiple ways family planning could be deployed to liberalize Russian society, from transforming clinical services and expert behaviors to guiding new interactions in intimate relationships.

By delving into the critical schools of thought that inspired Popov's research and the zeitgeist of late Soviet popular culture that shaped his values, this chapter reveals the specific forms of liberal thought that informed Russian family planning. While the impact of the global family planning industry's support should not be underestimated, it is crucial to understand how local critical concerns and debates shaped Russian proponents' approaches. Russian family planning was the creative response of experts who reflected on and aimed to solve problems they experienced in the Soviet system. It differed in notable ways from the visions underlying global family planning, which emphasized women's bodily autonomy as a feminist principle and general social good. Indeed, this book argues that the liberal biopolitics that Russian family planners sought to establish prioritized the rationalization of public policy and re-enchantment of intimate relationships. Russian family planners were inspired by humanistic concerns to establish scientific and pragmatic approaches to health in place of ideologically-inspired aims, approaches that respected individuals' needs over state interests and enacted caring interpersonal relations between experts and laypersons. Beyond illuminating historical changes to the specific field of reproductive health, therefore, an analysis of the visions and strategies of the Russian family planning movement can help us understand some of the key values and concerns that guided liberalizing reformers in Russian society more generally.

Global Collaboration, Friendship, and the Puzzle of Cultural Difference

Buoyed up by our lively discussions, Andrej and I began planning to collaborate on the study of abortion in Russia, joining his quantitative and historical inquiries with my ethnographic methods. In imagining this collaboration, I didn't know what to make of Andrej's view of Soviet abortion as an "enormous problem." His commitment to improving women's reproductive options certainly aligned with values of human rights, but I noticed he didn't use the language of rights or feminism. When I straightforwardly asked him, "You want to reduce abortions, but do you also believe that women have a right to get abortions on demand?" he responded with a definite but disinterested "of course." He had no doubt that keeping abortion legal was necessary, but it wasn't an issue that worried him. This dramatic difference between our concerns gave me pause. It left me intrigued to learn more about the Soviet context of abortion politics, about Andrej's own perspective on them, and about his view of the global abortion debate.

Hints emerged that Andrej was part of a community of critically minded intellectuals in Russia and found common cause with liberal health agendas. Once, he showed me an acquaintance's manuscript about hazing in the Soviet army, a still dangerous topic that the author was hoping to publish abroad. There were other moments, however, when I found his comments confusing. Returning from a weekend trip, he announced with reverence that he had visited an Orthodox priest in upstate New York and been baptized. I recall my surprise at this, for he had recently told me that the Russian Orthodox Church was vocally opposing abortion. Decades later, when I had already begun working on this book, I learned he had been a devotee of Alexander Men', an Orthodox priest with humanistic and ecumenical leanings who inspired numerous intellectuals disillusioned with the mechanistic orientation of Soviet atheism to explore Orthodox spirituality.

My confusion about Andrej's perspective on abortion politics subsided some when he introduced me to Henry P. David, a world-renowned researcher on abortion and reproductive rights advocate; David's Prague Study had shown the negative effects that denying women access to abortion had on their and their resulting children's mental health.[1] They met at a 1990 conference on family planning and abortion in Tblisi, Georgia, and David had recommended Andrej for the New York–based Population Council's postdoc that got him to Princeton. I now understood that even if Andrej's language and focus didn't entirely sync with the standard script of American pro-choice activism, he positioned himself within the reproductive rights movement. Translating its values to the Soviet context meant increasing the availability—and legitimacy—of contraceptive supplies in order to reduce women's need for abortion. This was a key juncture where the promotion of women's interests was clearly aligned with liberal, post-Soviet change.

Still, some interpersonal aspects of Andrej's behavior continued to bewilder me, and figuring these out would ultimately offer insights into Russian cultural contours of reproductive and gender politics. Andrej opened doors for me, insisted on carrying my books, and kissed my hand when our get-togethers ended. On my birthday, he brought me a bouquet of roses. These were moments that felt culturally awkward, though not personally unnerving. Andrej knew I was happily married and never hinted at romantic intentions. Like his wearing a jacket and tie when we first met, his gestures were clearly intended as displays of respect, even if reflecting unfamiliarity with the local social milieu. They did make me wonder what Russian cultural understandings he was reflecting regarding friendship, platonic relations between men and women, and the role of gender equality in daily life.

There was another aspect of our interactions that was unusual. Andrej invited me to accompany him at various professional and social occasions he attended, both at the university and in the community. In the context of my other experiences at Princeton, these overtures stood out as odd: people didn't go to the holiday parties of colleagues from other departments, just as they didn't bring guests other than their life partners to social events. But there was a spirit of generosity in his invitations. I noticed that Andrej was delighted to make connections between his acquaintances. He spent time talking with everyone at the Population Center, and eagerly introduced me to them as well. One weekend in the spring of 1992, my husband and I drove Andrej to Boston. The plan was to visit separately with our respective friends before returning to Princeton together. But Andrej insisted I join him for tea with Igor Kon, the eminent Russian professor of sociology and sexology on sabbatical at Harvard. I was doubtful that such a renowned scholar would want to meet a young graduate student with a barely formed project, but Andrej knew Kon and was confident I should come. Later, when Henry David supported his grant proposal to the MacArthur Foundation for researching Soviet abortion and contraceptive policies, Andrej insisted that some of the funds be allocated to my research, too.

Through all these experiences, I saw how Andrej created strong connections with many people and attentively nurtured his friendships. Later, when I became well-acquainted with dozens of people while conducting fieldwork, I realized that many of Andrej's interactions that I found confusing were culturally normal in Russia. Individuals brought others to interviews I had imagined would be just between the two of us, and friends invited themselves to join me at events I was attending. Even more impressively, people offered to introduce me to their friends to help broaden my connections. Unlike my own (American) assumption that being independent was necessary for professional and personal integrity, Soviet-era Russians intuitively knew that nurturing friendships by offering care was key to self-esteem and a rewarding life.[2] So while Andrej's warmth and big-heartedness were personal traits, his practice of introducing me to colleagues and linking me into his networks reflected a culturally appropriate mode of attending to relationships—by showing proactive care.

Additionally, Andrej's gestures that evoked what once would have been celebrated as "chivalry" were normal ways of communicating respect and friendship, and not necessarily love interest, among educated people in the late Soviet era. Such styles of interaction were part of broader cultural shifts that began in the post-World War II era. Exhausted from decades of revolutionary zealotry, political terror, and war, many Soviet people longed for a revival of intensely personal connections and a platonic romanticism in interpersonal relations. They associated the idea of "women's equality," by contrast, with the Bolsheviks' promotion of worker and comrade mannerisms among men and women alike, and the Soviet policy of assigning women to jobs involving hard manual labor. Reacting against this politics of enforced equality—associated with a symbolic and physical brutality—intellectual men by the 1980s commonly performed gestures reminiscent of social codes of honor and gallantry. Lost in translation to a Western feminist milieu, Russian men's "chivalry" was meant as a means a reclaiming beauty, comfort, and interpersonal joy from Soviet control—through an aesthetic of gender *in*equality.

Regrettably, my collaboration with Andrej would never occur. When a research opportunity arose to study maternity care reforms underway in St. Petersburg, I decided to base my year-long dissertation fieldwork there, visiting Moscow when possible. Knowing that reforms in maternity care would be relevant to the study of abortion, I decided to temporarily postpone our collaboration. Andrej had established a Moscow branch of Henry David's Transnational Family Research Institute; I hoped to affiliate with the Institute after finishing my PhD. Sadly, in April 1995, Andrej had a heart attack while trying to fight a fire at his remote dacha near Vychnyi Volochok, and died. He was thirty-nine years old, and his wife was eight months pregnant with their first child.

Soon thereafter I received a phone call from someone introducing himself as Sergei Zakharov, who explained that he was ensuring the completion of Andrej's MacArthur grant and needed me to report my findings to him. Shocked and distressed, I went to Moscow, relieved to meet with others who were also grieving Andrej. We spoke at length about the events that had happened. Their Moscow liberal demographic community was reeling from this loss, and the future of Andrej's research agenda was bleak. There was no one who had his sense of mission to focus on addressing Russia's

FIGURE 3.1. From left: Andrej Popov, the author, and Nina Khrushcheva, Princeton, New Jersey, 1992. Photo from author's personal collection.

abortion and contraception trends in either scholarly or applied approaches.

Over the years that followed, Sergei, his family, and I became good friends. Zakharov, as Andrej called him, illuminated crucial insights for me. His research on fertility became extremely important for my understanding of Russian reproductive health and politics. Sergei generously read and commented on my work, shared his research, debated with me, and introduced me to his demographer colleagues. This community of scholars had also been Andrej's community, and so by getting to know them, I was able to learn more about Andrej's work and life, as well as about shifting population trends in post-Soviet Russia. No less importantly, these relationships taught me about the history of Soviet demographic and social sciences and their transformations in the post-Soviet context.[3] When in 2011 I decided to return to the study of abortion in Russia, this scholarly community, now based at the Institute of Demography at the Higher School of Economics in Moscow, welcomed and encouraged my research.

Replacing Sanitary Enlightenment with a Liberal Model of Health Promotion

Andrej Popov was the most prolific and innovative Russian researcher of abortion and contraceptives in the 1980s and 1990s. This chapter explores

Popov's contraceptive education booklet as a springboard for introducing
the significant transformations he inaugurated in several aspects of health
promotion. Beyond imparting accurate information that was extremely
hard to come by, this booklet modeled a new way of performing expertise
with lay persons. By comparing Popov's approach with the sanitary enlightenment texts we saw in Chapter 2, we will see how he aimed to transform
public health outreach into a manifestly liberal endeavor. The chapter also
explores the late Soviet era intellectual and cultural inspirations that shaped
Popov's thinking. Grasping the liberalizing framework that shaped Popov's work on contraceptives will provide a baseline from which to compare
later family planners' efforts to unmake the country's abortion culture in
subsequent chapters.

The cartoons shown in Figure 3.2 grace the covers of Popov's 1990 booklet, *How to Prevent Pregnancy Effectively, Comfortably, & without Harm to
Your Health*.[4] These lighthearted depictions of sexuality and medical services immediately announce the booklet's distinction from the sober and
intimidating disciplinary approach that characterized sanitary enlightenment texts. Dobrovol'skaia's *Harm of Abortion* text has an austere cover with
no illustration, while Khodakov's *To the Young Married Couple* depicts a
young man standing romantically behind his love nuzzled in chaste intimacy. Popov's cover illustrations, with a silly looking cartoon couple holding an oversized condom (and nude on the front!)-- suggests that sex is fun
and perhaps even occurs outside of marriage. Yet the text itself is filled not
with jokes but with scientific facts and user-friendly advice. Its thirty-one
pages define the criteria for effective contraceptives as a method's reliability, reversibility, simplicity of use, physical accessibility and expense, safety,
and acceptability in both psychological terms and with regard to the sexual experience. Examining the condom, the IUD, oral contraceptives, withdrawal, the calendar, and temperature methods, the text describes how each
method works, how to properly use it, and its advantages, disadvantages,
and risks. Further, the booklet examines different kinds of IUDs and pills,
asserting their overall superiority in terms of reliability and compatibility
with sexual pleasure; it also acknowledges their inaccessibility in the Soviet
deficit economy.[5] But much of this book's innovations stem from what it
does not say, and the tone in which it presents its ideas. Popov introduces
key features of a liberal biopolitics in contraceptive education by decou-
pling discussions of pregnancy from fertility and avoiding issues of pronatalism altogether; by acknowledging the value of (hetero-) sexual pleasure

FIGURE 3.2. Front and back covers of Andrej Popov's *How to Prevent Pregnancy Effectively, Conveniently, & without Harm to Your Health*, 1990. Used with permission of Sergei Zakharov.

for its own sake and without regard to a couple's relationship status; and by abandoning socialism's emotional style of paternalistic expertise and replacing it with a friendly expert tone oriented towards helping fulfill consumers' self-defined needs. Notably, Popov's booklet also promoted caring gender relations without the patriarchal bias of earlier texts, which, as we saw, aimed to preserve men's comfort or buttress their power in the relationship.

Interestingly, while rejecting these characteristic features of socialist biopolitics, Popov accepts that the state should establish the socio-economic conditions needed for public health. But unlike social hygiene thinkers, he also recognizes that this requires understanding and addressing people's own concerns, not merely dictating these conditions from above. Thus, Popov recognizes the complex interplay between systems and individual agency; he neither envisions a state entirely withdrawn from collective well-being nor an abstract ideal of individual autonomy. His goal is to re-enchant relationships between experts and laypersons and between men and women as sites of care.

In the following sections, we toggle back and forth between analyzing this booklet and exploring the sources of Popov's thinking, including the multi-disciplinary, maverick scholars who shaped his research and also the popular cultural milieu that spurred his creativity. It is notable that Popov began his career as a physician who specialized in social hygiene, not as a clinician. He was therefore dedicated to bridging medicine, population studies, and the social sciences. He began researching abortion and contraceptives in the early 1980s, seeking out mentors who creatively transcended the disciplinary boundaries and ideological frameworks of their era, such as Mikhail Semenovich Bednyi, Anatoly Vishnevsky, and Igor' Semenovich Kon. Indeed, training with Bednyi in the new field of medical demography that the latter had established encouraged Popov to recognize the strengths and limitations of social hygiene as it developed within the Soviet state's administrative-command system. Popov's 1986 dissertation for the *kandidatskaia* (Soviet PhD) degree was entitled "Medical-Demographic Factors in the Regulation of Births."[6] He demonstrated the severe problems that resulted from the centralized planning of contraceptive supplies, which ignored questions regarding consumer demand. Through focusing attention onto people's own perspectives, he re-envisioned the work of public health as based on a feedback system between the population's interests and state policy making.

Popov also sought friends who similarly reveled in the spirit of truth-seeking.[7] His friend, demographer Sergei Zakharov, recounted how Popov sought out opportunities—which required forging connections and securing permissions—to attend lectures all over the city on topics ranging from demography to sexology. And in turn, many people sought out Popov to understand issues for which information was in short supply—such as how to prevent pregnancy effectively. With the new opportunities of Glasnost, Popov wrote for leading intellectual journals like *Ogonyok* and *Vek XX i Mir* to initiate transformative discussions about reproductive health and social relationships for the broader educated public. Popov highlighted lay people's interests and ignored state-defined collective ones; he replaced the moralizing communist tone with an empathic, caring, and friendly one; and rather than titrating sanitized information for teaching people how to achieve the state's goals, he shared broad-based scientific information to empower people's personal decisions. In these ways, Popov's work heralded a liberal alternative to both sanitary enlightenment and other fields of Soviet expert discourse. As later chapters will show, subsequent efforts to promote contraceptives took less progressive forms, and still endured a debilitating nationalist backlash. Making sense of the dismantling of family planning organizations during the 2010s requires grasping the historical inspirations and constraints that shaped their development.

Decoupling Contraceptive Education from Fertility Concerns

In a notable departure from writings in the "harms of abortion" genre, Popov's booklet omitted any mention of state family politics or fertility. He argued that deliberately planning one's reproductive life is necessary to avoid bearing children one doesn't want or love, which, he suggests, often results in abuse.[8] Arguing for reproductive planning as emotionally beneficial for the children one ultimately bears was entirely new in Soviet reproductive health education. Another innovation was Popov's explanation that preventing pregnancy is a normal, universal human action. In contrast with the pronatalism haunting Dobrovol'skaia's begrudging comment, "If for some reason a woman does not want children," Popov asserted, "If a woman doesn't regulate her fertility, she may have ten to twelve children over the course of her life," whereas most Soviet people have one or two.[9] He then explained that at stake is not *whether* to control fertility but *how* to do so reliably, safely, and with the least inconvenience and disruption to one's sexual pleasure. Striving to replace Soviet forms of biopolitics with a liberal one, Popov positioned the scientific expert as recognizing the naturally occurring regularities of human behavior and educating people about the effective technologies for pursuing their own interests.

Popov's intellectual shifts away from emphasizing state pronatalist interests and toward a notion of fertility control as normal and necessary were shaped by the broader intellectual and social influences of his education in demography. Popov's dissertation supervisor was Mikhail Semenovich Bednyi, the founder of the Soviet field of medical demography.[10] Bednyi's empirical research began in the 1960s and focused on improving life expectancy, but his broader intellectual concern was to create intellectual and institutional bridges between demography and social hygiene. To make his case, he argued a medical demographic approach to fertility trends would consider factors currently ignored by demography alone, such as the health of spouses, the prevalence and causes of infertility, and the impact of abortion on women's ability to conceive.[11] At stake for Bednyi was the need to overcome the ideological rejection of biological factors that had shaped

Soviet demography and social hygiene since the 1950s (as biological deter-minism was associated with US population research). Incorporating both biological and social factors in the study of human population health, Bed-nyi argued, was to search for the truth, build on empirical and theoretical knowledge, and recognize the laws of nature.[12]

Popov was inspired by Bednyi's holistic, interdisciplinary analyses and his commitment to using research for improving health. Popov's 1986 dis-sertation illuminated the failures of Soviet funding and procurement meth-ods to meet the population's demand for reliable, modern birth control. He demonstrated the absurd situation in which the amount of funding allocated for pharmacies to purchase contraceptive supplies was based on whether or not the previous year's funding allotment had been exhausted. Yet allot-ments came at inconsistent times in the year, and the types of contracep-tives procured were not in line with the kinds that buyers sought.[13] With no existing research into the population's actual demand for contraceptives, and no methodology for doing such research, Popov argued, a more ratio-nal system for meeting people's needs could not even be imagined. His the-sis developed just such a method through mathematical modeling. He rec-ommended this method be adopted by regional pharmaceutical managers in formulating their order-requests for contraceptive methods and by state planners "to significantly expand" production of IUDs and "to start produc-tion or increase purchases of imported oral hormonal contraceptives."[14] In later work, as representative survey data on contraceptive use became avail-able, Popov clarified the spurious character of apparent findings. For exam-ple, when 88 percent of respondents from the Russian Republic stated in 1990/91 that it was "not difficult" to buy contraceptives, Popov recognized this as a sign they were unaware of widespread shortages. Since 56.8 per-cent of respondents stated they "did not use" contraceptives, and 31.5 per-cent claimed they "always" or "sometimes" did, Popov demonstrated how, since most of these users relied on the calendar method, withdrawal, and douching, they probably never attempted to procure deficit items.[15]

Another area of Popov's research investigated women's reasons for using abortion in general and out-of-hospital abortions in particular. In 1982 he conducted a representative sample survey of 2,300 Muscovite women and found that abortion often resulted from unsuccessful efforts to prevent pregnancy with unreliable methods.[16] Some women concluded that attempt-ing to prevent pregnancy was futile, an idea echoed in women's informal discussions. In addition to the dire need for expanding contraceptive sup-plies, Popov concluded that official sanitary-enlightenment work about the harms of abortion was failing to reach women, and new methods of communication were urgently needed.[17]

Severe health repercussions often resulted from abortions provided outside medical facilities, known as "criminal" abortions. Popov found several causes for why, despite the wide availability of hospital abortions, women still risked obtaining terminations in unsafe conditions. He found that a major cause was the need for confidentiality. Hospital abortions were inpatient procedures that required a woman to miss work and thus to present her employer with a certified medical note documenting her temporary inability to work. These notes listed induced abortion as the reason for a woman's absence, and some women sought illegal abortions to protect their confidentiality.[18] Time off from work due to abortions was deducted from a woman's salary, another reason for avoiding official hospital abortions.[19] He also found that the social stigmas projected onto women with out-of-wedlock pregnancies and those who conceived in their forties led women to prioritize confidentiality, sometimes over safety.[20] Popov urged that the existing approach to medical certification be discontinued and confidentiality ensured. Through his work on scientifically calculating estimated demand for contraceptives and surveying women on their reasons for terminating pregnancies and for obtaining out-of-hospital abortions, Popov presented empirically verified insights into the causes of abortion. Like his mentor, Mikhail Semenovich Bednyi, Popov recommended policy changes be based on "real demographic processes," and not ideological assumptions, and he devoted his career to investigating them.[21]

Yet unlike Bednyi, who was a committed pronatalist, Popov did not argue the need to raise fertility. His one study addressing fertility contrasted the impact of birth control versus abortion on the birth rate. Echoing Sadvokasova's argument that contraceptives did not reduce fertility, he showed, by contrast, that secondary sterility caused by abortions could reduce fertility by 30 percent.[22] In his rejection of pronatalism, Popov was influenced by Anatoly Grigorevich Vishnevsky, whose work we encountered in the introductory chapter. Vishnevsky's pathbreaking contributions began in the early 1970s, soon after leading Soviet demographers pronounced low fertility in the country's European regions a serious problem.[23] Then a researcher at the Demography Unit of the Central Statistical Administration of the USSR (TsSU SSSR), Vishnevsky wrote "The Demographic Revolution" to explain human population trends in a strikingly divergent framework from the dominant Soviet view.[24] Vishnevsky defined fertility decline as the result of unprecedented decreases in mortality, themselves facilitated by industrialization and scientific-medical advances in the nineteenth century. In a striking departure from Marxist theory, he cast demographic changes as occurring independently from transformations in relations of production, and as generating more substantial changes in human consciousness.[25] Moreover, Vishnevsky saw fertility decline as a desirable sign of the progress all societies, sooner or later, underwent. Its universality—in other words, inevitability—meant that pronatalist interventions were pointless.

The courage required to make this argument in 1973 is notable. Recall that Soviet ideology steadfastly opposed Malthusianism, the idea that the need to control fertility emerges when resources were scarce, that is, in Soviet terms, under the unjust conditions of capitalism. Under socialism, mainstream Soviet ideology asserted, citizens' basic material needs were guaranteed and so population growth should proceed uninhibited.[26] By the mid-1960s, however, it was clear that reality was not fulfilling ideology. The birth rate had been declining for over four decades, which augured ill for future labor reserves and the economic imbalance of an aging population.[27] This decline was seen as posing threats to the Soviet Union's geopolitical stature. Disparities between fertility rates in Slavic and Muslim regions of the Soviet Union suggested the potential for future ethnic conflicts. And low fertility was interpreted as a symptom of decaying family life.[28] The crisis affected virtually every dimension of the nation's vitality, and experts in numerous fields avidly proposed strategies for reversing this trend.[29]

Vishnevsky, however, contested the fear that decreasing fertility threatened the socialist society. Considering smaller families as a sign of social progress, he argued that the deliberate control people exercised in creating them reflected the development of "free thinking" and the individualization of human psychology.[30] True to the foundations of liberal biopolitics, Vishnevsky and his supporters embraced such individual and family-based self-determination as beneficial to society.[31]

Popov knew Vishnevsky's work and, being close friends with his PhD student Sergei Zakharov, attended Vishnevsky's lectures. Popov used Vishnevsky's work on Russia's demographic transition to characterize Russia's dramatic regional differences in abortion rates.[32] And he shared the overall commitment to democratizing Russian society that distinguished Vishnevsky's school of thought from other demographic paradigms. In 1990, the same year Popov released his booklet, Vishnevsky and Zakharov published a refutation of the argument that Russia was facing a demographic crisis.[33] They began by acknowledging that the Soviet population had suffered catastrophic historical events over the twentieth century that had artificially distorted the modernization process. But these severe losses, they contended, did not derail the inevitable trajectory of social change. Demographic modernization was underway and inevitable; the existential question at stake was what kind of political regime would shape modernization's future trajectory. Rejecting pronatalist campaigns as characteristic of totalitarianism and militarism, Vishnevsky and Zakharov argued that "low fertility and small families are linked with improvements in quality of life, more individual freedom, the genuine emancipation of women, etc."[34] They further noted that internationally, nontraditional families were gaining recognition and rights, and urged Soviet leaders to accept these shifts as signs of the "democratization of the family, the broadening of its sovereignty, and the possibility of self-realization for each of its members."[35]

To achieve a more balanced age structure, Vishnevsky and Zakharov echoed Bednyi's concerns to reverse the country's high mortality rates, low life expectancy, and high rates of abortion.[36] They argued that pursuing socioeconomic development along the paths of Western countries—from economic reforms to a Western approach to public health—would strengthen the population and deliver social, political, and public health prosperity.[37] Popov's omission of any discussion of fertility and state interests from contraceptive education applied Vishnevsky's theories to transform the expert governance of reproduction. In its silence on pronatalism, this text aligned with popular (and liberal) understandings that bearing children to improve the state's population interests was utterly ridiculous.[38]

RECOGNIZING SEXUAL PLEASURE AND CARE

Popov's booklet emphasized that contraceptives should not negatively impact sexual pleasure. This was entirely absent from the 1960s texts from the "harms of abortion" genre; as we saw in Chapter 2, pleasure (implicitly for men) became a recognized concern in books promoting harmonious marriages in the late 1970s.[39] For Popov, sexual pleasure was not confined to marriage and was not a means of ensuring stable and more productive (fertile) marriages; it was a goal in and of itself. By using the term "female partner" (*partnersha*)—highly unusual in the Soviet context— Popov markedly did not assume that sex occurs only in marriage. Being able to acknowledge this in an official publication was a marker of Glasnost enabling discussions of sex without moralizing. It underscored the author's concern to promote readers' health rather than instruct them in the "proper" (communist) way to live.

Most notably, Popov recognized sexual pleasure for both women and men and addressed the multiple factors involved in women's sexual pleasure. His discussion of condoms is illustrative. Addressing men, Popov cautioned that proper use of the condom is essential for ensuring both their preventive effect and women's pleasure. He addressed women's physical comfort and pleasure, noting that "stopping in the middle of lovemaking to put on a condom can lead to vaginal dryness" and "higher friction can lead to vaginal irritation."[40] In another example, Popov called on men to address women's sexual needs: "Ending love play abruptly immediately after ejaculation is not good sexually. Many women at exactly those minutes have the strongest sexual feelings. Lack of attention to her and even worse, her partner's absence, sharply diminishes the point of the sexual act for her."[41] Popov also explained to men that women needed confidence in their contraceptive method to fully enjoy sexual intimacy. This was important for men to know, especially if relying on condoms: "it is women who are most interested in the issue of prevention of pregnancy, while men, on the contrary, very often treat this dismissively. Therefore the woman must trust her partner very highly or she will develop anxiety over fears of getting pregnant."[42]

He further argued: "In not preventing pregnancy, a man must remember that his partner will face the need to avoid pregnancy with the help of an abortion" and, "Remember that the health of the female partner (*partnershi*) depends on the carefulness (*akkuratnosti*) of the male partner. Not following even one of these rules strongly reduces the effectiveness of the method and puts the female partner at risk of getting pregnant."[43] In contrast to the American markers of feminism that I sought when initially reading Popov's booklet—affirmations of women's reproductive autonomy—Popov's progressive gender politics is evident in these calls for men to take responsibility for preventing pregnancy. Unlike health experts' earlier efforts to enlist men in convincing their already pregnant partners not to obtain abortions, Popov strives to get men involved in contraceptive practices and concern themselves with women's emotional health and sexual pleasure.[44] While resonating with the women characters in Ulitskaya's story discussed in Chapter 1, "Orlovy-Sokolovy," this was a radically new agenda for Soviet health education.

Inspiring Popov in these ideas were leading scholars in Soviet sexology—Igor Kon, Sergei Golod—and public debates emerging gradually since the late 1970s about sex and gender. Kon was well known as the country's

FIGURE 3.3. Andrej Popov and Igor Kon, Cambridge, Massachusetts, 1992. Photo by the author.

eminent historian of sexuality and a leader of efforts to enlighten the Soviet and later Russian public about the biological, historical, and cross-cultural dimensions of sexuality. Yet Kon's intellectual interests were far broader, spanning psychology, sociology, and history, the philosophy and methodology of social sciences, theories of the self (*lichnost'*), and the sociology and psychology of youth.[45] He described assuming the role of sexual educator as driven by his sense of obligation to help people understand this black box of life, somewhat at the cost of his research interests. His 1970 article "Sex, Society, and Culture" ("Seks, obshchestvo, kul'tura") published in the journal *Innostranaia literatura* (Foreign literature), "was the first, and for many years the only effort in the Soviet Union to more-or-less seriously discuss questions about sexual-erotic culture."[46] Kon was courageous in addressing these topics directly and undaunted in insisting on standards for robust research and substantive discourse. Serving on the editorial board for the third edition of the Great Soviet Encyclopedia, when an entry on "sexual life" could again be published after years of Stalinist censorship, Kon opposed the initial draft texts as entirely inadequate: it explained "sex" by solely discussing the silkworm; the section written by pedagogues and philosophers provided no knowledge, only "the habitual moralizing" (*privychnaia moralizatsiia*). Kon revised the entry for "sexual life" to address human sexuality and authored a new entry on sexology. He began examining the place of sexology among scholarly disciplines beyond medicine. In 1976, he gave a series of lectures about young men's sexuality to the Psychoneu-rological Institute named for Bekhterev. There was so much interest that notes taken during the lectures began circulating (uncorrected) in samiz-dat. And while he managed to publish sporadically on sexuality during the early 1980s, Kon's work focusing on sexuality as a "normal" part of life was often censored; the authorities feared that such work would arouse accu-sations of "unhealthy sexual interests" or "sexual perversion."[47] Still, for young researchers like Popov, Kon modeled the multidisciplinary study of sexuality in both its theoretical and applied dimensions.

Sharing these commitments was sexologist Sergei Golod—a former PhD student of Kon—and Anatoly Vishnevsky. Noting that the state's premarital consultations on "family life" weren't addressing people's concerns out of fear that talking about sex would be degrading, Vishnevsky dedicated the April 14, 1976, edition of his column on family issues in the newspaper *Kom-somol'skaia pravda* to his conversation with Golod about sex in marriage.[48] Noting that youth were getting some degree of "information" from graffiti in public toilets, Vishnevsky and Golod countered by emphasizing the need to instill a "culture of feelings" and develop "soulful subtleties" and "emo-tional openness." Implicitly critiquing Soviet ideologues, Golod cautioned against relating to sex as "secondary," "vile," or "sinful" for people who are in love. Both strove to emphasize that sexuality was a natural and import-ant part of relations, not equivalent to perversion and pornography, while cultivating its expression with sensitivity and care. Yet this was going too far for Soviet authorities, who responded to this topic by cancelling Vish-nevsky's column altogether. This same restrictive viewpoint meant that Kon's book *Introduction to Sexology* would not be published in Russia until 1988, but Popov and other Moscow intellectuals were able to learn from him directly. Sergei Zakharov remembered going with Popov to a talk Kon gave at Moscow State University in which the room had overflowed to such an extent that people were standing outside the building, hungrily listening through the open windows. Interestingly, this was not entirely hidden, as the talk took place in the old university building near Manezhnaya Square, in the very heart of Moscow.

Sex and Abortion in Popular Culture

The openness to thinking about sex thoughtfully and in terms beyond Soviet repression was not confined to scholarly elites. A brief glimpse into popular culture provides a telling lens onto emerging lines of debate on these issues. The 1977 film *School Waltz* (*Shkol'nyi val's*), directed by Pavel Liubimov and released by Mosfilm, provides an illustrative example of the emerging liberal perspectives on sex and how these related to the perceived crisis of masculinity that Popov and his mentors were trying to address.

The film depicts the gentle love affair of high school seniors Zosia and Gosha. Yet when Zosia gets pregnant and tells him she'd like to keep it, Gosha emerges as confused and far less decisive and responsible than Zosia. The film aroused vibrant debates, but not about issues American viewers might expect, such as their failure to prevent pregnancy, the possibility and morality of abortion, or the ways teen childbearing involves virtually unsurmountable obstacles to economic self-sufficiency.[49] Instead, viewers debated the film's lack of moral judgment about teenagers' sexuality. In negative letters to the editor, viewers decried the immorality they perceived in Zosia allowing "her noble feelings of love to degrade into lust" and expressed indignation that the film offered no judgment about these actions, for youth required positive role models.[50] The positive reviews, by contrast, took a resigned view toward teen sex. "Gosha and Zosia sincerely love each other—there's no doubt. Is that promiscuity? Immature frivolity? It's a pity if some viewers decide to judge their behavior so categorically and in a way that's essentially untrue."[51] This reviewer further argued that depicting "worrisome, adverse phenomena" that still plague society can be pedagogically valuable, by presenting "lessons of ethical and superb citizenship in sharp, impartial images, using the method of 'evidence from what is unpalatable.'" Applauding the film's deliberate "avoidance of evaluations of behavior, ready recipes, prescriptions, and condescending lessons"—the very issue that critics of the film found most troubling—this reviewer highlighted how Zosia modeled the admirable action of following her conscience. He argued that one of the strengths of *The School Waltz* is that it confronts viewers with the need to think for themselves.[52]

Interestingly, Soviet viewers widely agreed that the film effectively portrayed their society's lamentable "crisis of masculinity." The *Sovetskaia kul'tura* reviewer depicted Gosha as irresponsible, "a spineless rag," and saw his unassertiveness, indecisiveness, and failure to actively struggle for Zosia as exemplifying problems common among Soviet men. The reviewer claimed that while girls matured sooner and honed leadership skills, boys languished, turning to alcohol and dubious crowds; in time, they became men who were most comfortable with their drinking buddies who neither judged them nor asked anything of them. For this reviewer, the urgent problem portrayed in the film was the need to teach boys courage and steadfastness.[53]

Debates over films like *The School Waltz*, Vishnevsky and Golod's discussion in the family issues column, and the widespread fascination with Kon's work revealed that Soviets were actively grappling with the place of sex in society. Many people construed the key ethical concern as the need for loving and caring relationships. And here, the most pervasive problem appeared to be men, not women. Popov's booklet, by providing specific knowledge to men and women and directly addressing men in encouraging healthy, caring, responsible sexual practices, offered practical steps to improving gender relations marred by the crisis of masculinity.

Re-Enchanting Relations and a New Emotional Style of Expertise

In addition to Popov's new attention to men's care for women through taking responsibility for contraceptive use, his booklet also modeled a new emotional tone in communication between experts and laypersons. Rejecting the use of threats and paternalism to motivate behavior change, Popov established a friendly tone between expert and lay person from the booklet's introduction. When defining the process of "planning the family" as "your efforts to give birth to a specific, desired number of children at a time that's convenient for you," Popov added, "I hope you will succeed in this, just as I hope your children will."[54]

The booklet's conclusion combined this emotional transformation with an explicit shift in power relations. The last contraceptive method discussed is the temperature method, which Popov describes as "very good [in the sense] that it is effective and absolutely not harmful for either partner's health . . . but [which has] serious disadvantages—its difficulty to use and the sexual inconvenience it presents." He then concludes:

> Happily, you already have opportunities to use other, modern methods of pregnancy prevention that are more effective, less harmful, and more convenient to use. You have a choice. And can you [choose] independently? Now you can. Now you can choose for yourself the most suitable method. You are able to do so now because you know what constitutes effectiveness and sexual acceptability.

To do so, look at the chart we've included and try to find the contraceptive method that works for you. We wish you success![55]

The booklet's illustrations further communicate a light-hearted tone. In the cartoon in Figure 3.4, describing the disadvantages of withdrawal, Popov shifts away from earlier arguments that this method is "harmful" and highlights its disruption of pleasure.

Beyond depicting withdrawal as incompatible with personal pleasure, this cartoon communicated scientific expertise with humor and care. By expressing authorial "hopes" and "wishes" to the reader, by noting that the situation created by reading this booklet and becoming informed is a "happy" one, by encouraging the reader to feel capable of controlling their fertility effectively and conveniently, and by using humor and emphasizing pleasure, Popov's booklet strove to re-enchant expertise and the relations between experts and laypersons through an emotional style that differed significantly from the stern, fear-inducing style of Soviet biopolitics. Moreover, in contrast to *The Harms of Abortion*'s insistence that the choice of contraceptive method *must* be made by a doctor, Popov's booklet included a chart for readers to use to figure out the best contraceptive method for

FIGURE 3.4. Cartoon about the withdrawal method from Andrej Popov's *How to Prevent Pregnancy Effectively, Conveniently, & without Harm to Your Health*, 1990. Used with permission of Sergei Zakharov.

themselves. Friendly expertise involved providing resources and respecting lay people's capacities to determine their own paths forward.

RE-ENCHANTMENT: HUMANISM IN LATE SOVIET POPULAR CULTURE

Popov's emotional attunement in this booklet reflected his own personal warmth as well as cultural ideas circulating in late Soviet culture. The relatively liberal atmosphere that emerged after Stalin's death, "the Thaw" era, saw a broad retreat away from revolutionary zealotry and war-time mobilization as Soviet people yearned to recapture personal and intimate aspects of life.[56] Soviet art and media critics felt emboldened to express dissatisfaction with socialist realism's one-dimensional image of heroism, and called for a new relationship between culture producers and the public—highlighting a needed aesthetic of "sincerity."[57] They sought narratives shaped by social complexity and contradiction, less attuned to achieving ideological correctness than to resonating with emotional truths about human relationships and suffering. In popular literature and film, romantic relations became an arena in which the value of sincerity over ideology became particularly significant. As we saw with debates over *The School Waltz*, Soviets were grappling with the notion that art should avoid simple answers and invite audiences to "think for themselves." A brief excursion into some of the cultural sources inspiring late Soviet humanism will help contextualize and bring into relief the progressive work Popov's booklet was doing.

The reclaiming of personal struggles outside of ideology is expressed in the much loved 1968 Soviet film *We'll Survive until Monday (Dozhivem do ponidel'nika)*, directed by Stanislav Rostotski. Set in a high school, the Russian literature teacher embodies the ideologically correct Soviet school marm, a stickler for rules and defender of propriety. The plot develops after she announces a writing opportunity for students to explore their views of the meaning of "happiness," but then decries many students' attention to their own feelings as a "discursive striptease." She reproaches one girl's statement as particularly shameful and tells her to tear up her draft. Prompted by her classmates' curiosity, Nadia proudly insists on reading her statement aloud:

When speaking about happiness, it should be done with sincerity, not through rationalization. Many of us are ashamed to write about love, even though every girl dreams of it, even the least pretty one who no longer has any hope. But I think one should always have hope. I would like to meet the sort of man who would love children. Because without children, a woman can't be truly happy. If there won't be a war, I'd like to have four children, two girls and two boys. . . . Then, for the rest of their lives, no one will feel alone.

There is silence in the class and the camera hones in on the students' sympathetic faces, which turn toward the teacher with incredulity. One, and then another, asks, "What's wrong with that?," and a third humorously reminds the teacher that Nadia "plans to have [the children] with her legal husband, not someone else's!" Yet the teacher rebukes them as lacking shame and conscience.[58] The camera then pans to the film's protagonist, a quiet boy named Gena, who responds to the public humiliation Nadia has just endured with the single sentence, "happiness is when others understand you!" (*shchast'ia-eto kogda tebia ponimaiut!*) Going beyond the sympathetic gestures from the students, the film affirms its critique of ideological and moralistic rigidity just a few scenes later, when we see the shaming teacher weeping as she admits to herself her own loneliness.

This scene expresses the supreme value of affirming connections and loving relationships, which Nadia links directly to motherhood and family, for a meaningful life. The possibility of defining one's own desires and definitions of happiness, without regard to the collective's interests, seemed to replace ideological ideals with a deeper truth about human existence. "Happiness is when others understand you!" emphasized the value of intimate connections and personal emotional truths as profoundly needed by both women and men. This statement became a cultural truism reiterated for decades to come.

That Andrej immensely valued relationships was obvious in his way of being in the world; he never shied away from expressing love and concern for people dear to him. The feminist journalist and professor Nadezhda Azhgikhina recalled in a discussion with me how Andrej generously gave up his hotel room to ensure she had a safe place to sleep when her accommodations fell through at the 1994 UN Population Conference in Cairo. She and Andrej had planned to collaborate on providing information about contraceptives for public education.

Through this vignette and numerous other examples, I came to understand that Andrej's valuing of trustworthy friends was nourished by his awareness of how the state and bureaucracy harmed individuals; he recognized that providing informal care and protection to those one loved was essential.

I recount these mundane interactions because they provide a key to Andrej's worldview and similarly the cultural zeitgeist of late Soviet humanism. Blinded by my American cultural assumptions, there was so much I failed to understand about him. The absence of "women's rights" language in his booklet, which I initially considered a possible sign that he opposed legal abortion, was likely his effort to avoided any association with state ideology. For most Soviet people of the time, invoking "women's equality" would have been perceived as ideological claptrap. The 1979 hit film *Air Crew* (*Ekipazh*), directed by Alexander Mitta, reveals this in two notable storylines. First are the changes experienced by pilot and playboy Igor, who points to the policy of women's equality for avoiding commitment. In an early scene, he informs his young stewardess lover of his approach to romantic relations:

> In our country women have equal rights with men, correct? So you should *use* them! . . . Why this absurd, wild, atavistic desire to marry? The idea of marriage stems back to the cave dwellers. The male hunted mammoth while the woman waited for him by the fire. No husband—no mammoth, no food. That was the rock solid logic. She had to stick to someone to survive. But now? She's got a PhD, her salary is even higher than a man's because she doesn't drink. But she has to cling to some creep with both hands because of the grand idea of a husband—a *husband*—a family. Isn't it ludicrous?! (*bred*) (31:25).

Yet when Igor and Tamara face a horrific brush with disaster and death, Igor realizes he has fallen in love and wants to marry Tamara. At the film's climax, Tamara cries out that "all [women] want to get married and have children and spend their whole life with that person," giving the lie to Igor's opportunistic, if playful, take on Soviet ideology. Love and commitment win the day as foundational truths of a meaningful life; women's equality is forgotten as irrelevant to fulfilling relationships.

Another pilot's story goes even further in undermining the value of Soviet women's "emancipation," here depicted in a controlling personality, not economic equality. Valentin is a deeply loving father who patiently tolerates his wife's unrelenting harangues. When they finally decide to split, she falsely accuses him in court of alcoholism and abuse, smearing his reputation and depriving him of parental rights.[59] This malicious character is one of many Soviet-era representations which implicitly associates women with access to state levers to manipulate men.[60] Indeed, in everyday thinking, "women's equality"—whether as socialist policy or assertive personality—appeared disconnected from caring interpersonal relations. Andrej, by contrast, omitted explicit discussion of women's rights; he wanted his information to reach people, and this required it be perceived as apolitical. Yet he recognized the dire need for changes in gender relations for men to address women's physical and emotional needs. In ways resonating with late Soviet humanism, he did so through emphasizing caring and an openness to sexuality embedded in love in place of terminology or frameworks linked with Soviet ideological language.

Re-Enchantment, Liberalism, and Critical Politics in Late Soviet Humanism

Finally, Popov was moved to re-enchant relations as a means of ending the immense suffering that women endured in a society that failed to provide them with safety—in pregnancy prevention and all other matters. In a 1991 article in the literary journal *Vek 20 i Mir*, he reflected on his visit in the late 1980s to Kamchatka, a peninsula in Russia's Far East where he joined a team of researchers from the Academy of Sciences' Institute for Sociological Studies and conducted a survey on family, fertility, and health issues. Popov saw in Kamchatka's extraordinarily high abortion rates (which he cited as officially registered at 245.8 abortions per 100 births) "an index and realistic model of everything that is going on with us . . . here is the most extreme expression of everything that is in our Soviet life." Observing "open manholes to sewer lines, many, everywhere. . . . But, notably, gaping [*ziiaiushchie*] holes in the street didn't worry anyone. There were no signs of efforts to protect oneself and others from the dangers." He further surmised the connection between failed infrastructure, the lack of prevention or planning, and utter human despair:[61]

> the bottomless emptiness of [women's] eyes, the abandoned foundations of unfinished buildings, ditches, careers, zones, industrial projects and destruction, destruction. . . . It is everywhere: in people's eyes and souls, it is everywhere on this earth. Here so much is meaningless that it gives a certain aroma of . . . doom to life on the edge of the Soviet earth. Why should we therefore plan our families? All children are going to live badly in this world.[62]

At stake in family planning, Popov asserted, is freedom. Specifically, "freedom of reproductive choice: freedom to decide the timing and number of children to have."[63] And this freedom entails people's ability to imagine that they are the subjects of their own fate, a privilege he perceived as unavailable in Kamchatka, and far too rare in mainland Russia.[64] Yet he concluded with an abrupt refusal to despair, seeking hope and affirming the love that childbearing can bring:

> Only who can explain to me what is the historical cause, and what is the consequence? Isn't the kingdom of God within us ourselves? Are we ourselves not the cause? Are we ourselves not the consequence of our own actions? Are we not rewarded in accordance with our belief, and only it? But this is what surprises and inspires: we live and we bear children. No matter what—we live and we give birth. I don't know of anything that is a more impressive, convincing and hopeful example of human resilience [*stoikosti*] and dignity.[65]

Conclusion

Popov's contraceptive education focused on providing people with knowledge to manage their sexual and reproductive lives for their personal goals; in the process, he also strove to re-enchant relationships both between men and women and between experts and laypersons. In this way, Popov's liberalism aimed to replace a form of expertise that asserted prescriptive norms for how to live a proper life; and if he recognized a wide range of lifestyles that could be pursued, he maintained a commitment to disseminating scientific knowledge for people to rationally manage their sexual lives in the name of care, pleasure, and health. Had I approached him with the critique that his work was not promoting people's "freedom" but striving to renew Russian medical authority, I expect he would have agreed. Popov felt that the Soviet state had put a socialist ideological straitjacket on health care and that a new, legitimate foundation for expert authority was urgently needed. He would not have conceptualized scientifically-grounded expert knowledge as a constraint on personal freedom but as a precondition for it. Nor did he envision people attaining anything like complete, individual autonomy, as Western myths appear to promise (and Foucaultian critics love to debunk). Popov's liberal humanism aimed to improve social problems created by the Soviet regime, not establish a utopian social order.

Contraceptive education was only one component of Popov's multifaceted vision for liberal transformations. He fought expert and bureaucratic ignorance through presenting globally sourced scientific data and recommended practices. This included investigating the centralized health system's failures to estimate and reasonably fulfill contraceptive demand and devising a formula for doing so; lobbying for policy changes to secure oral contraceptives and other globally common, effective methods; researching the reasons women often sought risky, out-of-hospital terminations and advocating for policies ensuring patient confidentiality to prevent them; and actively supporting the fledgling nongovernmental RAFP to become a local resource for professionals and the public.[66]

In one of his final and most compelling publications, Popov provided a historical and political explanation for the rise of Soviet abortion culture: policy and legislation on abortion had been repeatedly instrumentalized, for political purposes and social experiments, at individuals' expense. He described the 1920 legalization of abortion as useful for the Bolsheviks' goals of destroying the traditional large and religious family and creating a new, secular Soviet woman-worker; the 1936 abortion ban was a tool for maximizing women's reproductive capacities for the state; and abortion's 1955 relegalization—along with the state's continuing neglect of contraceptives—was yet another attempt to engineer higher fertility (this time, without women dying from illegal terminations). Decrying "the cynical and ignorant manipulation of abortion legislation by authorities pursuing their own political ambitions and economic goals," he envisioned a shift away from a society shaped by "the combined absence of personal freedom and responsibility in childbearing" to a society of "personal reproductive choice and responsibility."[67] Popov's faith in liberal biopolitics was rooted in the humanist ideals of late Soviet culture and the aspirations it nurtured for cultivating respect for individual needs and relations of care. It promised a profound alternative to the suffering he witnessed among "single mothers and adolescent mothers" without support, and the even more common phenomena of "unwanted children, parental cruelty, infanticide, child abandonment, and coerced parenting."[68]

In 1994, Popov won support from the MacArthur Foundation to research abortion and contraceptive policy in Russia. With mentorship from the US-based global abortion rights researcher Henry P. David, Popov established a Moscow branch of David's Transnational Family Research Institute, which was poised to conduct research, advocacy, and applied projects promoting contraceptive use. It was Popov's sudden death in April 1995 that tragically ended these efforts.

CHAPTER 4

Adopting Global Family Planning with Neoliberalism

Glasnost and the end of the Soviet era opened the door to innovations in reproductive health by enabling an entirely new infrastructure for family planning. Contraceptive advocates within and beyond the Ministry of Health recognized that their decades-long fight against abortion had failed. Maternal morbidity and mortality remained high, fertility was low and declining. Existing public health strategies were not effectively reaching the population; the services established specifically to reduce abortions, the so-called "offices of marriage and family," had not achieved significant success. Family planning proponents realized some of the reasons—these offices were neither open to men nor welcoming to teenagers, and they offered no sex education.[1] Health leaders also recognized that clinicians' widespread misinformation about oral contraceptives was contributing to these problems. In January 1992, the deputy prime minister of the Russian Federation, A. Shokhin, issued an order endorsing "the establishment of the Russian Association of Family Planning, whose main activities are improving the demographic situation . . . [and] lowering the rates of abortion, maternal and infant mortality."[2] The order also provided the new association a two-hundred-square-meter facility free of charge.[3] On July 30, 1992, the Russian deputy minister of health, N. N. Vaganov, affirmed the need for ob-gyn and pharmaceutical services to collaboratively ensure contraceptives' supply and distribution in a manner *maximally convenient for the population* (*naibolee dostupnykh dlia naseleniia*).

Significant transformations ensued. The Russian state provided funding to repurpose more than two hundred existing women's clinics into new centers for reproductive health and family planning. With interdisciplinary staffs of physicians, psychologists, and lawyers, these were well supplied with contraceptives and began providing sex education.[4] The mandate for these new institutions to improve the demographic situation—i.e., raise fertility, is politically notable. Contraceptive supporters and leaders of the family planning association recognized that it was crucial to enable the deliberate timing of pregnancies according to people's own interests through access to effective contraceptives. They saw safe abortion as a backup necessary to ensure women's continuing fertility, and believed that the reduction in abortions made possible by regular contraceptive use would ultimately strengthen fertility rates. But this new strategy would become intensely contested by those who insisted on the need to explicitly and solely promote births as the path toward demographic vitality.

As we will see, contraceptive advocates found various ways of justifying the prevention of pregnancy as a means of promoting demographic renewal. In the early 1990s, virtually no family planning activists highlighted a liberal commitment to ensuring women's reproductive freedom. Instead, they portrayed contraceptives as a step toward improving reproductive health and even increasing births by preventing health complications from abortions— such as uterine scarring from the use of curettage in poor conditions, as was typical in Soviet clinics.[5] Family planning supporters considered their approach not ideological, but scientific, pragmatic, and compatible with family-focused politics.[6] Nationalists, by contrast, defined the systematic prevention of pregnancy as dangerous, ideological work to further reduce Russia's demographic strength on behalf of enemy agendas.

The need to defend family planning led its Russian supporters to downplay discourses on reproductive rights even as they adopted global family planning's approaches. Moreover, they accepted support from global antiabortion movements, now networking throughout Eastern Europe.[7] In the 1990s, Russian family planning leaders did not imagine that such collaboration entailed advocating for abortion's criminalization, and they would not have supported such an idea had it been proposed to them. But in "fighting against abortion" as they promoted contraceptive use, they saw common cause with both global family planning and antiabortion movements. Notably, while small, isolated groups of intellectual feminists were beginning to organize in Russia, they remained disconnected from the family planning movement for decades to come—and most Russian family planners remained disengaged from Western feminist concerns with bodily autonomy.[8]

Family planning work saw rapid and impressive success. In 1995 alone, the rate of abortions decreased by 12 percent.[9] By 1997, oral contraceptive use had quadrupled.[10] Abortions continued to decrease between 6 and 7 percent yearly, with the number of women using hormonal contraceptives and IUDs consistently rising.[11] Yet by 1998, after intense conservative objections and lobbying, federal funding for family planning was eliminated.[12] Although a group of almost thirty highly ranked Russian health experts advocated reinstituting financial support, that never occurred.[13] Campaigns to discredit family planning continued apace.

Understanding this paradox is the goal of this chapter and Chapter 5, which trace the emergence of a family planning infrastructure and Russian efforts to legitimize such work amid avid pronatalism and hostility toward the West. During Glasnost, researchers clamored for more effective approaches to combatting abortion. Their appeals were answered in the early 1990s, as global family planning initiatives came to Russia. Drawing on archival materials, published sources, and my fieldwork experiences, we will see how Russian experts adopted global recommendations for reorganizing their clinical services while strategically navigating the foreign advisors' emphasis on reproductive rights. We hone in on two new family planning institutions, an advocacy/ training NGO and a clinic for teenagers, which served as models for countrywide developments. This chapter's final section examines a confrontation between Russian family planning leaders and their conservative opponents in a 1997 television talk show debate. Family planners defended their programs by invoking the authority of science and their commitment to care. The campaign to discredit them exploited Russia's post-truth media landscape while preying on public misgivings about Western-driven liberal reforms. Although Russian justifications for family planning—framed as rationalizing policy and re-enchanting relations—were culturally salient forms of liberal humanism, the neoliberal landscape had begun eroding the persuasiveness of those very arguments. They were contested with lies and sensationalism. The fate of family planning illuminates the struggles facing liberal humanist reforms more generally in post-Soviet Russia.

Researchers' Demands for Change Come to Fruition

With Glasnost, Soviet researchers' published arguments about reproductive health expanded significantly beyond what had been possible to say openly in previous decades. Researchers explicitly criticized Soviet policies. They decried the ban on oral contraceptives with impassioned arguments that it had left Soviet health behind other developed countries and that, even in the highest doses—which were no longer being widely used—the possible complications of hormonal contraceptives would not be as serious as those of repeated D&C abortions.[14] Researchers explicitly linked the use of unreliable birth control methods, such as douching, with shortages of effective contraceptives and acknowledged that people who practiced withdrawal saw no other options.[15] These researchers pushed for contraceptive services to be individually tailored to each person and couple, not standardized for the masses.[16] They called for contraceptives enabling psychosexual well-being.[17]

In November 1991, the RSFSR Minzdrav established the first ever nationwide family planning system by creating some two hundred centers for family planning and reproduction on federal, regional, and local levels.[18] In 1992, the Russian deputy minister of health, N. N. Vaganov, emphasized how the involvement of various ministries and agencies, as well as societal organizations, in this new project, was an important innovation: "for the first time at a government level, the issue of family planning is not defined solely as a medical concern."[19] Yeltsin's government endorsed the newly founded Russian Association of Family Planning and provided funding. The emergence of this nongovernmental organization networked globally and poised to help shape policy and expert practices was a crucial step away from the state-dominated social hygiene regime central to socialist biopolitics.[20]

These Glasnost era discourses and institutional changes thus undermined Soviet state ideology and reimagined the work of the state in two ways. First, they acknowledged the state's failure to provide for citizens' basic needs and turned to the global market and nongovernmental sector to do so. Second, they abandoned expectations that citizens' personal interests would align with state goals. Researchers acknowledged that people's timing of childbearing and number of children would be determined by personal factors unmanageable by state engineering. Notably, contraceptive supporters also largely rejected early socialist policies of gender equality—as did most late-Soviet elites, from Gorbachev to the liberal intelligentsia. They explained high rates of abortion as the downstream outcome of Soviet society's irrationalities, from economic deprivations to the erosion of patriarchal gender relations, which, they claimed, reduced men's ability to care for their families and women's ability to nurture. Reviving "traditional" masculinity and femininity was described as part of prioritizing family life and raising the "spiritual level" of society.[21] Given this, it is not surprising that some Russian family planning advocates in the early 1990s welcomed support from global abortion opponents.[22] At the same time, they recognized that abortion must remain legal and available, recalling the terrible mortality and secondary sterility that ensued during Stalin's eighteen year abortion ban.

As we saw in Chapter 3, liberal aspirations in the late 1980s and early 1990s imagined policies prioritizing science and care, the rationalization and re-enchantment of relations. Russian health experts saw the family planning paradigm as an effective means of realizing these changes, but they were ambivalent about its focus on reproductive autonomy. They intuitively recognized that to become culturally and politically legitimate, the global family planning paradigm would need to be framed as enhancing *societal* well-being. New habits of preventing unwanted pregnancy, they argued, would reduce abortion and strengthen families; contraceptives were the rational and humane path toward enhancing fertility.[23] The fact that Yeltsin's presidential program "Children of Russia" funded the federal project of Family Planning epitomizes this logic. Russian family planning leaders thus navigated Western reproductive rights discourses with caution, selecting from them strategically while promoting their goals in locally salient terms. For example, the RFPA quite explicitly highlighted the idea that children have the right to be born wanted and loved. The association's approach to women's rights, while never placed in doubt, was less central. In its inaugural issue of the journal *Planirovania sem'i* (Family Planning) in 1993, the editorial board, headed by Dr. Vladimir Kulakov, the director of the Scientific Center for Obstetrics, Gynecology, and Perinatology, distinguished professor of the Russian Academy of Medical Sciences, and president of the RFPA, stated:

> women's intimate life is accompanied by a perpetual fear of unwanted pregnancy. In actuality, the population of Russia is deprived of a guaranteed right to safe sex and contraception, while throughout the civilized world modern contraceptives, as well as information about them, are available. The situation is exacerbated by the rise of STDs, especially among youth, and AIDS.[24]

This use of "rights" language echoes the collective form of rights central to the Soviet, socialist political-economy more than an individual "right to choose."[25] In describing the Russian population as deprived of rights otherwise guaranteed "throughout the civilized world," the editorial board cast the society as lagging behind global standards. A loaded acknowledgment, this statement was part of the journal's introduction of the newly founded Russian Association of Family Planning. Declaring that the RAFP would "implement the ideology and strategies of the International Planned Parenthood Federation, the world's largest voluntary organization that unifies national associations of family planning of 134 countries," the statement highlighted Russia's integration into the global expert community after decades of isolation.[26] Still, with the media and conservative politicians often eyeing "the West" as a threat to national well-being, collaborating with foreign contraceptive advocates involved a degree of risk. The article thus began by situating the embrace of family planning firmly within Russia's national demographic needs: "The demographic situation in the Russian Federation can certainly be called catastrophic. The health of women and the future generation is in clear danger. Since 1988, the country has experienced an annual significant decrease in fertility. For the first time since the end of the War, the number of people dying has surpassed the number being born."[27] It further linked these dynamics to the high abortion rate, noting that on average a woman in Russia will have four to five abortions over her lifetime, with approximately 30% of maternal mortality linked to abortions. Thus, just as the journal spoke of "the population's right" to safe sex and contraception, their overriding justification emphasized Russian national interests. Ambivalence about promoting women's individual rights emerged in family planning experts' continuing assumptions that women should be mothers; they did not endorse absolute reproductive autonomy if that meant rejecting childbearing altogether. For example, while Russia legalized voluntary surgical sterilization in 1993 for people aged thirty-five and older or for those with two or more children, clinics did very little to educate people about this as an option.[28] Discussions of contraceptives rarely mentioned sterilization.

Thus, while these new institutions established dramatic transformations in reproductive health care, it would be a slower, more contested process to create ideological changes. Globalization was involving painful economic consequences and arousing troubling backlashes against "the West," leading family planning leaders to treat markedly foreign phrases like "reproductive rights" with caution. They adopted ideas from the global family planning paradigm strategically and strove to legitimize these ideological changes as beneficial for the Russian nation and society. As we will see, promoting family planning involved an enduring tension—managing Russian pronatalist concerns on the one hand, and the global family planning world's women's rights agendas on the other.

The Global Reproductive Rights Movement Comes to Russia: WHO and Western Pharma

Prior to Glasnost, there was little connection between the population industry and Russia, although Russian experts had some international relationships on health more generally: Soviets hosted the famous 1977 Alma Ata conference calling for universal primary health care. But ideologically, the population industry and fertility control movement were Western products of Cold War anxieties about the spread of Marxist rebellions to poor populations. The Soviet state obviously rejected this logic, arguing for alleviating poverty by redistributing economic resources, not pushing contraceptives. And given the universal literacy, equal rights, industrialization, and low fertility in the Soviet Union's European regions, the socioeconomic context shaping population and reproductive health differed dramatically from that in the developing world. Finding the terms through which connections between Western and Soviet population experts could even be established thus required negotiations.

When the Soviet Union opened its doors to Western collaborations in the late 1980s, reproductive health stakeholders flooded the country, eagerly seeking locals interested in reducing the high abortion rates. Global health experts saw training Russian clinicians in contraceptive counseling as a low-cost strategy that would simultaneously reduce abortions and promote women's rights. Yet in the political-economic and social chaos of Russia's 1990s, global collaborations on reproduction were politically fraught in ways outsiders did not recognize. Russian politicians mostly assumed that contraceptives would lower fertility, and therefore questioned their relationship to population welfare and national vitality. Clinicians, while interested in learning about the latest forms of hormonal contraceptives, doubted the morality of prescribing contraceptives to teenagers or remaining value-free regarding their patients' choices. As global family planning experts tried to sell the value of reproductive rights to their Russian peers, they knew little if anything about the concerns these doctors and policy makers faced.

One of the main ways global advocates introduced reproductive rights was by teaching Russian clinicians a consumer-based model of interacting with patients. What the foreigners did not appreciate was that all of Russian health care were rigidly hierarchical; neither patients nor clinicians experienced the individual choice model that consumer health care presumes.[29] Persuading clinicians to acknowledge patients' individual rights in the absence of meeting clinicians' own interests would be a hard sell. Numerous Western-sponsored projects tried. In one that took place from 1996 to 1999, a USAID-funded program taught select Russian gynecologists in two cities (Yekaterinburg and Ivanovo) the GATHER method of contraceptive counseling, which aims at eliciting women's concerns and desires about contraception and providing them information that fits their individual situation.[30] The name of this method represents the key steps a counselor should undertake to provide "competent, caring counseling": Greet the client in a friendly, respectful manner; Ask open, nonjudgmental questions eliciting their feelings and needs with active listening; Tell them information tailored to their particular situation; Help clients consider their options; Explain how the client can implement their decision; Return—invite clients to return for a follow-up appointment as desired.[31] Participating clinicians received up-to-date information about contraceptives aimed at dispelling common myths, and their clinics received a free six-month supply of contraceptives to provide women the method they chose. Contraceptive services were advertised on national media outlets. Some clinicians were selected to become master trainers. Based on client-focused health care practices, the GATHER model minimized clinicians' paternalism and aligned with a rights-based model.

To study the impact of these interventions, two panels of surveys were undertaken at the start of the project (1996) and three years later (1999) with two thousand women per site; a control group of women in a city where the workshop was not conducted (Perm) was also surveyed. The findings did not show the desired impacts: among women attending the project sites, neither the likelihood of receiving contraceptive counseling nor the use of any contraceptives increased. In 1999, at the project's conclusion, all three sites showed significant increases in the number of pregnancies identified as "unwanted."[32] The study's authors explained the project's failure simply due to "the model's uneven implementation," and did not offer further explanation.[33]

While I was not involved in that project, I conducted fieldwork in a similar contraceptive counseling workshop in St. Petersburg in March 1995, implemented within a collaboration between the European Regional Branch of WHO and the city of St. Petersburg.[34] Training workshops for Russian health care planners, physicians, midwives, and nurses in St. Petersburg were organized by a delegation of Western reproductive health experts and committed feminists; they had no expertise in Soviet history or society, and minimal knowledge of the devastating socioeconomic ruptures Russians were concurrently experiencing. Russian participants' responses to their counseling approach reveal some of the major obstacles to introducing a women's rights agenda in Russian clinics at the time.

Leading the workshop was a marketing specialist from a Western pharmaceutical firm that produced contraceptives; he also had a graduate degree in education, which prepared him to both pursue a new market for the pill and facilitate clinician training in a reproductive choice framework. He opened his presentation to the thirty-some Russian participants by asserting that ensuring "contraceptive acceptance and compliance" required providers to learn "appropriate" communication skills with women. The challenge was to adopt a nonjudgmental, value-free attitude so a woman's individual needs could be fulfilled:

> When a woman or couple decides to use contraception, there are a lot of questions. Women bring their own understandings, fears, what they heard from their mother, their level of education, culture. And we also, as medical personnel, have biases. As providers of information, we need to be aware of our biases and give good information. Even if I think oral contraceptives are the best, and my colleague likes IUDs, we must give information to the women so that they'll have choices. . . . It's very important to be supportive of her choice.

As with the GATHER method, this workshop presented counseling as the process of describing possible contraceptive methods and helping fulfill the choices people make. The delegates' recommendation to downplay their expert authority and facilitate clients' choices exasperated Russian clinicians. "Our women have a low level of culture," they declared, asserting the need for medical paternalism because laypeople were incapable of reaching sound decisions. Elsewhere I have argued that Russian physicians' reactions to such models were shaped by the combination of social and political-economic conditions they faced.[35] On the one hand, they were taught to expect deference from patients and authority in society. Yet physicians were occupationally disenfranchised from any decision-making authority, at either the macro-policy level or even the micro-level of their own clinics. Moreover, their salaries during the economic crisis of the 1990s were barely enough to cover their minimal survival needs while inflation ran amuck. Seething with resentment and vulnerability, clinicians emphasized their high status and authority in their interpersonal interactions with patients. Moreover, the notion of taking a "value-free" approach toward patients seemed antithetical to demonstrating professional concern, inasmuch as a physician's active advising was seen as revealing her commitment to a patient. Russian doctors defended paternalism toward patients as necessary for promoting patients' health and demonstrating their genuine care; training workshops by foreigners who did not understand these realities were unlikely to transform habitual practices.[36]

The MacArthur Foundation's Initiative in the Former Soviet Union

A very different effort to promoting women's reproductive rights and health was undertaken by The MacArthur Foundation, which included this topic in its broader program of initiatives in the Former Soviet Union (FSU) between 1991 and 1998.[37] Unlike USAID and WHO, which worked through Russian government channels, MacArthur's status as a private foundation allowed it to partner with individuals and nongovernmental organizations. The Foundation's aim was to "support the intellectual community in the former Soviet Union" and "to support researchers to remain in their countries of origin and to apply their intelligence and skill to building new societies there."[38] A key feature of its approach was to seek out Russian professionals whose goals dovetailed with those of the Foundation, providing support for their individual research work and institution-building efforts.

A central intermediary in this effort was the abortion researcher Henry P. David, PhD, director of the Transnational Family Research Institute (TFRI) in Bethesda, MD. As we saw in Chapter 2, David had been researching abortion in Central and Eastern Europe since the 1960s, visiting top Ministry of Health officials since that time. He persistently strove to engage Soviet experts on the topic by meeting with scientific counselors at the Soviet Embassy in Washington, arranging visits to meet with population and maternal health experts at the Soviet Ministry of Health; inviting them to population conferences; and getting them his relevant publications. Yet he continually faced Soviets' evasiveness. In a letter to David dated August 11, 1970, the second secretary of the US Embassy in Moscow, Harry Gilmore, warned that the Soviets were reluctant to discuss their high abortion rates with foreigners for fear of exposing the country's poor social conditions, which

David found out himself with leaders at the Ministry in Moscow later that year. Undeterred, David continued his research, publishing monographs on reproduction in the region in 1981 and 1982.³⁹ In 1990, at a WHO conference in Tblisi, "From Abortion to Contraception," David met Andrej Popov and soon thereafter nominated him for a postdoctoral fellowship sponsored by the Population Council. Popov's award led him to Princeton to work on his project, a comprehensive Fact Book of research on abortion from 1880 to 1990 and the main laws, policies, and statistics on abortion during the entire Soviet period.⁴⁰ Opportunities for collaborating were finally emerging. As one of the most knowledgeable experts on the social aspects of abortion in the world, including in the former Soviet bloc, David became a key consultant to MacArthur's initiatives in the FSU and served on the project's advisory board. In April 1993, David's Transnational Family Research Institute received a grant to undertake initial explorations for programs to support related to women's rights and reproductive health.⁴¹

In April 1993, David and Carmen Barroso, director of the Foundation's Population Program, traveled to Moscow and St. Petersburg to meet with The MacArthur Foundation's Moscow staff office and "already identified individuals and organizations" who were being encouraged to develop requests for support from the Foundation on reproductive health and women's rights.⁴² This trip would also help MacArthur prepare for an August workshop with potential Russian grantees on reproductive rights in Montreal. In addition to Andrej Popov and his proposed historical study of Soviet abortion and contraceptive policies, a proposal was underway by Vladimir Shapiro and Valeriy Chervyakov, from the Institute of Sociology at the Russian Academy of Sciences, to survey Moscow teenagers about their knowledge and perceptions of sexual behavior. Inga Grebesheva, director of the Russian Family Planning Association, wanted to discuss expanding the RFPA's sexuality education program. David and Barroso also met with the director of the new Moscow Center for Gender Studies (MCGS), Anastasia Posadskaya.

David was highly sensitive to the socioeconomic ruptures tearing at Russia, noting how Moscow's streets were "bazaars of poverty as people sell their possessions to make ends meet"; he astutely recognized how the economic crisis was expanding gendered inequalities, including the "increasing commercial exploitation of women as sex objects . . . the life of hard currency prostitutes is glamorized in the media. Women are told that unemployment permits them to devote more time to family life and housework; day care centers are closing for lack of state support; and the divorce rate is declining, in part because of women's greater economic dependency on men."[43]

David urged the Foundation to assist, in particular, with reproductive rights:

> The incidence of AIDS and STDs is increasing but not widely discussed. There is some evidence that the liberal abortion law is being undermined, in part by pressures from the Russian Orthodox Church (abetted by U.S. Right-to-Life groups) and by "patriotic" groups who are concerned about the death rate exceeding the birth rate. Professional women are labelled as "anti-family" by some, but the term "family planning" is overcoming its association with past centralized planning activities. . . . Now is the time to strengthen women's organizations, support women's rights (including reproductive health), and facilitate the emerging research on gender and sexuality.[44]

Barroso agreed, noting specific challenges in Russia: feminists "had not paid much attention to health, reproduction, and population policies" because they were overwhelmed with other issues; while the sex and reproductive health researchers "have not benefitted from a gender perspective." She hoped the foundation could bring these groups together for mutual benefit.[45] Moreover, she reflected:

> greater attention to women's rights and reproductive rights, in addition to addressing one of the major social problems in ex-Soviet societies, would also have a public image benefit. As an American foundation . . . [MacArthur] still has to grapple with (I suspect) a widespread and thinly disguised suspicion about its ulterior "political" motives. To be able to list activities that are not narrowly defined as political certainly helps to build trust.[46]

David kept these dynamics in mind when seeking local advocates to support. Realizing that Russians might not use the reproductive rights movement's terminology, he aimed to discern whether a particular expert was inclined to value women's reproductive self-determination or construe motherhood as a social and biological imperative. For example, in writing about Valentina Bodrova, a senior demographer at the All Union Center for the Study of Public Opinion, David stated:

> While she does not view herself as an active feminist, she is a bridge builder, questions the values of her own generation, and is prepared to work with [M]CGS. The more we talked, the more respect I gained for her efforts. Very

knowledgable [*sic*] about the entire former Soviet Union with superb contacts and access to trained interviewers, she is an excellent resource for [M]CGS and the Foundation.[47]

David observed whether his interlocutors appeared sincere and enthusiastic to exchange ideas or close-minded and contentious. In his trip report, David wrote that one person "talked nonstop for an hour"; someone else seemed to be more of "an operator rather than a collaborator," while another impressed him as "willing to compromise" . . . "sophisticated . . . and probably marches to her own drummer."[48] He attended to how they spoke about other Russian experts whom David knew, from Igor Kon and Andrej Popov to Irina Manuilova. MacArthur's strategy of supporting an infrastructure for reproductive rights thus took a ground-up approach: the Foundation sought to empower local scholars and professionals who were open to this cause. And unlike the international development industry, David and Barroso also recognized that what it meant to support reproductive rights would need to be gauged from within Russia's political and cultural circumstances. They selectively modified their feminist rhetoric to accommodate Russian state pronatalism, as when Barroso suggested, "we can argue that healthy mothers and babies are part of the reproductive rights agenda."[49] Notably, however, their use of this important strategy seems to have remained intuitive; unfortunately, they did not promote research into how the gaps between Russian and Western cultural concerns, between feminist and pronatalist reproductive politics, might become bridged.

During David's years consulting with MacArthur's Population program, he transformed the lives of select scholars and activists by mentoring them to navigate the professional sphere of global health. Several significant developments resulted. David helped Moscow and St. Petersburg reproductive rights professionals form a networking consortium, hoping to minimize the competition that haunted fledgling NGOs in Russia. Those invited to join the consortium were people he and Barroso identified in their April 1993 trip; David provided them extensive advice and technical assistance for developing funding proposals, from teaching them the basic skills of grant writing—unknown in Soviet society—to helping them revise multiple drafts. He also recommended ways MacArthur could effectively navigate the complex dynamics these professionals faced, including bureaucratic and personal frustrations related to the grant process. Most members of the consortium received MacArthur funding, and some were able to leverage other support, too. Henry David provided unflagging moral support and friendship to the grantees until his death in 2009.

For a variety of reasons, the project's outcomes were less than David and the Foundation hoped. Andrej Popov's project, "Family Planning and Public Health Policy in Russia: Shift from Abortion to Contraception in Transitional Society" received MacArthur funding.[50] In 1994, he established the Moscow office of the Transnational Family Research Institute and intended to use it as a base for research and advocacy; his death in April 1995 sadly cut these projects short.[51] The Moscow Center for Gender Studies conducted several workshops on reproductive rights, and their affiliate Elena Ballaeva published a 1998 book on the legal dimensions of women's reproductive rights in Russia.[52] Despite David's assisting Grebesheva in preparing a grant to support a peer counseling project with the Russian Association of Family Planning, she did not receive MacArthur funding, but David kept abreast of her work with Lyn Thomas of IPPF, which did support the organization. Sociologist Valery Chervyakov conducted surveys on sexual attitudes and behaviors among teens intended to be used for developing sex education curricula; in a similar survey (but not funded by MacArthur) his work ended with the most contention, as I discuss in later in the chapter. While the fate of each project inevitably differed, MacArthur's support launched research on reproductive rights that did not previously exist, and the IPPF's funding for the RAFP enabled scientific evidence and information about global practices to reach clinicians throughout the country.

Anchoring Family Planning in Scientific and National Revivals: The RAFP and Yuventa

While global activists were striving to shape Russian developments, local experts were also establishing initiatives. In 1989, Irina Aleksandrovna Manuilova—the Minzdrav expert and contraceptive researcher who denied that abortion continued to be a problem when Henry David met her in 1970—founded the first association for reducing abortion and promoting contraceptives.[53] With state funding channeled through the Soviet Child's Fund named for V. I. Lenin, the Family and Health (Sem'ia i zdorov'e) association was established to create: "a new approach to the optimal planning of families, and protection of maternal and child health" due to the country's "poor demographic situation" . . . "characterized by small families [and] a large number of induced abortions in the European regions." Key to Family and Health was "establishing teenagers' and young people's preparation for family formation, childbearing and raising a healthy child."[54]

Family and Health brought together committed experts but did not organizationally survive. In a 1993 report to the MacArthur Foundation, David's comment about his meeting with Manuilova provides insights into some of the reasons this may have happened:

> Because I had known Dr. Irina A. Manuilova since the late 1960s and her name had been repeatedly mentioned in meetings with others, we arranged a luncheon with her at the Foundation's office on our last day in Moscow. In the 1960s she had been head of Ob/Gyn training in the USSR Academy of Medical Science and subsequently held very senior positions in the medical establishment. It was she more than anyone else who had been responsible for establishing and sanctioning the poor conditions under which abortions were performed. Currently Director-General of the International Association of Family and Health, she won and lost IPPF affiliation; her association now earns money by sponsoring clinical drug trials and organizing tuition-paid seminars for physicians. Manuilova had a low opinion of everyone whose names we mentioned, often dismissing them as "sociologists," including Grebesheva, Momdjan, and Popov. Deeming unwanted pregnancy a woman's fault, she discounted poor abortion conditions by stating that anesthetics and other supplies were needed for cases of more serious illness. In many ways, Dr. Manuilova represents an example of the autocratic nomenklatura of the old regime.[55]

Although this first initiative floundered, a new organization emerged from its rubble. As the Soviet system was about to collapse, Inga Ivanovna Grebesheva established the Russian Association of Family Planning (RAFP), launching an exodus of Manuilova's colleagues and the end of Family and Health. Grebesheva had long experience in the Soviet health bureaucracy, having been the head of the administration of Treatment and Preventive Assistance to Children and Mothers of the USSR Minzdrav. Indeed, she was the one demanding reports from regional Minzdravs on their efforts to fight abortion that we analyzed in Chapter 2. In 1990, she was appointed the deputy Representative of the Soviet Ministers of the Russian Federation for Social Issues and Representative of the Committee of Family and Demographic Politics, another sign of her authority with state leaders. In addition to Grebesheva, the president of the RAFP was Vladimir Ivanovich Kulakov, the director of the Scientific Center for OB-Gyn and Perinatology and Russian Academy of Medical Sciences.

With Grebesheva and Kulakov at the helm at the RAFP's founding, in December 1991 the Soviet government provided rent-free premises for an office and clinic. The IPPF withdrew its affiliation from Family and Health and also provided the RAFP support.[56] In 1993, the RAFP became an official branch of the IPPF. The RAFP's mission focused on "improving the population's reproductive health, first and foremost of youth, decreasing the number of abortions, and STDs" through disseminating knowledge and methods of contraceptives, undertaking "sexual moral education [*seksual'-noe vospitanie*] of youth," and "establishing a network of regional RAFP branches and supporting their activities."[57]

While maintaining the focus on youth sexual moral education—providing "scientific information" alone was presumably not sufficient—the RAFP dropped the ideologically correct Soviet euphemism of "preparing teenagers for family life" that was central to Family and Health. RFPA leaders implicitly recognized that teens become sexually active long before marriage and that education is needed to ensure this involves preventive measures.[58] And whereas Family and Health explicitly highlighted the need to improve the country's demographics, the RAFP focused more on reproductive health without, however, dropping the focus on fertility and motherhood. Noting Grebesheva's "many contacts throughout the country," Henry David lauded "her organizational capacities and resources, and her willingness to change to a new perspective and approach."[59] In his visit to the RAFP in spring 1993, David noted that "Grebesheva is supported by a staff most of whom worked for her previously at the Ministry of Health or left the original family planning association founded by . . . Manuilova."[60] Yet the RAFP's ideological orientation was not yet firm, as David recounted being shown a video there about abortion that, "unhappily, contained images of a meat grinder that prompted purchase inquiries by a Right-to-Life Group; the producer had been previously associated with Dr. Manuilova."[61]

As one of its first endeavors, in 1993 the Association began publishing the journal *Planirovanie sem'i* (PS) with an editorial board composed of the country's leading scientist-clinicians and Ministry officials. Their prestige and their central role in health policy making underscored the scientific and political authority of the RAFP. Upon its founding, the RAFP developed branches throughout the country. It was the country's only NGO that trained professionals in the scientific and clinical aspects of family planning services and advocated for it to the Russian government.

That family planning could help Russia advance scientifically and clinically, and also improve reproductive health and fertility rates, was also key to the establishment of the reproductive health clinic for teenagers, Yuventa.[62] Rooted in the Leningrad Pediatric Medical Institute's new discipline of Children's Gynecology established in 1988, Professor Yuri Aleksandrovich Gurkin, who had recently defended a doktorskaia dissertation on ovarian dysfunction among girls and women, became its head in 1989. Gurkin justified Children's Gynecology as a separate discipline due to "the necessity of physicians observing additional ethical and legal requirements [with minors]; the presence of natural anatomical-topographical particularities in girls that change throughout childhood; the preference to use noninvasive methods for diagnosis and treatment; the necessity of minimizing medication use for treatment (including hormonal steroids) . . . and using instead physical reflex methods, herbal medicine; and a focus on combining therapy and rehabilitation for the well-being of future generations."[63]

Thus, while in the US Planned Parenthood introduced sexual health services specifically for adolescents in the very early 1970s to prevent early childbearing for moral and economic reasons, in Russia the field known as "children's gynecology" emerged from local efforts to develop pediatric science and address the serious problems that routine abortion posed for women's reproductive health.[64] Yuventa's founders realized that a gap existed in the coverage of adolescents; while pediatricians were referring patients aged fifteen and older with gynecological needs to women's clinics, the teenagers were not seeking assistance.[65]

Pavel Naumovich Krotin, an advanced professor (dotsent) in the department of Children's Gynecology at the St. Petersburg Pediatric Medical Academy, became Yuventa's chief doctor. Recounting its founding to me in a 2013 interview, Krotin explained that in 1992, Yuventa opened as an office serving girls aged fifteen to eighteen, but quickly faced such a torrent of patients that the city provided them with a budget and a facility; a former maternity hospital that had been closed due to "poor sanitary-technical conditions" would become the site of a full-fledged, multidisciplinary teen center for reproductive health.[66] I first visited Yuventa in the summer of 1993 and it was, indeed, both run-down and buzzing with activity. Krotin told me that they provided approximately two thousand abortions for girls under age eighteen annually during the Center's first years, and "in 1997, there wasn't a day when we didn't find a case of syphilis."[67] But over time, their work bore fruit. As a clinical base for the children's gynecology department, Yuventa ran continuing education courses for physicians, and later also for psychologists and social workers, from throughout Russia.[68] In

1998 Yuventa began founding branches—small clinics for teenagers—in the city's neighborhoods. By 2016, twenty-two teenage centers were working in seventeen regions of St. Petersburg. They described themselves as providing "an individual approach and ability to connect with teenagers" which enables them to "instill in youth the importance and necessity of responsibility for one's own health."[69] Professionals trained at Yuventa went on to open teenage clinics in other Russian cities as well.[70] By 2013, Krotin told me proudly, "Last year we didn't have a single case of syphilis among teenagers; this year there was one." And abortions also dramatically fell: in St. Petersburg teenagers had about 370 abortions annually, with about 320 performed at Yuventa. "They all know that here . . . everything is very . . . good, they will be fussed over, given attention, no one will judge them."

Thus although the RAFP was an NGO and Yuventa a state clinic linked with a medical institute, both were founded by leading scientist-clinicians with close ties to the health bureaucracy, which provided moral or financial support. Moreover, they shared an overarching set of goals: to reduce abortions through establishing a society-wide routine of habitual contraceptive use within a mindset of deliberative family planning. Both institutions were central to the professional retraining of physicians from all over the Russian Federation. For the professionals themselves, this mission was compelling as a pathway for revitalizing Russian science and contributing to the good of the nation by helping strengthen the family and increasing fertility (as decreasing abortions would mean less secondary sterility, more wanted pregnancies, and more overall births). Krotin explicitly linked preventive services and education in family planning for teenage girls with improving the country's demographics:

> Young women under eighteen years of age compose 8 percent of the entire female population who are in their fertile years. According to the WHO's data, if this indicator is less than 15 percent, there is a severe depopulation—and we have half as many than this recommendation. We are in a critical situation, because things depend on them more than on the boys. Therefore, it is necessary . . . to maximally preserve their health. Otherwise, there will be no one to fulfill our demographic [needs].[71]

To realize these goals, family planning advocates recognized that establishing ties with international colleagues was invaluable.[72] The IPPF provided necessary know-how and material resources by helping Russian family planners establish and disseminate a new scientific publication, *Paniro-vanie sem'i* (*PS*; Family Planning: International Medical Journal), founded in 1993. The journal presented original Russian language research and Russian translations of international research on contraceptives, abortion techniques, sexually transmitted infections, infertility treatment, menopause, premenstrual syndrome, men's role in family planning; it documented legal codes on citizens' rights, minors' rights, teenage sexuality, ethical privacy, and confidentiality; it described practical matters related to the organization of family planning services; announced international conferences, training seminars, and publications; communicated messages of support from international colleagues in the IPPF; and published ideological statements, recommendations, and best practices from the IPPF. The scientific basis of contraceptives and strategies for promoting family planning were also communicated in conferences and training seminars the RAFP regularly held, which brought professionals together in a community of learners and turned many into advocates.

Foreign influence, however, was also a source of ambivalence. Amid the devastating loss of national pride and the country's severe economic depression, Russians found themselves grateful but also humiliated recipients of humanitarian food aid from the US—the so-called "Bush [chicken] legs" (*nozhki Bushki*). Well beyond the sphere of family planning, debates swirled as to whether Western influences were helpful or harmful for Russia, whether they could be trusted, to what extent, and at what costs. At stake was the fateful dilemma of what kind of society Russia should become and whether Western influences would enhance or hinder this development. Grebesheva faced this question repeatedly, as when an interviewer questioned the "need and usefulness" of international contacts. She replied:

They are essential. There is a very high culture of sexual education abroad. They have already gone through the heightened sexual activity and rise in abortions and pregnancies among teenagers that we are now going through. They have already formed an attitude toward these issues that allows them to avoid the losses we are now having. There is a totally different approach toward interacting with the population, with youth there—people are informed and led to realize that they must make decisions, and that raises their sense of responsibility. Our organization is an affiliated member of the IPPF. In essence, it finances the majority of our programs, and we have free access to all their information. Without this our country would lose a lot, since we wouldn't be able to acquire the literature that we publish and the clinical training which we use, without the assistance of the IPPF.[73]

For its part, the IPPF-Euro seems to have sought a tactical balance between speaking to Russian concerns and maintaining a focus on women's rights. In *PS*'s first issue, for example, Lynn Thomas, Director of the European Region of IPPF, provided the RAFP with a welcome statement. Noting her close work with RAFP founders over the previous eighteen months, she expressed admiration for their efforts. She then defined the objectives of IPPF: "The goal of the Federation is to teach the methods of family planning to people around the world, to raise parents' responsibility, and also to protect the spiritual and physical health of parents, children, and youth through the provision of effective family planning services."[74]

These references to "parents' responsibility" and "protect[ing] spiritual and physical health" notably resonated with Russian ideals of moral order and national interests. Thomas then proceeded to deploy a Western feminist language of rights and choice, highlighting the consumer framing of family planning services, oriented toward "clients," not patients, and attentive to women's socio-emotional concerns:

> If we could characterize the work of the Federation and national branches in one word—it would be CHOICE. Family planning relates to people's fundamental human right to decide for themselves the number of children they want and the timing of birth. People's quality of life can be dramatically changed through the provision of free access to family planning services. These are not only medical services, but also the opportunity for women to interact, to exchange personal impressions and experiences, to have open conversations about their health, their worries, and their needs. These discussions should take place with medical experts who can help clients choose the most acceptable and convenient method for planning the family.[75]

Similarly, the inside cover of the second issue of *PS* (1994) presented the IPPF's key conceptual framework:

> Rights of the Client: Every client who seeks family planning services has the right to information; accessibility of services; choice; safety of methods; privacy

[*uedinennuiu obstanovku*], defined as "the opportunity for a private consultation"; confidentiality; dignity, defined as "a respectful, kind, and attentive attitude from providers"; comfort "to feel comfortable during the consultation";
continuity, access to contraceptive methods throughout the entire time period
they are needed; and the right to express one's own opinion with regard to the
services provided.[76]

The IPPF's terminology and solicitude differed sharply from Soviet era
language and tone. As noted earlier, Soviet literature discussed "rights"
in terms of collective citizenship entitlements to services (e.g., abortion,
maternity leave); there had been no acknowledgment of individual rights to
"dignity, . . . respectful, kind, attentive attitudes" or the emotions of health
service users, as in the right "to feel comfortable."[77] Nor was there a right
"to express one's own opinion" about health care services. Additionally, in
presenting IPPF recommendations on topics such as providing contraceptives for HIV+ people and for teenagers, and on sexuality, fertility, and pregnancy among women and men with disabilities, the journal covered topics
that had been ignored if not taboo in Soviet health experts' writings. Such
new concepts marked the text as emphatically non-Soviet; for some readers, this was likely alien, for others, intriguing.

Family planning advocates in RAFP and Yuventa treated these changes
with caution, first adopting them in official publications. The new liberal
terminology and frameworks highlighted the value of the individual as a
client rather than a patient and recognized that personalized, not mass-
focused, care was needed. When asked about Poland's recent ban on abortion in an interview published in the second issue of the RAFP's *PS*, Grebesheva explicitly used the language of women's and human rights: "The right
to family planning, to reproductive choice—is one of women's inalienable
rights. It is present in the Declaration of the Human Rights and in the Declaration of the Rights of the Child."[78]

Shifts away from alluding to sex through Soviet-era phrases such as
"marriage and family," "husband and wife," and "young married couples"
(*molodozhenov*) to terms such as "family planning," "partner," and "youth/
teenagers" (*molodezh, podrostki*) tacitly acknowledged that sex occurs in
multiple kinds of relationships. As we saw in Chapter 2, previous Soviet
texts did so mainly through stigmatizing warnings against venereal disease.

In their 1997 *Manual for Family Planning* aimed at clinical experts, RAFP
president Kulakov and head obstetrician of the Minzdrav of the Russian

Soviet Federation of the USSR, Vladimir Serov, cited internationally recognized rights to legitimize these concepts:

> The right to family planning or, in other, more correct words, "to free and responsible parenthood," is an internationally recognized, inalienable right of each person. It is strengthened by the extremely important documents of the UN: the Universal Declaration of Human Rights (1948), the Appeal [*vozzvaniem*] (of the) International Conference on Human Rights (Tehran 1968), the Convention on the elimination of all forms of discrimination against women (1979), the Nairobi future strategies to improve the status of women (1985).[79]

Undertaking family planning was thus an explicit way of aligning Russia with the international community. The authors also cited the 1994 Cairo conference's statement on individuals' and couples' reproductive rights.[80] Given these obligations, they affirmed, family planning "should be based on encouraging equal rights between the sexes," and "addressing teenagers' needs for education and services that enable them to positively relate to their sexuality."[81]

But Russian family planning professionals also insisted on retaining discretion over what their programs would include, specifically asserting: "the optimal population use of contraceptives . . . should not be built according to Western ideas nor based on opinion."[82] They policed liberal ideologies they considered unacceptable—most notably, radical feminism. During our 2013 interview, Yuventa's director, Pavel Krotin, noted that international organizations differ among themselves, and that his Center benefitted tremendously when the collaboration included respect for Russian experts' maintaining control over the programs they adopt:

> we had a brilliant project with the Swedish organization LAFA. LAFA is an anti-AIDS. . . . And Sida, they do sexual enlightenment, Sida is Swedish . . . The most valuable aspect was [they agreed on our condition] that they would not insist on their model, but would offer us the opportunity to develop our own, taking into account their experience . . . well, they tried, of course, to say . . . "this works well for us, this promotion of homosexuality" . . . and we immediately told them, we're not going to have this. . . . Also, we had that same [kind of relationship with] the Dutch, we had a project, MATRA—this organization, also didn't force us to do what they did. We have a completely different culture, absolutely different from the Dutch! But—they have brilliant success, and we

learned how to do it, and we took a lot from them, but I want to say—the most valuable was that they did not demand that we fully copy them. Some American projects from the beginning established very rigid requirements: You have to do it this way. [Laughs.] There were projects like that.

Krotin's rejection of LGBT rights underscores his ideologically conservative approach to family planning: for him, it was ultimately a movement to strengthen heteronormative families and childbearing.[83] Many Russian family planners similarly drew on the global movement's gender equality language selectively while maintaining a focus on moral social change and discipline, rather than women's rights. Grebesheva represented family planning as instilling a new worldview in people based in scientific knowledge and generating deliberative, personal responsibility toward forming families:

> family planning is responsible and conscious parenthood, which assumes a great deal and is ultimately expressed as a person's attitude toward life. For parenthood to be responsible, for wanted and healthy children to be born, first and foremost a person must have free access to information about what reproductive health is, what sexual culture and sexual behavior are, what one does so the child will be healthy.[84]

Grebesheva's message is that access to information should cultivate a moral sensibility, not the simple existence of "choice," as IPPF's rhetoric sometimes suggested. But even as Grebesheva remained unenthused about her global colleagues' discourses of feminism and individualism, she appreciated how their family planning model strove to combine accurate scientific knowledge with humanistic care:

> The IPPF asserts that each woman undergoing an abortion should feel that the personnel is doing everything possible to preserve her reproductive health and support her psychologically and morally. We have made abortions into something horrible. In other countries . . . there's an enormous effort to achieve maximal safety by using modern technologies and medicines.[85]

For Krotin, the radical feminist ideas that he found among some global reproductive rights activists were off-putting. As he told me in an interview, "I always understood that a woman should receive great respect in general . . .

[and] there should be equal rights to some extent," but he recoiled at what he perceived were rude interpersonal interactions by activists who emphasized their feminist politics. As an example, Krotin recalled his impatience with the "aggressive" pronouncements about women's equality he heard from a French minister of social politics he met on a study tour, to whom he replied, "You know, I have only one question for you. Do you think it's acceptable for a woman to work in a mine, with radiation? [And she's like—] 'Yes, we are no worse . . .' And I say, 'That's all, I don't have any other questions. That's all.'"

For Krotin, a feminism that valued women's equality over women's health, that rejected protectionist policies and allowed women's exposure to dangerous and toxic labor conditions was specious. His concern was not hypothetical, but alluded to the early Soviet mobilization of women into heavy labor in backbreaking conditions, justified in the name of women's equality, which he considered an ideological extremism that contravened both common sense and humanism.[86] Krotin saw "respect" for women as a value compatible with medical paternalism, and he remained wary of feminism and any extreme insistence on women's "equality."

Given the abysmal reality of women's lives amid Soviet claims to having achieved "women's equality," many family planning experts similarly prioritized health concerns and deemed feminist ones largely irrelevant. Moreover, their eagerness to reduce abortions led many to collaborate with Western antiabortion organizations, even while working with the IPPF. Some endorsed messaging that ignored women's own views of their priorities in favor of the "interests" of the fetus. For example, when touring a St. Petersburg Center for Reproduction and Family Planning in 1993, I noticed color photos of aborted fetuses on the clinic walls where women waited before their abortions. A bold-faced title proclaimed these photos showed "The Silent Scream of the Unborn Child during an Abortion." When I asked the clinic's deputy director why the clinic displayed these photos, she answered without hesitation. "Women need to understand that this is not a positive form of family planning. They should start using contraceptives," she explained with a Soviet-style paternalism.[87] In the end of the 1990s, I saw further evidence of Western antiabortion groups' influence in family planning clinics when I visited a branch of the teen services and saw newly painted walls, comfortable furniture, video players, and the *Silent Scream* film, which providers told me they screened for youth as a documentary account of the fetus' suffering during abortion. In a sense, family planners' willingness to entertain antiabortion messaging made sense: Preoccupied with women's health and healthy reproduction, they strove to establish society-wide habits of contraception and higher birth rates; gender equality was not among their major priorities. They couldn't fathom abortion as a form of women's empowerment, for it was a symptom of the state's failures to fulfill its promises, of men's failures to care and take responsibility. Abortion was a sign of the lack of choice. And their devotion to reducing unwanted pregnancies and terminations meant they saw no need to justify abortion as a potentially prudent decision or morally neutral decision—even if, in individual discussions, they recognized that women needed access to safe and legal abortion.

Grebesheva herself employed the language of women's rights selectively and strategically. In August 2003, the Ministry of Health ended almost all access to second trimester abortion, except in cases of rape, imprisonment, the death or severe disability of one's husband, or the loss of parental rights.[88] While from a feminist perspective this change signaled a disturbing restriction on women's autonomy, Grebesheva chose not to criticize the policy, explaining that her organization "did not vigorously object to the regulations since they would not greatly affect a woman's access to abortion."[89] This comment ignored the fact that repealing criteria related to poverty would disproportionately affect the most marginal women in Russia. Grebesheva repeatedly justified contraceptive programs rather than defending abortion. In a *Moscow News* article, Grebesheva articulated the logic guiding her perspective: "Where do I say that abortion is a norm? Nowhere! Our position is that abortion is profound psychological stress for a woman which can also have dreadful consequences for her health. . . . That is why a woman should have access to birth control."[90]

If family planners felt ambivalent about adopting feminism's emphasis on autonomy, they unconditionally endorsed laypeople's need for scientifically valid knowledge about contraceptives. Grebesheva noted that the Soviet ban on hormonal contraceptives had spread falsehoods and ignorance that now required hard work to reverse.[91] Kulakov's assertion that people have the right to both contraceptives and information about safe sex, as guaranteed "throughout the civilized world," reflected a commitment to increasing knowledge, catching up to global standards, and improving health.[92]

Interestingly, where Grebesheva did emphasize women's need for self-determination was in the context of discussing state-citizen relations. In response to an interviewer's question (which itself expressed liberal assumptions): "How is the right to reproductive choice linked to the rights of the person [*lichnosti*]?" Grebesheva replied:

> The right of choice is above all access to information. Any woman, any man, has the right and should know what methods of contraceptives exist, what the problems of abortion are. . . . If a woman is pregnant, she herself must decide whether to have get an abortion or bear a child.
>
> But to protect women from the necessity of such an extreme choice, the government should, besides providing a certain level of knowledge, also provide the essential choice of contraceptive methods. And it should be not only a declaration but a real right. If it exists only on paper, but not in reality, then you can actually talk about the violation of reproductive choice. Undoubtedly, the right to choose is still the unlimited access to family planning services. It's essential to create a special structure where a woman can go several times, where she can open up fully, and solve her problems. It's very important not to limit the time devoted to the consultation. And it must always be remembered that the doctor should not decide what method of contraception is suited to a woman, this must be the woman's own decision, consulting with the doctor.[93]

In this passage, Grebesheva partly echoed social hygiene's idea that the state holds responsibility for ensuring the social conditions for health. But she also made several liberalizing shifts beyond the socialist social hygiene framework: She acknowledged that the state "violates" reproductive choice if it does not ensure that people actually experience the rights they are guaranteed. She recognized that having reproductive choice requires both accessible information and available services delivered in a nonpaternalistic manner. This exemplifies family planners' shifting views of the appropriate relationship of the state and experts toward citizens' bodies. Put simply, family planners rejected the idea that citizens' bodies are the property of the state and could be engineered to fulfill state agendas.

But Grebesheva did not embrace the liberal global vision of unrestricted "freedom" for bodily autonomy, either. She retained her commitment for a strengthened heteronormative family: "during such difficult economic and social shocks, with the enormous psychological pressure that every person in our country is experiencing . . . the significance of the family can increase . . . the family always was a refuge for the individual and helped him escape stressful situations or ease them. Throughout the world there is currently a certain resonance of the family, the revival of family values."[94]

FIGURE 4.1. New Year's Celebration at Organon Information Center, Moscow. Lyubov Erofeeva, director of the Center; Ekaterina Lakhova, Duma member and head of the Committee for Issues of Women, Family, and Demography in the Russian Federation's Presidential Administration (1993–2000); deputy directors of the committee Galina Gul'ko and Emma Zaporozhets; Dina Ze-linskaia, head of the Administration of Treatment—Preventive Assistance to Children and Mothers of the Russian Ministry of Health; and Larisa Gavrilova, deputy head of the administration. Photo courtesy of Lyubov Erofeeva.

Family planners thus recognized women's reproductive health concerns as legitimate matters, as long as they did not appear to pit women against men or the family. Ekaterina Lakhova, founder of the political party Women in Russia who explicitly endorsed women's equality, also supported family planning. Lakhova's own mother died from an illegal abortion and she spoke out against proposals to restrict the procedure. Notably, however, her statements about family planning emphasized health, while she cast gender equality as relevant for addressing women's economic and political exclusion and domestic violence. Strengthening family life, not women's reproductive autonomy as a principle, inspired Lakhova's endorsement of family planning.

Grebesheva's commitment came from her concerns for children's well-being. When asked how she came to see the need for an association of family planning, the pediatrician explained:

It was the children that young women left in the maternity hospital and that stayed in clinics or orphanages for years, it was hard and painful to look at them. It was young mothers who gave up their children due to confusion, fear to remain alone with the problem—they were cut off from society and their parents. And they wouldn't have made such a decision if they had had timely access to the necessary information and contraceptive methods, if they didn't think that sexual activity always had to result in a wedding and childbirth. And . . . the situation of our boys. . . . Our medical system is totally unprepared to treat boys.[95]

Notably, Grebesheva was clear that men need to accept responsibility for preventing pregnancy and for supporting their families, while women must retain the right to define their reproductive lives. Responding to the question, "Does a man also have the right to reproductive choice?" Grebesheva argued:

A man should, first and foremost, figure out his behavioral standards in sexual relations. He should relate to his partner [*partnershe*] with responsibility, and if she wants to have a child, decide together with her. But it's savage [*diko*] to force a woman to carry an unwanted child. If a man decided in a totally responsible way to become a father, then he should establish the conditions for the future mother to feel confident about her and her child's future.[96]

The logic that family planning leaders adopted thus drew selectively on reproductive rights concepts; they invoked such ideas to contrast their model from certain Soviet tactics, especially regarding cases where they perceived the state had overreached in its efforts to control women's bodies. But they retained a Soviet-era focus on women's responsibilities and highlighted the new idea that children should be born wanted. Proponents avidly disseminated global scientific research and findings about reproductive health and contraceptives, citing international declarations of human rights to legitimize the family planning approach. They aimed to teach providers to focus on individual contraceptive needs, addressing both women's comfort and men's responsibilities, but did not emphasize women's autonomy. They navigated between recognizing that women's personal decision making was important for obtaining their contraceptive compliance, on the one hand, and protecting them from pathological social and environmental conditions, on the other. Retaining a commitment to medical paternalism that essentialized women as (future) mothers, RAFP and

Yuventa leaders justified their efforts with reference to the demographic crisis and perceived need for increased fertility (unlike Popov, who ignored these issues entirely), but their commitment ultimately lay in ensuring healthy pregnancies and childbearing, not the narrow promotion of state politics.

Sex Education for Teenagers: Moral Panic and the Limits of Liberal Persuasion

Reconciling tensions between pragmatism and paternalism proved much harder when family planning practitioners developed sex education for teenagers. The anxieties at stake emerged during the WHO's 1995 contraceptive counseling workshop for St. Petersburg clinicians. During a role-playing exercise designed to help clinicians practice communicating in a value-free way, the WHO delegate (who was also a pharmaceutical company representative) gave a series of hypothetical cases describing a woman's reproductive goals and medical history. After discussing the cases in small groups, participants were to explain the contraceptive methods they would recommend, and the pros, cons, and any contraindications they would consider in making their decisions. One scenario elicited particular outrage: "A fifteen-year-old girl with no previous births, abortions, or pregnancies comes to you because she wants contraceptives. What do you do?"

A loud hum overtook the room, and one Russian doctor burst out only half in jest, "First we're going to investigate the kindergarten that gave her such a bad upbringing!" A round of laughter followed, with many participants nodding in agreement. After the translator explained the comment in English, the Russian respondent continued by offering the kind of answer expected in the role-playing exercise: "Then we'll do a standard exam, try to talk to her and to her partner if there is one. We'll suggest barrier methods until her period, and then we'd suggest monophase [oral contraceptive] pills from the beginning of her period."

Pleased with the correct response, the pharmaceutical representative smiled appreciatively and stated, "Great! I think it's good to use oral contraceptives."

While he commended the participant, other Russian participants expressed diverging opinions in asides not intended for translation. A second doctor exclaimed, "Lock her up in her house!" And a third physician, a highly positioned public health planner in St. Petersburg, concurred, "Well, taking into account that she's changing partners and can get gonorrhea, I think I'm wasting my time here!"[97]

Such reactions were typical. Many Russian providers at the time saw the idea of adolescents openly seeking contraceptives as shameful, and they condemned adolescent sexual activity as morally and physically degrading.[98] Moreover, recall that family planning services were funded through the federal program Children of Russia: advocates emphasized that planning families would ensure healthy childbearing and improve the nation's demographic vitality. But the possibility that contraceptives could negatively affect fertility haunted family planning activities from its inception. Soon after they began, nationalists seized on its incipient sex education efforts to portray family planning as perverting children by teaching them "how to have sex." Citing historical campaigns such as Margaret Sanger's push to lower poor women's fertility and the global population industry's work to decrease fertility rates, nationalists maligned family planning as a Western ploy to reduce Russian birth rates, too.[99] Family planning became portrayed as the nefarious work of the hostile West and its unpatriotic Russian toadies. The pragmatic acceptance of nonprocreative teenage sexuality was thus fraught with moral and national dangers.

During fieldwork between 1994 and 1995, I observed and recorded thirteen sex education lectures in St. Petersburg, many of them sponsored by Yuventa. The topics and approaches ranged; gynecologists tended to emphasize the value of abstinence and harms of abortion, not only to the woman but also the fetus—increasingly depicted as a "child" with conscious thoughts, fears, and pain. Lectures by psychologists, contrastingly, emphasized personal responsibility for one's health, the prevention of unwanted pregnancy, and the emotional aspects of (always heteronormative) gender relations and sexuality. These varying approaches reflected broad uncertainty about what sex education should involve: should it teach youth the mechanics of sexual activity? Although some considered this plausible, many worried it facilitated deemphasizing love, care, and kindness, with sex defined as an animalistic instinct devoid of morality. RAFP leaders endorsed communicating scientific information about human nature alongside "moral education" about healthy intimate relationships.[100] Yet there was little opportunity to explore these debates in-depth, for a scandal broke that put an end to these initiatives for decades to come.

In 1997, conservatives became aware of a survey being conducted at schools about sexual behavior and attitudes among teenagers. The survey was devised by a Moscow-based group of scholars collaborating with Dutch colleagues; they won financial support from UNESCO and received approval from Russia's Ministry of Education. The project began by surveying seventh through ninth graders, their parents, and teachers in sixteen schools in eight Russian cities, eliciting "students' knowledge of sexuality problems, their interest in these matters, sources of information, and the dynamics of their sexual behavior."[101] The goal of the project was to develop recommendations for the content and format of age-appropriate sexuality educational materials. The survey's report states that "about 4,000 students' questionnaires, 1,300 parents' questionnaires and 400 teachers' questionnaires were approved for computer data processing."[102]

The survey asked students to rank the following topics according to their relative importance for sex education courses to cover:

1. Psychology of relationships between sexes;
2. Conception, prenatal human development and childbirth;
3. Diversity in sexual orientations: homosexuality, etc.;
4. Sexual techniques: how to receive more pleasure from sex;
5. Anatomy and physiology of sexual system;
6. Marriage and family life;
7. Hygiene of sex organs;
8. Methods of birth control;
9. Sexual abuse and avoidance of unwanted sex;
10. Prevention of sexually transmitted diseases and AIDS; and
11. Improvement of sexual health.

While noting that "children approach this subject absolutely instrumentally, envisioning training aids and underestimating the significance of basic knowledge," the project's authors argued that this very finding demonstrates students' need to "understand . . . how the human body functions," "the psychological mechanisms of interpersonal interaction for creating an adequate approach to human sexuality," and "the possible negative consequences of early sexual contacts and the dangers of early sex itself."[103]

The authors also found that girls (but not boys) indicated a strong need to learn about "problems of sexual abuse, including rape, and means of avoiding unwanted sex."[104] Parents and teachers acknowledged their own inability to educate teens about sexual issues and welcomed pedagogical resources and training. In summary, the report concluded:

The absolute majority of the respondents spoke in favor of introducing sex education into school curricula. Its content, according to the opinions of students, their parents, and teachers, must deal with a wide spectrum of topics, including anatomy and physiology, psychology of sexual relationships, practical issues of avoiding sexually transmitted diseases and unwanted pregnancy, and moral aspects of cross-gender relationships.[105]

But long before these survey data were analyzed, some parents at the schools where the surveys were conducted complained, fomenting a hostile campaign not only against sex education, but the entire fledgling family planning movement.

In spring and again in fall 1997, Orthodox activists began lobbying against the Family Planning program. They first circulated a letter among Duma members criticizing the RAFP for wanting to make abortion safe, "like extracting a tooth."[106] Then, an organization called On the Moral Regeneration of the Fatherland submitted petitions to eliminate its federal funding. Igor Kon described the organization as having collected these thousands of signatures by approaching people on Moscow streets asking, "Do you want your children to be taught in school how to make [*sic*] sex? If not, please sign the petition to ban this evil project."[107] In response, a Duma roundtable was convened, "Family Planning in the Context of Russia's National Security." On October 16, 1997, a report issued by the Analytic Administration of the Governmental Parliament called for the Family Planning program to be discontinued.[108] Orthodox activists also took matters into their own hands, vandalizing a tram used to disseminate contraceptives and safe sex information, painting graffiti on advertisements for the contraceptive firm Organon, and characterizing themselves as warring against Satan.[109] The campaign worked: by February 1998, federal funding for family planning was eliminated.[110] Although a group of almost thirty highly ranked Russian health experts advocated reinstituting the funding, it never was.[111]

In both the Duma report and similar screeds in Russia's press, contraceptives were portrayed as instruments in enemy conspiracies to decrease Russia's demographic power and exacerbate the country's already low fertility levels.[112] As evidence, critics detailed the eugenics goals that inspired early twentieth-century birth control advocacy in the West and identified this history with contemporary agendas, as if no political or ideological changes had developed in the subsequent decades. Nationalist and religious activists blamed family planning for perverting youth by teaching them about having sex and preventing pregnancy. In contrast to sex education supporters' arguments that a growing number of adolescents were sexually active and needed information to stay safe, opponents presented alternative statistics showing that most teenagers were not sexually active.[113] Conservatives presented themselves as unmasking the real motivations for Western organizations' promoting contraceptives in Russia: their desire to raise profits for pharmaceutical companies and support their governments' goals of decreasing Russia's geopolitical power by reducing its population size.

Contraceptives were thus portrayed as a threat used by enemy outsiders and their cynical Russian collaborators to convince women against childbearing, destroy the Russian family, and undermine Russia's national security.

Kon traced the program's fate to bureaucratic incompetence and confusion:

> Unfortunately, Ministry of Education officials, without consulting serious experts, made a fatal mistake: they declared the beginning of such a delicate work without an adequate political and psychological preparation. Even worse, the Ministry sent to 30,000 schools a package of 5 selfmade [sic] and unrealistic (some of them . . . require more than 300 class hours) "alternative sex education programs." These programs had nothing to [sic] with the so called "UNESCO project" but they have been perceived as a part of it. . . . So before it was even born, the project is already under a heavy attack as a Western ideological subversion against Russian children. . . . [instigated by the] world "sexological-industrial complex" "which has manipulated the Russian government to act . . . against the best interests of its own country."[114]

Federal funding for family planning would not be reinstituted, and sex education courses such as those held at Yuventa in 1994 through 1996 were eliminated. But proponents did not give up without a fight.

Defending Family Planning with Russians' Liberal Biopolitics

A 1997 episode of the national TV talk show *Odin na odin* (One on One) illustrates how family planners' hopes for rational debate and science-based policy making were thwarted by opponents' sensationalism and lies.[115] Two conservative Duma representatives relentlessly discredited family planning, using tactics that ranged from shaming its women leaders as promiscuous to feigning politeness but trivializing family planning and accusing its proponents of corruption. Family planning leaders responded by jus-tifying their activities as rationalizing health policy and promoting loving, caring families, but this was not a media genre dedicated to investigating and clarifying the truth. The talk show host did nothing to adjudicate the conflicting accounts, and so family planning leaders and their opponents were depicted as presenting equally plausible accounts.[116] The twenty-six-minute episode typified 1990s debates about family planning.

The episode opened by screening video footage of a recent, scandal-ous confrontation in Russia's Duma. Deputy Ekaterina Lakhova forcefully argues, "Communist Shandybin told me that contraceptives are harmful and imported condoms spread diseases, without understanding that domes-tic condoms are not being produced." The camera pans over to her male addressee, Duma representative Vasilii Shandybin from the Communist Party, who bellows in response, "Deputy Lakhova has mastered sex in all forms, with and without our [Russian-made] condoms." The Duma speaker immediately announces that Shandybin was now prohibited from talking, and the video ended. In the studio, the *One-on-One* host, Aleksandr Liubi-mov, then explains that following this incident's broadcast on a major TV channel, the state restricted media access to Duma proceedings. With this introduction, Liubimov introduces two topics for the day's show: whether and how to regulate sexually explicit material on TV, and the legitimacy of state support for family planning services. In the following discussion, I examine how they debated family planning in this episode.

At a table in the studio another conservative Duma member, Sergei Kalashnikov, sat facing Lakhova and tried to distinguish himself from the behavior of his colleague on the video. Apologizing for Shandybin's insult, he immediately lamented society's moral degradation, asserting, "This stream of pornography that flows around us all day long, and I mean all day, not night, it's of course, I don't know, some kind of enemy act against us." In this opening pronouncement, Kalashnikov displaced attention from his own colleague's contributions to public obscenity and instead blamed it on "enemies." Then Kalashnikov trivialized the family plan-ning program for failing to promote child well-being. He falsely claimed that the Family Planning program was allocated twenty billion rubles in 1996 and its sole product was publishing a booklet, "Your Best Friend, the Condom."[117] This grossly minimized the manifold work of the family planning program and hugely overestimated its funding, while implying it also misused its funds.

Excuse me, is there nowhere in the country to spend this approximate 20 bil-lion rubles except for publishing this brochure? If 200 billion rubles are being allocated for the Children of Russia program, and of these, 25 billion on family planning, I naturally asked myself, maybe this 25 billion could be better spent on children's food rations . . . because many school children don't go to school due to not having anything to eat.

The budget numbers Kalashnikov presented were wholly inaccurate, but his point was rhetorically powerful: children were hungry, they may need medical care, and investing scarce funds into mere "paper" amid such suf-fering seemed absurd.[118] Lakhova did not contest the numbers, but after the host interjected another litany of social problems (domestic condom production practically eliminated, AIDS and prostitution burgeoning), she pressed on with her own list of horrors, and argued that family planning's sex education programs were providing solutions:[119] "Seriozha . . . we have six thousand teens under fifteen getting pregnant. About a half of them get abortions and half give birth. Parents today don't know how to talk about these sexual moral education topics. Teachers can't do it. Doctors aren't obligated to. The Deputies' society isn't ready, this is a topic that isn't talked about."

Lakhova continued by presenting more examples of suffering that the Family Planning program aimed to reduce. She strategically offered both sta-tistical and anecdotal accounts of personal tragedies resulting from the lack of family planning services and argued the need to understand what family planning entailed. She asserted, "syphilis among teenagers has increased 31 times . . . Congenital syphilis has appeared . . . and according to predic-tions by Valentin Ivanovich Pokrovskii, the academician who studies AIDS, by 2000, . . . we will have a million HIV+ people."[120] Lakhova then shifted to explain what "family planning" entailed—"the birth of a healthy and wanted child," "responsible parenthood," and, citing global authorities, "the WHO speaks of family planning as primary medical-sanitary care. And family planning services provide consultation and treatment first and foremost to those who need it. And that, of course, is young people."

Opponents of family planning entirely misunderstand its basic pur-pose, Lakhova argued. Recalling an exchange along these lines she had with Shandybin, she states: "He asks me, 'Katerina, what's this family plan-ning? We in Briansk have already blocked the program.' I say—"How can you block a program without even knowing what it is?!"[121]

Lakhova continued with examples of the problems arising from the birth of unwanted children, including hundreds of unwanted babies abandoned at the maternity hospital to be raised in orphanages. With neither parents nor teachers able to educate their children about sex, it was the Family Planning program that was communicating information to teenagers in competent, age-appropriate ways. In all these points, Lakhova highlighted family planning's benefits to children, not adult women.

Standing up from the audience, Grebesheva did defend women's interests, declaring, "The attempt to defame the [family planning] programs is mostly linked to the fact that the government wants to pass its social and economic problems onto women to resolve."[122] Her comments shifted between highlighting children's suffering and women's rights:

> You know, our state always said, no matter how many children you give birth to, we'll raise them. But as a pediatrician I need to say first and foremost that every child needs individual love in a family where he's accepted, and no matter what he's like, they will love him. This is first. Second: Only a woman can ultimately decide if she'll give birth or not. And in order for her to have the right not to have an abortion, but to choose her situation, at any given point in her life, she needs contraception. It's a real pity that the issue of contraception in the Duma is only focused on condoms. I think only a hundredth of the funding was spent on the purchase of condoms. There are hormonal contraceptives and other methods . . . used in the entire world . . . and only 5 percent of our women use them. If we don't provide free contraceptives, our women will get abortions.

Lakhova expanded the discussion on women, without using the term "rights" but invoking both the ethics of self-determination and the protection of women's health:

> Prior to 1955 . . . abortion was criminalized. Due to this law, for twenty years a woman was an instrument of the government. The number of criminal abortions and maternal mortality rose by several times. Today in three years of family planning work, mortality from abortions has fallen by 25 percent. . . . a woman shouldn't be an instrument of the state, and abortion should not be the main method of regulating fertility.

Lakhova and Grebesheva alternated between providing anecdotes about the personal tragedies resulting from lack of family planning and clarifying family planning's goals. They did not directly respond to the accusations of corruption or waste and did not address the booklet Kalashnikov raised as problematic. While affirming women's reproductive self-determination, they kept the discussion centered on children and family. Overall, they emphasized the link between family planning and childbearing; they avoided mentioning that contraceptives would enable an autonomous self who rejects reproduction.

If family planning proponents could cite global authorities such as WHO to justify their claims, this episode shows how illiberals drew on a broader range of tactics. Beginning with Shandybin's outburst in the Duma video, they cast family planners as promiscuous women; in the television studio, they trivialized family planning as an implausible means of reducing children's suffering and accused its proponents of misusing funds. Through these and similar ploys, patriarchally-minded opponents of family planning claimed to be the true protectors of the nation's children. As Lakhova insisted, these modes of de-legitimation side-stepped the actual substance of family planning services. But they were successful in eliminating federal support for family planning. In part, their success derived from a tactic that many Russian politicians, including Vladimir Zhirinovsky and Vladimir Putin, found to be an effective legitimating strategy: making patriarchy a vehicle for national renewal. .[123]

Conclusion

When Russian liberal health experts founded family planning institutions, the prevailing political attitude deemed the country's low fertility highly dangerous and the concept of personal freedom suspicious. Promoting the systemic prevention of pregnancy, therefore, needed to be justified as achieving national well-being. The justifications they devised entailed efforts to make contraceptives 'safe' for demographic interests and thus politically acceptable; analyzing these justifications allows us to highlight the specific kinds of liberalism family planners sought to create.

Family planners rejected the Soviet biopolitical treatment of citizens' bodies as resources for the state and opposed continuing efforts to engineer reproduction for such purposes. Commenting in 2001 on the government's recently approved "Concept of Demographic Politics for the Russian Federation through 2015," Inga Grebesheva stated: "Families have children not out of governmental interests but first and foremost out of their own interests. The state's task is to create the kind of conditions in which a family wants to have children. And for that, the family's interests need to be considered."[124] Yet unlike Andrej Popov, whose work we explored in Chapter 3, they reiterated the framing of low fertility as a serious problem.[125] Most family planning leaders proclaimed the need to strengthen families and increase fertility. They did not embrace a liberal vision of unrestricted "freedom" for bodily autonomy, and they refused to encourage respect for LGBTQ rights. They insisted that abortion was a harmful procedure to be avoided, even while recognizing that the ultimate decision about a pregnancy should remain the woman's alone. Here we see how sanitary enlightenment and liberal biopolitics shared a key principle —that experts inform laypeople about healthy ways of life. At the same time, family planning leaders understood that these models enact expert authority in different ways, and they expected the globally recognized scientific framework of family planning expertise to help renew their authority as professionals.

Russian leaders of family planning also emphasized specific values and approaches of liberal biopolitics that differed from sanitary enlightenment practices, including the redesign of clinical services to address individual needs. This went beyond earlier liberalizing stances of calling for privacy in doctor-patient discussions, as earlier contraceptive advocates had proposed, or refusing to push state agendas for higher fertility onto people's personal lives, as Sadvokasova had modeled. In the 1990s, family planning leaders adopted a liberal form of professionalism in which experts elicit and strive to meet clients' wishes. This change had been presented by foreign advisors in workshops promoting USAID's GATHER model and WHO's value-free model of contraceptive counseling, where it was met with disquiet and rejection by many Russian physicians. Russian Family planning leaders strove to legitimate this new mode of performing expertise by linking it with broader concerns in Russian society related to both humanistic change and demographic needs. They argued that by eliciting and fulfilling clients' needs for effective, personally compatible contraceptives, they would encourage (heterosexual) couples to conceive wanted pregnancies, avoid abortions, and presumably enjoy happier family lives.

Certainly, these physician-leaders remained ambivalent about global family planning. They described themselves as antiabortion in the sense that they aimed to minimize its use, even as they presumed its continued accessibility. In contrast to global reproductive rights rhetoric, Russian family planners emphasized that contraceptive habits were a rational and healthy form of interpersonal discipline, not a means toward achieving individual autonomy as a principled end goal. Still, their engagement with the global family planning paradigm opened the door to modestly reducing medical paternalism and increasing Russians' reproductive self-determination.[126]

The debate over family planning did not proceed as a rational analysis about its contributions to national well-being. Conservatives found family planning useful to condemn because it was linked to the West and women's sexuality; they could readily denounce it with symbols of enemy conspiracy and patriarchal bravado. Indeed, combatting family planning and sex education as the hostile agendas of Western interests became a means of resurrecting national pride. Shandybin's spectacle in the Duma was exemplary: his aggressive attack against Lakhova simultaneously shamed her as sexually promiscuous, stigmatized family planners as the stooges of Western enemies, and represented conservatives as bringing a performatively tough masculine leadership to public policy and family protection.[127] Later, during the talk show, the illiberal argument took on a more polite tone but expanded this logic by additionally accusing family planners of corruption and waste, of prioritizing profit over children's well-being. This nationalist, pronatalist vision would become an enduring threat to family planning's legitimacy.

CHAPTER 5

Creating and Defending Liberal Health Professionals

"Does your manner of behavior help the patient to feel that her presence is desired? Does your behavior change depending on the specific characteristics of the patient? Do you express well-meaning intentions [*oblik dobrozhelatel'nost'*] to the patient?"

—Questions psychotherapist VIKTOR EVGEN'EVICH SAMOKHVALOV asked gynecologists at the reproductive health clinic Yuventa, in helping them reflect on their interactions with teenagers.

It was here that my confidence was shaken regarding the fact that I am a government-minded person. I stopped being someone who works on behalf of state interests [gosudarstvennik], probably. It was some, little by little, some ideas came to me, some understandings, reflections, . . . I became a feminist. It was simply a revolution, a revolution took place inside me. Absolutely.

—DR. LIUBOV EROFEEVA, on her experiences studying family planning in London under the auspices of the Dutch pharmaceutical company Organon.

While the foreign-run workshops on contraceptive counseling discussed in Chapter 4 largely failed to persuade their audiences, some Russian family planning leaders agreed that showing respect for the individual patient was an important step toward unmaking Russia's abortion culture.[1] What inspired this concern and how did they define it in practice? In exploring these questions, this chapter focuses on the careers of a psychotherapist and sex educator, Dr. Viktor Samokhvalov, and a gynecologist and director of the RAFP, Dr. Liubov Erofeeva. Through their experiences we will see how family planning became a vehicle for pursuing specific kinds of liberal aspirations in Russia.[2]

As many ethnographies of post-Soviet Russia show, proactively creating oneself became a possibility if not a cultural imperative for the aspiring middle class, and various models of the self as an individual emerged. There was the self-sufficient, ambitious entrepreneur (available in hyper-masculine and feminine versions); the sexually liberated woman who controls her own body and effectively manages her reproductive capacities; and the emotionally managed self produced by Russia's emerging therapeutic culture.[3] Although ideals of an "autonomous, choosing . . . socially unobligated" individual have gained increasing acceptance in Russia in the wake of global market forces, this image of personhood remains contested.[4] Many Russians continued to identify themselves through their significant relationships. Studies of alternative healing in Russia, for example, underscore visions of persons as inherently vulnerable from, and potentially healed through, relations with others.[5] And since the image of women's reproductive autonomy could be associated with the rejection of childbearing and lower fertility, conceptualizing individualism as a benefit for Russian society was difficult and dangerous. Both Samokhvalov and Erofeeva faced frightening repercussions for their efforts.

It is worth interrogating the specific kind of "individualism" that family planners endorsed. As we saw in Chapter 4, Russian experts rejected foreigners' calls to adopt a "value-free" approach to contraceptive counseling as a means of respecting individual self-determination. Such models did not resonate with the concerns and commitments of the professionals whom foreign workshops targeted for change. It was when they saw in family planning a source of updated scientific knowledge and echoes of their own, humanistic values, of renewing expert authority and undertaking active care, that the idea of redesigning expert interactions with lay people on the basis of respect for persons began to appeal.

I draw on numerous in-depth interviews, discussions, and long-term relationships for this analysis. Dr. Viktor Samokhvalov assisted teenagers, their families, and health providers at the St. Petersburg clinic for reproductive health, Yuventa, from its opening in 1993 until his retirement in 2017. I first met him in 1994 while touring the clinic. Introducing myself, I asked his permission to attend and study his sex education talks for teenagers. He not only agreed, but generously shared his ideas and answered my questions with eagerness and thoughtfulness. His interest in analyzing interpersonal dynamics and sociopolitical change, his excellent listening skills, and his vivid storytelling made for many important conversations; I wrote about him in my 2005 book and in 2009, we published a co-authored, Russian-language article that I draw on here.[6] Beyond my research, I have benefitted enormously from his sage and empathic advice on childrearing and other personal issues. Viktor requested that I use the informal, second-person pronoun, *ty*, and call him by his first name only, without his patronymic, a sign of our friendship.[7] And Viktor has been immensely important to me: I always visited him when coming to St. Petersburg and we stay in touch through phone calls and Skype.

Dr. Liubov Vladimirovna Erofeeva, an ob-gyn turned public health expert, became the most prominent Russian activist defending women's access to legal abortion and contraceptive services. Sergei Zakharov introduced me to Liubov Vladimirovna Erofeeva after I mentioned reading an article she published that greatly impressed me with its explicit embrace of human rights and women's reproductive autonomy.[8] Liubov Vladimirovna kindly agreed to several interviews in Moscow, and in 2017 I invited her to Chapel Hill, where she gave a talk at UNC about Russian reproductive politics and her activism.

Notably, neither of them endorsed liberal ideas based on abstract deliberations; Russian historical concepts and particular life experiences shaped both of their commitments to valuing individual interests over state and medical authority. For Viktor, it was the profession of psychotherapy, a field he realized was his calling after practicing psychiatry and becoming disillusioned with its focus on illness and its frequent politicization in the Soviet era. For Liubov Vladimirovna, it was training in London as a family planning practitioner that taught her the importance of patients' rights and feminism, and inspired a commitment to individual interests. Their professional and intellectual histories reveal two key ways that models of individual selfhood—and consumer approaches to personal empowerment—became disseminated and legitimated in Russia. Finally, the ordeals they experienced for promoting family planning reflect broader trials endured by many Russian liberal humanist groups in the years leading up to Putin's third term—the era that saw these institutions' demise.

Lichnost' As a Humanist Project for Sexual and Reproductive Health

Viktor explained that his interest in psychology and respect for the person, *lichnost'*, came from his biography. He was born in the early 1940s and raised in a family of doctors; his mother was a pediatrician and his father a military doctor.

As he told me in 2019,

My father treated people injured in war, and, you understand, they both helped people in need. And after the war he was sent to a military zone in Lvov. Lvov in Western Ukraine was the most western, it was on the border with Poland. And there, by the will of fate, I first heard American jazz on the radio. In all of Russia they jammed its broadcasts . . . but in Lvov, to my great joy, and which shaped my whole life, it was there. And therefore American music could be freely heard there. I listened to a whole lot of it . . . I liked it, it was harmony, it was new. It was swing, it was what my heart and soul, the waves of this swing were so in tune with my thinking, my reasoning and everything. Glenn Miller, Arty Shoi, Tommy Dorsey, etc.

Viktor's father opposed his listening to jazz, and once "took a belt and whopped me really well" when he caught him doing so.

I fought with my father for a very long time. . . . And once, when I was a pioneer, with a tie, I talked [to other kids] about listening to the Polish radio and jazz. And one of my classmates, probably in fourth or fifth grade . . . told on me to the school principal.[9] And in Russia the situation was that if you report on someone, that means you're a good person. The syndrome of Pavlik Morozov.[10] . . . Well. They called me to school. In front of everyone at the school, they put me in the center, they beat a drum of military rhythm—brrrr trrrr, burrrr-rrr-trr tuum-du duum—and they removed my pioneer tie in front of the 250 people in the school. They said, "He listens to jazz. He deserves to be kicked out of the pioneers." It was a big trauma for me. After that, I began stuttering, I couldn't say a word. Well, that's all not important. It led to my first beginning to think about what kind of person [*lichnost'*] I am. They excluded me from the pioneers—am I really guilty because I listen to music? They thought it was the music of our enemies . . . and so from then on I was shaped by this opposition. I wasn't ever a dissident, but from that time I stopped believing in the *bright Soviet future* . . . I didn't join the Komsomol', I wasn't a communist, despite the fact that everyone in our family was supposed to be a Party member. It's not important—why am I talking about all this—it's because it made me think, reflect on what to become, who to be, how to live. [*kem byt', kak byt'*].

Viktor continued listening to the Voice of America jazz in secret. After finishing high school, he studied medicine at the Leningrad Pediatric Medical Institute. For his first job placement in 1968, he requested a position in the "periphery." "I didn't want to stay in . . . the prosperous city. I wanted to know how I'd manage somewhere remote. So I want to Onezhskoe lake, the village of Voznesenie, northeast of Leningrad, a really remote place. I did the work of all kinds of medical specialties, attended childbirths, did everything but surgery."

Over time, Viktor realized he was fascinated by the human psyche and, again "in the periphery," he found a colleague with a personal library that included books otherwise unavailable, including pre-Revolutionary printings of Freud, Jung, and Otto Weininger. He became interested in "where, how, and why in the contemporary world women have problems." He dreamed of becoming a psychotherapist, "to gain knowledge not of sick people, but healthy people in challenging conditions." But there was no training in psychotherapy, and so he returned to Leningrad and trained as a psychiatrist, subsequently becoming the first psychiatrist for teenagers in the city. He worked as a psychiatrist at a Leningrad outpatient clinic from 1975 to 1988. Realizing that his patients were mainly not ill, but simply "not fulfilling society's norms," further strengthened his desire to work as a psychotherapist.

> You have to behave as the school principal says, as the *komosomol* organization says, as is written in the newspapers, as in the writings of our dear Leonid Ilych Brezhnev, etc., etc.[11] And so when a certain boy was disobedient, they suspected he had mental illness. He's breaking away from society, from how a Soviet teenager is supposed to live. Does that mean he's mentally ill? And there were some situations when they simply pressured me, saying, "There's this Vasia, you need to admit him to the hospital . . . during the holidays—May 1, November 7, Revolution Day, because this Vasia might print flyers and throw them down from a balcony onto the parade." . . . Well. I didn't agree with that. There were many, many conflicts, but I had to work, and you know, I got the idea that I needed to leave psychiatry. Because, you see, psychiatry in general is the science of mental illnesses. Schizophrenia, psychopathology, manic-depression. . . . But I wanted to work with people who didn't have mental illness. And I started to learn about sociological issues . . . who was accused, incarcerated; about repressive forms of action, prison, and alongside all that, I started studying sexology, Freud, Erik Bern.[12] And I realized I needed to find an opportunity to leave psychiatry and work as a psychotherapist.[13]

As Tomas Matza has described, humanistic psychotherapeutic approaches that assist people in achieving "inner freedom," self-esteem, and satisfying relationships began developing in the Soviet Union in the 1960s.[14] The concept of *lichnost'* played a key role in this shift away from Pavlovian approaches, which were behaviorist and mechanistic.[15] Corresponding roughly to the concept of the "creative individual," *lichnost'* is historically rooted in nineteenth-century intelligentsia discourses about educated, "morally developed" selves. But in the 1960s the term also came to be used to mean personality or a developed self; it was frequently used to refer to an exceptional social figure.

During Glasnost the salience of *lichnost'* burgeoned, with educational reformers and psychologists urging "the intellectual, moral, emotional and physical development of the personality," and "the liberat[ion of] its creative potential."[16] Having prized a sense of inner freedom his whole life, and professionally dedicating his work to strengthening people's sense of self—*lichnost'*—Viktor was part of this zeitgeist.

In 1988, he became the first professional hired by St. Petersburg's psychological hotline, and in 1993 he was hired as a psychotherapist by the newly opening Yuventa clinic. Describing Pavel Naumovich Krotin, the founder of the clinic and its chief doctor until his death in 2016, as a "smart, decent person," Viktor says, "he opened the doors to my new life." Viktor worked at Yuventa for twenty-seven years, providing therapy to youth and their parents, and guiding physicians in their interactions with clients. Between 1994 and 1998 he gave sex education lectures to teenagers at the clinic, before the political scandals we saw in Chapter 4 led to their elimination. For Viktor Samokhvalov, valuing individuals' personality over conformity to the collective was a lifelong commitment. Training in psychotherapy and sexology gave him disciplinary forms of knowledge for conceptualizing and cultivating *lichnost'* for well-being, and the welcoming approach of Yuventa's chief doctor, Pavel Naumovich Krotin, made pursuing this work feasible.

As I described elsewhere, Viktor's sex education lectures with youth in the mid-1990s provided knowledge about human anatomy and sexuality as natural aspects of human life; he cast this approach in opposition to Soviet ideology's banishment of sex from the sphere of respectability.[17] Viktor's approach, indeed, dramatically contrasted with lectures delivered by his gynecologist colleagues, which depicted sex as shameful and contraceptives as a marker of immorality. He affirmed the importance of sexual pleasure in human life and encouraged young women to understand their own bodies and sources of pleasure. He cast sexuality as acceptable in all forms when undertaken without coercion. All his interactions with teenagers, from his sex education lectures to his therapy sessions and hotline counseling, aimed to develop *lichnost'*, which he described as helping clients develop self-respect and the skills to navigate interpersonal relationships with care for oneself and one's partner. As most professionals in his generation, he considered motherhood a woman's "natural" destiny, but his lectures did not dwell on this issue. Rather, he strove to help young women understand common dynamics in heterosexual relations and develop the skills to protect themselves physically and emotionally. He cautioned young women that they may face pressure from men, and the desire for attention and love might lead them to agree to sexual activity that they may not want and/or that was not safe. He offered them skills for figuring out their own needs and standing their own ground, while also advising them to keep a condom in their purse just in case it became needed. "Tell your mother, 'doctor Viktor Evgen'evich told me to carry it with me, to be safe,'" he suggested, to help them de-escalate potential conflicts with parents.[18]

Notwithstanding the cancellation of his sex education courses, Viktor continued providing therapy at Yuventa. He also ran monthly support sessions for the clinic's staff modeled on the Balint support groups for physicians.[19] Encouraging gynecologists to think anew about the young women they were treating, and in the process, to think anew about themselves, he told them:

> In principle, you work for a client, you serve a person for their health [*ty sluzhish' cheloveku dlia ego zdorov'ia*], so why should your personal opinions lead you to think [about a patient], "Oh, you're a fool, you're a nobody [*nichtozhestvo*], you, ugh, you're having sex with whoever fell your way, you're carrying contagion . . . " You understand? A girl can't be reproached for being a certain way [*nel'zia ee uprekat' v tom shto ona v dannyi moment takaia*], for who she sleeps with, or what she does. That's her deep problem. A gynecologist may have a totally different mentality than a client. But as I see it, the doctor, first and foremost, must not say the word "must" [*dolzhen*]. Because each person must decide for themselves [*dolzhen-to sam chelovek samomy sebe*].

Viktor's strategy in this statement is particularly noteworthy as an explicit challenge to Russia's long-standing hierarchy of values. When the notion of the "creative individual" first emerged among the Russian intelligentsia in the mid-nineteenth century, it referred to "an exceptional consciousness, a person whose erudition and cultural achievements place him above the throng."[20] In prizing the creative individual as naturally superior, the

Russian intelligentsia saw philosophies of "moral individualism"—which attribute equality and autonomy to every person regardless of social status or behavior—unappealing.[21] Yet in this statement, Viktor took the concept of *lichnost'* in a radically new direction. He highlighted the need for doctors to treat each person as a *lichnost'*—recognizing her as having complex motivations, perhaps problems, and the potential for change.[22] Regardless of the person's behaviors, Viktor argued, paying her respect is imperative. Indeed, he used the new, and contested, consumer terminology to oppose the conventional doctor-patient hierarchy, asserting that doctors "work for a *client*" (as opposed to the standard phrase of, 'treating a patient') and "*serve* a person for their health."[23] By declaring that each person deserves to be treated as a moral equal, Viktor aimed to transform doctors' understandings of both their young patients and themselves. He outlined specific verbal and nonverbal gestures in which such respect could best be conveyed during clinical *interactions* for family planning:[24]

> Speak to the teenager one-on-one and tell them about their rights to confidentiality. . . . Support the decisions of those who have not yet become sexually active to remain abstinent, and also recommend this to all others as a possible option. . . . Ask those who haven't yet become sexually active how they feel about contraception and whether they will use it in the future. . . . Discuss with the teenager what they know about methods of preventing unwanted pregnancy; what the teenager him/herself prefers.

Throughout his recommendations, Viktor encouraged clinicians to elicit clients' questions, problems, complaints, to offer possible solutions, and to offer necessary psychological support and information. He framed the clinicians' task as "assisting her in making an informed choice" (*informirovannyi vybor*). Notably, in attempting to guide clinicians into new modes of interacting with clients, he simultaneously envisioned teenagers as deserving respect and as vulnerable to the power plays of others. He aimed to balance a view that individuals should become responsible for their own lives and decisions with a recognition that complete self-sufficiency is an impossible condition, for people need each other, and, he believed, youth need expert guidance. To cultivate trusting relations in which the expert demonstrated care and respect for the client, Samokhvalov instructed doctors to examine their role in establishing the patient's trust for discussing uncomfortable issues, providing them specific ways to become aware of their own behaviors and to adapt them to help their clients. For example, he prepared a list of training questions that a consultant should ask herself for developing the optimal skills in the process of psychological counseling:

1. Does your manner of behavior help the patient to feel that her presence is desired?
2. Does your behavior change depending on the specific characteristics of the patient?
3. Do you express well-meaning intentions [*oblik dobrozhelatel'nost'*] to the patient?
4. Do you have a calm look?
5. Do you smile at appropriate moments?
6. Do you look the patient in the eyes and from time to time look away?
7. Do you nod your head as a sign of agreement or encouragement?
8. Do your gesticulations demonstrate understanding of the feelings the patient expresses?
9. How natural does your voice sound?
10. Do you think you speak in an "official" tone?
11. Do your feelings and the patient's feelings get expressed in your tone of voice?
12. Do you convey your concerns and good intentions to the patient through your tone of voice?
13. Do you think that you ask the patient questions according to the "official protocol"?
14. Do you behave according to the generally accepted ethics of behavior?
15. Are you able to attentively and actively listen?
16. Can you recognize [*raspoznat'*] and reflect [*otrazit'*] the patients' feelings?
17. Are you able to ask "open" questions?
18. Are you able to provide the patient with necessary information in an accessible language?
19. With what words and actions are you able to support a patient's decisions?
20. Are you able to draw conclusions from the consultation, draw the session to a close, and end the interaction?

Viktor deployed a psychotherapeutic framing of *lichnost'* and the analysis of interpersonal relations to transform physicians' interactive style. His approach did not assume an ideal of individual autonomy or a political vision of "rights." Rather, he cultivated physicians' capacities to undertake emotional labor—to reflect on and modify their own body language, tone of voice, and phrasings to communicate respect and not judge patients.

He also strove to help physicians become attentive to their patients' emotional state as a central part of medical care. Knowledge of emotions and emotional labor were Viktor's strategies for transforming medical power in the consulting room.[25]

While I did not have opportunities to observe these Balint sessions or interview physician participants, my informal conversations with doctors at Yuventa revealed that they highly respected and admired Viktor Samokhvalov. I did sit in on several of his therapy sessions with teenage clients, and saw him implement his own recommendations. Viktor listened attentively to the young women who called the hotline or came to his office—teens dealing with an unintended pregnancy or other highly challenging situations. He also met with these teenagers' parents, likewise in great distress. Viktor presented a calm and nurturing presence. He expressed concern about a client's situation and avoided any appearance of morally judging them. He asked clients questions to elicit their feelings and concerns, prompting them to observe their own feelings about their situation. He guided them in figuring out the decisions they needed to make by looking inward and articulating their feelings and fears. He asked them to play out alternative scenarios regarding where different decisions might lead. In our discussions about teenagers, Viktor often told me about his efforts to avoid saying "must" or "should" (*nado*), in order to enable the client to be the decision maker; he also tried to get parents to understand the advantages of this approach. With psychotherapy still rather new and unusual during the years I visited Viktor's office, I was not surprised to see the teenage clients I observed meet Viktor's approach with a palpable sense of relief.[26]

Yet beyond the clinic, his discussions of sexuality became a target for the ire of conservatives. As antiabortion political organizations became increasingly mobilized in St. Petersburg and nationally, Viktor Samokhvalov, Yuventa's chief doctor, Pavel Krotin, and the clinic itself, were maliciously slandered as a danger to children and threat to Russian society.[27] This rhetoric cast them as perilous, traitorous individuals, who further deepened the nation's vulnerability.

The most frightening attack took place on July 4, 2010, when Russia's national television channel 1 broadcast an episode of the program *Special Correspondent* titled, "School in the Twenty-First [Century]—Sex Enlightenment" (*Seksprosvet*). It featured a film made by Arkadi Mamontov, one of several extremist media producers who peddle conspiracy theories in Russia.[28] Mamontov's episode purported to be a documentary about sex education programs in Russia, and on that basis, he deceived Viktor into agreeing to be profiled for it. I draw on a verbatim transcript of the episode that Viktor gave me to show the slander he endured.[29]

To establish the political stakes of the topic, the film began with selected demographic data: Russia has the largest territorial expanse in the world, but is sparsely populated. In Russia's far eastern region, the Kamchatka peninsula has 1.4 persons per square kilometer, and the Republic of Sakha has only 0.3. By comparison, we are told, Japan's population density reaches 337 persons per square kilometer, and China, the world's most populous country, has more than 1.5 billion people. But "we" have a 2010 total population of 141,900,000.[30]

The next introductory framing of the film presented highly selective historical anecdotes to establish the urgent threat confronting Russia's moral order:

> Before 1917 in Tsarist Russia the law of God was taught in schools and universities . . . it provided youth moral education about love, chastity, and the need to protect one's honor . . . communists spoke about almost the same thing—that it's harmful to become sexually active from a young age. . . . Now it's all different. Entirely different understandings have come to the country that were opposed to the people's traditions [*protivny narodnym traditsiiam*] and the most severe stage in the demographic crisis has begun—the destruction of the family.[31]

Noting that "Western patterns of behavior" are being planted in youth and schools are imparting a different mentality (than Russian), Mamontov poses the question that foments the film's moral panic: "How will our children live? With faith, according to the traditions of their own land, or professing an ideology of self-destruction that is being doggedly imposed on us?"[32]

The film then cuts to the clinic Yuventa, where, it tells the viewer, "in the vestibule a cartoon is screened nonstop of a professor telling a little girl about sex." The voice of a woman lawyer recounts how "the Center's staff started a fight [*ustroili draku*] with parents who asked to see the manuals and get an explanation of what they're teaching the children whose schools bring them there. An obscure sexual enlightenment that threatens us all."[33]

Having set up the story as exposing evil doers who pervert innocent children, turn them away from their cultural inheritance, destroy families, and fight off parents' attempts to protect them—Mamontov reveals this occurring behind the walls of wrongly legitimated medical clinics. The film then spotlights Viktor: "A certain Samokhvalov, who represents himself as a psychologist, is legally employed at Yuventa. Parents themselves bring their children to him."[34] The conspiratorial plot then thickens as the film seems to grant us a glimpse of nefarious action behind a different set of walls, not the clinic, although there is no clarification as to what, precisely, we are viewing. In truth, we are briefly seeing the home of a close friend of Viktor's who established, in his home, the first hospice in Russia. This old, fantastic St. Petersburg building had an unusual architecture, with a large wooden staircase to a roof top patio filled with wind chimes and a working belfry. The large apartment's living spaces were filled with musical instruments and exotic-looking knick-knacks from all over the world. Antique furniture and high ceilings gave the apartment an atmosphere of another era, while the sounds of all kinds of music also transported visitors beyond the mundane life outside. People confronting terminal illness were not only cared for there but also given opportunities to dress up in costumes and theatricalize their dreams, fears, and wishes. Viktor had taken Mamontov and his film crew to this home because it was an immensely special place for him, a refuge where people gathered to experience the intensity of facing one's mortality in community with others who welcomed emotional expressions in numerous registers—melancholy, fear, play, fantasy, connection, and love. As he later explained ruefully, Viktor had been led to believe Mamontov would profile his work with appreciation and honesty. Instead, the director cut and spliced footage manipulatively, added ominous music, and omitted the context of Viktor's discussion in order to create a deceptive and sensationalist portrait. After framing the topic of sex education as antithetical to Russian culture, a moral outrage that perverts children by instructing them in sexual activities, the film shows Viktor himself stating:

> Children sit together on their potties, right? This is normal erotica. They see each other's organs and even touch them. There is an alternative form of so-called sexual interpersonal relations. The progressive Western world and civilization says that you can begin to teach people to feel their sexual reactions and to use them, not necessarily having genuine sexual contact of an adult type. This is petting culture which is really developing now and among teens it is generally very popular. . . . The concept of sexual health, accepted by WHO, says that in part, sexual health is the absence of pressure, shame and guilt feelings.[35]

While Viktor was discussing the various forms of sexual awareness and its expressions in different stages of human development, the film casts this worldview as sinister. Mamontov further accused Samokhvalov: "For this teacher, in quotes, of course the understandings of 'chastity' and 'innocent children' don't exist and have no meaning. What can such a psychologist teach? Tens, if not hundreds of children have passed through his hands. Why aren't such types isolated from society instead of being allowed to work with children and considered normal?"[36]

As Borenstein shows, conspiracy narratives unfold in the genre of melodrama: characters are cast in simple roles of hero or villain, and the plot unravels a battle of good against evil.[37] Placing himself in the superhero role of the muckraking reporter patriotically exposing internal enemies, this film director slandered Viktor and Yuventa as corrupting Russian children and promoting Western agendas to destroy Russia's future.

Viktor Samokhvalov's life work was devoted to supporting teenagers emotionally, helping them gain the confidence and skills to protect themselves in a world of multiple risks, and to care for their sexual and reproductive health. He strove to erase the Soviet-era shame surrounding sex in order to help children, teens, and adults gain an understanding of human sexuality and make responsible decisions in favor of health. While withholding moral judgments about teenagers' past behaviors, he also urged young women to protect themselves emotionally and physically from people who sought to exploit them. Indeed, by soberly recognizing that many teens become sexually active whether or not adults desire this development, Viktor presented them with harm reduction skills; yet he never encouraged teens (or anyone) to have sex. Viktor's own workshops with clinicians urged them to "support the decisions of those who have not yet become sexually active to remain abstinent, and also recommend this to all others as a possible option," and he suggested that young women facing pressure for sex consider whether pressure belongs in a loving relationship. He recommended that women ask themselves, "what do I need this for?" But the film entirely ignored such nuances; true (only) to the genre of conspiracy, it provided viewers with the thrill of peering behind doors to disclose supposed horrors.

Mamontov's film was one of many personal and institutional defamations. On October 14, 2010, Pokrov, the interinstitute Association of Spiritual-Moral Enlightenment, and Parental Standing, a civic coalition in defense of Russian traditions of moral upbringing and education, undertook a protest against alcoholism, drug abuse, molestation, homosexuality, and juvenile justice at the centrally located Kazan Cathedral in St. Petersburg.[38] Reporting on this demonstration, the website of the Orthodox and nationalist organization Russkaia Narodnaia Liniia noted that these "ulcers of our society" are being defended by "democratic-liberal-tolerant activists" who "hide beyond masks of smart and kind" people "defending the rights of children."[39] In addition to naming two Russian talk show hosts and Elton John, the website stated:

> The names of those people who disgrace our city and country were also announced at this demonstration . . . activists from the notorious Petersburg Center Yuventa, director Pavel Krotin and the psychologists with the prefix "sex-," Viktor Samokhvalov and Stanislav Kazanskii. Representatives of the Coalition Parents' Standing and Petersburg regional branch of the Narodnyi Sobor movement have begun to put out a series of color posters with the faces of "heroes" which people need to know. The first awarded to lead this "gallery" are Yuventa workers. And this is not simply a one-time action, it is the beginning of a cleansing of our city, within the framework of the law, of people who propagandize fornication, homosexuality, abortion.[40]

In a society where millions, within living memory, had been labeled "enemies of the people," taken to forced labor camps, and often destroyed, the act of identifying individuals publicly and circulating their photographs in a process of "cleansing of our city" carried terrifying implications. And this was not the last public denunciation. More protests took place against Yuventa, with deputy of the St. Petersburg Legislative Assembly (*Zakonodatel'noe sobranoe*) Vitalii Milonov describing the clinic as a "death factory," lecturing the staff about abstinence and chastity, and calling for doctors to report all pregnancies among teenagers to the police.[41] In reporting on this with a critical lens, one newspaper likened the scene to the "theater of the absurd," as Yuventa's chief doctor Pavel Krotin was accused of all the deadly sins: "receiving grants, harboring pedophiles, perverting minors, and, of course, murders."[42] In response to the activists "harping on" their opposition to abortion, Krotin is reported to have stated, "I'm also against [them]. But it's a legal operation and our clinic must do them. Pass a law prohibiting them and we won't." When they demanded that the clinic promote "abstinence and chastity," he explained, "Unfortunately, those who come for abortions are those for whom it's too late to discuss abstinence and chastity. We have to 'rake out' [*razgrebat'*] the inadequate work of parents and society."

Krotin's response, notably, did not assert rights or explain harm reduction, but reiterated his "opposition" to abortion while blaming society for not appropriately educating teenagers to avoid abortion. Defending himself and his clinic as the technicians carrying out the law, he recommended—dared—that conservatives turn to political venues to criminalize abortion rather than picketing his clinic. While Krotin expressed his frustration and annoyance with Milonov's disruptive theatrics, he could not bring himself to justify the need for abortions to remain legal in the face of this crude attack.

Antiabortion activism began to take place among Orthodox youth in 2006. A young man named Maksim Vorob'ev became inspired to undertake dynamic civil protests of abortion clinics after reading Russian translations of the American books *Why Can't We Love Them Both?: Questions and Answers about Abortion* (1997) by John and Barbara Wilkes, and *Forbidden Grief: The Unspoken Pain of Abortion* (2002) by Theresa Burke.[43] With permission from Life, Russia's antiabortion center, Vorob'ev and associates began picketing clinics that provide abortions in June 2006.[44] They subsequently received materials and training from international colleagues.[45] Staff of Yuventa told me about being annoyed by the noise of picketers outside the clinic but feeling powerless to stop the protests.

Change would come from an unanticipated twist of fate. On March 21, 2016, Dr. Pavel Naumovich Krotin died at age sixty-nine. The city appointed a new chief doctor, Marina Federovna Ippolitova, who introduced profound changes in the clinic, inviting a Russian Orthodox priest to run a prayer room and perform weekly prayer services in the clinic. The clinic's website devotes extensive attention to the immorality of abortion, asserting that women who abort must atone for the rest of their lives. It also describes the Orthodox view that contraceptives are a tool for those who are too weak to follow Church morals. While at this time of this writing, the clinic continues to provide abortions, its website no longer mentions doing so.

Finding Inspiration for Feminism in the Consumer Model of Patients' Rights

In 2010, Dr. Liubov Vladimirovna Erofeeva, an ob-gyn and director of the nongovernmental Russian Association for Population and Development (RAPD) (the new name of the Russian Association of Family Planning, a change I discuss later in this chapter), published the results of a survey she and colleagues undertook on Russians' knowledge about reproductive health and patients' rights.[46] The study included interviews with 549 individuals, 22 focus groups, and 37 observations of abortion procedures and patient consulting, and concluded:

> The absolute majority of [survey] respondents, both health care users and providers in family planning, did not know that laws exist in many countries protecting reproductive health and rights. They did not know whether Russia has a similar law. . . . There is an extremely low level of knowledge about the social and medical criteria for terminating pregnancy, about the rights of adolescents (over age fifteen) to decide whether to terminate or prolong a pregnancy, and about contraceptives.[47]

When I first came across this study, I was amazed at these authors' concern with the population's knowledge of their reproductive *rights*—it differed dramatically from the vast majority of Russian discourses on reproductive health I had read, and particularly from the RAFP's rhetoric as presented by Grebesheva, Kulakov, and Lakhova. I mentioned my keen interest in this article to Sergei Zakharov, who filled me in on the fact that he and his colleagues at the Institute for Demography were allied with the RAPD in advocating for abortion rights and offered to introduce me to Dr. Erofeeva. I was fortunate to interview her in 2013 and 2016; I invited her to speak at UNC-Chapel Hill and we spent a week together during her visit in 2017. Upon first meeting her, I learned that she had known Andrej Popov from Manuilova's first family planning initiative, the Association of Family and Health, and she greatly respected him. I explained that I was writing about the development of Russia's family planning movement, which I sensed was not generally presenting as a "feminist" organization. I asked her about her professional history and how she came to embrace feminism and advocate for reproductive "rights."

Erofeeva's career is a story of access to leading educational institutions and outstanding achievements throughout her life. Growing up in Moscow and attending an English-focus school, she graduated from medical studies in 1984 and spent two years in a clinical internship, after which she pursued a PhD. She conducted research and wrote several dissertations, but due to bureaucratic problems (which Soviet graduate students often faced), didn't defend them. Undeterred in her pursuit of women's health, she went to work for the Moscow city public health department where she participated in analyses of maternal mortality. Every death was examined at a clinical-anatomical conference where the entire leadership of the city's 137 women's outpatient clinics gathered. As she told me, "Maternal mortality was very high. These were deaths from criminal abortions and self-induced abortions; some women wouldn't go to a hospital if you put a gun to their head—they didn't want their mother to know, or their husband—and they harmed themselves instead, and they died. And so this was the impetus [for my interest]."

A lecture by Irina Manuilova, who was researching oral contraceptives at the All Union Scientific Research Center for Obstetrics and Gynecology, deeply impressed Erofeeva; it was the first time Erofeeva heard the pill discussed as a means of preventing abortion. She realized her goal of reducing maternal mortality would require introducing new technologies at the population level rather than pursuing a career in clinical work. In 1988, she became involved in the Moscow public health department's unfolding experiment to introduce vacuum aspiration (VA, or what Russians called "mini-abortions") into the city's women's outpatient clinics. Vacuum aspiration removes the contents of the uterus through suction, a less-invasive procedure than dilation and curettage (which involves scraping with a hard metal instrument); VA results in far fewer complications. Working under Professor Yuri Mironovich Bloshanskii, the chief ob-gyn of Moscow for thirty years and "an unusually brilliant" visionary, and Yakov Grigorevich Zhukovskii, who introduced the technology into the clinics, Erofeeva helped prepare the clinical instructions, protocols for the operating theatre and recovery room, and all technical and organizational details.[48] Clinicians "needed to see how it worked, and there had to be anesthesia," she told me. This innovation met with skepticism from the Soviet Minzdrav's authorities:

> It was a huge leap forward, but only for Moscow, not in the eyes of Minzdrav. They didn't like it and began looking for criminal elements. Minzdrav launched an investigation. Irina Aleksandrovna Manuilova was a member of the investigatory committee—that's how I met her. But the results of the commission were so good, it was such an excellent report, that VA came to be introduced everywhere in the country.

With Glasnost well underway, this was a time of possibilities and innovations. Erofeeva recounted that Gorbachev's wife, Raisa Maksimovna, put women's health on the agenda of Soviet leaders. "She put in a good word for contraception—that not only condoms existed but more modern methods, too," and new opportunities in this sphere opened. Manuilova established a new kind of contraceptive advocacy organization—the Association of Family and Health—which was also provided with clinical and research facilities and the right to provide some commercial services.[49] Erofeeva explained:

> This was the era when all hospitals of the Central Committee of the Communist Party, so-called hospitals of the fourth administration, were being transferred to the Moscow municipal public health organ. This was the beginning of the democratization process, members of the elite sort of began to partly reject their entitlements. . . . They of course built themselves other hospitals, but some of the facilities were transferred to the head of the Moscow public health administration, where I was then working. And one of these was a very small maternity hospital on the Arbat, practically behind the Ministry of Foreign Affairs, which served wives of the Kremlin. And it was transferred to the Association!

Having already established ties with Western pharmaceutical companies while at the Center for Obstetrics and Gynecology, Manuilovna left the Center and continued conducting trials on oral contraceptives at the new Family and Health clinic. She invited Erofeeva to work for her as a clinician and researcher, undertaking vacuum-aspiration abortions, treating women for infertility, and leading a team of seven doctors in trials to determine whether specific oral contraceptives should be approved by the Russian Federation's pharmaceutical committee. Erofeeva's English skills came in very useful for collaborating with pharmaceutical representatives, who, she emphasized, taught her team the value of blinded, controlled studies.[50]

When I asked how the pharmaceutical companies established relations with Soviet colleagues, Erofeeva recounted:

> They all had different marketing techniques. Representatives came here and some invited people on trips or gave them gifts. . . . But Organon, in my opinion, chose the most appropriate technique. The first thing they did was open an office on Maloi Bronnoi [Street]. Second, they opened the Organon Information Center for Human Reproduction . . . for doctors, inside the Center for Obstetrics. The center undertook seminars off-site, it trained doctors in contraception, prevention, and treated infertility, questions of andrology, etc. . . . It was about two hundred square meters, everything was very beautiful inside, a blue velvety rug on the floor, offices inside a library, a hall for screening videos,

a discussion room. . . . Organon had very wise people, and I think [the company] stood out in the best way.

Organon, a Dutch firm with a production site in Northern Ireland's offshore region, began producing the low dose oral contraceptive Marvelon (generic: desogestrel and ethinyl estradiol) in 1981. I first heard about this brand in St. Petersburg, when I began my PhD research in 1994 and was asking young women whether they were familiar with oral contraceptives. I got two kinds of responses—negative ones citing the harsh effects of Postinor, a Hungarian-made postcoital contraceptive, and positive ones, in which women's face lit up and they specified the brand by which they had come to know the pill: "you mean Marvelon?" I later learned that Organon had opened its first subsidiary in Eastern Europe in 1991 (in Hungary), and merely three years later, in Russia, Marvelon had achieved genericization. One of the ways this happened was through establishing an Information Center on Human Reproduction on the premises of the Center for Ob-Gyn, (which, at the time, was directed by Dr. Vladimir Kulakov, the founding president of the Russian Association of Family Planning).[51]

Erofeeva herself first clinically observed Marvelon courtesy of Organon's senior medical advisor for Eastern Europe, Nico Briunyks. When visiting the Family and Health Association's clinic, he invited Erofeeva to attend conferences they were organizing throughout the Russian Federation. Erofeeva remembered:

> He gave us one hundred sample packets of Marvillon, so that we would later make a presentation at the conference and report that we received and distributed them, whether the women liked them or didn't like them, what negative side effects there were, what subtleties. . . . I fell in love with this drug. It won me over! It's so easy, it's simply fantastic, women had good experiences with it. Everyone thanked us, that is, many continue to use it to this day because it was so good.

Soon thereafter, Briunyks sent Erofeeva to study family planning at a clinic in London with close colleagues of his. This experience proved transformative for Erofeeva, as she explained when I asked about the origins of her feminism:

> MRF: As a person who was socialized in the Soviet medical worldview, how

did you come to the view that a woman should make her own decisions? This is a huge difference.

LE: [It was] probably the education I got in Great Britain, when I first became a family planning doctor, and then became an instructor of family planning . . . this new understanding of the rights of the patient. These changes in worldview were concerned with the client-oriented view [*klientoorientirovannost'*]. Everything is oriented toward the patient's interests. It was here that my confidence was shaken regarding the fact that I am a government-minded person [*Vot zdes' pokolebalas' moia uverennost' v tom, shto ia gosudarstvennik*]. I stopped being "government-minded," probably. . . . It was some, little by little, some ideas came to me, some understandings, reflections . . . I became a feminist. It was simply a revolution, a revolution took place inside me. Absolutely.

MRF: Because at that time the word "feminism" was almost a curse word, and it still is. At that time there wasn't much literature; did you understand it intuitively, that this [idea of feminism] is a vision for the person, not for the masses, not for the state/government?

LE: And not for the statistics, not for the state, it was to protect health, to support each person's health, even the smallest person. This was entirely revolutionary.

With the Soviet Union's collapse at the end of 1991, additional, heady institutional changes developed. As we know from Henry David's archived papers, the Association of Family and Health was initially granted member status in the IPPF, but thereafter had it revoked (David does not mention why, but notes that Manuilova was focusing her time on collaborating with global pharmaceutical companies).[52] Erofeeva told me that she had been on the Association's Presidium and there were serious internal conflicts with Manuilova's authoritarian-style of leadership. When Inga Ivanovna Grebesheva formed the RAFP in 1992, Erofeeva and Andrej Popov, and many of the regional branch representatives of Family and Health broke away from Manuilova and affiliated themselves with the RAFP. It received office space from the new Russian Ministry of Public Health and was recognized as a member of the IPPF in 1993, the same year that Yeltsin established the federal program of Family Planning to provide clinics throughout Russia with funding for contraceptive services.

Then, in 1992, the Russian director of Organon's Information Center emigrated and Erofeeva was offered her position. With the Center physically housed in the most prestigious ob-gyn clinical-research institution in Russia, Erofeeva was perfectly situated to disseminate contraceptive knowledge among doctors. Directing the Center for seven years, she found the experience exhilarating. In a time of grave economic upheaval, the Center offered ob-gyn professionals something they deeply yearned for—access to new scientific knowledge:

> The first people who responded to us were the staff of the Center for Obstetrics. . . . the department heads, the leaders, all leading professionals. How could they walk past us? They'd come in and say "Hello, what is this?" And we'd explain everything to them . . . [because] even they didn't all know [about contraceptives and family planning]. There wasn't much international literature available then, and to subscribe to the journal *The Lancet*, you had to pay—so who, who could have had access to it? Only the Information Center had a library—and they were like, "Please, come, look around, fresh issues of journal, older issues . . . please, look at the journals in Human Reproduction." It was the kind of place where you could always come and discuss issues.
>
> If a person comes by a second time, that is, he comes by, comes by again, we'd ask to write down his contact information. He asks us what we need it for. And we say, "We'd like to invite you to our conferences," or, "We'll inform you when we put out a new device." That was first. Second, Organon put out a journal . . . it was glossy, in English, and we told them, "We'll send you the upcoming issue of our journal."[53] For some people, that was enough. And some people came back a second, third, fourth time . . . "Oh, there's a conference, would you be able to please include me in the list of attendees?" Our door was always open. This was AWE-SOME work, it was such an important part of my life.

Erofeeva described how, conveniently located on the first floor of the Center for Obstetrics, the Information Center became a hub of activity. It drew leading reproductive medical specialists from around Moscow and other regions. In a time when the country was pervaded by crisis and uncertainty, Organon's Information Center was a sign of hope and progress, innovation and opportunity. In recounting the next developments in family planning to me, Erofeeva emphasized the importance of "historical *lichnosti*" in paving transformative social changes:

> LE: I'll tell you—this was a time of creative individuals [*lichnosti*] in history. Because in Minzdrav there were such people who were willing to listen,

who were prepared for changes and were willing to take responsibility for these changes . . . and we must talk take off our hat to Ekaterina Filippovna Lakhova.

MRF: The leader of the political party Women of Russia?

LE: [Yes, but she] began before Women of Russia. She was a deputy of Parliament even in the Soviet era. Her closeness to Boris Nikolaevich Yel'tsin was also greatly impactful. And . . . while being a Duma deputy [in the first Congress of People's Deputies of Russia], she also worked with the presidential administration and directed the Commission for Women, Family, and Demography. And it was precisely on the governmental level and as the leader of Women of Russia that she did a lot for the idea of family planning, for introducing it and for realizing this program. When Organon came to her (represented by myself) and we began to talk, it was pretty easy to organize a family planning service. She said, let's take some Russian territory far from Moscow, and show how it's done.

Lakhova had good relations with a member of the regional government of the Russian Republic of Udmurtiia, Galina Ivanovna Klimantova, through women's societal activity, which began emerging throughout Russia in the 1990s.[54] Erofeeva and Lakhova approached Klimantova and explained their idea of developing a model family planning service, describing its purpose and necessity. "Although she was educated as a journalist, she always participated in women's movements, she was a real social activist." Klimantova agreed to establish family planning services in Udmurtiia, and the regional government supported it.

Udmurtiia is a Republic in central Russia, with a population of about 1.5 million inhabitants, about 600,000 of whom live in the capitol, Izhevsk, and about 30 percent of whom live in rural areas. During the Soviet era, Udmurtiia was closed to foreigners because of nearby military industry. I expressed surprise that Lakhova and Organon located their model in what seemed, from the vantage point of Muscovites, a rather remote location. Erofeeva explained the strategy: "it was yet another rupture, I think— specifically to show that it's not difficult [to establish family planning services], that the most important thing is to change your ideas, to change the system of interaction."

Moreover, Udmurtiia's authorities welcomed the foreigners from Organon and their British colleagues who arrived to share their experiences of running family planning clinics. Together, they set up model family planning services, locating them both in a rural setting and in the large, republic-level hospital. The goal was to show that "family planning was everywhere, in all kinds of places. . . . We taught all administrators at the level of Minzdrav and trained all the doctors."

Erofeeva and Organon representatives went to Udmurtiia two or three times a year and held cycles of two week long professional trainings, supported by a leading professor of ob-gyn there, Dr. Klara Georgievna Serebrennikova. Erofeeva instructed Russia's ob-gyns in contraceptive counseling and prescribing practices, organizing family planning clinics, following global best practices. She brought in British specialists to offer training participants comparative insights: "[we discussed] how they organized their services, what they encounter, what we may encounter, what would be possible to improve. It was an exchange of opinions, very interesting and important." Erofeeva and her colleague Larisa Vladimirovna Gavrilova developed clinical recommendations for the organization of family planning services in Russia and used them in the courses.[55] Doctors from all over Russia came to these trainings and participants received a diploma certifying them as specialists in family planning. This certification became essential to qualify to work in the newly established family planning services, so "all doctors in the Russian Federation who would work in the system of family planning were trained by me, at the Udmurtiia department of ob-gyn."

Unclear about the extent of Organon's influence, I asked Erofeeva whether there was a relationship between the company and the RAFP. She denied any connection on the basis of conflict of interest: "No, because it wasn't permissible for a societal organization in Russia to have activities with a pharmaceutical company—because pharma is business. It's an income. And in order to maintain a neutral position and not recommend one or another contraceptive brand, the RAFP kept an equal distance from all of them. And that was appropriate; it's not possible to serve several gods."

Still, local public health departments did welcome Organon's involvement, and the RAFP, funded by the International Planned Parenthood Federation, was another partner. As Udmurtiia's training program brochure states:

> the implementation of the program was facilitated by the introduction of scientific developments of the Izhevsk Medical Academy in the field of family planning and protection of reproductive health, adapted to regional particularities of the republic. Coordination and organizational-methodological direction for activities of family planning services in Udmurtskoi Republic is undertaken by the administration of protection of maternal and child health

of Minzdravmedprom [name of Ministry of Health between 1994 and 1996] of Russia with participation of the societal organizations (RAFP, and the Information Center in Human Reproduction of the firm Organon International and others).

Such opaque intertwining of state, pharmaceutical corporation, and nongovernmental organization recalls similar findings from numerous studies of institution-building after the collapse of state socialism.[56] While Western democracy advisors imagined that after 1991, nongovernmental organizations would arise to represent citizens' interests and politically empower them, the economic calamity that ensued and absence of legal regulation created an arena more aptly described as wild marketization. Global corporations were in the position of both defining the kinds of consumer "demands" possible to imagine and supplying them. As much research has shown, persistent global inequalities in access to medications are directly linked to the unrelenting drive for profitability by global pharmaceutical firms; these firms' use of marginalized populations for testing new drugs without ensuring these same people's access to proven medication involves troubling layers of exploitation.[57] My data on Organon's work in Russia's 1990s offers insights regarding how the firm legitimated itself in local expert circles. By establishing a long-term presence on the ground in Moscow and developing relationships with both the Ministry of Health and RAFP leaders, Organon provided Russian physicians with knowledge and resources otherwise unobtainable at the time for helping women avoid abortions by using effective contraceptives. Trainings co-sponsored by the Ministry of Health, RAFP, and Organon became central to Russia's certification of family planning professionals, and Organon's support was welcomed during a time of severe crisis. Erofeeva noted how the doctors receiving this training returned to their localities and helped to create family planning clinics. They were provided with translated scientific literature through the RAFP's Russian-language journal *PS* (Family Planning) and became part of a vanguard group of experts. Russian physicians' concerns about the profit-focused nature of pharmaceutical corporations would be raised only later, in the form of unverified accusations and conspiracy theories circulated by extreme conservative opponents.[58]

In our interview, I asked Erofeeva whether she faced pushback when introducing family planning.

MRF: Were the doctors who came to your classes in Udmurtiia already in
favor of it?

LE: Not all. Some of them didn't understand anything about it at all. . . . We
needed to reorient doctors from treatment-focused work to prevention,
to listening, consulting, motivating, changing their attitudes, to get rid
of the paternalistic approaches, to stimulate women to make their own
decisions. This was insanely difficult.

If persuading physicians already interested in family planning to forsake
paternalism was one huge challenge, Erofeeva's career would soon take on
another colossal trial: in 2007, Inga Grebesheva retired and asked Erofeeva
to become the director of the Russian Family Planning Association. The
organization faced both internal and external trials: the renowned ob-gyn
professor Vladimir Kulakov, who had served as the Association's president
since its founding, had recently died. Opposition to family planning was
growing due to virulent nationalist defamations and ubiquitous qualms
about contraceptives' potential to lower fertility. Regional branches of the
RAFP were facing manifold pressures, as exemplified by the Family Planning organization in Stavropol' krai, which a conservative activist group
took to court twice, prompting an investigation by the city administration
for negatively affecting fertility.[59] In response to this pressure, the organization known as "Family Planning" changed its name in 2007 to Responsible Parenthood and entered into relationships with the Stavropol' diocese,
made presentations at the first Congress of Orthodox Women and other
conferences highlighting family values. It proclaimed its goals as "strengthening the prestige of the family, the moral education of responsible attitudes toward family formation, preventing social orphans and homeless
children; ensuring a child's right to harmonious development in the family; forming healthy lifestyles and protecting reproductive health among
youth"; and "defense of reproductive rights that are acknowledged in international documents as part of basic human rights, including the right of
each person, each family, to free and responsible parenthood."[60]

In assuming the RAFP's directorship that same year, Erofeeva became
the country's most prominent defender of family planning and confronted
these objections head-on. She recalled the profound impact of Lynn Thomas,
the European office head of the IPPF, during this experience: Lynn "listened
to people, she was interested in them . . . she never imposed anything on
anyone. She felt that a person is only going to do something well if they feel

it's needed." It seems Erofeeva adopted this model as she devised rhetorical strategies for defending family planning in the RAFP. Erofeeva astutely recognized that legitimating family planning required speaking to cultural concerns, including the value of global scientific knowledge and technical progress, while carefully and selectively advancing feminist ideals.[61]

Strategies for Legitimating Family Planning: Selective Uses of Feminism and Family Values

In 2009, the Presidium of the RAFP also decided to change the organization's name, to the Russian Association of Population and Development. In a 2014 published interview, Erofeeva tied the new name to the UN's 1994 Conference on Population and Development in Cairo, which made reproductive health and rights global priorities.[62] Since the Association addressed far more than family planning, she explained, the term "population" was more fitting. Population can mean "the number of people, the dying out of the population and its continuation, the quality of life and health." In addition to protecting the reproductive health of youth, preventing sexually transmitted diseases and unwanted pregnancy, and providing contraceptive services, RAPD also undertook "advocacy," a term "that's not always understood" in Russia: "Advocacy is help for those who aren't able to stand up for their own rights. It's patients' rights, the right of new technologies to be invented, informing the authorities and decision makers what's needed to improve the situation. We gather information from the population to learn about what they need and then discuss this with expert communities and convey the information to the authorities."[63]

If advocacy meant the right of collectivities to have their interests represented to policy makers, in the case of teenagers, this meant their right to access scientifically grounded information. Her 2009 article "'Tolerance' in Dutch means nothing less than the fewest abortions in the world!" challenged the widespread association in Russia between "tolerance" and moral dissipation.[64] Indeed, she underscored that sex education promotes responsibility for preventing pregnancy and sexually transmitted infections. Erofeeva thus balanced the goals of promoting both teenagers' responsibility and practitioners' and politicians' respect for individuals' autonomy. In the process, advocacy also involved Erofeeva in debunking conservative myths, calming pronatalist anxieties, and strategically introducing her feminist objectives when finding an efficacious way to do so. In response to a journalist's question, "What does family planning mean?" Erofeeva asserted:

> I want to address my answer also to critics. Family planning helps infertile cou-
> ples have their long-awaited child or children; families who have a child with
> difficult genetic illnesses may avoid bearing a second child with this pathology,
> etc. That is, the idea of family planning is nature that has listened to science,
> nothing more. There is nothing artificial, no infamous limiting of births. . . .
> A Russian woman should be a respected member of society, we must listen to
> her life goals and urgent tasks, respect her right to have as many children as
> she can afford, as many as her family is able to care for, and no more.[65]

Erofeeva's argument for listening to individual women and respecting
their sense of how many children they can raise, offered the basis for critiquing medical paternalism. In the same interview, she argued that people seeking contraceptives are acting responsibly and should be assisted,
not instructed, by medical professionals:

> the idea of family planning includes the idea of consulting, which didn't exist
> either in the Soviet Union or in the 1990s, when the doctor's approach to pa-
> tients was purely paternalistic. . . . the patient began to transform into a client
> for whom information and assistance in choosing became essential. I think
> medical personnel have become accustomed to these ideas, for which we're
> very glad. However, we've recently observed a return to [paternalism, with doc-
> tors scolding women] "Do as I say!" . . . The opportunity to choose the medical
> facility and doctor helps. Returning to the main issue: the foundational idea
> of family planning is the patient's rights.[66]

In mentioning that women can now choose the medical facility and
doctor, Erofeeva alluded to a 2007 state policy to introduce competition
between maternity care institutions. The national health care plan began
treating mothers-to-be as consumers who would choose their caregivers,
which Erofeeva lauded for reducing medical paternalism.[67] Notably, her
description of family planning did not cite the abstract principle of wom-
en's autonomy—a concept that would explicitly challenge the "family values" framing that seemed necessary for legitimating family planning. Erofeeva advocated respect for individuals by articulating its relevance to issues
people increasingly recognized as important in their lives: the need to time
childbearing in accordance with one's personal and economic readiness,

and to have medical professionals who support one's choices rather than dictating the correct decisions. The media offered ample opportunities for debating the notion of deliberately planning childbearing, as this idea met with both demographic skepticism and moral criticism. As we will see, the scenarios Erofeeva (and other family planning defenders) offered to make their cases highlighted constraints and relational insecurities women commonly face, not an abstract notion of "choice" or "autonomy." Another example of Erofeeva's smart and pragmatic advocacy is evident in the January 1, 2008, episode of the TV talk show *Russkii Vzgliad* (The Russian view).[68] The host introduced a panel discussion on family planning with Erofeeva, an Orthodox priest, an Orthodox father of many children, a teacher of "personal safety behaviors education" (*Osnovy bezopasnosti zhiznedeiatel'nosti*), and a woman writer. He introduced the discussion's themes as "the demographic crisis and families with many children, . . . happy mothers and contemporary ambitious women, . . . the social, moral, and material aspects of family planning."[69]

Erofeeva asserted that family planning ensures that children are born wanted, that parenthood is entered into responsibly. She then offered an example related to women's own readiness: "If a woman is married, busy with a thesis or creative project, she may experience pregnancy as a problem, because she's busy with other goals. Why force nature? Pregnancy and children are given to women as a joy, so she can dedicate herself to the child at a specific time [of life]." Erofeeva strove to balance a focus on the multiple reasons that women and couples may want to prevent childbearing, even as she aimed to demonstrate that the RAFP was not "against" families and all the symbolic meanings associated with "family values." She discussed the economic constraints preventing having many children, the unreliability of men, and the medical importance of spacing pregnancies. She also emphasized that family planning's embrace of "choice" meant that she did not reject the decision to have many children, as her fellow guest on the episode had, saying, "The Russian Association of Family Planning is in favor of such families! A couple should be allowed to have as many children as it wants," and later, "I can only wish Russian women such husbands as [father-of-many-children] Sergei, loving, responsible, caring, taking on the full responsibility for decisions taken." Still, Erofeeva cautioned, "We should also ask the state whether it's able to support such families in the case something happens."

The host's reverence for the ideal of family emerged repeatedly, as in her statement: "the desire to bear a child arises in little girls when they play with dolls. What's happened to our consciousness?" Erofeeva responded by normalizing small families, noting that they are the norm throughout Europe; she asserted that women's personal life goals beyond motherhood also deserve respect. Toward the episode's closing, the host presented her own romantic view of sex and childbearing: "I think that it's wonderful when people don't plan their families, when they just give birth to children. As a rule, children who weren't planned bring much happiness and joy." She then asked the priest, "What can you say to our viewers who somehow plan their lives?"

Father Mikhail took aim broadly at this idea, saying:

> it's necessary to avoid egotism—it's a frightening evil that can completely subjugate a person and allow him to always find justification for any wicked life choice. . . . In the ancient Christian tradition there is a phenomenon called "literature of two paths" . . . [that describes how] "there are two paths: the path of life and the path of death." The path of fulfilling one's own comfort is the person's path of death. No one is insured against infirmities or poverty. But the person who is surrounded by grateful descendants, or even maybe ungrateful descendants, nonetheless will never be alone. Children, as St. John Chrysostom said, are the riches of the poor. And who among us can call himself rich? No one! Therefore, our riches are our children.

Erofeeva's reply did not directly address the priest's claims, but emphasized that family planning was similarly concerned with providing moral education:

> I think that there's much that's very reasonable in the Orthodox Church representative's view. And I think we should stop juxtaposing the Russian Association of Family Planning to some Church doctrine. We have far more points of connection, despite what divides us . . . concern about the ethical atmosphere in society, about moral education for responsible attitudes toward oneself, one's partner, and one's future children—this is extremely important! And we think that's our cornerstone. That's what we do and will continue to do![70]

Unquestionably, Erofeeva disagreed with the priest's rejection of individuals living according to their own values and priorities (dismissed as pursuing "comfort" and the path of death). Yet in this concluding comment, she steered away from dispute. In the face of Russian Orthodoxy's self-presentation as leading the country's moral revival by embracing family life, Erofeeva emphasized family planning's own contributions to moral education as promoting people's responsibility for childbearing. This strategic effort to legitimate family planning reveals how conservative discourses had largely succeeded in shaping the terms of debate, such that contributing to the "social good" required adhering to a foundational mission: embracing family, fertility, and the moral responsibilities aligned with these values. Advancing ideals of patients' rights would remain firmly situated within this broader rubric, rather than endorsing unlimited degrees of individual freedom and autonomy over one's body.

Conclusion

The calling to nurture professionals' respect for individuals came to Samokhvalov and Erofeeva from different sources. Viktor found in the concept of *lichnost'* his own lifelong struggle against authoritarian forms of control over inner freedom. Cultivating *lichnost'* became central to the humanistic psychotherapy he practiced. By asking clinicians to monitor their own verbal and nonverbal expressions with patients, to show care through attentiveness, not authoritarianism, he urged them to respect patients' dignity as a *lichnost'* (a full human self/personality)—and also to transform the basis of their professional authority. Instead of a sanitary enlightenment approach communicating expert knowledge to ignorant patients along with moral judgments about their improper behavior, Viktor's approach based professional authority on principles of humanistic well-being. And while similar ideas would later emerge under the marketized rubric of consumer services, for Viktor—who was dismayed at the gross inequality emerging with Russia's "wild capitalism"—these ideals were rooted in humanistic values that he did not link with economic systems.

Erofeeva was inspired by the concept of "patients' rights" through her extensive engagement with representatives of a global pharmaceutical company seeking to create a Russian contraceptive market. She saw both moral and pragmatic advantages to the concept of patients' rights for establishing a culture of family planning: like Lynn Thomas from IPPF, who listened and "never imposed" her ideas, the concept of patients' rights guided clinicians to listen to laypersons and respect them as clients with their own concerns and interests. Closer to the consumer model of relations than the

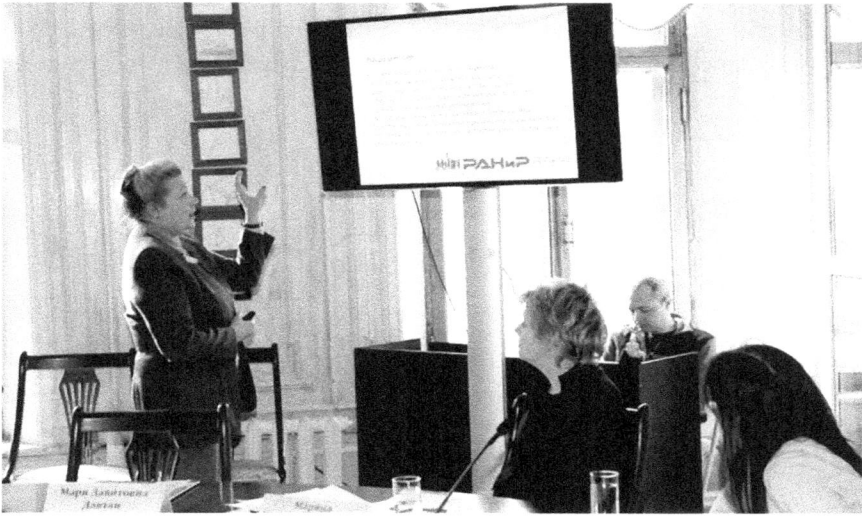

FIGURE 5.1. Lyubov Erofeeva, director of the Russian Association of Population and Development

social hygiene model, patients' rights gave rise to consulting, rather than instructing. In these ways, the concept of patients' rights led Erofeeva to rethink her stance as a *gosudarstvennik*—someone who works on behalf of the state interests—and to see herself, instead, as a feminist.

Through these notions of cultivating *lichnost'* and respecting patients' rights, Samokhvalov and Erofeeva moved health care relations away from the paternalistic social hygiene model and toward a liberal model focusing on individual interests and aligned with consumer-service provision. Notably, this was not a vision of consumer *sovereignty*: these advocates maintained a view of sex education as moral education promoting responsibility for one's own and one's partner's health. They de-emphasized the dominance of medical authority over patients in select ways and maintained a focus on the hetero-normative family. These concepts constituted a liberal biopolitics that did not proclaim radical political individualism or unmitigated freedoms while also enabling a conceptualization of people as relational selves.[71]

Despite their support of heteronormative family life, Viktor and Liubov Vladimirovna and their organizations faced virulent accusations and unceasing threats. Conservative campaigns against family planning and abortion compromised their institutions' abilities to do their work. But neoliberal economic constraints were also changing lay people's consciousness. As campaigns against abortion intensified, defending family planning finally became a concern for members of the public beyond professionals. Demands for women's rights soon entered Russian public debate.

CHAPTER 6

Defending Legal Abortion through New Civic Activism

When Dr. Erofeeva told me that the first concept she presented in her 1990s family planning training was patients' rights, I was more than a little surprised. As we saw in previous chapters, Western health consultants had actively promoted respect for individual rights to Russian medical practitioners since the early 1990s, and Russian physicians repeatedly dismissed the idea as irrelevant. When I asked how her physician-trainees reacted to this idea, she took the conversation to a broader level, remembering the zeitgeist of the era:

> In various ways. Inasmuch as this was a time when the winds of change were blowing, it was the time of democratic transformation, and we so wanted to believe that the West and we were on the same side, that we are friends and Europe supports us, we're going to have exclusively friendly contacts with the USA. But we would instead be disappointed. [We were] beckoned, screwed, and dumped [*Pomanili, pomatrosili i brosili, nazyvaetsia*].[1]

We had this conversation at the end of 2016, by which time Erofeeva had realized the naiveté of such hopes for Russian-Western relations. The RAPD's relationship with global NGOs had been both a necessity—as a source of funding and practical strategies—and a liability—as nationalists cast these ties as political treason and the support itself ultimately disappeared. With the Russian Orthodox Church and its supporters persistently seeking legal restrictions on abortion, new forms of local activism were needed. Abortion was being intensely debated in the media, with lay people voicing a range of perspectives. And while many Russian physicians remained against restrictions, some ob-gyns were accepting Orthodoxy and its rejection of abortion as a sin. These shifts thrust Erofeeva far beyond promoting respect for patients' rights when training medical professionals, to campaigning for abortion access itself as a political right. During this experience, she learned firsthand about the instability of global support for NGOs and the retreats many international organizations make from defending abortion rights.

At the same time, the struggle for liberalizing reproductive politics was spreading to the grassroots. By the 2010s, movements of younger women and queer people were actively forming, enabled by internet access and the global information it made available.[2] Interestingly, similar processes were underway elsewhere in the former socialist bloc. In Romania, for example, where abortion and contraceptives had been banned under socialism, the post-socialist era saw similar challenges as in Russia: the need to retrain health experts and the public about modern contraceptives and to devise ways of addressing sexuality in educational formats, all amid a strongly patriarchal culture.[3] Since 2012, Romanian nationalists have been proposing restricting abortion, conveniently forgetting the horrific consequences of repressive pronatalism.[4] Anton discusses Romania's first reproductive rights movement as an outcome of this illiberal turn.[5] In Poland, where abortion was banned soon after the end of socialism, reproductive rights activism and family planning organizing developed in tandem in the early 1990s. Poland's foremost family planning expert, Wanda Nowicka, formed ASTRA, the Central and Eastern European Network for Sexual and Reproductive Health and Rights, which provides information exchange and networking for experts around the region.[6] Mishtal shows that while efforts to make abortion more accessible in Poland have so far failed in the face of the powerful Catholic Church, resistance to this illiberalism has manifest in a growing feminist consciousness. While the Church's claims to moral authority had long been politically uncontestable, the violence and repression resulting from Poland's abortion ban have made the concept of reproductive rights increasingly legitimate.[7]

To preserve abortion access in Russia against restrictive legislative proposals in 2011 and 2015, the RAPD created a coalition with grassroots feminists in Moscow and St. Petersburg. This chapter traces how their struggles crystalized significant cultural transformations and inaugurated a new stage of reproductive politics in Russia. More specifically, in the process of justifying abortion access, activists also narrated their visions of ethical personhood and state-citizen relations. The concept of "reproductive rights," embedded in these broader expressions of people's lived realities and aspirations, gradually grew salient. Understanding this process requires first examining the intensifying drama of Russia's antiabortion and anti-Western politics.

Russian Cultural Politics in the Era of Putin's Third Term

In the spring of 2011, conservative politicians proposed an array of severe restrictions on abortion. Deploying tactics inspired by the US antiabortion movement, Russian legislators sought waiting periods before receiving an abortion; compulsory listening to the fetal heartbeat, viewing of ultrasound images, and counselling against abortion; prohibition of second-trimester abortion except for pregnancies due to rape; and requirements for women to sign consent forms indicating they are aware of "the negative consequences of abortion for women's health, including the risk of infertility" and the husband's written permission for abortion.[8] Moreover, physicians would be able to refuse to provide abortions through conscientious objection.[9]

To oppose these drastic proposals, an online petition drive launched by a coalition between the RAPD and grassroots feminist groups advocated "Fight Abortion, Not Women" (*borot'sia s abortami, a ne s zhenshchinami*). The petition insisted women should be able to "choose motherhood freely" (*za svobodnoe materinstvo*), while its URL highlighted the authors' stance "against abortion" (*protivabortov*). The site featured a metal coat hanger superimposed upon a woman's stomach—an image rooted in US abortion-rights struggles—with a verbatim (and thus non-native sounding) Russian translation of the English-language phrase "This should never again be used as a surgical instrument. We won't go back to the past!" This campaign thus joined symbols of the US reproductive rights movement and calls to address women's interests, on the one hand, with specifically Russian sensibilities regarding abortion as a problem needing to be "combatted" and an implicit invitation to the Russian state to do so, on the other.

This campaign was the first grassroots, public opposition to proposed abortion restrictions as a matter of women's interests in Russia ever. A momentous development, it emerged amid vibrant political and social denunciations of abortion. Presidents Putin, Medvedev, and the Russian Orthodox Church had earlier found common ground in publicly opposing abortion as key to the revitalization of both Orthodox morality and national demographics. The Ministry of Health issued administrative orders in 2003 and 2007 restricting second trimester abortions; in 2009, Svetlana Medvedev (wife of then president Dmitry Medvedev) established an annual "week of silence" during which abortions would be prohibited. Street level activism and online antiabortion messaging were commonplace.[10] Although some feminist activism was developing in cities around Russia, no civic opposition to these moves took place—a silence that was not surprising when seen in historical perspective.[11] As we have seen, decades of moral panic over the nation's "dying out," and both official and unofficial discourses loaded abortion with implications of selfish destruction. Moreover, young Russians considered abortion as a Soviet-era barbarism. Although physicians warned that restrictions would lead to illegal and unsafe procedures, as occurred during Stalinism, the overall antipathy toward abortion made generating activist enthusiasm in support of abortion rights especially challenging.

Indeed, pervasive discourses celebrating nationalism and family values made it difficult to legitimate the very notion that women have interests apart from the Russian nation and their family. Widespread arguments called for reviving Russia's traditional values, that is, patriarchal gender norms, both to overcome the consequences of Soviet women's "emancipation" and ostensibly to protect against Western feminism, portrayed as an ideology of hateful women who reject men and family life.[12] Conservatives proposed numerous creative interventions to incentivize women to give birth instead of having abortions: one parliamentarian proposed creating a database of men who have divorced because of their infertility, enabling those of them who are willing to marry single pregnant women; and he urged supporting research into the transplantation of embryos from pregnant women who do not want the pregnancy to women who want to get pregnant.[13] Putin's administration agreed that addressing low fertility required supporting families, and in 2006 established the "maternity capital" entitlement, financial support equivalent to $10,000 as an incentive for mothers to have a second or third child.[14]

Simultaneously, as the global LGBTQ rights movement blossomed, Russia's Orthodox Church aggressively tied heteronormative sexuality to patriotism.[15] Russian conservatives increasingly harnessed hostilities against feminism, abortion, and LGBTQ rights for political gain; the marked rise of authoritarianism at the start of Putin's third term became justified in part as necessary to protect Russia's "traditional values" from the supposed antifamily ideology of the West.[16] When widespread citizen protests erupted in 2011 through 2013 against irregularities in parliamentary and presidential elections, the state imprisoned hundreds. Then came the 2012 performance protest of the all-women's group Pussy Riot in Moscow's Cathedral of Christ the Savior, which called for God to depose Putin.[17] Pussy Riot members were sentenced to two years in a penal colony for "hooliganism motivated by religious hatred." In summer 2013, Putin signed laws against offending religious believers and prohibiting the "propaganda of nontraditional sexual relations" among minors.[18]

And in 2014, Russia annexed Crimea and began a war with Ukraine, inciting more nationalist vitriol. These events spurred the establishment of civic organizations such as the Sorok sorokov (Forty Forties), "a public movement consisting of Orthodox Christians, but open to anyone who wishes to defend their country and its traditional spiritual-moral values."[19]

With Russian politicians, Church leaders, and civic groups endorsing abortion restrictions and using US antiabortion strategies as templates, activism to preserve abortion access took courage and ingenuity. A coalition between the Russian Association of Population and Development and grassroots feminists, dubbing themselves the Rowan Berry Bunch coalition, issued a petition and organized street protests in 2011.[20] In 2015, they undertook more street protests and creative performance art to defend abortion access again, in opposition to another set of proposed restrictions.[21] I conducted in-depth interviews and email correspondences with leaders of the coalition and analyzed their YouTube campaign, #pravonaabort (right to abortion), which includes 132 short video statements submitted by Russians throughout the country expressing their opposition to restrictions. By analyzing the meanings of abortion, gender, and state-citizen relations shaping this activism, this chapter examines what the emergence of feminist reproductive politics looked like, and what kinds of transformations it reflected in Russian society.

More specifically, given the cultural antipathy toward abortion, this activism required conceptual innovations that also resonated with local values. What inspired this new feminist claims-making, and what kinds of feminism did it enact? While family planning activists had invoked the value of a relational self—as when Popov, Grebesheva, and others at the RAFP linked contraceptive habits to ensuring children would be wanted—could *abortion* be defended for its ability to strengthen relationships and nurturance? Or did activists defend abortion by insisting on women's autonomous selfhood—and if so, how did they culturally legitimate that kind of subject? What were the outcomes of their efforts?

As we will see, activists for abortion access made both kinds of arguments. In 2015, they reiterated the "Fight Abortion, Not Women" slogan and also made explicitly pro-choice claims for "the right to abortion" and "my body—my business." The seemingly paradoxical combination of slogans to "fight abortion" and ensure women's "right to abortion" reflected their insights about the numerous challenges women faced. Implicit in "Fight Abortion, Not Women," was the argument that reducing abortions—a worthy goal—requires providing contraceptives. In their 2015 performance protests, activists elaborated on the argument that restricting abortion harms women. They explained what it meant to consider childbearing without a firm social safety net or reliable partner; some spoke of their longing to experience motherhood—but only if they could do so in decent conditions. Through these statements, activists argued that women's labor in reproducing the next generation—a contribution to families and society—obliges fathers and the state to provide financial support and assistance. And yet, they reminded, such support is rarely forthcoming. By highlighting a widely shared understanding of mutual expectations and values about reciprocity, a moral economy, advocates claimed that abortion access was necessary because the state and men were failing in their obligations.[22] They echoed state leaders themselves on the importance of family life.

Simultaneously, feminists also increasingly asserted liberal claims to personal autonomy and rights. Some defended self-realization outside family formation. Activism to preserve abortion access thus became a venue for explaining personal aspirations and making political claims—for articulating new connections between the state's responsibilities to citizens, and its citizens' rights as individuals. In the process, activists revealed how neoliberal conditions had changed Russians' ideals and goals for life. They recognized that reproductive autonomy was necessary to pursue personal economic well-being as well as to be a caring parent. Control over reproduction was key to a new and necessary life orientation where the state provided minimal support—planning one's future.

"Fight Abortion, Not Women": The 2011 Formative Campaign

When I interviewed Dr. Erofeeva in 2013, she acknowledged that the slogan "Fight Abortion, Not Women" did not emphasize women's rights and agreed that the implied welcome of state intervention into women's reproductive decisions could be problematic. But the coalition needed salient messaging they could agree on and so disrupting the Soviet-era image of abortion as normal remained a key theme. Erofeeva captured the coalition's main messaging as articulated in the symbol it adopted of the rowan berry bunch, and described its meaning on their website:

> In Russia the rowan has been a symbol of the family and the prosperity of the domestic hearth, a protection against the evil eye and unclean spirit forces. For our coalition, the rowan symbolizes: Cohesion as bunches of berries, because only unified efforts can achieve social change; the woman, who was traditionally associated with rowan in Russia. Independent, mature woman, who cares about her family and wants to make her own decisions about her own life. The family, which is the key to prosperity in life and the health of the society. The blood-red berries of the rowan bunch also symbolize the memory of women who were killed, who became the victims of criminal abortion. One of the goals of our coalition is not to allow a return to the frightening page of our history when there was such a high level of criminal abortions.[23]

This statement frames women as focused on caring for their families while mentioning their need for independence; it is not primarily an argument for freedom of choice over how to live one's life, including deciding not to become a mother at all. It casts restrictions to abortion access as a threat to families' prosperity by putting women at risk of death through unsafe abortion.

Activists connected with the Coalition of the Rowan Berry Bunch undertook street protests (later uploading photographs of these protests online), arguing "A Child Must Be Wanted." This communicated two arguments: that forcing women to bear children against their will is wrong, and that conception should be allowed to happen in a timely manner through contraceptive use. Another of the activists' slogans, "We're Against Abortion" (*#protivabortov*), highlighted that support for legal and accessible abortion does not necessarily mean approving of abortion. It can entail viewing abortion as a necessary evil rather than a neutral personal choice, the least bad among bad decisions.

The slogan "Fight Abortion, Not Women" differed significantly from reproductive rights arguments that assume a private sphere insulated from state interference; it brought into relief that reproduction entails citizenship obligations between the state and families as well as intimate obligations between men and women, parents and children. And it acknowledged the fact that these obligations of caregiving are enmeshed in profound uncertainty, very often going unfulfilled. This advocacy thus envisioned a different approach to state support, one that acknowledges the importance of women's desires and the quality of the mother-child relationship in reproductive decisions. It recognized that in conditions of women's and children's economic and social abandonment, an ethical decision can involve terminating a pregnancy. In stating "we're against abortions" and using the phrase *"protiv abortov"* (against abortions) in their URL, Russian feminists construed abortion as a morally undesirable act undertaken in morally compromised situations. They cast the state as a necessary participant in a moral economy of reproductive decision making, including by ensuring abortions remained freely available and safely provided.

This initial organizing effort revealed both the vast support for antiabortion policies among Russian governing leaders and the persistent need to seek allies for effectively preventing their success.[24] Erofeeva recounted the overwhelming urgency that ensued when Parliament member (deputy) Elena Borisovna Mizulina held a press conference announcing her draft law "On the protection of life of unborn children." It was June 1, the Day of Protecting Children. Although this bill hadn't yet been registered in the Duma, another, similar bill was registered by United Russia's deputy Valerii Draganov, who was working separately from Mizulina.[25] Erofeeva explained, "It turned out several priests in Mizulina's working group thought she was moving too slow in not yet registering the bill; they went to Draganov, another ally of the ROC. So he became the initiator of bill." As noted above, this bill proposed numerous restrictions: requiring the husband's written permission for married women and parental permission for minors; requiring consent forms stating the woman understands "the negative consequences of abortion for women's health, including the risk of infertility," and "possible negative consequences of prenatal diagnostic procedures for woman's and baby's health"; prohibiting second trimester abortion for any "social reason" except rape; ending insurance coverage for abortion; and establishing waiting periods, mandatory counseling, and the right of doctors to conscientious objection. Erofeeva initially thought it would take time before the bill came up for a vote, as there are numerous rounds of review, but the conservative parliamentarians were savvy and in a rush: "In 2010, the Ministry of Health Protection signed an agreement with the ROC. At first we thought this was about returning chapels that had been on hospital premises to the Church. But actually, the number one issue was restricting abortion." Mizulina added her proposed restrictions to another bill that had already proceeded through several reviews, "On the basis of protecting the health of the population of the Russian Federation."²⁶

Calling it "an undeclared war," Erofeeva and her partners undertook a nerve-racking period of frenetic, around-the-clock activism to oppose it:

> [Parliament's] work on the bill advanced like a locomotive, without much at-tention to details and all behind closed doors. It was such a difficult time. We had July, August, and the beginning of September, two and a half months un-til the first reading. Everyone was away on summer vacation. The deputies weren't around, they only return from summer vacations the first week of Sep-tember. It was awful, really. But we bit the bullet—we realized this was now or never—they were trying to pass so many restrictions. It was a terrible time, a nightmare. Sleepless nights.

Erofeeva described spending enormous effort seeking financial and tactical support. The coalition formed between the RAPD and grassroots feminists included representatives of the forty-three local branches of the RAPD, vol-unteers who advocated to their regional governments. The Russian Society of Obstetricians-Gynecologists and the Society for Children's and Teenagers' Gynecologists joined the coalition. "But the [Scientific Research] Center for Obstetrics and Gynecology did not support us, did not oppose this legisla-tion; apparently they didn't feel it threatened women's rights."

The refusal of Russia's leading clinical-research institute on ob-gyn to oppose the bill was galling, yet they were not the only ones who rejected Ero-feeva's request for endorsement. Global institutions were also unreliable:

> We wrote [numerous] requests to the special representative for women's is-sues at the Organization of United Nations. But unfortunately, we didn't re-ceive any reply. And the most insulting, we didn't get anything from the WHO. They were in negotiations over Russia's contributions to the WHO, and money determines everything. They started to explain to us, "Well, you're a societal organization, if a scientific research institute had written to WHO—but we're an intergovernmental structure." That is, civil society asks the professional UN community, the WHO, to help argue and they won't get involved in any-thing. It's terrible. Shameful.

Some private foundations, by contrast, provided support. While RAPD's general financing came only from the International Planned Parenthood Federation (IPPF), the coalition's 2011 campaign received assistance from the Open Society Foundation to create their website.[27] This required extensive translations of international material into Russian, as virtually no literature defending abortion access previously existed. The global abortion rights organization Ipas gave them the right to publish the brochure "The Evidence Speaks for Itself: Ten Facts about Abortion," which the coalition gave to Russian lawmakers to provide them with basic information.[28] Erofeeva also appreciated the valuable strategic support received from the Center for Reproductive Rights in New York and Stockholm. "We spoke with them by Skype almost daily. They offered very professional assistance, since they knew how things had been in Slovakia, Hungary, and Romania. [Antiabortion campaigns] all use the same clichés, scenarios. And they helped us present argumentation, the international data, juridical bases; they helped a lot."

Erofeeva described "bombarding" Russian lawmakers with letters, commentaries, and evidence from international experiences about the consequences of restrictions on abortion. "We contacted the committee for Health Protection and those parliamentary deputies with whom we had some relationship. Of course, we tried to reach those who'd support us. There were very few—you could count them on your fingers. Reasonable people, experienced people, professional doctors who could raise their voice in opposition."

They highlighted the negative medical consequences of long waiting periods:

> We explained that during early weeks of gestation, you can't wait two weeks because then a woman won't be able to have a [less invasive] medical abortion or vacuum aspiration. And also in the eleventh week you can't have a long waiting period because then she won't be able to get it at all. So the waiting period we have is unlike anywhere in the world: from four to eight weeks gestation, the waiting period is forty-eight hours; from eight to eleven weeks, seven days; from eleven to twelve weeks, again forty-eight hours.

When the law passed in November 2011, Erofeeva expressed relief that only conscious objection and waiting periods were adopted, far fewer restrictions than had been proposed. Yet soon thereafter, Minzdrav issued administrative orders banning abortion advertisements by private clinics; any other abortion advertisements were now required to also state the procedure's possible risks.²⁹ And more restrictions would soon be established.

The RAPD-grassroots coalition's strategy of emphasizing women's maternal commitments and their "opposition" to abortion made sense given that many women's activists who politically supported family planning and legal abortion—such as Ekaterina Lakhova—did not express a *feminist* view of reproductive rights.³⁰ Many of these leaders served as directors of the RAFP/RAPD's regional branches. Yet Erofeeva noted that these same activists sometimes revealed they did not fully understand or endorse family planning's holistic approach to women's autonomy. "They think, 'Well, abortion's bad. It's better if we talk [women] out of abortion.'" In frustration, Erofeeva told me how she tried to disabuse these activists:

> People! She's made this decision herself! She's not some stupid little woman, she's super-responsible! She may have a traumatic family situation. [The man] may be an alcoholic, or mentally ill. . . . She'll come and ask for an abortion "on request" without stating this actual reason. And what are you doing—why are you interfering in a person's personal life? What right do you have? [*shto vy delaete, vy pochemu v lichnuiu zhizn' cheloveka vmeshivaetes', kakoe vy pravo imeete?*]

While in 2011 the coalition was divided among those who preferred the "Fight Abortion, Not Women" slogan and those who favored calls for "free motherhood" and "the right to abortion," the next round of protests saw many more activists sharing Erofeeva's explicitly feminist approach. Simultaneously, the push for abortion restrictions expanded.

Joining Calls for State Support with Claims for Women's Autonomy

In 2015 conservatives proposed eliminating public payment for abortion and criminalizing the procedure altogether. One of the grassroots feminist leaders, a St. Petersburg artist I call Rita, was thirty-three years old when I interviewed her in 2015.³¹ She had been an activist for four years and described what inspired her emerging critical perspective: "At first I thought everything in Russia was really good, because finally, I was getting a salary on which I could buy myself clothes and even go to a resort somewhere for vacation. Things hadn't been so good for a long time and therefore, I figured, everything in the country was probably all going well."

"You remember the 1990s as a very difficult time?" I asked.

Yes, yes. My mother was single, raising two kids alone here in Piter, and of course we were very poor. And I have a small salary as a government worker, but I can earn some extra money on the side and now I practically don't hold back from things I want: I don't think about how much such an item of food costs and I can go buy something at the cosmetics store, I can buy my friends nice gifts. But then, a lot of political murders were happening: Politkovskaya, Estemirova, Magnitsky, Litvinenko, I think he was murdered abroad, and so it was clear that something was not right.[32] And then . . . a bill was proposed to decrease education financing. It required state institutions such as hospitals, schools, theaters, libraries, even hospices, to become partially self-sustaining.[33] So we understood that . . . in kindergartens and schools there are lessons you'd have to pay for. And I've heard conversations with some moms who say, "Well, we wouldn't choose to sign them up for paid lessons, but they take those kids whose parents have paid, and then ours begin to cry, they also want to go, say, to dancing or drawing class. So we have to find another two or three thousand [rubles]." It's really hard on people, salaries are very low, and this pressures them. It's also happening in medicine.

Mobilized by these events, Rita joined protests against Putin's re-election in 2012, asserting it was "entirely falsified," and then demonstrated in support of Pussy Riot. She was inspired by feminism soon thereafter, encountering activists with the domestic violence crisis center and the Russian production of the *Vagina Monologues*.[34] And she saw St. Petersburg's feminist community grow: "On May 1, 2013, three feminists came out with purple flags. And then last year on May 1, a group of feminists came out, and on March 8 [International Women's Day], about 100 to 150 people came." Rita's story reflects significant shifts underway among many young people in Russian cities: having become active internet and social media users, their popular culture was globalized, and some were increasingly interested in feminist thinking, LGBTQ rights, and human rights.[35]

Globalization also promoted the importance of seeing oneself as an individualized self. Ideas from global therapeutic culture recruited people to undertake self-help and personal improvement as a means to a rewarding life and satisfying relations.[36] A core goal expressed in Russian therapeutic culture was the value of becoming a "master of the self" (*khoziain/khoziaika*)—relying on the self alone and being skeptical of institutions.[37] Nonetheless, self-help also paradoxically remained gendered, often teaching women to improve themselves by cultivating their femininity and caring for their relationships with others.[38] The spread of consumerism has also impacted Russians' notions of personhood. The goal of earning profit has spurred salespeople, service providers, and professionals to become reflexive about how they treat "customers" or "clients" (which, unlike "patients," implies some status and entitlement). Individualistic and utilitarian goals are emerging in the cultural scripts about the sexual self increasingly common among Russian women raised since the 1990s. These express a willingness to take initiative and responsibility in sexual relationships, to seek pleasure, and to view sex instrumentally as an exchange.[39] Indeed, in contrast to the Euro-American "sexual revolution" of the late 1960s, when sexual freedoms were tied to political action and collective solidarities, the individualized, sexualized self culturally prevalent in neoliberal Russia was largely depoliticized.[40]

But not entirely so. In early 2015, Rita and her friends saw that conservative proposals to limit abortion access were yet another weapon in the country's ongoing conservative turn and named it as a form of gendered oppression. "We analyzed it historically: Beginning with Ancient Rome, whenever imperial conquests intensified, abortion became criminalized. It happened under Napoleon, Hitler, Ceausescu, and here you go, now [they're trying it]."

Under the rubric of the informal grassroots group Left-Fem, Rita and her friends devised performance protests in downtown St. Petersburg as a collective political action. Women and men posed with signs and props enacting and explaining their opposition to the proposed policies and posted the scenes on social media.[41] Additionally, they organized a video campaign on YouTube with people explaining why they support women's right to abortion (*#pravonaabort*).[42]

The performance protests and videos reveal two overarching logics about why abortion should be available: a socialist-inspired argument that the state has failed to establish the conditions necessary for raising children, and a liberal political argument highlighting women's right to choice and bodily autonomy. Whereas in 2011 the defense of abortion access explicitly deplored abortion and affirmed views of women as nurturers and caregivers, discourses of personal choice and freedom were more prominent in the 2015 grassroots actions. Yet they did not displace socialist logics. Hybrid combinations of socialist, liberal, neoliberal, and related ideologies abound in contemporary Russia.[43] In the following sections I present examples of the video statements and street performances that exemplify the socialist, liberal, and hybrid arguments with an eye to understanding how these statements reflected Russian feminists' shifting sense of gendered struggles for justice. I find it significant that even when arguing for bodily autonomy, feminists did not entirely reject state involvement in family life as a correlate of their autonomy claims; rather, the majority embedded the right to abortion within broader presumptions about the mutual obligations between state and society, between women and men, and between parents and children— the moral economies of government and family life. In other words, many evolving approaches to Russian feminist claims-making built on the moral economy of care rooted in socialist ideals and tied their justifications for bodily autonomy to problems arising from the state's and men's neglecting these obligations. Individual rights and reproductive autonomy arguments gained legitimacy as the campaigns for restricting abortion strengthened and Russia's moral economy of state-citizen reciprocity unraveled.

Relational Personhood, Individual Autonomy, and Ruptures in the Moral Economy of Reproduction

In video no. 46, a middle-aged woman argued,

> I believe that before banning something, for any prohibition is a sign that the government isn't able to influence the issue with any other means, before prohibiting, the government must guarantee a mother and her child a decent human life. It should guarantee the parents work, or at least the father, if the mother is staying home with the child; should guarantee accessible, free, and worthy health care; should guarantee education; should guarantee well-functioning pre-school programs, and only after all this can the question even be posed about intervening in personal life and in the planning of the future family and of any person's future.[44]

Notably, this logic leaves open the hypothetical possibility that, given an ideal economic situation, it could be ethical for the state to restrict abortion.

Grassroots activists' performance art protests reiterated the irony of criminalizing abortion when the state and men routinely betray their responsibilities for supporting children. In the photo in Figure 6.1, the image of an abandoned, impoverished mother supporting many children alone starkly

FIGURE 6.1. Left-Fem protest, St. Petersburg, 2015. "70 percent of women getting abortions are mothers / 80 percent of fathers do not provide for their children / 50 roubles per month [$1.35] the welfare payment for a child from 1½ years old–5 years old. Abortion is murder—life is hell." Photo by Maria Rakhmaninova.

contrasts with the romanticized imagery of large families that pronatalists celebrate as reviving traditional values and spiritual well-being.

These examples exemplify the socialist-inspired logic: the state is held responsible for providing basic conditions of welfare for families. Having failed in this obligation, the state is to blame for abortion by providing ordinary people with no choice but to commit regrettable acts.

In a less common socialist logic, some advocates invoked Marxist ideology as a bulwark against the Russian Orthodox Church's power. Video statement no. 61 says:

We are now confronting a full-on attack on the secular principles of our society[45] . . . and for me as a union member, and as a Marxist and as a worker, simply for the worker's struggle for the secular principles of our government, the struggle for women's opportunity to have control over their own body, their future, independent of any strange men in cassocks, bearded people who consider themselves entitled to decide our fate for us, for me, this struggle is a very important one.[46]

The diverse ideas inspired by socialism underscore that there is no essential core of a socialist logic justifying abortion access and no absolute boundary between socialist and liberal approaches to reproductive rights: both share the Western heritage of the Enlightenment. Yet significant distinctions between the orientations of these frameworks are evident. "Socialist" statements highlighted structural conflicts and contradictions that justify women's access to abortion. The statement by a self-described Marxist exposed the conflict between a secular social order and a religious regime that underlies the politics of abortion. More frequently, socialist-inspired statements called on the state to fulfill its obligations to citizens for ensuring a minimal degree of economic well-being. In these ways the socialist-inspired logics understand persons as embedded in broader socioeconomic systems, and they conceptualize personhood as relational.

In contrast, a few videos justified abortion through the rhetoric of choice and spoke to issues of privacy. Video no. 101 exemplifies this liberal framing:

I'm not in favor of abortion, but choice, choice. It's the personal business of every person and no one has the right to instruct a woman what she should choose and how she should use her own body, and even more so men, who will never in their lives be able to give birth physiologically. So that's why I am in favor of the right to abortion.[47]

Here we see a vision of individual autonomy conceptualized in the form of "personal business" that as such deserves protection from others' influence. This is an implicit understanding of a private sphere, quite distinct from an argument that calls on the state to support families' needs. While some advocates deployed either a socialist or liberal logic of justification, the most elaborated statements brought them together in creative, hybrid logics that joined concerns about the uncertainties of support with women's need for bodily autonomy. Reminding listeners that parenting first and foremost entails obligations, advocates insisted that women must have the autonomy to decide whether or not to accept these obligations. For example, many who noted that women alone carry the burden of childrearing concluded that women should therefore not feel obligated to give birth but instead be able to do so only voluntarily, as in video no. 108: "Women should have the inalienable right to autonomously decide on how they will use their own

FIGURE 6.2. Left-Fem Protest, St. Petersburg, 2015. "These are the wet stockings that a destitute mother used for beating her unwanted child, A. Chikatilo [a serial killer], who was born during Soviet abortion ban. 56 people became his victims. Prohibit abortion / preserve life." Photo by Maria Rakhmaninova.

FIGURE 6.3. Left-Fem protest against a proposed abortion ban and the war in Ukraine, in St. Petersburg, 2015. "Save an embryo, give birth to a soldier. Abortion is murder, war is sacred." Photo by Maria Rakhmaninova.

body. Pregnancy is reproductive labor. To undertake it through conscription [*povinnost'iu*], as a slave, as a debt to society, as a service to one's partner or spouse, is absolutely unethical and absolutely wrong. Every woman must have the right to abortion."[48]

In this quote the advocate identified a range of possible relational forms through which a woman can end up mothering—equating anything besides free decision making to be wrong, akin to slavery. Similarly, the next advocate insisted that women do not owe it to anyone to reproduce, not their own parents nor society, figured here (video no. 50) as an abstract and irrelevant concept:

There is a responsibility that parents need to take on, and that a woman, first and foremost, needs to have the opportunity to take on. This is the responsibility for a child that's been born[49] . . . Physiologically, women's uniqueness is based in the fact that she can bear children. That doesn't mean, not in any way, that she must. She doesn't owe anyone anything—not her parents, not her partner, her husband, not some "society." But the fact that she can bear children leads to an oppressive norm that she "should." Under no conditions should men in the governmental parliament or in everyday life situations make this decision for women. It is solely her individual right.[50]

Parenthood is a responsibility to the child, and therefore women should have full decision-making autonomy about reproduction. Video statement no. 104 provided an elaborated vision of this logic and concluded that women's sense of contentment and happiness should be defined individually, not on the basis of cultural images of essential womanhood:

In a situation where the social infrastructure is inadequate, as in our post-Soviet space, women's reproductive capacity gets transformed from her strength, her iron raison-d'être, into her vulnerability. Unfortunately, our society treats us in an irresponsible manner, since it doesn't provide any universal, available resources to support women's independence after giving birth. Women often end up in the grip of necessity, and one way or another they are forced to be subordinate to those who give them the means to survive while caring for the child. And rather than provide mechanisms for preserving women's independence, society first frees itself from this responsibility, and then considers woman's rejection of an unplanned pregnancy to be its own [society's] loss. As a matter of fact, the prohibition of abortion is violence against women by society.

In addition to discussing women's personhood, advocates argued that a child has needs that must be met for him or her to acquire social personhood and not become a danger to society. This requires relationships; being alive—life itself—is not sufficient to be a person in the full social sense of the concept. A child must be needed by specific others to become a full, moral member of society.[51] As video no. 49 asserted, the competitive organization of neoliberal society makes the need for socially connected relationships even greater, and disaster looms if these relationships are not formed:

Who do these legislative proposals, these abortion bans really hit? The most unprotected strata of society, those women who don't have money for an abortion. Why then do you think that she'll have money for a child? In such cases, you ought to think about it, you prosperous, happy, satisfied men who lobby for these laws louder than everyone—for it is those children that are going to compete with your cared for, loved, cultivated children—they are angry children, sure of the fact that they ruined their own mothers' lives and that no one loves them. Are you really not afraid of this?

This image of a society divided into wanted and unwanted children, those who have been raised in loving homes and those who have grown up knowing they were not loved, was also expressed in a performance art protest in St. Petersburg on February 1, 2015. In the poster in Figure 6.2, the advocate asserted that an infamous Russian serial killer was an unwanted child born during the abortion ban who endured violence from his destitute mother.[52]

The poster's ironic conclusion, "Prohibit Abortion, Preserve Life," underscored the absurdity of forcing women to bear unwanted children as a means of protecting life, inasmuch as unloved and unwanted children are at risk of growing up to become brutally violent killers, taking the lives of others.

In other statements we see a new form of subjectivity shaped by neoliberal conditions: autonomous and reflexive decision making is necessary to become a mother capable of caring because women also have their own aspirations to fulfill; they have obligations to themselves (video no. 16):

> Depriving women of the right to abortion is equal to murdering her as a fullfledged mother. As a rule, when a woman decides to have an abortion, she has serious reasons for this. She understands that she can't be a complete mother for this child, she can't provide for him economically, she will be dead as a mother for him emotionally or psychologically. To say that the man can take part of the obligations for raising this child on himself is meaningless, because we know that the majority of the obligations lie on women's shoulders. If I was to get pregnant now, I'd have to have an abortion. Because to give birth would mean to reject my own interests, to reject my professional aspirations, to refuse to have a career. It's possible that it would mean complete loneliness. And I wouldn't be able to be the full-fledged mother whom I'd like to sometime become. I don't want to be a dead mother, and therefore, I'm in favor of women's right to abortion.[53]

In stating, "I don't want to be a dead mother," this advocate metaphorically conjured up an image of a mother who has buried her own ambitions. Autonomous decision making is essential for pursuing the ideals of relational personhood, a relationship in which a mother wants and needs her child while also fulfilling her obligations to herself. While certainly compatible with liberal concepts of autonomy and choice, this statement presented an elaborated vision of the kind of person making reproductive decisions: not an isolated individual calculating solely according to personal interests but a person in relation to herself and others, embedded in obligations of care.[54] She makes reproductive decisions having recognized these obligations and having considered the uncertain support of others (men, the state, even other kin) in helping her fulfill them. Autonomy is thus wedded with relational notions of personhood, inspired by an ethic of reciprocity that a woman, as a self-reflective and self-caring subject, holds as she considers embarking on the obligations of motherhood.

"Abortion Is Murder—War Is Sacred": Highlighting State Hypocrisy

Among the performance protests that took place in Moscow and St. Petersburg February 1, 2015, two stand out for their ironic, biting critiques of state hypocrisy by juxtaposing its supposed concern for the unborn with its militarism and violence. In one photo (fig. 6.3), a man sits on his knees on the ground, with his legs tucked under him, portraying a double amputee.[55] He holds a sign stating "Save an Embryo—Give Birth to a Soldier. Abortion is Murder—War is Sacred."

Following Russia's invasion of the Donbas and annexation of Crimea in March 2014, Russians committed to human rights and international law spoke out against these illegal actions. In this performance protest, activists critiqued the state's cynical pretense of caring about families while launching violent war. The protest sign identified the state's goal in restricting abortion as increasing fertility to ensure future military prowess, not the protection of "life." In light of the state's and Church's treatment of the war in Ukraine as a religious war, their claim that "abortion is murder" appeared wholly opportunistic.[56]

Another biting critique reminded viewers of the horrible consequences of Stalin's ban on abortion. The performance sign shown in Figure 6.4 reads, "After the Ban on Abortion in the Soviet Union, Thousands of Women Were Killed by Criminal Abortions, but Fertility Did Not Rise. Will We Do This Again? (*Povtorim?*)"

At first glance, this statement appeared to be a straightforward cautionary tale about not repeating a grim policy decision from Soviet history.

FIGURE 6.4. Left-Fem protest, St. Petersburg, 2015. "Will we do this again?" Photo by Maria Rakhmaninova.

FIGURE 6.5. Rowan Berry Bunch Coalition protest, Moscow, 2015. "My Body – My Business." Photo courtesy of Lyubov Erofeeva.

Yet at the time of this protest in February 2015, the slogan "We will do it again" (*Povtorim*) was being used by Russian nationalists to hail the ongoing military invasion of Ukraine. To justify this war, Putin depicted Ukraine's Maidan revolution as the work of "fascists"—the term associated with the Nazis in World War II. A provocative image circulating in 2015 compared Russia's impending triumph in the current war against Ukrainian fascists to the Soviet state's victory over the Nazis, claiming, "We can do it again."[57]

The image consisted of two stick figures whose heads were replaced with the symbols of the USSR (hammer and sickle) and Nazi Germany (swastika), respectively. The hammer and sickle figure was leaning over the back of the swastika figure, suggesting anal penetration. This image trades in homophobia to demean the prostrate loser; the slogan "we can do it again" asserts that the Russian army will visit the same fate upon contemporary Ukraine. By appropriating the phrase "we will do it again" for her own purposes, this feminist activist thus communicates another layer of meaning about revisiting the past—this time, regarding a possible abortion ban. By enacting the suffering of a woman bleeding to death from a criminal abortion (notably, undertaken with a clothes hanger), she recasts the nationalistic and violent meme as a question about repeating a bad decision—"Will we do it again?" In so doing, she exposes the state's bad faith in its goals to both restrict abortion and wage war, implying that the idea of repeating the past should be doubted, not applauded.

Another performance art protest by a Petersburg feminist group in February 2019 condemned both abortion restrictions and military conscription. Wearing camouflage and gas masks, the protestors held bundles wrapped to look like newborns and tied with the St. George ribbon, sign of support for Russia's military. Inside the bundles were pieces of raw meat, and above the protesters hangs a banner, "Give birth to meat," making the claim that the state's pronatalism is directly related to militarism, whose soldiers are treated as "cannon fodder."[58]

In Place of a Conclusion

Culturally, these campaigns reveal that significant changes have occurred in what is possible to think about reproductive politics, personhood, and state-citizen relations in Russia. The political-economic and social realities of market society have made the idea of reproductive autonomy meaningful in ways it had not been in the Soviet and early post-Soviet eras. Therapeutic

FIGURE 6.6. Vandalism at Russian Association of Population and Development, an accusation of being a "foreign agent." Photo courtesy of Lyubov Erofeeva.

and consumer cultures, combined with the lack of support from the state and often by individual men, had led women to become increasingly reflexive about their sense of self and relational obligations.[59] They saw reproductive decision making, like proactive and responsible sexuality, as necessary for enjoying and managing their lives.[60] This involved using contraceptives to plan pregnancies when possible and assessing their own psychological, emotional, economic, and social ability to provide a child what it needs and deserves before becoming a parent. In this light, they recognized abortion as a moral decision when undertaken on the basis of one's ethical obligations to existing relationships—to one's (potential or existing) child(ren) as well as to oneself.[61]

I emphasize that activism to preserve abortion access developed organically from the constraints of people's lives and concerns, not from abstract liberal ideologies imported from abroad.[62] Liberal concepts of individual rights and autonomy became salient among Russian activists when they offered a meaningful tool for confronting the political-economic and social dilemmas issued by a tattered state welfare system. When bills arose to criminalize abortion and/or end its public financing, these activists responded with critiques of their society's dismantled moral economy. They exposed the stark hypocrisies of the state and individual men who would limit women's reproductive rights while neglecting to fulfill their own responsibilities to families. This strategy brilliantly underscored long-standing values about reciprocal responsibilities and revealed how the collapse of this moral economy was leading women to embrace autonomous selfhood. Liberal principles of bodily autonomy were not replacing relational selves; they were invoked to ensure women could still realize relational selfhood amid continuing economic precarity and increasingly authoritarian governance.[63]

Despite this creative and courageous activism, defenders of abortion rights are a small group of isolated activists. When in 2016 Erofeeva described her dashed hopes for strong relations with the West, she had witnessed support from Western organizations come and go, become a necessity and a liability. WHO and UNFPA refused to support the coalition's opposition to abortion restrictions; the IPPF ceased funding the RAPD in 2014, and then, in 2015, the Russian state labeled the RAPD a foreign agent (a particularly ironic event, since it was no longer receiving global financial support). Domestically stigmatized, internationally abandoned, the organization could not function, and gradually reduced its activities almost completely. Facing the virulent influence of Russian antiabortion adherents, even in the Ministry of Health, Erofeeva was deeply pessimistic about the future.

Liberal Aspirations and Neoliberal Realities

Soviet and Russian efforts to replace a culture of routine abortion with habits of contraception provide insights into more than a series of public health campaigns to overcome deficits of supplies and knowledge. As this book has shown, such projects initially strove, over the course of the late Soviet era, to realize the potentials of the social hygiene regime. From the time abortion was (re-)legalized in 1955 through Glasnost, contraceptive advocates responded to the tensions between social hygiene's approach to providing the material necessities for healthy living and pronatalist goals of promoting higher fertility. We traced how different experts responded to the state's continual failures to increase contraceptive supplies. While most reoriented their strategies of advocating for contraceptives to focus on persuading women against terminations, one particularly creative and committed researcher, Andrej Popov, pushed for a series of innovative approaches. Popov designed a new model for determining contraceptive demand for the purpose of supply requisitions, helped write new recommendations for clinicians' contraceptive prescriptions, and designed new forms of health communication about preventing pregnancy. If the push for contraceptives reflected a relatively liberalizing orientation within social hygiene, Popov's visions heralded the emergence of a wholly distinct, liberal form of reproductive governance. It was a culturally particular liberalism, one calibrated to the specific needs of unmaking Russia's abortion culture. It emphasized both the rationalization of public policies and reproductive decisions for deliberate preventive practices, and the re-enchantment of relationships between experts and lay persons and between intimates for prioritizing care.

With the end of the Soviet system and arrival of market reforms, the bio-political regime of social hygiene would gradually be displaced by a liberal biopolitical regime—and the Russian experts who founded family planning institutions were among the most active agents of this transformation. The rise of family planning institutions reveals the new visions for policy mak-ing, modes of expertise, and intimate relationships that liberals aimed to implement in order to improve Russians' health. Theirs was a liberalism inspired by the humanism of the late Soviet era and the new opportuni-ties made available through global scientific relationships, and specifically, outreach and assistance from the global family planning apparatus. They strategically drew on the conceptual and institutional frameworks modeled by colleagues abroad to establish new modes of professional training and clinical services in Russia. While some expressed ambivalence towards the more radical aspects of feminism they perceived in the reproductive rights movement, Russian family planning supporters held fast to the value of ensuring women's control over their reproductive lives. If they emphasized goals of strengthening (heteronormative) families and the well-being of children, their overarching vision echoed that of Andrej Popov: they envi-sioned liberal biopolitical transformations that would rationalize policy and re-enchant relationships in the name of individual health and social and interpersonal care.

Understanding the distinctions between the social hygiene and liberal biopolitical regimes has required examining them at both ideological and practical levels. Ideologically, we have seen how social hygiene recognized the state's responsibility for establishing the material conditions for well-being. The state, however, determined what constituted society's needs for wellness, limiting both what could be advocated for and what would be provided. In the Soviet Union, the state continually invoked its univer-sal social welfare and health care systems as evidence that it provided for the population's needs. And despite the poor quality of health services— for instance, the lack of effective anesthesia during an abortion—citizens could not mobilize to charge the state for failing to live up to its promises. Simultaneously, the state held demands of citizens; socialist biopolitics pushed women to both increase their childbearing and participate fully in the labor force. When it became obvious that state planners were ignoring bureaucrats' requests for increased contraceptive supplies, health authori-ties relied on techniques of sanitary enlightenment to teach people how to behave properly. As a form of reproductive governance, then, social hygiene comprised a top down, unilateral determination of needs that lacked a feedback system for addressing the population's own perceived interests.

Ideologically, social hygiene did not rule out the provision of birth control, but the pill's impact on fertility was a source of concern that gave some health bureaucrats pause. More generally, Soviet planners did not prioritize any intimate consumer items, and contraceptives too faced continual deficits. Health information was also titrated: sanitary enlightenment involved didactic processes of communicating only what people "needed" to know, with heavy doses of political ideology, gender essentialism, and often scientific errors. With the dearth of effective contraceptives and lack of accurate information, socialist biopolitics made abortion into the most commonly used form of fertility control. The state described abortion's availability as a policy protecting women's health from illegal, unsafe procedures, but abortion experiences—with their lack of privacy, poor anesthesia, and disrespectful treatment—gave the lie to socialism's broader ideological conceits.

With the new openness of Glasnost and market reforms, family planning offered professionals a means of re-establishing their authority by aligning with global scientific standards. This was a paradigm that seemed poised to help solve problems widely recognized in Russia—fragile marriages, unwanted children, women's poor reproductive health from repeat abortions. Early advocates for family planning, therefore, focused on addressing such social wounds; they clearly affirmed that women should have ultimate say over their reproductive lives but did not celebrate family planning as helping realize individual autonomy. In the 1990s, I believe they would have heard in phrases such as "pro-choice" a rhetoric that sounded ideological and illusory (as they saw socialism), for the very idea of "individual autonomy" was then considered alien-- at best, a fantasy. In conditions of immense economic and social hardship, family planners maintained a concern with one fundamental value of social hygiene- the idea that the state held responsibility for establishing the conditions for the public's health, including prevention. They sought a middle ground between obligating the state and promoting individual responsibility for health. Similarly, while endorsing women's bodily self-determination, they were also committed to strengthening (heteronormative) family life and did not associate their services with voluntary childlessness. Proponents of family planning justified the new mode of clinical services and the intimate practices they promoted on the basis of the idea that "A person is born in order to be happy," and not to serve as an instrument for the state.[1] Still, they also strove to establish family planning as a significant means of reviving Russia's demographic future.

But the liberal humanistic aspirations family planners envisioned—the rationalization of policy and re-enchantment of relations—were overtaken by broader shocks from neoliberal capitalism, which subjected society to tremendous economic instability, a crumbling welfare system, and a deregulated media awash in porn and violence. Conservative political contenders saw catastrophic signs of national demise in rising mortality and plummeting fertility. Their Soviet-era concerns that women's equality had undermined men and thrown the family into crisis became inflamed. By the mid-1990s, Russian conservatives began discrediting family planning by portraying it as a threat to patriarchal and national revival. In making family planning a concrete target for broader ire, conservative political contenders found a means of channeling anti-Western sentiment and envisioning the ideal of national demographic sovereignty.

Supporters responded to the attacks against family planning in diverse ways. Regional family planning experts largely recast their goals as "pregnancy planning" and emphasized their contributions to family values; by contrast, the leadership of the Russian Association of Population and Development and the fledgling, grassroots groups of Russian feminist activists began more explicitly highlighting values of bodily autonomy. Without abandoning the value of state support for families, including contraceptive services, they also made explicit claims for bodily autonomy. The phrase, "pro-choice," and the Russian equivalent slogan, *moe telo-moe delo* (My body is my business) became meaningful concepts in Russians' vocabulary beginning in 2011, when threats to legal abortion access first appeared probable. In the years since, notions of bodily autonomy and reproductive choice have joined a host of globalized concepts reflecting progressive social and political visions of the world that are being taken up by people in Russia, including queer rights, disability rights, and therapeutic culture.[2] Still, progressive discussions about abortion continue to address the historically specific experiences of 'punitive gynecology,' framing the ethical questions about terminating pregnancies with the reminder that "Russia's abortion culture is steeped in blood, pain and contempt for women."[3]

From Family Planning to Invasive Pronatalism

The defunding of Yeltsin's presidential program known as "Family Planning" in 1998 and ongoing campaigns discrediting the terms "family planning" and "pregnancy prevention" in favor of "pregnancy planning" and "traditional values" paved the way for a severe illiberal turn in reproductive politics. While contraceptive supporters had long considered the routine use of abortion a problem and described themselves as "opposing" abortion, they never endorsed restrictions on access. By the second decade of Russia's twenty-first century, an "anti-abortion" perspective called for exactly such changes. The Russian Orthodox Church took the lead in such proposals both in the name of protecting "life" and promoting Russia's demographic revival. Despite the unflagging decrease in abortion use among all age groups and at all stages of pregnancy, campaigns to restrict abortion access proliferated in federal and regional parliaments, the mass media, and street-side protests. Activists pursued anti-abortion agendas through proposing (and sometimes passing) legislative and policy restrictions; by disseminating "traditional values" discourses emphasizing large, patriarchal families in institutions, mass media, and popular culture venues, and by stigmatizing abortion. Some of these tactics imitated Western anti-abortion movements—such as policies of establishing waiting periods and "counseling" before obtaining an abortion; presenting scientific falsehoods in a manipulated process of obtaining clients' "informed consent"; requiring clients to first undergo ultrasound procedures so as to hear and see the fetal heartbeat in the hope of changing their plan to terminate the pregnancy; and pushing for an end to public funding of abortions.[4] Other tactics drew on and expanded Soviet approaches of trying to persuade abortion applicants to change their mind.[5] Indeed, with the concept of "decreasing abortion" disconnected from promoting the prevention of unwanted pregnancy, it became associated with realizing the nation's "demographic reserve," a view that any pregnancy is a potential resource for the state's pronatalist agenda.

Anti-abortion efforts became an arena where conservative gender values and state demographic interests converged. Various coalitions between the Russian state, social organizations, and the Russian Orthodox Church promote these goals through both symbolic and economic outputs. For example, Svetlana Medvedeva, the wife of former President Dmitry Medvedev, inaugurated several projects through her foundation (Fond sotsial'no-kul'turnykh initsiativ). These include encouraging local regions to schedule a temporary moratorium on abortions to coincide with the new national holiday celebrating Family, Love, and Fidelity that she helped establish in 2008. In this and similar projects, clichéd, sentimental messaging about family values became ubiquitous, and language defining the fetus as "an unborn child" and equating abortion with the "sin" of "murder" proliferated.[6] In

June 2015, the Russian Federation's Ministry of Health signed an official agreement with the Russian Orthodox Church outlining areas in which the two institutions would cooperate. Article 9 of the agreement specifically addresses joint projects to prevent abortion, including establishing Orthodox crisis pregnancy centers inside reproductive health care centers and including Orthodox priests in the state funded pre-abortion counseling services women are to undergo before obtaining abortions.[7] We saw an example of this in chapter 4, when the new chief doctor of the teenage clinic Yuventa brought a priest onto the staff to fight abortion among its clients.

The state and Church have thus created extensive infrastructures for pronatalist, anti-abortion activity that reach into clinics, schools, the media, and even the national calendar. Non-governmental organizations with names such as Sviatost' materinstva (The Sanctity of Motherhood) receive state grants to work at federal and regional levels, holding conferences on topics such as the "Large Family and the Future of Humanity" and implementing school curricula on "traditional family values."[8] This invasive anti-abortion work has also transformed the work of ob-gyns; doctors face pressure to convince women seeking abortions to change their mind. And to ensure such work takes place even if doctors demur, the state established paid positions for psychologists and social workers to agitate against abortion in reproductive care clinics. Descriptions of their pre-abortion "counseling" normalize invasive and manipulative techniques, as evident in the new descriptor of a woman who seeks an abortion as "*nakhodiashchikhsia v sostianii reproduktivnogo vybora*" (facing a situation of reproductive choice).[9] Embedded in this use of the phrase is the assumption that a choice, in the sense of a decision, has not yet been made, but is merely an expressed preference amenable to being reversed. To recognize professionals' "success" in convincing pregnant women seeking abortions to carry the pregnancy to term, national competitions have been established that award financial prizes to ob-gyns, clinics, and psychologists/social workers. Hundreds of people from throughout Russia participate in the annual event.[10] Through these multi-pronged activities, the state-Church alliance has ensured that propagandizing "traditional values" and persuading pregnant women against abortion offers Russians substantial social and economic resources.

Existing evidence suggests that many physicians have adopted assertive anti-abortion and pronatalist stances. Improving women's reproductive health indicators, attracting clients to maternity services, and promoting childbearing are all means by which physicians acquire prestige and remuneration.[11] Some physicians have become practicing Christians and refuse to provide abortions on the basis of their "conscience." Yet even for those who do not profess religious opposition, distancing themselves from providing abortions has become a means of expressing moral virtue.[12] It is also becoming a measure of safety: In many regions, fines have been introduced for "coercing" women into abortions.[13]

Certainly, there remain health professionals and social advocates who remain unmoved by state pronatalist ideology. They work cautiously and courageously in public and private clinics and women's crisis centers, and in underground social movements such as the feminist anti-war movement. Their struggles—whether aimed at preserving their own medical authority over reproductive health or at upholding women's rights to make their own reproductive decisions—certainly require investigation.

Reproductive Politics and the Global Illiberal Backlash

The rise and demise of Russian family planning institutions illuminates some of the key stakes in the troubling global crisis of liberalism. Since the end of state socialism, leaders in almost all Central and Eastern European and former Soviet countries have sought to limit abortion access and revive a patriarchal social order.[14] The liberal politics they did institute, in the sense of multiparty elections, market economics, and some individual rights, did not guarantee bodily autonomy or respect for minority bodies.[15] Indeed, democratic governance per se does not ensure reproductive autonomy, as the 2022 Supreme Court reversal of *Roe v. Wade* in the United States demonstrates.[16]

As this book has shown, understanding such phenomena requires recognizing the many forms that a liberal sensibility can take. In both the late Soviet and post-Soviet contexts, liberal reformers in health care focused on creating legitimacy for services to address individuals' (instead of only state) interests. In women's health care, the signs of liberalizing change Russians described as appealing involve aesthetically attractive designs, technologically advanced equipment, and polite experts.[17] In other words, the promise of consumer services granted legitimacy to market-based health care and physicians' power. But profit-driven, consumer-based medicine often compromises individual health. And if it sometimes offers the pretense of upholding individual "rights," it certainly does not prioritize social equality.

True, the liberalism that Russian family planners established attended to some forms of inequality: the decision to establish physicians' certification courses in the remote region of Udmurtiia, rather than in Moscow or St. Petersburg, acknowledged that family planning services should be available to everyone in the country, not only the most privileged urbanites. Establishing clinics for teenagers was an important recognition of a population highly marginalized from reproductive health care. But Russian family planning leaders did not see eliminating inequality in access to services for other marginalized groups (such as migrant populations) as a major priority. Partly, the task of establishing basic family planning services for mainstream populations was so enormous that they did not yet manage to consider groups with special needs. And then defending the very idea of preventing pregnancy against vitriolic pronatalist attacks precluded family planning experts from attending to the more specific barriers that impeded access to minority populations. This is an important way that Russia's family planning movement differed from the US reproductive justice movement. The latter's commitment to justice for racially marginalized and poor communities presents a critique of the liberal reproductive rights focus, one that is urgently needed worldwide.

The basic commitments underlying liberal family planning in Russia—a commitment to science and care, the rationalization of public policy and social practices, and re-enchantment of relationships—were thus imperfect from the perspectives of both social justice and individual autonomy. Embedded in health care institutions, family planning services aim to discipline the population, even as their techniques were less blunt and more attuned to individual concerns than typical Soviet-era expertise. Yet in light of the fact that Russia's family planning institutions have been dismantled, and the pursuit of demographic and sexual sovereignty has expanded to a previously unimaginable level of genocidal destruction in Ukraine, I find another question most pressing: what might have been done to prevent Russian illiberalism's ascent?

If the liberal reforms after socialism had focused more directly on the kinds of changes Russian family planning activists sought—cultural and economic developments that addressed social cohesion, the needs of vulnerable groups, (e.g., mothers, children, the elderly), and the value of caregiving—then perhaps a backlash against both the West in general and family planning in particular wouldn't have been as likely.

Similar arguments are being made to explain the rise of illiberalism in the West. The feminist legal scholar Robin West suggested that if the reproductive rights movement had pursued more than a narrow focus on abstract choice, if it had promoted family well-being and expansive conditions for care, the backlash against *Roe* might not have been as successful.[18] Mark Lilla offers a compelling dissection of how the liberal Left failed to respond to Reagan's demolition of the social welfare compact with a new approach to collective solidarity. While progressives turned to identity politics as a means of addressing injustice, they have not formulated a vision for social cohesion, community, and reciprocal care.[19] Neoliberalism has grossly exacerbated inequalities on global and local scales, and the illiberal resentment and backlash emerging in response are increasingly nationalist.[20] Some illiberal campaigns attack global institutions of governance (Brexit), while others get directed at cultural and domestic arenas of social life—promoting patriarchal revival, protecting white supremacy against minorities and immigrants, buttressing family values against feminist and transgender activism.[21]

The architects of Russian neoliberalism—Western and Russian alike—didn't attend to the diverse array of Russian people's priorities, anxieties, and aspirations: they were sure that creating markets was the most important path forward, ignoring questions about social well-being. Russian supporters of family planning held onto the need for social commitments to well-being for a very long time. Even as many advocates started claiming not only the practical need for abortion access but also the more liberal value of individual "reproductive rights," their discussions also included reflections about what genuine caring requires. They emphasized that parenting requires emotional and economic readiness, capacities and skills they want the opportunity to develop. Their recognition that reproductive autonomy can only truly exist within a broader framework that ensures social well-being raises powerful food for thought. What would the post-Soviet era have looked like had reforms prioritized social well-being instead of marketization through shock therapy? And what kinds of developments would have been possible in Russia and beyond had the global family planning movement been embedded in a reproductive justice framework explicitly focused on enabling childrearing in auspicious conditions? Amid the troubling spread of illiberalism in Europe and the US, scholars and activists committed to preserving reproductive rights may find such questions valuable in devising new and better strategies.

TIMELINE OF KEY DEVELOPMENTS DISCUSSED IN THE STUDY

1955 Abortion is legalized, but without establishing the right to contraception

1970 Soviet physicians hold symposium and release statement advocating approval of widespread use of hormonal contraceptives

1970 Henry P. David meets with Soviet Ministry of Health experts hoping to develop collaborations on abortion and contraception

1974 Minzdrav issues instructional letter warns of the dangers of hormonal contraceptives, effectively banning their use for contraceptive purposes

1979 Minzdrav orders local (Republic) health authorities to report on their efforts in the fight against abortion

1983 Minzdrav's methodological instructions allow limited use of some hormonal contraceptives for contraceptive purposes

mid-1980s Vacuum aspiration method for "menstrual regulation" becomes used throughout the country

1985 Minzdrav issues order stating current efforts to prevent abortion in the RSFSR are unsatisfactory and must be improved

1988 Liubov Erofeeva begins working at Moscow city health department and introduces vacuum aspiration abortions into the city's women's outpatient clinics

1988 Viktor Samokhvalov is hired as the first professional for St. Petersburg's psychological hotline

1989 Irina Alexandrovna Manuilova establishes the Family and Health Association to promote contraceptives, (January)

1990 The Supreme Soviet of the RSFSR passes a decree to develop the Children of Russia program

1990 Henry P. David and Andrej Popov meet at the conference, "From Abortion to Contraception" in Tblisi, Georgia

1991 Federal program "Family Planning, 1991–1995" is developed under the direction of the Committee for Family and Demographic Politics under the Soviet of Ministers of the RSFSR

1991 Andrej Popov begins a postdoctoral fellowship at Princeton's Population Center, sponsored by the Population Council; he and the author (then Michele Miller) meet at Princeton University, September

1991 Pharmaceutical firm Organon opens its first subsidiary in Eastern Europe (Hungary)

1991 Minzdrav establishes centers for family planning and reproduction

1991 The MacArthur Foundation begins its initiative in the Former Soviet Union

1991 Gorbachev resigns, the USSR ends, and Russian Federation is established, 25 December

1992 Negative population growth is recorded, nationalists respond with alarm about the "nation's dying out"

1992 Government Resolution establishes the Russian Association of Family Planning, whose main purpose is to improve the demographic situation of the Russian Federation, and reduce abortions, maternal and infant mortality

1992 Inga Ivanovna Grebesheva establishes the Russian Association of Family Planning

1992   Liubov Erofeeva becomes the director of Organon's Information Center, housed in the Research Center for Obstetrics, Gynecology, and Perinatology in Moscow

1992   The Women's Health and Family Planning program is established by the Udmurtiia (regional) Republic Government with Izhevsk State Medical Academy

1992–1995   Republic of Udmurtiia opens family planning clinics and offices

1993   RAFP becomes a member of the IPPF

1993   First National Conference, Issues of Family Planning in Russia, is held in Moscow, December 7–9

1993   The legal right to abortion is established in the Russian Federation.

1993   Inaugural issue of the journal *Planirovanie sem'i* (Family Planning) is published

1993   St. Petersburg Center for the Reproductive Health of Youth, Yuventa, opens in March; Pavel Naumovich Krotin is chief doctor and Viktor Samokhvalov is hired as a psychotherapist

1993   Henry David's Transnational Family Research Institute receives a grant to undertake initial explorations for programs to support the MacArthur Foundation initiatives related to women's rights and reproductive health; David and Carmen Barroso travel to Moscow and St. Petersburg to meet potential collaborators

1993   "Life," an anti-abortion movement at the Orthodox Medical and Educational Center, is founded by Fr. Maxim Obukhov in Moscow

1993   MacArthur Foundation holds a workshop in Montreal for its FSU initiative grantees in the sphere of women's rights; David begins organizing them as a consortium for networking purposes (August)

1994   International Conference on Population and Development is held in Cairo, Popov attends

1994   The "Family Planning" project (part of the larger "Children of Russia" program) is confirmed as holding the status of a Presidential program by the President of the Russian Federation

1994   Andrej Popov wins a MacArthur Grant from the initiatives in the FSU program for his research

1995   Andrej Popov dies suddenly at age thirty-nine

1996   Social criteria for accessing legal abortion during the second trimester are expanded to include a woman's unmarried status, homelessness, refugee status, a disabled husband or disabled child, a woman's or her husband's unemployment, and a salary lower than the minimum living standard for one's region

1997   Proposal presented to Government Duma by Nina Krivel'skaia of the Liberal Democratic Party of Russia to end federal funding of family planning as a matter of national demographic security

1998   Funding for the Family Planning program is eliminated from the federal budget

1998   Yuventa clinic for teenagers' reproductive health begins to open youth consultation branch offices in municipal regions of St. Petersburg

1999   Total fertility rate (average number of children per woman) in the Russian Federation falls to a record low of 1.16

2001   Government issues the "Concept of Demographic Development of the Russian Federation until 2015"

2002   Foundation for the Protection of the Family, Motherhood and Childhood, founded by Fr. Maxim Obukhov, advocates measures to increase the birth rate

2003   Social criteria for accessing abortion in the second trimester reduced to only rape, imprisonment, death or severe disability of the woman's husband, or loss of parental rights

2006   Putin announces state maternity capital program to incentivize second
       and third births in Annual Speech to the Federal Assembly, (May)

2007   Explicit pronatalist plans announced in the President's "Concept of
       Demographic Politics of the Russian Federation until 2025" (revised
       and re-confirmed in 2014)

2007   Russian Ministry of Health and Social Development issues an Order
       for obtaining informed consent for abortions in first trimester
       emphasizing possible negative consequences

2007   Russian Ministry of Health and Social Development issues an Order
       limiting the medical indications for abortion

2007   Inga Grebesheva retires and Liubov Erofeeva becomes director of the
       RAFP

2007   Regional branches of RAFP begin changing their names to de-
       emphasize the phrase "family planning"

2008   The Foundation for the Protection of the Family, Motherhood, and
       Childhood initiated the all-Russian non-profit organization For Life!

2008   Russian Federation announces the "Year of the Family," and
       undertakes numerous antiabortion initiatives

2009   The Russian Association of Family Planning (RAFP) changes its name
       to the Russian Association of Population and Development (RAPD)

2010   A film libeling Viktor Samokhvalov is shown on Russia's national
       television channel 1 (July)

2010   Protests occur in St. Petersburg against the Yuventa clinic doctors and
       personally defame Drs. Krotin and Samokhvalov (October)

2010   Russian Ministry of Health establishes an official method for pre-
       abortion "counseling" to persuade pregnant women seeking abortions
       to keep the pregnancy

2011   First public feminist protest held against proposed abortion restrictions, with the slogan "Fight Abortion, Not Women"

2012   Putin establishes the legal category of "foreign agents" to limit the influence and activities of NGOs

2013   Law adopted criminalizing the "propaganda" of nontraditional sexual relations among minors (June)

2014   IPPF ends its funding of RAPD

2015   RAPD and feminist groups protest against new proposed abortion restrictions

2015   RAPD labeled a "foreign agent" by the Russian government

2016   Pavel Naumovich Krotin dies; a conservative Christian is appointed the new chief doctor of Yuventa

2016   Russian Ministry of Health issues an Order re-confirming the requirement for obtaining informed consent from women seeking abortions

APPENDIX 2
TABLES

TABLE 1: Total Fertility Rate (TFR) in Russia, 1970–2015

YEAR	TOTAL POPULATION	URBAN POPULATION	RURAL POPULATION
1970	2.00	1.75	2.60
1975	1.97	1.76	2.63
1980	1.89	1.70	2.51
1985	2.05	1.86	2.67
1990	1.89	1.70	2.60
1995	1.34	1.19	1.81
1996	1.27	1.14	1.70
1997	1.22	1.10	1.62
1998	1.23	1.11	1.64
1999	1.16	1.04	1.53
2000	1.19	1.09	1.55
2001	1.22	1.12	1.56
2002	1.28	1.19	1.63
2003	1.32	1.22	1.66
2004	1.34	1.25	1.65
2005	1.29	1.21	1.58
2006	1.30	1.21	1.60
2007	1.42	1.29	1.80
2008	1.50	1.37	1.91
2009	1.54	1.41	1.94
2010	1.57	1.44	1.98
2011	1.58	1.44	2.06
2012	1.69	1.54	2.21
2013	1.71	1.55	2.27
2014	1.75	1.59	2.34
2015	1.78	1.68	2.12

Average number of children per woman over the reproductive lifetime, ages fifteen to forty-four. Source: Sergei Zakharov "Naselenie Rossii 2015. Dvadtsat' tretii ezhegodnyi demograficheskii doklad" (Moscow: Izdatelskii dom Vysshei shkoly ekonomiki, 2017), 135. Rates from 1995 through 2003 exclude data from the Republic of Chechnya.

TABLE 2: Registered Abortions in Russia, 1990, 1995, 2000, 2005, 2015

	NUMBER OF ABORTIONS			
	ACCORDING TO ROSSTAT			ACCORDING TO THE MINISTRY OF HEALTH OF RUSSIA, IN THOUSANDS
YEAR	IN THOUSANDS	PER 1000 WOMEN AGED 15–49	PER 100 LIVE BIRTHS	
1990	4,103.4	113.9	206	3,920.3
1995	2,766.4	72.8	203	2,574.8
2000	2,138.8	54.2	169	1,961.5
2005	1,675.7	42.7	117	1,501.6
2010	1,186.1	31.7	66	1,054.8
2011	1,124.9	30.5	63	989.4
2012	1,064.0	29.3	56	935.5
2013	1,012.4	28.3	53	881.4
2014	919.1	26.0	48	803.8
2015	836.9	23.9	44	735.9
Ratio 1990:2015	4.9	4.8	4.7	5.3

Source: Zakharov, "Naselenie Rossii 2015," 168. Calculations for 1995, 2000, 2005 exclude data from the Republic of Chechnya. Calculations for 2014, 2015 exclude data from the Crimean federal district.

NOTES

Preface

1. Laruelle, "Illiberalism," 303–27; and Krastev and Holmes, *The Light That Failed*.
2. Hilevych, "Abortion and Gender Relations," 98; Remennick, "Epidemiology and Determinants of Induced Abortion," 841-842.

Introduction

1. Maria Arbatova, *Menia zovut zhenshchina*, 266–67.
2. Hilevych, "Abortion and Gender Relations," 90; Polina Bachlakova, "Talking to My Grandma about Her 12 Abortions." *Vice*, July 6, 2016, https:// www.vice.com/en/article/ ypaagw/talking-to-my-grandma-about-her-12-abortions. Poet Igor Kholin's lines from his 1950s *Zhiteli baraka* cycle presents a laconic, powerful illustration: "Marusia's body is buried here. / She never married, / People say she didn't want to. / She had 22 abortions. / By the end of her life she looked like hell." Kholin, *Izbrannoe: Stikhi i poemy*, 29. I thank Kirill Tolpygo for sharing this poem and Stas Shvabrin for help with translating it.
3. Prior to the reproductive justice movement, women activists from the global South established the Development Alternatives for Women in a New Era (DAWN) framework, which emphasized the imperative of ensuring holistic socio-economic needs as well as reproductive rights. Petchesky, *Global Prescriptions*, 6. See also Luna and Luker "Reproductive Justice"; Ross and Solinger, *Reproductive Justice: An Introduction*; and Price, "What Is Reproductive Justice?"
4. Hilevych, "Abortion and Gender Relations," 98; Remennick, "Epidemiology and Determinants," 841–42.
5. Inspiring my approach are feminist works including Funk, "Feminist Critiques of Liberalism"; Hemment, *Empowering Women in Russia*; Holmgren, "Bug Inspectors and Beauty Queens"; Morgan, "Afterword"; and Turbine and Riach, "The Right to Choose or Choosing What's Right?"
6. Feminist activists acknowledge that reproductive rights campaigns are inevitably shaped by local concerns and thus may differ across geographical space and time. But few analyses have delved into the conflicts that arise from such differences. This book calls for attention to the serious challenges of establishing a "shared ethical core" for reproductive and sexual rights across different cultural and political-economic contexts. Petchesky, *Global Prescriptions*, 7–8.

7. Zakharov, ed., "Naselenie Rossii 2018," 179.
8. Zakharov, ed., "Naselenie Rossii 2018," 177. These data are estimates because in 2012, the central statistical administration, Rosstat, broadened the categorization of miscarriages to include phenomena such as pregnancies that were not developing, which in turn affected the data on induced abortions. Another estimate for this indicator, based on Ministry of Health data, shows a decline of 9.3 times over this same time period (from 78.9 to 8.5) (Zakharov, ed., "Naselenie Rossii 2018," 179). Between 1991 and 2014, the average number of abortions a woman in Russia would have during her reproductive lifetime declined fourfold, from 3.39 to 0.85; in 2015, the last year statistics were collected on a woman's age at abortion, the rate was 0.56, and by 2020, it was estimated at approximately 0.34. Viktoria Sakevich, "Ot Aborta k kontratseptsii," *Demoscope Weekly*, May 23, 2016. http://www.demoscope.ru/weekly/2016/0687/demoscope687.pdf; Zakharov, personal communication, June 6, 2020.
9. After the Soviet era, conservatives began proposing bills to criminalize abortion in 1997 and 1998, and the first restrictions went into effect in 2003 and 2007, limiting access to second-trimester abortions. See Bateneva, "Na sobach'em urovne"; "Neve-zhestvo"; Myers, "After Decades".
10. Some important exceptions include David, *Family Planning and Abortion*; David, *From Abortion to Contraception*; David and McIntyre, *Reproductive Behavior*; Kligman, *The Politics of Duplicity*; and Sobotka, "The Stealthy Sexual Revolution?"
11. Gal and Kligman, *The Politics of Gender after Socialism*; Gal and Kligman, *Reproducing Gender*; Kuzma-Markowska and Ignaciuk, "Family Planning Advice," 23; Nakachi and Solinger, *Reproductive States*.
12. On the need for anthropological analyses of contemporary demographic and health trends including below-replacement fertility, see Greenhalgh and Winkler, *Governing China's Population*; Johnson-Hanks, "Demographic Transitions and Modernity"; and Petit et al., *The Anthropological Demography of Health*.
13. Deomampo, *Transnational Reproduction*; Siegl, *Intimate Strangers*; Inhorn, *Cosmopolitan Conceptions*; and Inhorn, *Mating Gaps*.
14. Krause, "'Empty Cradles'"; Krause and DeZordo, "Introduction: Ethnography and Biopolitics"; Krause and Marchesi, "Fertility Politics"; Kligman, *The Politics of Duplicity*; Marchesi, "Reproducing Italians"; Rivkin-Fish, "Anthropology, Demography"; Rivkin-Fish, "From 'Demographic Crisis'"; Rivkin-Fish, "Pronatalism, Gender Politics"; Grzebalska and Peto, "The Gendered Modus Operandi"; and Teitelbaum and Winter, *A Question of Numbers*.
15. Roudakova, *Losing Pravda*.
16. Lipovetsky, "The Poetics of ITR Discourse"; Lipovetsky, "Clarifying Positions"; Vald'shtein, "O liberal'nom meinstrime'"; and Zubok, "Technologies of Bringing a 'True' Freedom."
17. Krastev and Holmes, *The Light That Failed*. They also argue that Western leaders never accepted Central and East European nations as full-fledged democracies, which gave local elites leverage for an anti-Western, nationalist revival, especially in Hungary and Poland.
18. Szacki, *Liberalism after Communism*; Laruelle, "Illiberalism."
19. Berlin, *Liberty*; McGowan, *Pragmatist Politics*.

20. Laruelle, "Illiberalism," 9–11.
21. Funk, "Feminist Critiques of Liberalism."
22. Connelly, *Fatal Misconception*; Connelly, "Population Control Is History"; Hartmann, *Reproductive Rights and Wrongs*; Gordon, *The Moral Property of Women*; Hodgson and Watkins, "Feminists & Neo-Malthusians"; Krause and de Zordo, "Introduction: Ethnography and Biopolitics," 145; MacNamara, *Birth Control and American Modernity*; Morgan and Roberts, "Reproductive Governance in Latin America"; Rivkin-Fish, "Anthropologies of Abortion"; Roberts, *Killing the Black Body*; and Russell, Sobo, and Thompson, *Contraception across Cultures*.
23. Hartmann, *Reproductive Rights and Wrongs*; Solinger and Nakachi, *Reproductive States*; Ali, *Planning the Family in Egypt*.
24. Halkias, *The Empty Cradle of Democracy*; Ignaciuk, "Reproductive Policies"; Ignaciuk, "No Man's Land?"; Kościańska, *Gender, Pleasure, and Violence*, 46–48, 92–94; Paxson, *Making Modern Mothers*; Varley "Islamic Logics."
25. Ali, *Planning the Family in Egypt*; Arousell et al., "Unintended Consequences"; De Zordo, "Programming the Body"; Halkias, *The Empty Cradle of Democracy*; Kościańska, *Gender, Pleasure, and Violence*; Krause and de Zordo, "Introduction: Ethnography and Biopolitics"; Ignaciuk, "No Man's Land?"; Ignaciuk, "Reproductive Policies"; Paxson, *Making Modern Mothers*; Temkina, "The Gynecologist's Gaze"; Varley, "Islamic Logics."
26. Efforts to repress abortion rights emerged immediately after the end of socialism and have continued apace. See Gal and Kligman, *The Politics of Gender after Socialism*; Susan Gal and Gail Kligman, eds., *Reproducing Gender*; Mishtal, "Irrational Non-Reproduction"; Mishtal, *The Politics of Morality*; Mishtal, "Quietly 'Beating' the System"; Mishtal, "Reproductive Governance"; Rivkin-Fish, "Anthropology, Demography"; Rivkin-Fish, "Moral Science"; Rivkin-Fish, "Pronatalism, Gender Politics"; Grzebalska and Peto, "Gendered Modus Operandi"; Leykin and Rivkin-Fish, "Politicized Demography." For the US, see Ginsburg, *Contested Lives*; Bjork-James, *The Divine Institution*.
27. L. I. Remmenick, "Epidemiology and Determinants"; David, *From Abortion to Contraception*; Goldberg Sherwood-Fabre, and Bodrova, "Impact of an Integrated Family Planning Program";. Zakharov, "Fertility, Nuptiality"; Zakharov, "Rozhdaemost' v Rossii"; Zakharov and Ivanova, "Regional Fertility Differentiation"; Zakharov and Ivanova, "Fertility Decline"; Zakharov and Sakevich, *Osobennosti planirovaniia sem'i*; Sakevich, "Ot aborta k kontratseptsii"; Sakevich, Denisov, and Rivkin-Fish, "Neposledovatel'naia politika"; Vishnevsky, *Demograficheskaia modernizatsiia Rossii*; Vishnevsky, Denisov, and Sakevich, "Zapret aborta"; and Vishnevsky, Denisov, and Sakevich, "Contraceptive Revolution in Russia," 96. An important contribution of this research debunks Russian government officials' claims that their pronatalist policies generate fertility increases, as scholars caution against drawing conclusions from momentary statistical dynamics. A demographic perspective reveals that socio-historical developments, such as varying sizes of different generations entering childbearing age (i.e., cohort effects), significantly impact population trends. Vishnevsky, "Konservativnaia revoliutsiia v SSSR"; Vishnevsky, "Russkii krest"; Vishnevsky, ed. *Demograficheskaia modernizatsiia Rossii: 1900–2000*; Vishnevsky, "Byli li 90-e demograficheskoi katastrofoi dlia Rossii?"; Vishnevsky, Denisov, and Sakevich,

"Zapret aborta"; Vishnevsky, Denisov, and Sakevich, "The Contraceptive Revolution in Russia"; Frejka and Zakharov, "Apparent Failure."

28. Gal, "Gender in the Post-Socialist Transition"; Krause and de Zordo, "Introduction: Ethnography and Biopolitics"; Mishtal, *The Politics of Morality*.

29. Detwiler and Snitow, "Gender Trouble"; Graff and Korolczuk, *Anti-Gender Politics*; Grzebalska and Peto, "Gendered Modus Operandi."

30. The total fertility rate is a statistical calculation undertaken each year that provides a sense of the number of children an average woman would have by the end of her reproductive years based on aggregate fertility in the society at that time. Demographers recognize a total fertility rate of 2.1 children per woman as a sign of population stability. Clearly, no woman can have a fraction of a child, but the fraction helps gauge how close the average number of children per woman is to two, three, or more.

31. Andrei Gudkov, "Bol'she novykh rozhdenii," *Vedomosti*, January 16, 2008, http://www.demoscope.ru/weekly/2008/0317/gazeta09. php.

32. Hockstader, "Antiabortion Activists"; Heuvel, "Right-to-Lifers Hit Russia."

33. Vishnevsky aligned his school of demographic research with global population experts.

34. Latikhina, "Demografiia s pliusom." The newspaper continues: "Golikova presented sad statistics: in 2008 the number of newborns almost equaled the number of abortions—1,714 million births and 1,234 million cases of induced pregnancy termination. And that is actually an achievement: earlier, for every 100 live births there were 130 abortions, but in 2008, there were 73."

35. *Demoscope Weekly*, "Russkii antikrest'."

36. *Demoscope Weekly*, "Russkii antikrest'."

37. Vishnevsky was the founder and director of the Institute of Demography at Moscow's prestigious Higher School of Economics until his death in early 2021. This comment was published on the biweekly Demoscope.ru website, which Vishnevsky founded in January 2001 with funding by international foundations including the UNFPA, MacArthur Foundation, French National Institute of Demographic Research (INED), and others. The site offers a rich array of resources for studying population dynamics; notably, the kind of criticism seen here—of scientific miscalculations, demographic ignorance, and ideological blinders among policy makers—is distinguished from all other sections of the site by its placement in an editorial column that Vishnevsky wrote anonymously called, "What Do We Know about the Fox? . . . Nothing. And That's Not All," a quote from the Soviet children's poet Boris Zakhoder that announces its critical content by alluding explicitly to the multifaceted, contradictory nature of knowledge and truth.

38. Westoff and Ryder, *The Contraceptive Revolution*; Zakharov, "Rozhdaemost' v Rossii."

39. "There are only three countries in Europe that have criminalized abortion," explained Liubov' Erofeeva, director of the Russian Association for Population and Development: "Ireland, Malta, and Poland, where the Church is closely tied to the state. In none of these countries has the population grown." Liubov' Erofeeva, "Aborty naprashivaiutsia na zapret," *Gazeta*, January 29, 2010, http://demoscope.ru/weekly/2010/0409/gazeta01.php.

40. See, for example, Sakevich, "Abort ili planirovanie sem'i?"; Sakevich, "Novye ogranicheniia"; Sakevich, "Ot aborta k kontratseptsii"; Sakevich and Denisov, "Birth

Control in Russia"; Zakharov, "Fertility, Nuptiality"; and Frejka and Zakharov, "The Apparent Failure."

41. Leykin, *Caring Like a State*; Leykin, "Vernacularizing Demography"; Rivkin-Fish, "Anthropology, Demography"; Rivkin-Fish, "From Demographic Crisis."
42. Geertz, *Interpretation of Cultures*.
43. Accusations that liberal demographers pursue ethnocide against Russians are found on sites such as KM Onlain, as on this page: KM.RU, October 15, 2008, https://www.km.ru/news/anatolij_vishnevskij_seryj_kardi.
44. Anthropologists studying cultural logics of reducing harm around the world have found similar strategies of strengthening relationships rather than cultivating individual autonomy. See, for example, Kowalski, *Counseling Women*.
45. Solomon, "Social Hygiene in Soviet Medical Education," 607–8; Hutchinson and Solomon, introduction to *Health and Society*; Solomon and Hutchinson, *Health and Society*; Solomon, "Social Hygiene and Soviet Public Health." As these historians discuss, Soviet social hygiene had its roots in German social medicine and pre-Revolutionary Russian community medicine. Revolutionary visions for social hygiene imagined physicians who would consider the patient in the context of his work life and occupational and social interests, and both prevent and cure illness. Solomon, "Social Hygiene in Soviet Medical Education," 615.
46. Hutchinson and Solomon, introduction; Bernstein, *The Dictatorship of Sex*, 185–86; Starks, *The Body Soviet*, 135–61.
47. In 1920, the reasoning for legalization claimed that women's "low material and cultural level" under the tsarist regime made abortion a temporary necessity; with socialism's development, the need to limit childbearing was supposed to disappear. Nakachi, "Liberation without Contraception?," 313.
48. Solomon, "The Demographic Argument."
49. Hoffmann's "Mothers in the Motherland" demonstrates that a concern with increasing population to ensure national greatness was not unique to Stalinist pronatalism but common throughout western Europe.
50. Nakachi, *Replacing the Dead*; Michaels, *Curative Powers*.
51. In 1944, the average sex ratio in rural areas was twenty-eight men per one hundred women. Nakachi, "Replacing the Dead," 2.
52. Nakachi, "Liberation without Contraception?"; Nakachi, *Replacing the Dead*.
53. Nakachi, 153.
54. Nakachi, 180.
55. Nakachi, 181.
56. Due to a lack of information and sex education, as well as misogyny, abortion was a major form of fertility control despite the relative availability of contraceptives in these countries. Dolling, Hahn, and Scholz, "Birth Strike"; David and McIntyre, *Reproductive Behavior*; David, *From Abortion to Contraception*; Ignaciuk, "No Man's Land?"; Drezgić, "Policies and Practices"; Hilevych and Sato, "Popular Medical Discourses."
57. Romania's draconian pronatalism made contraceptives even harder to find there than in the Soviet Union. Couples in Romania relied on withdrawal and other ineffective methods. Baban, "Women's Sexuality and Reproductive Behavior"; Kligman, *Politics of Duplicity*. Andaya tells of Cuban women making homemade contraceptive rings from fishing wire, which itself was in short supply. *Conceiving Cuba*, 43.

58. David and Macintyre, *Reproductive Behavior*, 108.
59. David and Macintyre, *Reproductive Behavior*, 108–9.
60. Amy Randall, "Abortion Will Deprive You of Happiness!"
61. Another sign of a culture of post-conception decision making was the high frequency of births taking place less than nine months after a couple's marriage, as Soviet demographic research detailed. See Tol'ts, "Kharakteristika nekotorykh komponentov"; Zakharov, "Vozrastnaia model' braka."
62. David and Macintyre, *Reproductive Behavior*, 112.
63. David and Macintyre, *Reproductive Behavior*, 112; Anderson, "Role of Abortion"; Popov and David, "Russian Federation."
64. Popov, "Aborty v Rossii," 115.
65. I first observed this normalization of post-conception decision making and abortion during fieldwork in a St. Petersburg maternity hospital in 1994, when I asked the chief doctor when a woman begins prenatal care. She began her response with the phrase, "If she keeps the pregnancy . . ." Similarly, instructions for women's outpatient clinic services issued by the Russian Ministry of Health Protection in 1981 state: "At a woman's first visit to the clinic about pregnancy, if she desires to keep it . . ." ("Pri pervom obrashchenii zhenshchiny v konsul'tatsiiu po povodu beremennosti i pri zhelanii zhenshchiny sokhranit' ee"). Prilozhenie No.1 k prikazu Minzdrava RF ot 22 aprel'ia 1981g N. 430 "Instruktivno-metodicheskie ukazaniia po organizatsii raboty zhenskoi konsul'tatsii." The Soviet Ministry of Health official instructions document was given to me by Andrej Popov.
66. Vail' and Genis, *60-ye*; Zubok, *Zhivago's Children*; Yurchak, *Everything Was Forever*; Shlapentokh, *Strakh i druzhba*.
67. Patico, *Consumption and Change*.
68. Ries, "Russian Talk"; Burawoy, Krotov, and Lytkina, "Involution and Destitution"; Humphrey, *The Unmaking of Soviet Life*; Dunn, *Privatizing Poland*; Rivkin-Fish, *Women's Health in Post-Soviet Russia*; Hemment, *Empowering Women in Russia*; Kideckel, *Getting By in Post-Soviet Romania*; Morris, *Everyday Postsocialism*; Matza, *Shock Therapy*.
69. Gessen, *Dead Again*.
70. Azhgikhina, *Propushchennyi siuzhet*; Caldwell, *Living Faithfully*; Caldwell, *Not by Bread Alone;* Hemment, *Empowering Women*; Hemment and Uspenskaya, "The 1990s Wasn't Just a Time of Bandits"; Lindquist, *Conjuring Hope*; Luehrmann, "Innocence and Demographic Crisis"; Posadskaya, *Russia: A New Era*; Sperling, *Organizing Women*; Wallace, "Father Aleksandr Men'."
71. Gessen, *Dead Again*, 12.
72. Patico, *Consumption and Change*; Matza, *Shock Therapy*; Lerner and Zbenovich, "Adapting the Therapeutic Discourse"; Lerner, "Changing Meanings of Russian Love"; Temkina, "'Childbirth Is Not a Car Rental'"; Temkina and Zdravomyslova, "The Sexual Scripts and Identity"; Temkina and Rivkin-Fish, "Creating Health Care Consumers."
73. Natalia Roudakova, *Losing Pravda*.
74. See also Borenstein, "Selling Russia"; Borenstein, *Overkill*.

75. Lipovetsky, "Clarifying Positions"; Lipovetsky, "The Poetics of ITR Discourse"; Vald'shtein, "O liberal'nom meinstrime'"; Zubok, "Technologies of Bringing"; Nathans, "Coming to Terms"; Malinova, "Konstruirovanie 'liberalizma.'"

76. Funk and Mueller, *Gender Politics*; Renne, "Disparaging Digressions"; Snitow, *Feminism of Uncertainty*; Snitow, "All Were Rebels."

77. Höjdestrand, *Needed by Nobody*; Parsons, *Dying Unneeded*; Watson, "Explaining Rising Mortality."

78. Other significant forms of inequality and suffering were less visible to Western feminist observers but are demonstrated in numerous detailed scholarly accounts, ethnographic descriptions, and popular texts that reveal how censorship about sexuality, shortages of contraception, violence, and woefully inadequate housing (with entire families often living in a single room of a communal apartment) greatly impeded Soviet women's agency and well-being.

79. Funk and Mueller, *Gender Politics*; Gal, "Feminism in Civil Society"; Ghodsee, "Feminism-by-Design"; Watson, "Civil Society and the Politics of Difference."

80. Funk and Mueller, *Gender Politics*; Hemment, *Empowering Women*; Snitow, *Feminism of Uncertainty*; Snitow, "All Were Rebels"; Sperling, *Organizing Women*; Sopronenko, *Feminism: Twenty Years Forward*.

81. But in a new twist on the Western-feminists-encountering-women's-lives-in-Eastern-Europe playbook, Ghodsee cites 1980s survey data in which East German women indicated higher levels of sexual satisfaction than their West German counterparts to generalize that "women had [have] better sex under socialism." Ghodsee, "Why Women Had Better Sex"; Ghodsee, *Why Women Have Better Sex*. Targeting her polemic at American audiences to advocate stronger welfare and economic rights in the US, she argues that when women don't need men for financial support, they can engage in sexual relations on relatively more equal and freer terms. Without contesting the latter point, a variety of sources on sexual experiences under Soviet state socialism clearly demonstrates that their relative economic independence did not determine the quality of their sexual experiences. For a few examples, see Haavio-Mannila and Kontula, "Single and Double Sexual Standards"; Kon, *Sexual Revolution in Russia*; Popovskii, *Tretii lishnii*; and Voznesenskaya, *The Women's Decameron*. For a helpful analysis of the debates between Ghodsee and leading feminist scholars, see Hinterhuber and Fuchs, "Neoliberal Intervention."

82. Gal and Kligman, *Reproducing Gender*; Nanette Funk, "Feminist Critiques of Liberalism."

83. Snitow, "All Were Rebels," 148.

84. Funk, "Feminist Critiques of Liberalism"; Sarah Phillips, *Women's Social Activism*; Gapova, "Gender Equality vs. Difference; Rivkin-Fish "Moral Science"; Rivkin-Fish, "Conceptualizing Feminist Strategies." See also: Borovoy and Ghodsee, "Decentering Agency in Feminist Theory"; Ghodsee, "Feminism-by-Design"; Hemment, *Empowering Women*; Holmgren, "Bug Inspectors"; Mazzarino, "Entrepreneurial Women"; Sperling, *Organizing Women in Contemporary Russia*; Johnson, *Gender Violence in Russia*; Zhurzhenko, *Sotsial'noe vosproizvodstvo*; Snitow, *Feminism of Uncertainty*.

85. Phillips, *Women's Social Activism*.

86. Two important examples are the Network of East-West Women in Poland (Snitow,

Feminism of Uncertainty; Snitow, "All Were Rebels") and the Moscow Center for Gender Studies in Russia (Sperling, *Organizing Women in Contemporary Russia*); see also Gal and Kligman, *Reproducing Gender*, for case studies in Central-Eastern Europe; and Kuehnast and Nechemias, *Post-Soviet Women Encountering Transition*, for former Soviet cases.

87. Katalin Fábián, *Contemporary Women's Movements in Hungary*; Posadskaya, *Russia: A New Era*; Hemment, *Empowering Women*; Phillips, *Women's Social Activism*; Johnson, *Gender Violence in Russia*; Gapova, "Gender Equality vs. Difference."

88. Phillips, *Women's Social Activism*, 80.

89. Ghodsee, "Feminism-by-Design"; Fraser, "Feminism, Capitalism"; Funk, "Contra Fraser on Feminism and Neoliberalism"; Hall, "Resistance to Right-Wing Populism"; Bystydzienski, "Women's Organizations."

90. Posadskaya, *Russia: A New Era*; Hemment, *Empowering Women*; Hemment, *Youth Politics*; Snitow, *Feminism of Uncertainty*; Snitow, "All Were Rebels."

91. Joanna Mishtal, *Politics of Morality*, 68–73; Hall, "Resistance to Right-Wing Populism"; Bystydzienski, "Women's Organizations."

92. Perheentupa, *Feminist Politics*, 56.

93. Nikolas Rose. *Politics of Life Itself*; Lemke, *Biopolitics*; Bröckling, Krasmann, and Lemke, *Governmentality*.

94. Foucault, *History of Sexuality*; Foucault, Senellart, and Burchell, *Birth of Biopolitics*; Barry, Osborne, and Rose, *Foucault and Political Reason*.

95. Nasir, "Biopolitics, Thanatopolitics"; Nasir, "Biopolitics, Thanatopolitics." For an account of a biopolitics that joins technoscience to the redesign of life itself to cultivate an unending future, see Bernstein, *Future of Immortality*.

96. Morgan and Roberts, "Reproductive Governance," 241.

97. Murphey, *Seizing the Means of Reproduction*.

98. For an example of biopolitics undertaken by nonstate, community actors, see Kravel-Tovi, "Specter of Dwindling Numbers."

99. Foucault, *History of Sexuality*; Foucault, Senellart, and Burchell, *Birth of Biopolitics*; Lemke, *Biopolitics*; Bröckling, Krasmann, and Lemke, *Governmentality*.

100. Barry, Osborne, and Rose, *Foucault and Political Reason*; Cruikshank, *Will to Empower*.

101. Despite this shift away from repressive power, Dean has argued that liberalism also deploys authoritarian technologies, combining governance through freedom with liberal policing functions of civil society. Dean, "Liberal Government and Authoritarianism.

102. See, for example, Lansing, "Cognitive Machinery of Power"; Koopman and Matza, "Putting Foucault to Work"; and Kharkhordin, *Mishel' Fuko i Rossiia*. In a particularly useful analysis of Foucault's engagement with Stalinist history and Cold War politics more broadly, Plamper observes that "the genealogical method effected a leveling of sources that made distinctions between different types of evidence impossible." "Foucault's Gulag," 256. Further describing Foucault's approach to the East-West dichotomy as "underhistoricized" and "undertheorized," Plamper joins other scholars who argue that the critique of liberalism could only have emerged from a thinker well-ensconced in its privileges. Engelstein, "Combined Underdevelopment"; Zhivov, "Chto delat' s Fuko, zanimaias' Russkoi istoriei?"

103. Dickinson, "Biopolitics, Fascism, Democracy"; Makarychev and Medvedev, "Biopolitics and Power."
104. Varley, "Islamic Logics."
105. Collier, *Post-Soviet Social*; Prozorov, *Biopolitics of Stalinism*.
106. Prozorov, *Biopolitics of Stalinism*, 66.
107. Certainly the boundary regarding what liberalism considers outside of governability is debated and shifting, but the distinguishing characteristic of liberal political rationality is the *assumption* that spheres of life exist external to governance. The view of the market as the natural form of human intercourse is exemplary: acts of government can regulate the market but not eradicate it.
108. Collier, *Post-Soviet Social*, 64, 73–74. Prozorov explains, "liberal biopolitics intervenes in the society in order to secure its immanent functioning, which presupposes that this society must retain its self-identity, remain *what it is* in the course of and as a result of governmental interventions. The violent interventions of liberal government must therefore be limited to the cases when the object of government does not (appear to) follow its own natural laws, that is when its very existence is posited as a threat to the self-identity of the society as a whole." Still, "this critique of liberal governmentality that exposes its perpetual transgression of its own limits in the projects of immunitary re-naturalisation of the social realm attunes us to the implausibility of any simplistic contrast between liberalism and totalitarianism as between 'limited' and 'unlimited' government. Nonetheless, it would be equally implausible to efface all differences between, for example, liberal and Stalinist biopolitics on the grounds that liberalism does not respect its own limits." Prozorov, *The Biopolitics of Stalinism*, 99.
109. Collier, *Post-Soviet Social*, 64; Prozorov, *Biopolitics of Stalinism*, 66–67.
110. Prozorov, *Biopolitics of Stalinism*, 105.
111. Prozorov, *Biopolitics of Stalinism*, 123.
112. More specifically, Prozorov argues that the Bolshevik Revolution established the reign of the socialist idea; Stalinism involved forcing the idea into reality, a rationality for governance that Putin also courts. Prozorov, *Biopolitics of Stalinism*, 13–37, 93–94.
113. Greenhalgh and Winkler, *Governing China's Population*, 17–18.
114. Antonov and Medkov, *Vtoroi rebenok*; Antonov and Sorokin, *Sud'ba sem'i v Rossii XXI veka*; for Poland, see Ignaciuk, "No Man's Land?," 1,339.
115. Kligman, *Politics of Duplicity*; Anton, "On Memory Work"; Anton, "For the Good of the Nation."
116. Kligman, *Politics of Duplicity*, 11.
117. Kligman, *Politics of Duplicity*.
118. Kligman, *Politics of Duplicity*, 13.
119. Gail Kligman, *Politics of Duplicity*, 148; Andaya, *Conceiving Cuba*.
120. Greenhalgh and Winkler, *Governing China's Population*. Gammeltoft's research on the ways Vietnamese doctors and couples negotiate the tragic situation of fetal anomalies offers an important example of paternalistic techniques of socialist biopolitics that were not seen as coercive. Like China, Vietnam has proclaimed the importance of child "quality"; the state deploys medical doctors to guide women with affected fetuses to terminate. For their part, women construe childbearing as an obligation to family and nation. The importance of preserving belonging to these collectives

led Vietnamese couples to accept medical and community advice and end their pregnancies. Individual autonomy is an irrelevant concept here, but cultural ideals about belonging and responsibility to community are central. Gammeltoft, *Haunting Images.*

121. This is not to deny the suffering caused by the one-child policy or to imply that all Chinese women accepted the state's ideology. For a poignant account of forced abortion, see Chen, "Globalizing, Reproducing, and Civilizing."

122. Note that when reproductive coercion is used against stigmatized minority communities, the dominant population may accept state power as legitimate. The decades-long state use of coerced sterilization to curb Roma births in Czechoslovakia, and public refusal to reckon with this oppression after communism, is a notorious example. Marks, "The Romani Minority"; Sokolová, "Planned Parenthood." See also Varsa and Szikra, "'New Eugenics,' Gender and Sexuality" for a significant analysis of such historical trends and their current implications across the region.

123. Paxson, *Making Modern Mothers*; Pigg and Adams, "Introduction"; Schneider and Schneider, *Festival of the Poor*; Bledsoe, *Contingent Lives*; Russell, Sobo, and Thompson, *Contraception across Cultures.*

124. Carbaugh, "Competence as Cultural Pragmatics," 191; Carbaugh, "'Soul' and 'Self.'"

125. Carbaugh, "'Soul' and 'Self,'" 189.

126. This is similar to what Yurchak identified as happening when people voted in favor of a resolution during official Soviet-era meetings: rather than expressing their authentic beliefs, they were performing their accommodation to the social process. Alexei Yurchak, *Everything Was Forever.*

127. Ries, "Russian Talk"; Pesman, *Russia and Soul.*

128. Carbaugh, "'Soul' and 'Self.'" Notably, such emotionality was not articulated through the psychologized register shaping Western cultures. Illouz, *Intimacies*; Lerner, "Changing Meanings."

129. In some personal contexts, they also used an obscene language, considered emotional and vulgar.

130. Carbaugh, "Competence as Cultural Pragmatics," 176.

131. In another episode of Donahue's dialogues with Soviet audiences, a middle-aged Soviet woman blurted out "There is no sex in the Soviet Union," implying that the concept of "love," rather than "sex," was culturally salient. Yet the literal absurdity of this phrase became widely cited (and ridiculed) by Soviets and Americans alike for decades. Otkroi glaza, Rossiia, "Fraza 'U nas v SSSR net seksa.'"

132. Solomon, "Social Hygiene and Soviet Public Health"; Solomon, "Demographic Argument"; Krylova, "In Their Own Words?"; Chatterjee and Petrone, "Models of Selfhood and Subjectivity"; Kharkhordin, *Collective and the Individual*; Prozorov, *Biopolitics of Stalinism*; Collier, *Post-Soviet Social*; Halfin, *Terror in My Soul.*

133. Kotkin, *Magnetic Mountain*; Halfin, *Terror in My Soul*; Makarychev and Medvedev, "Biopolitics and Power"; Makarychev and Yatsyk, *Critical Biopolitics*; Prozorov, "Foucault and Soviet Biopolitics"; Prozorov, *Biopolitics of Stalinism.*

134. Solomon, "Social Hygiene in Soviet Medical Education"; Solomon, "Social Hygiene and Soviet Public Health"; Solomon, "Demographic Argument"; Hutchinson and Solomon, "Introduction"; Bernstein, *Dictatorship of Sex*; Starks, *Body Soviet.*

135. Vishnevsky, Denisov, and Sakevich, "Zapret aborta."

136. Zavisca, *Housing the New Russia*; Collier, *Post-Soviet Social*.
137. The comparative availability of contraceptives across European and non-European regions of Russia is an important research question. Public rhetoric includes frequent comments about preserving the Russian "ethno-gene pool" and in public images promoting childbearing, the babies pictured are always white. See Figure 0.1, "To the Idea of Increasing!"
138. Informally, doctors struggled against being identified with the state—for example, by asserting their professional integrity as the basis for wielding legitimate power and authority. Rivkin-Fish, "Moral Science." On professional journalists' relationships with the Soviet state, see Roudakova, *Losing Pravda*.
139. Examining the historiography of the Stalin era, Krylova observes a tendency to portray human agency as unflaggingly rational by describing Soviet people as either heroically resisting totalitarianism or cleverly making deals with the state for their own interests. The assumption of a "tenacious liberal subject" underlying such arguments paradoxically ignores how the "chaotic and socially fragmented" conditions of life during Stalinism "unsettled" people's subjectivity. "Tenacious Liberal Subject," 140. This book examines how a group of medical experts critical of the Soviet abortion culture strove to promote the rationalization of reproductive capacities, without assuming a universally rational or coherent subject.
140. Szacki, *Liberalism after Communism*; Funk, "Feminist Critiques of Liberalism"; Murphey, *Seizing the Means of Reproduction*.
141. Szacki proposes a "situational definition of liberalism." *Liberalism after Communism*, 23.
142. Laruelle, "Illiberalism."
143. Literally, the engineer / technical employee (*inzhenerno-tekhnicheskii rabotnik* or ITR). Lipovetsky, "Poetics of ITR Discourse"; Magun, "They Were Genuinely Liberal"; Zubok, "Technologies of Bringing"; Gessen, *Dead Again*; Gessen, *Future Is History*.
144. Gessen, *Future Is History*, 37.
145. Boym, *Common Places*, 346.
146. Vishnevsky, *Demograficheskaia modernizatsiia Rossii*, 458–66.
147. Vishnevsky advocated addressing the imbalanced dependency ratio by increasing immigration. Vishnevsky, *Demograficheskaia modernizatsiia Rossii*, 503–13.
148. Roudakova, *Losing Pravda*; Bergman, *Meeting the Demands of Reason*.
149. This view was officially propounded starting in the mid-1930s to temper any radicalizing effects that women's political "equality" might have on family formation.
150. Pomerantsev, "Ob iskrennosti v literature"; Mendel, "Hamlet and Soviet Humanism"; Boym, *Common Places*.
151. In this, I follow Verdery, *What Was Socialism, and What Comes Next*? and Gal and Kligman, *Reproducing Gender*.
152. Lipovetsky, "Poetics of ITR Discourse"; Zubok, "Technologies of Bringing"; Gessen, *Dead Again*.
153. Prezidium Verkhovnogo Soveta SSSR, Ukaz ot 23 noiabria 1955 g.
154. Nakachi, in *Replacing the Dead*, argues that Kovrigina, the minister of health who likely drafted the law, defended it as necessary due to the social consequences ensuing from maternal mortality—especially the thousands of orphaned children—and cast it as a pronatalist measure.

155. Vishnevsky, Denisov, and Sakevich, "Contraceptive Revolution in Russia."

156. Prikaz Minzdrav RF of December 28, 1993 N 302 "Ob utverzhdenii perechnia med-itsinskikh pokazanii dlia iskusstvennogo preryvaniia beremennosti." Accessed at https://base.garant.ru/4174920.

157. Health authorities first expanded the category of "social indicators" in 1987 and again in 1996 to prevent women from resorting to illegal, unsafe abortions. The 1987 criteria included only severe injury or death of one's husband, divorce, incarceration of the woman or her husband, loss of parental rights, having three or more children already, and pregnancy resulting from rape. In 1996, the Russian Ministry of Health expanded the criteria to include economic hardship, including a woman's unmarried status, homelessness, or refugee status; having a disabled husband or disabled child to care for; loss of the woman's or her husband's job; and having a salary lower than the minimum living standard for one's region. Women with medical complications could still access abortion at any time until birth. Mishle, *Iuridicheskii spravochnik;* Kulakov et al., *Rukovodstvo,* 26–27.

158. Boym, *Common Places,* notes the subtle change in intonation characterizing the Thaw.

159. Rivkin-Fish, *Women's Health in Post-Soviet Russia;* Rivkin-Fish, "Moral Science."

160. Pravitel'stvo Rossiiskoi Federatsii, "O perechne sotsial'nykh pokazanii"; Timashova, "Mediki vvodiat ogranicheniia."

161. Myers, "After Decades."

162. Price, "What Is Reproductive Justice?" 201.

163. Rosefielde and Hedlund, *Russia since 1980,* 112–13.

164. Rosefielde and Hedlund, 109.

165. Rosefielde and Hedlund, 115.

166. Rosefielde and Hedlund, 117–18.

167. Ries, "Russian Talk"; Shevchenko, *Crisis and the Everyday.*

168. Lindquist, *Conjuring Hope,* xiv.

169. Borenstein, *Overkill.*

170. Shevchenko, *Crisis and the Everyday.* Young adults in the 1990s identified neither as Soviet nor as a "new Russian" (a pejorative label for the ultra-wealthy). They lacked a vocabulary for articulating who they wanted to become through their country's transformation. Oushakine, "In the State of Post-Soviet Aphasia."

171. Borenstein, *Plots against Russia;* Gorham, *After Newspeak;* Malinova, "Konstruirovanie 'liberalizma,'" 28.

172. Vishnevsky, in "Byli li 90-e demograficheskoi katastrofoi dlia Rossii?," notes that the early 1990s spike in excess deaths occurred after two decades of rising male mortality between 1964 and 1984, and did not continue increasing after 1994. Moreover, there were more elderly people in Soviet society at the end of the 1980s than in the previ-ous decades, since many men in earlier cohorts died young in the war. Fertility rates in the 1990s also echoed longer-term effects of the war. Cohorts giving birth then were the children of parents born during the war, who themselves had fewer children than earlier generations. Vishnevsky argues that understanding demographic trends in the 1990s requires accounting for this changing population structure, which popu-lar demographic discourses rarely did.

173. Rosefielde and Hedlund, *Russia since 1980,* 109, 131. Immigration is complex to calculate, as it is may be unregistered and even reversible. Official data show that

more than 791,000 Russian citizens emigrated between 1993 and 2002. While this was partially offset by legal and illegal immigrants from former Soviet republics, exact numbers of immigrants to Russia have been difficult to calculate. Chudinovskikh, "Statistika migratsii znaet ne vse"; Denisenko, "Emigratsiia iz Rossii v strany dal'nego zarubezh'ia."

174. Rivkin-Fish, "From 'Demographic Crisis.'"
175. Zdravomyslova and Temkina, "Crisis of Masculinity"; Dumančić, *Men Out of Focus*.
176. Attwood, *New Soviet Man and Woman*; Antonov and Medkov, *Vtoroi rebenok*; Rivkin-Fish, "Anthropology, Demography."
177. Blium, *Rodit'sia, zhit' i umeret' v SSSR*; DaVanzo, *Russia's Demographic "Crisis"*; Demko, Ioffe, and Zayonchkovskaya, *Population under Duress*; Feshbach, "A Country on the Verge"; Feshbach, "Russia's Population Meltdown"; Vishnevsky, *Demograficheskaia modernizatsiia Rossii.*
178. Antonov and Sorokin, *Sud'ba sem'i*; Derzhavina, "Russia Has 100 Years to Live"; Khorev, "Rynok"; Khorev, "V chem ostrota"; Kostyuk, "Contracts for Babies."
179. Medvedova and Shishova, "Demograficheskaia voina protiv Rossii."
180. Makarychev and Medvedev, "Biopolitics and Power," 59–60.
181. The Russian name is Rossiiskaia Assotsiatsiia Narodonaselenie i Razvitiia and so the acronym RANiR is often used in English. I use RAPD for readers'convenience.
182. Gurkin, "Deputat Milonov predlagaet."
183. Malinova, "Konstruirovanie 'liberalizma' v postsovetskoi Rossii."
184. Laruelle, "Illiberalism."
185. Gal and Kligman, *Politics of Gender.*
186. Mishtal, *Politics of Morality*; Romania is an important exception, decriminalizing abortion immediately after the execution of dictator Nicolae Ceaucescu, but anti-abortion campaigns have not receded.
187. Like Russia, Poland's state has promoted fertility and family while severely attacking concepts of gender and gay rights. Mishtal, *Politics of Morality*; Detwiler and Snitow, "Gender Trouble in Poland."
188. Gal and Kligman, *Politics of Gender.*
189. Ginsburg, *Contested Lives*, 7.
190. Ginsburg, *Contested Lives*, 7.
191. Kumar, "Disgust, Stigma."
192. Holland, "'Survivors of the Abortion Holocaust.'"
193. Hamilton, "Two Antiabortion Activists."
194. Kelly, "In the Name of the Mother"; Haugeberg, *Women against Abortion*; Bryant and Levi, "Abortion Misinformation"; Chan et al., "Patient Experiences."
195. Kelly, "In the Name of the Mother," 210.
196. Kelly, "In the Name of the Mother," 220.
197. Cooper, *Family Values.*
198. The Operation Rescue organization is examined in Maxwell, *Pro-Life Activists in America*, 176–91.
199. Maxwell, *Pro-Life Activists in America*, 176–91; Ginsburg, "America's Souls." That white nationalists also endorse antiabortion messages indicates that the "moral order" to be restored is sometimes also framed in racial terms. Bjork-James, *Divine Institution*. Explanations of the broader rise of conservative populism, a movement

that has embraced antiabortion politics, further expand on these dynamics. Wendy Brown observes that among groups who face pronounced exclusion, hating those who appear to be Other offers a sense of power and pride, which authoritarian leaders like Trump and Putin instigate to their advantage. The search for meaningful connections and worthwhile missions becomes embedded in nostalgic visions of a golden past when order reigned and traditional hierarchies were stable: men and whites and Christians were on top, others subordinated. Abortion bans become a means of trying to re-establish this hierarchy, justified as defending the "innocent" (unborn) and limiting feminist assertions to power. Brown, *In the Ruins of Neoliberalism.*

200. Luehrmann, "Innocence and Demographic Crisis"; Kondakov and Shtorn, "Sex, Alcohol, and Soul"; Zdravomyslova and Temkina, *V poiskakh seksual'nosti*; Zdravomyslova and Temkina, "Crisis of Masculinity"; Zdravomyslova, "Hypocritical Sexuality."

201. Attwood, *New Soviet Man and Woman.*

202. Burawoy, Krotov, and Lytkina, "Involution and Destitution."

203. Leon et al., "Huge Variation." For perspectives that show how a gendered, cultural understanding of being "unneeded" fueled these behaviors among men, see Shkolnikov, McKee, and Leon, "Changes in Life Expectancy"; Danilova et al., "Changing Relationship"; Watson, "Explaining Rising Mortality"; Parsons, *Dying Unneeded.*

204. Some demographers and political elites insisted that increasing fertility was more important than reducing premature mortality and increasing migration (Konygina, "Spiker Mironov"); but more often, the task of increasing fertility was linked to the broader prioritization of family values, itself defined as the key societal need. Antonov and Sorokin, *Sud'ba sem'i v Rossii XXI veka.* Even when some regulatory efforts were made to control alcohol consumption, from Gorbachev's infamous rationing campaign to later efforts in the 2000s to control alcohol production and sale and also improve cardiovascular services, these initiatives were not framed as efforts to "save the nation." State officials barely mentioned homicide and suicide, other key causes of men's death. Danilova et al., "Changing Relationship."

205. Verdery, *What Was Socialism*; Ghodsee, "Feminism-by-Design"; Sperling, *Sex, Politics and Putin.*

206. Laruelle, "Illiberalism."

207. Medvedev, *Return of the Russian Leviathan*, 119–20.

208. Morris and Garibyan, "Russian Cultural Conservatism Critiqued."

209. Chernova, *Semeinaia politiki v sovremennoi Rossii*, analyzes Russia's family and demographic politics.

210. Makarychev and Medvedev, in "Biopolitics and Power in Putin's Russia," call it "sexual sovereignty," but historically, the struggle for demographic sovereignty came first and expanded to include sexual sovereignty in reaction to the gay-rights movement's prominence in Euro-American contexts.

211. Krause, "'Empty Cradles.'"

212. Krastev and Holmes, *Light That Failed.*

213. Shpakovskaya, "How to Be a Good Mother"; Utrata, *Women without Men.*

214. Concerns about contraceptive deficits emerged as early as March 2022. See Kondrashkova, "Postavki budut"; and "'Aborty budut delat' po starinke.'"

Chapter 1

1. Makarova, "Na sokhranenie."
2. This story was published in the respected literary journal *Novyi mir*. For a critical assessment of Baranskaya's writing and this story in particular, see Kelly, *History of Russian Women's Writing*, 397–410.
3. An apartment in which a kitchen, toilet, and maybe a bath are shared by numerous families, each generally occupying a single room. Communal apartments were very widespread in the Soviet era and are invoked as an archetype of the country's poor living conditions.
4. Rivkin-Fish, "Moral Science."
5. For a cogent literary analysis of several of the texts and authors I discuss that also analyzes the reception of writing about the mundane and quotidian in Russian literature, see Sutcliffe, *The Prose of Life*.
6. I take inspiration from other anthropologists' analysis of literature. For examples see Bourdieu, "Is the Structure of Sentimental Education"; Handler and Segal, *Jane Austen*; Narayan, "Ethnography and Fiction"; Narayan, *Alive in the Writing*.
7. The famous violinist example in moral philosophy (published in 1971) was explicit in setting the right to life of the individual fetus against the right of a woman to have jurisdiction over her own body. Thanks to Jane Thrailkill for reminding me of this.
8. Ginsburg, *Contested Lives*.
9. Ginsburg, "America's Souls," 57.
10. State demographers undertook numerous surveys to understand why women limited births, although surveys about why they did so through abortion specifically would only emerge near the end of the Soviet era. See Popov's work, described in Chapter 3.
11. Platonov, *Chevengur*; Sholokhov, *Quiet Flows the Don*; Granat and Volgina, "Ispol'zovanie khudozhestvennoi literatury"; Randall, "'Abortion Will Deprive You.'"
12. Hubbs, *Mother Russia*; Kelly, *History of Russian Women's Writing*; Barker and Gheith, *History of Women's Writing in Russia*.
13. Oushakine's account of the organization of Soldier's Mothers offers an important example of this dynamic, whereby maternal claims regarding their fallen soldier sons garnered them public visibility, social respect, a sense of community, and objects of memory, but not political solutions. Oushakine, *Patriotism of Despair*, 202–33.
14. Critical analyses of the gendered character of Russian literature have extensively examined these tropes and their broader cultural implications. See, for example, Barker and Gheith, *History of Women's Writing in Russia*; Berry, *Postcommunism and the Body Politic*; Borenstein, *Overkill*; Goscilo, *Dehexing Sex*; Goscilo and Holmgren, *Russia—Women—Culture*; Goscilo and Lanoux, *Gender and National Identity*; Kaminer, *Women with a Thirst*; Kaminer, *Haunted Dreams*; Kelly, *A History of Russian Women's Writing*.
15. These are the dates of the original Russian publication. My discussion below draws on some other editions and translations.
16. Goscilo argues that the "the strategy of enfleshment" and frequent turn to the grotesque in Russian women's Glasnost-era writing were deliberate tactics of overturning the clichéd romanticism of "sacred motherhood." *Dehexing Sex*, 97, 99.

17. Unlike the images of Soviet people as wholly rational, self-interested subjects that Krylova critiqued in "The Tenacious Liberal Subject," these narrative accounts powerfully depict fragmented subjectivities shaped by perpetually unstable and contradictory if not violent circumstances.

18. Baranskaya, "A Week Like Any Other Week," 673.

19. Baranskaya, 671.

20. Baranskaya, 671.

21. While Baranskaya's text illustrated these dynamics and problematized the absence of collective discussion around them, her writing did not have the kind of influence that Betty Friedan's *The Feminine Mystique* (1963) did for awakening a generation's consciousness to the negative repercussions of gender inequalities. Baranskaya's story certainly does present a Soviet style rendering of "The Problem That Has No Name," but such broad public critique of the failures of the Soviet system could not happen during the Soviet era.

22. Similarly, other narratives depict women rejecting abortion without reaffirming patriarchal ideals of selfless nurturance (e.g., Voznesenskaya, *The Women's Decameron.*)

23. Baranskaya, "A Week Like Any Other Week," 671.

24. Makarova's rich narrative depicting her stay in a Moscow maternity hospital in the 1970s, "Na sokhranenie," (1989; In maternity hospital on bedrest), reveals the interpersonal dynamics in a ward inhabited by women variously striving to prevent miscarriage, get treated for infertility, and obtain and recover from an abortion. It details miseries for all these inmates in the hospital-prison. After reading this striking account, I contacted Makarova by Facebook to tell her about my research on abortion in the Soviet and post-Soviet contexts.

25. Makarova, "Ulitka v kosmose," 4.

26. Themes related to the Holocaust have been central to much of Makarova's work. She has written extensively about the artists Friedl Dicker-Brandeis and other Jewish intellectuals in the Terezin ghetto.

27. Makarova, "Ulitka v kosmose," 7.

28. Makarova, "Ulitka v kosmose," 16–17.

29. Makarova, "Ulitka v kosmose," 8. She continues with an allusion to God, "That's how HE will punish me," and later suggests the punishment could be by an impersonal fate—"Those without a conscience will be punished." Makarova, "Ulitka v kosmose," 9.

30. Epstein, "Post-Atheism."

31. Makarova, "Ulitka v kosmose," 30.

32. Makarova, 30.

33. Makarova, 31.

34. Makarova, 31. The original is "ukhodit' nado otsiuda, rvat' kogti." I thank Stas Shvabrin for this textured translation.

35. Elena shares Dostoevsky's skepticism toward an ideology of progress based in rational, utilitarian calculus. If saving the whole world isn't worth a single child's tear, she asks, what about "thousands, millions, an ocean of children's tears? Is the world staying still? It moves. On the path to PROGRESS." Makarova, "Ulitka v kosmose," 9–10.

36. Baraulina, "Moral'noe materinstvo." Interpreting abortion as a positive sign of a

woman's fertility and a man's masculinity is not uncommon in patriarchal contexts. See Hilevych "Abortion and Gender Relations," 101; Paxson, *Making Modern Mothers*.

37. "I eto strashno. Ne lichno mne. Eto voobshche strashno. Kakaia-to bessmyslennaia emblema bessmyslennoi tsivilizatsii . . . i takaia vo vsem etom bessmyslennaia obrechennost,' chto khochetsia pozvonit' v Verkhovnyi Sovet i skazat': 'Kozli, ili pridite i posmotrite na nee, ili zakupite, nakonets, protivozachatochnye sredstva.'" Arbatova, *Menia zovut zhenshchina*, 63.
38. "Otdelenie propavshchikh" is the original title.
39. Palei, "Losers' Division," 191.
40. Petrushevskaia, "Bednoe serdtse Pani," 32–35.
41. Petrushevskaia, 32–33.
42. Petrushevskaia, 32–33.
43. Petrushevskaia, 33.
44. Petrushevskaia, 33.
45. Petrushevskaia, 33.
46. Petrushevskaia, 34.
47. Petrushevskaia, 34.
48. Arbatova, *Menia zovut zhenshchina*, 11.
49. Interviewing women and their spouses in Kharkiv about their Soviet-era abortion experiences, Hilevych found that many did not discuss preventing pregnancy, even when they did not want more children. Hilevych, "Abortion and Gender Relations," 96–97.
50. Mother-daughter relationships are a common theme in Russian women's writing. Barker and Gheith, *History of Women's Writing in Russia*, 11.
51. This scene effectively captures the retrospective sense of deprivation that Soviet people experienced in many areas of life when they eventually encountered the material affluence and pluralistic forms of knowledge prevalent abroad. It supports Fehérváry's insight that perceptions of deficit arise in particular historical and social conditions. Fehérváry, "Goods and States," 434.
52. Ulitskaya, "The Orlov-Sokolovs."
53. Ulitskaya, "The Orlov-Sokolovs," 177.
54. Ulitskaya, *The Kukotsky Enigma*.
55. Ulitskaya, *The Kukotsky Enigma*, 23–24.
56. Ulitskaya, *The Kukotsky Enigma*, 61.
57. Ulitskaya, *The Kukotsky Enigma*, 61.
58. In February 2016, I interviewed Ulitskaya and asked whether she was commenting on Russia's contemporary abortion debate through the conflict between Elena and Kukotskii. In line with the Russian intelligentsia ethos of refusing to politicize art (and thus rejecting Soviet ideology), she firmly denied any connection. I see in this book a masterful effort to think beyond abortion as either a (simple) choice or a heinous murder that deserves criminalizing.
59. Ulitskaya, *The Kukotsky Enigma*, 149.
60. Ulitskaya, *The Kukotsky Enigma*, 157.
61. The connection between this event and the broader ethics of abortion becomes more explicit in the next scene, when Tanya returns home and asks her family's housekeeper, a religiously devoted, superstitious, and obedient older woman, Vasilisa,

the question that underlie Tanya's sense of horror at herself:

"Vas, what do you think: when does a soul attach itself to a child, immediately upon conception or only at birth?

Vasilisa bulged her one buttonlike good eye and answered without the slightest hesitation.

"Everyone knows: at conception. What else?"

"Is that church doctrine or what you think?"

Vasilisa ingenuously knotted her brow. She suffered from the persistent delusion that precisely what she thought was church doctrine, but now she suddenly had doubts: The second question seemed more complicated than the first . . . Ulitskaya, *The Kukotsky Enigma*, 159.

62. Ulitskaya, *The Kukotsky Enigma*, 161–62.
63. Arbatova, *Menia zovut zhenshchina*, 11.
64. Arbatova, *Menia zovut zhenshchina*, 11–12.
65. Arbatova is using hyperbole for emphasis here. In Russian and particularly Soviet-ese, the term "Actions" refers to political demonstrations.
66. Arbatova, *Menia zovut zhenshchina*, 53–54.
67. The Decembrist revolt took place in December 1825 by Russian men with liberal leanings in St. Petersburg. Participants not sentenced to death were exiled to Siberia, where many of their wives joined them. The concept of a Decembrist wife came to symbolize a woman's enduring loyalty to her husband.
68. Loseff, *On the Beneficence*.
69. Note that American public framings of pro-choice and pro-life do not exhaust the range of concerns American women themselves have about abortion; Gilligan found that women's moral deliberations over abortion also considered the well-being of important others in a woman's life. Gilligan, *In a Different Voice*.
70. Other narratives depict women inducing abortions themselves (Vasilenko, *Shamara and Other Stories*), or dying from those induced by folk healers (Sholokhov, *Quiet Flows the Don*, 1996), without detailing the exact procedures used.
71. See, for example: Mendel, "Hamlet and Soviet Humanism"; Boym, "'Banality of Evil.'"
72. Caldwell, in *Not by Bread Alone* and *Living Faithfully*, explores similar themes in the Post-Soviet Russian context.

Chapter 2

1. Granat and Volgina, "Ispol'zovanie khudozhestvennoi."
2. Granat and Volgina, "Ispol'zovanie khudozhestvennoi," 29. The authors cite an excerpt from the early twentieth-century Soviet epic novel *And Quiet Flows the Don*, by Mikhail Sholokhov, as a useful resource. In this scene, Granat and Volgina explain, we witness "the last hours of life and death from hemorrhaging after a criminal abortion undertaken by a village 'grandmother.'" If she survived, childlessness due to secondary sterility was deemed another risk. Notably, Randall found that an article published in 1957 by Nikolai Granat also suggested educators recount Sholokhov's novel to portray the harms of abortion. Randall, "'Abortion Will Deprive You,'" 17. This recurring recommendation leads one to wonder how Soviet educators

understood both the causes of illegal abortions and the impacts of their own antiabortion strategies.

3. Solomon, "Social Hygiene and Soviet Public Health"; Solomon, "Social Hygiene in Soviet Medical Education"; Bernstein, *Dictatorship of Sex*; Tricia Starks, *The Body Soviet*; Tatiana Chudakova, *Mixing Medicines*.

4. Solomon and Hutchinson, *Health and Society*; Bernstein, *Dictatorship of Sex*. For the concept's use in the early twentieth-century West, see Feder, "Social Hygiene."

5. Earlier efforts at sanitary enlightenment are discussed in Bernstein, *Dictatorship of Sex*.

6. Peterburgskii et al., "Opyt organizatsii bor'by s abortami"; Chernetskii, "Organizatsiia raboty."

7. Peterburgskii et al., "Opyt organizatsii bor'by s abortami," 151.

8. Michaels, *Lamaze*, 28–32. Michaels similarly documents deficits of anesthesia undermining state promises about childbirth care in the 1930s through the early 1950s.

9. Konovalova, Rivkin-Fish, and Vasil'ev, "Exploring the Material." Note that the bureaucrats were also scientists.

10. Verbenko, Il'in, and Chusova, "Effektivnost' protivozachatochnykh sredstv."

11. Katkova, *Rozhdaemost' v molodykh*, 79.

12. Nikonchik, "Problema kontratseptsii," 5.

13. Katkova, *Rozhdaemost' v molodykh sem'iakh*, 79.

14. Nikonchik mentions studies in Moscow, at the Vsesoiuznom nauchno-issledovatel'skom khimiko-farmatsevticheskom institute (dir. M. V. Rubtsov); in Kharkiv, at the Khar'kovskii khimiko-farmatsevticheskii institute (director M. A. Angarskaia) and Khar'kovskii institute okhrany materinstva i detstva (director A. I. Kornilova); in Kiev, at the Kievskom institute okhrany materinstva i detstva, which had a laboratory for developing new contraceptives directed by Prof. E. F. Shamrai; and in Riga, at the Rizhskom meditsinskom institute, lead by prof. R.L. Shub. Nikonchik, "Problema kontratseptsii," 5.

15. The Gramicidin paste study was directed by M. V. Rubtsov. Nikonchik, "Problema kontratseptsii," 5. Many important details for assessing the reliability of this study are missing from the article. The sample size was quite small; the researchers do not provide their measurements or definitions of correct/incorrect usage; and their methods and findings are also misleading. They used the data from the women's consultation clinics, but not from their own study of 222 women. Finally, the study does not include examination of why the method failed, or why the authors concluded that everyone who got pregnant used the method incorrectly. I thank Anastasia Zeegers for her assistance with this analysis.

16. Nikonchik, "Problema kontratseptsii," 5.

17. Nikonchik, "Problema kontratseptsii," 6; Chernetskii, "Organizatsiia raboty," 20.

18. Stepanov, "Organizatsionnye voprosy problem kontraktseptsii," 7.

19. Verbenko et al. *Aborty i protivozachatochnye*, 34.

20. Verbenko et al., *Aborty i protivozachatochnye*, 34.

21. Sadvokasova, *Sotsial'no-gigienicheskie*. This book was her doktorskaia dissertation, analogous to the German habilitation, establishing her senior professor status. For a short biography of Sadvokasova (1908–1971), see "K 95-letiiu so dnia rozhdeniia Elizavety Alikhanovny Sadvokasovoi," *Demoscope Weekly*, September 25, 2003, https://www.demoscope.ru/weekly/2003/0123/nauka02.php.

22. Sadvokasova, *Sotsial'no-gigienicheskie*, 13, 40, 91–92. Paul Ehrlich's book *The Population Bomb* had just been published in 1968 and popularized the neo-Malthusian approach in the West.

23. Sadvokasova cites V. I. Lenin's article "The Working Class and Neomalthusianism," published in the newspaper *Pravda* on June 13, 1913.

24. Sadvokasova, *Sotsial'no-gigienicheskie*, 93.

25. Sadvokasova, 109–11.

26. Sadvokasova, 13.

27. Sadvokasova, 65–66.

28. Sadvokasova, 67–68.

29. Sadvokasova, 115.

30. Sadvokasova's data were unique: having worked at the central research-methodological bureau of sanitary statistics of Narkomzdrav (the People's Commissariat of Public Health and precursor institution to the Soviet Ministry of Public Health), she had access to the records of every medically induced abortion and those that began outside of medical institutions after the procedure was criminalized in 1936. Sadvokasova analyzed the approximately 400,000 abortion records completed in thirty territories of the Russian Soviet Socialist Republic between 1937 and 1939, which constituted more than 80 percent of all registered abortions in those regions. She also had a representative sample of abortion records from six oblasts in the Ukrainian SSR from 1938. After the legalization of abortion in 1955, the recording of abortions shifted to hospital discharge records, and Sadvokasova analyzed abortions started inside or outside medical facilities between 1958 and 1959. She also examined a survey of 25,902 women who had abortions during those years in the Russian Republic. Sadvokasova, *Sotsial'no-gigienicheskie*, 6; Sadvokasova, *Nekotorye sotsial'no-gigienicheskie*, 46.

31. Sadvokasova, *Sotsial'no-gigienicheskie*, 152–55.

32. Sadvokasova, 152, 155.

33. Sadvokasova, 143–45; on similar trends in Czechoslovakia, 110.

34. Sadvokasova, 147.

35. Sadvokasova, 182.

36. Sadvokasova, 99 (referring to Hungary).

37. Sadvokasova, 182.

38. Sadvokasova, 135. Emphasis added.

39. Sadvokasova, 127.

40. Avdeev, Blum, and Troitskaya further critique the limiting character of Soviet ideology on Sadvokasova's analysis, which led to overemphasizing standard-of-living problems over other reasons abortions are necessary, and paradoxically treated contraception as solely a medical, rather than also a social, issue. Consequently, the authors argue, in the beginning of the 1930s, statistical surveillance of abortions was undertaken for health services planning purposes (to justify the number of beds needed), not to understand its social dynamics. Avdeev, Blum, and Troitskaya, *History of Abortion Statistics*, 50, 61.

41. Volgina, "Sotsial'no-gigienicheskaia," 12–13; Randall, "Abortion Will Deprive You." The reason given was to avoid iatrogenic sterility. The invasive process of curettage,

undertaken by scraping the uterus, often resulted in inflammatory processes that became exacerbated with each subsequent abortion. Moreover, physicians could not see what they were scraping, and sometimes accidentally perforated the uterus.

42. Katkova, *Rozhdaemost' v molodykh sem'iakh*, 3.
43. Katkova, 81, 83, 84.
44. Katkova, 71.
45. Katkova, 72–73, 85–86.
46. Katkova, 71.
47. Katkova, 43.
48. Readers may object to the assumption that medical experts were the only or best source for information about preventing pregnancy, and in many global cases, that objection would hold true. However, there was a dearth of information about preventing pregnancy in Soviet public discourse and the media, and folk remedies had largely been lost or were ineffective. Medical experts were not necessarily a reliable source of information, but they were one of the only sources. Katkova, *Rozhdaemost' v molodykh sem'iakh*, 80.
49. Katkova, 73.
50. Katkova, 84, 88.
51. Katkova, 75.
52. Katkova, 76; see also Bernstein, *The Dictatorship of Sex.*
53. Polchanova, "Analiz metodicheskikh oshibok," 40.
54. Nikonchik, "Problema kontratseptsii," 5.
55. Polchanova, "Analiz metodicheskikh," 37.
56. Polchanova, "Analiz metodicheskikh," 38.
57. Polchanova, "Analiz metodicheskikh," 40.
58. Katkova, *Rozhdaemost' v molodykh sem'iakh*, 84, 88.
59. Katkova, *Rozhdaemost' v molodykh sem'iakh*, 88.
60. Katkova, *Rozhdaemost' v molodykh sem'iakh*, 81–82.
61. Katkova, *Rozhdaemost' v molodykh sem'iakh*, 87; Korostelev and Petrakov, "Izuchenie praktiki planirovaniia sem'i."
62. Katkova, *Rozhdaemost' v molodykh sem'iakh*, 88.
63. For more details on these debates, see Rivkin-Fish, "Anthropology, Demography."
64. The Laboratory of Medical Demography, for instance, was situated under the Ministry of Health of the RSFSR and designed a formula for scientifically calculating contraceptive demand in order to assist planners. See Shneiderman and Popov, "Mediko-demograficheskoe izuchenie"; and Minzdrav RSFSR, "Opredelenie potrebnosti."
65. Minzdrav SSSR Prikaz no. 377 "O merakh po usileniiu bor'by s abortami," August 2, 1962, pg. 1, Gosudarstvennaia tsentr meditsinskaia biblioteka, o–68467, https://rusmed.rucml.ru.
66. The report also mentions Soviet republics of Kazakhstan, Kyrgystan, Armenia, Azerbeijan, Moldova, and Ukraine, including Dnepropetrovsk, Lugansk, Donetsk, and L'vovsk oblasts. Minzdrav SSSR, 1962, p. 2
67. Minzdrav SSSR, 1962, p.2.
68. Minzdrav SSSR, 1962.
69. Minzdrav SSSR, 1962, p.4.

70. Henry P. David (1923–2009) was a world-renowned researcher of abortion and founder of the Transnational Family Research Institute. After earning a PhD in psychology, he moved into the field of public health to address what he considered the root causes of mental illness and individual well-being. David, "Unwanted, 35 Years Later." Although not an anthropologist, Henry David understood and practiced the core principles of anthropological methods in his collaborations from the earliest years of his international work in the 1950s: building rapport by respecting one's interlocutors and recognizing the significance of history, politics, and cultural difference in his and his colleagues' lives.

71. The trip was supported, in part, by the Center for Population Research (NICHD) and the Ford Foundation.

72. David, *Family Planning.*

73. David, *Family Planning,* 9.

74. Geltzer, "Surrogate Epistemology." When abortion statistics became accessible, researchers extensively debated their validity. See Remennick, "Patterns of Birth Control," 47–48, 51; and Popov and David, "Russian Federation."

75. "Reshenie simpoziuma po gormonal'noi kontratseptsii" in *Vsesoiuznyi nauchno-issledovatel'skii institut akusherstva i ginekologii: Glavnoe upravlenie lechebno-profilakticheskoi pomoshchi detiam i materiam MZ SSSR,* Moscow, October 9, 1970. The statement also recognized that hormonal pills can treat numerous gynecological illnesses, preventing the need for invasive surgeries.

76. These were esliuton, noretin, infekundin, enovid, metrulen, stederil, anovlar, ovosisto, and ovulen. Minzdrav SSSR, *Vsesoiuznyi NII akusherstva i ginekologii,* 1970, 1. Document in author's personal files.

77. Minzdrav SSSR, "Reshenie simpoziuma," 1970, 1. Document in author's personal files.

78. Minzdrav SSSR, "Reshenie simpoziuma," 1. It is unclear which neutrotropic substances the text refers to, or what kind of research and development was underway.

79. Minzdrav SSSR, "Reshenie simpoziuma," 1.

80. Persianinov and Manuilova, "O rasshirennoi programme VOZ"; Persianinov and Manuilova, "O sostoianii nauchnykh issledovanii"; Konovalova, "Istoriia razrabotki gormonal'noi kontratseptsii"; Konovalova, Rivkin-Fish, and Vasil'ev, "Exploring the Material."

81. Marks, *Sexual Chemistry,* 138.

82. In Norway, sales of the pill were prohibited for about two years. Marks, *Sexual Chemistry,* 139. The Japanese government only legalized the pill for contraceptive purposes in 1999. Fruehan, "Reproductive Technologies," 15.

83. Marks, *Sexual Chemistry,* 149.

84. Marks, *Sexual Chemistry,* 139.

85. PBS, "Senate Hearings on the Pill."

86. According to the PBS film *The Pill,* there was an 18 percent drop in oral contraceptive use after the hearings.

87. Marks, *Sexual Chemistry,* 150.

88. Marks, *Sexual Chemistry,* 140. Emphasis added.

89. Minzdrav SSSR, "Informatsionnoe pis'mo."

90. Minzdrav SSSR, "Informatsionnoe pis'mo," 1–2.

91. Minzdrav SSSR, "Informatsionnoe pis'mo," 2.

92. Cites "S. M. Kalman, 19—" (copy illegible).

93. Minzdrav SSSR, "Informatsionnoe pis'mo," 3–5.
94. Minzdrav SSSR, "Informatsionnoe pis'mo," 5.
95. Minzdrav SSSR, Prikaz No. 620-DSP.
96. Minzdrav SSSR, Prikaz No. 620-DSP, 107.
97. Minzdrav SSSR, Prikaz No. 620-DSP, 107. Given these deficits, the Order's previous statement, "In the majority of hospitals the abortion procedure is undertaken through vacuum-aspiration, which ensures the fewest number of complications" (105), seems dubious.
98. Minzdrav SSSR Prikaz No. 620-DSP, 104. See also Randall, "Abortion Will Deprive You."
99. Minzdrav SSSR Prikaz No. 620-DSP, 106.
100. Minzdrav SSSR, 106.
101. Minzdrav SSSR, 106.
102. Minzdrav SSSR, 109.
103. Minzdrav SSSR, 109.
104. Minzdrav SSSR, 110.
105. Minzdrav SSSR, 109.
106. Minzdrav SSSR, 103–12.
107. Minzdrav SSSR, 108.
108. The text reads: "Podgotovit' pis'mo v Ministerstvo Meditsinskoi Promyshlennosti s pros'boi vkliuchit' v plany nauchnykh issledovanii na 1980–81 gody . . . raboty po izyskaniiu novykh effektivnykh protivozachatochnykh sredstv i usovershenstvovaniiu imeiushchikhsia" Minzdrav SSSR Prikaz No. 620-DSP, 110–11.
109. I reviewed a selection of six reports in Ministry of Health archives at the State Archives of the Russian Federation (GARF) covering the "experiments" in the cities of Leningrad (2), Minsk (2), and Kyiv, and the regions of Tatar ASSR, Altai Krai, Ivanovsk, Kaliningrad, and Kurgansk (1).
110. Marked "for internal use only," abbreviated DSP.
111. "Spravka po resul'tatakh proverki organizatsii raboty po profilaktike abortov i gineko-logicheskoi pomoshchi v g. Leningrade," January 16, 1987. GARF f. R8009, o.51, d. 2857, l. 17. A 1983 report from Tatar ASSR, Altai Krai, Ivanovsk, Kaliningrad, and Kurgansk regions boasts "practically no queue" for abortions, as maximum waiting times were three to five days. Report from V. A. Alekseev to the Deputy Head of the Main Administration of the Treatment-Prophylactic Assistance to Children and Mothers of MZ SSSR, Baklaenko, N.G., March 30, 1983. GARF f. R8009, o. 51, d. 92, 1. 21.
112. Alekseev report to Baklaenko, 1983, f. R8009, o. 51, d. 92, 1. 21–22. A neuroleptic analgesia is a sedative.
113. Kulakova, T. V (1984–[copy unclear]). "Plan organizatsionnykh meropriiatii Minister-stva Zdravookhraneniia RSFSR po dalneishemu snizheniiu chisla abortov v RSFSR," GARF f. R8009, o. 51,d. 653, l. 30.
114. Kulakova, T. V (1984–[copy unclear]). GARF f. R8009, o. 51, d. 653, l. 30.
115. Report from Paraskevich, L. V., to the Deputy Head of the Main Administration of the Treatment-Prophylactic Assistance to Children and Mothers of MZ SSSR, Baklaenko, N.G., March 3, 1983. GARF f. R8009, o. 51, d. 654, l. 1.
116. Paraskevich report to Baklaenko 1983. GARF f. R8009, o. 51, d. 654, l. 2.
117. Panov, V. G., report to comrade Shchepin, O. P., "MZ RSFSR dokladyvaet o khode vypolneniia resheniia kollegii MZ SSSR ot 22 avgusta 1985g." "O merakh po ustraneiiu

ser'eznykh nedostatkov v organizatsii raboty po snizheniiu abortov v RSFSR," GARF f. R8009, o. 51, d. 2258, l. 51.

118. Panov, V. G., to comrade Shchepin, O. P., GARF f. R8009, o. 51, d. 2258, l. 51.

119. T. V. Kulakova, report to comrade V. I. Lebedeva, Deputy Head of the Department of Treatment-Prophylactic assistance to Children and Mothers, August 6, 1982, GARF f. R8009, o. 51, d. 92. l. 11.

120. T. V. Kulakova, "Plan organizatsionnykh meropriiatii Ministerstva Zdravookhraneniia RSFSR po dal'neishemu snizheniiu chisla abortov v RSFSR, 1984–5"; GARF f. R8009, o. 51, d. 653, l. 30.

121. Minzdrav RSFSR, "Opredelenie potrebnosti," 6–13.

122. I. A. Manuilova et al., *Metody preduprezhdeniia beremennosti.*

123. Manuilova et al., *Metody preduprezhdeniia beremennosti*, 16–18. Chemical methods discussed are gramicidin paste, kontratseptin-T, a vaginal suppository; Liuternurin, a lotion; and Tratseptin, a suppository that gets softened in water prior to insertion.

124. Galascorbin is a complex compound of sodium salts of ascorbic and gallic acids; calcium permanganate is a compound with the chemical formula $Ca(MnO_4)_2$. It consists of the metal calcium and two permanganate ions. The Esmarch apparatus (*kruzhka Esmarkha*) is a rubber or plastic device outfitted with a tube and syringe, used for undertaking enemas or douching. Most Soviet households would have had these. Thanks to Anastasia Zeegers for her assistance on this.

125. Manuilova et al., *Metody preduprezhdeniia beremennosti*, 17. The booklet provides no citations to establish the effectiveness and safety of such concoctions. Doctors are told to recommend such contraceptives for women who have a shallow vaginal canal and whose uterus is positioned backward, whereas not to recommend them for women with deep vaginal canals or tears of the perineum. Manuilova et al., *Metody preduprezhdeniia beremennosti*, 16.

126. Manuilova et al., *Metody preduprezhdeniia beremennosti*, 19.

127. Manuilova et al., *Metody preduprezhdeniia beremennosti*, 19.

128. The US Food and Drug Administration considers postcoital contraceptives to be fundamentally different from typical oral contraceptives and only legalized them in the late 1990s. Food and Drug Administration, "Certain Combined Oral Contraceptives."

129. Manuilova et al., *Metody preduprezhdeniia beremennosti*, 21.

130. Manuilova et al., *Metody preduprezhdeniia beremennosti*, 24, 19.

131. Manuilova et al., *Metody preduprezhdeniia beremennosti*, 25.

132. Prikaz 590-DSP of July 25, 1985, Appendix 4, p. 20

133. Prikaz 590-DSP p. 21

134. Remennick cites 1980s survey data by Babin that found 94 to 95 percent of respondents considered the pill dangerous. Remennick, "Patterns of Birth Control," 56.

135. GARF f. R8009, o. 51, d. 2857, l. 6.

136. GARF f. R8009, o. 51, d. 2857, l. 25.

137. Randall, "'Abortion Will Deprive You.'"

138. Specifically, the law absolved men who fathered children while unmarried to the mother from child support, as a way of promoting conceptions and increasing fertility.

139. Randall, "'Abortion Will Deprive You,'" 18.

140. Khodakov, *Molodym suprugam.*

141. Dobrovol'skaia, *Vred aborta*, 3–4.
142. Dobrovol'skaia, 4.
143. Dobrovol'skaia, 5.
144. Dobrovol'skaia, 5.
145. Dobrovol'skaia, 5.
146. Dobrovol'skaia, 18–20.
147. Dobrovol'skaia, 18–20.
148. Dobrovol'skaia, 22.
149. Dobrovol'skaia, 22.
150. Cervical caps made from rubber were referred to by the initials KR (*kolpachki rezinovye*); those made from metal were called Kafka. The minimal amount of practical details about contraceptives, their proper use, and their success or failure rates was typical of Soviet era anti-abortion materials for the public. See Hilevych, "Abortion and Gender Relations," 94.
151. For more details on the communal apartment, see Boym, *Common Places*.
152. Dobrovol'skaia, *Vred aborta*, 27.
153. Khodakov, *Molodym suprugam*, 3.
154. Khodakov, *Molodym suprugam*, 9–10.
155. Field, *Private Life and Communist Morality*, 51; Kon, *Sexual Revolution in Russia*.
156. Khodakov, *Molodym suprugam*, 119–20.
157. Khodakov, 120–21.
158. Khodakov, 122.
159. Khodakov, 123.
160. Khodakov, 120.
161. Khodakov, 124–25.
162. Khodakov, 125.
163. Michaels, *Curative Powers*; Field, *Private Life and Communist Morality*; Bernstein, *Dictatorship of Sex*; Starks, *The Body Soviet*.
164. Drezgić, "Policies and Practices of Fertility Control"; Ignaciuk, "No Man's Land?"; Kuźma-Markowska and Ignaciuk, "Family Planning Advice."
165. Nakachi, *Replacing the Dead*.
166. Cruikshank, *Will to Empower*.
167. At the same time, it is important to recognize that beyond state messaging, cultural diversity contributed to distinct habits around sexuality, reproduction, and abortion. For example, Hilevych, in "Abortion and Gender Relations," found patterned differences in the ways married couples in Soviet-era Kharkiv and Lviv managed pregnancy prevention and abortions. In Central and Eastern Europe, debates over the meanings of gender equality under socialism blurred the messages communicated in family life education and local understandings of sexuality. Varsa, "'Respect Girls as Future Mothers.'"
168. Stawkowski, "'I Am a Radioactive Mutant'"; Koch, *Free Market Tuberculosis*.

Chapter 3

1. David et al., *Born Unwanted*.
2. Shlapentokh, *Strakh i druzhba v nashem totalitarnom proshlom*.
3. Rivkin-Fish, "Anthropology, Demography."

4. Popov, *Kak mozhno effektivno'*.
5. For Popov, the deficit of contraceptives in Soviet society, compared with the plethora of such devices in the West, served as quintessential signs of the "inhumane" nature of state socialism. Fehérváry, in "Goods and States: The Political Logic of State-Socialist Material Culture," explores this symbolic power of consumer goods under socialism.
6. Popov did this work at the Vsesoiuznyi nauchno-issledovatel'skii institut meditsinskoi i medico-tekhnicheskoi informatsii, the USSR's Ministry of Health All Union Scientific Research Institute of Medical and Medical-Technical Information.
7. Roudakova, *Losing Pravda*.
8. Popov, *Kak mozhno effektivno*, 3.
9. Dobrovol'skaia, *Vred aborta*, 22; Popov, *Kak mozhno effektivno*, 2.
10. In 1980, Bednyi became the director of the new Scientific-Research Laboratory of Medical Demography under the auspices of the Russian Ministry of Health, Moskovskii Nauchno-Issledovatel'skii Institut Epidemiologii i Mikrobiologii, im. G. N. Gabrichevskogo.
11. Feshbach, *Soviet Population Policy Debate*, 72. I thank Inna Leykin for this reference.
12. Bednyi, *Mediko-demograficheskoe*, 38.
13. Popov, "Regulirovanie rozhdenii," 18–19.
14. Popov, "Regulirovanie rozhdenii," 24.
15. In 1990–91, the Soviet statistical organ Goskomstat conducted a national survey of contraceptive use among ninety-three thousand married women. Popov, Visser, and Ketting, "Contraceptive Knowledge."
16. Popov, "Regulirovanie rozhdenii," 193. His study addressed numerous specific dilemmas facing women of different ages and social circumstances as well.
17. Popov, "Novye napravleniia sanitarnogo," 126–28; Popov, "O chastote i prichinakh," 29.
18. Popov, "O chastote i prichinakh," 29.
19. Popov, "O chastote i prichinakh," 30.
20. Popov, "O chastote i prichinakh," 29.
21. Bednyi, *Mediko-demograficheskoe*, 31.
22. Popov, "Demograficheskii aspekt," 76.
23. Perevedentsev, "Continuation of a Controversy," 9–13.
24. While using "revolution" in the Soviet context was provocative, Vishnevsky took it from Adolphe Landry's 1934 book *La révolution démographique*. Personal communication, Sergei Zakharov, June 22, 2001.
25. Kuznetsova, "Glazami zhenshchiny."
26. Vishnevsky, "Ideologizirovannaia demografiia."
27. Bondarskaia, *Rozhdaemost' v SSSR*; Vishnevsky, "Demografiia stalinskoi epokhi."
28. "Sotsial'no-filosofskie problemy demografii (Kruglyi stol)," *Voprosy filosofii* 11 (1974): 82–96; "Sotsial'no-filosofskie problemy demografii (Kruglyi stol)," *Voprosy filosofii* 9 (1974): 84–97; Urlanis, *Problemy dinamiki*; Perevedentsev, "Continuation of a Controversy"; Perevedentsev, "Neobkhodimo stimulirovat'"; Kvasha, *Demograficheskaia politika*.
29. Similar anxieties were cited in most Eastern European countries. David and McIntyre, *Reproductive Behavior*; David, *From Abortion to Contraception*; Gal and Kligman, *Politics of Gender*; Gal and Kligman, *Reproducing Gender*; Kligman, *Politics of Duplicity*.

30. Vishnevsky, "Demograficheskaia revoliutsiia," 59, 57.
31. Vishnevsky, "Demograficheskie protsessy"; Volkov, *Sem'ia —ob"ekt demografii*, 251, 253.
32. Popov, "Planirovanie sem'i na Kamchatke." For insights into the second demographic transition in Russia and its manifestations in changing practices of family formation, see Vishnevsky, *Demograficheskaia modernizatsiia Rossii*; Vishnevsky, *Serp i rubl'*; Vishnevsky, Denisov, and Sakevich, "The Contraceptive Revolution"; Zakharov, "Rozhdaemost' v Rossii"; Zakharov, "Russian Federation"; Zakharov, "Vozrastnaia model'."
33. Zakharov is currently deputy head of the Institute of Demography at the Higher School of Economics named for A. G. Vishnevsky, which the latter founded in 2007.
34. Vishnevsky and Zakharov, "Demograficheskie trevogi Rossii."
35. Vishnevsky and Zakharov, "Demograficheskie trevogi Rossii"; Ivanova and Mikheeva, "Unwed Motherhood."
36. Vishnevsky, "Russkii krest," part I; Vishnevsky, "Russkii krest," part II; Vishnevsky, "Russkii krest," part III; Vishnevsky, *Serb i rubl'*; Leon et al., "Huge Variation"; Vishnevsky and Zakharov, "Demograficheskie trevogi Rossii," 25; Vishnevsky, "The Demographic Situation."
37. Vishnevsky and Zakharov, "Demograficheskie trevogi Rossii," 28.
38. See Chapter 1 of this book for examples, as well as this sarcastic remark by Baranskaya's protagonist, Olga, to her colleagues: "I assure you that I had my two children with national considerations in mind exclusively. I challenge all of you to a competition and hope that you will beat me in the quantity as well as the quality of production! And now—I beg you!—somebody give me some bread." Baranskaya, "A Week Like Any Other Week," 673.
39. Temkina and Zdravomyslova, in "The Sexual Scripts and Identity of Middle-Class Russian Women," note increasing numbers of texts on intimate life and spousal relationships in the 1960s and provide helpful citations. Some translated texts, such as Neubert's *The Questions of the Sexes* (1960) and *The New Marriage Book* (1967), were re-edited for Soviet readers. The overriding message was that sexual relations were ideologically concerning for socialist society and not merely a private matter.
40. Popov, *Kak mozhno effektivno*, 11.
41. Popov, 11.
42. Popov, 11–12.
43. Popov, 7.
44. Hilevych and Sato note that the Soviet magazine *Zdorov'e* urged men to "protect" their women partners from pregnancy. "Popular Medical Discourses," 12. Polish experts urged the calendar method and periodic abstinence as an expression of spousal love. Ignaciuk, "No Man's Land?," 1,344. Many cases of involving men in reproduction aim to shore up patriarchy. See Randall, "Abortion Will Deprive You," 28–29; Paxson, *Making Modern Mothers*, 323; Drezgić, "Policies and Practices," 201; and the discussion of Khodiakov's text later in this chapter.
45. *Otkrytie 'Ia'* (1978, The discovery of the "I") and *V poiskakh sebia* (1984, In search of oneself). On his website, Kon explained that his first article on sexology, published in 1981, was given the ambiguous title "At the Junction of Sciences" ("Na styke nauk") to avoid "dangerous sensationalism."

Kon's efforts to publish on "normal" sexology were thwarted repeatedly throughout the 1980s despite having been published in Germany and Hungary as early as 1981. His *Introduction to Sexology* was published in Russia only in 1988. His later works include his 1995 English book *The Sexual Revolution in Russia*, and the first scholarly books about homosexuality and homophobia in Russia. Igor S. Kon, "O sebe i svoei rabote," personal website of Igor S. Kon, accessed February 18, 2021, http://sexology. incarne.net/about.html.

46. Igor Semenovich Kon, personal website of Igor S. Kon, "Sexology," n.d., https:// sexology.incarne.net/about.html.

47. The state arguably saw Kon's work as more problematic than Vasil'chenko's, which focused on sexopathology. See Rivkin-Fish, "Moral Science."

48. Vishnevsky and Golod, "Krylatyi eros vchera."

49. Viewers knew it would be hard but possible for Zosia to be achieve economic stability as a single mother given the Soviet socialist safety net.

50. Sem'ia Glavatskikh, letter to the editor, *Sovetskaia kul'tura*. February 27, 1979, 4; A. Zhitkov, letter to the editor, *Sovetskaia kul'tura*, February, 27, 1979, 4.

51. Nikolai Savitskii, "Tvoia otvetstvennost'. Kino," *Pravda*, April 5, 1979, 6.

52. Savitskii, "Tvoia otvetstvennost'."

53. Denina, "Eti vzroslye podrostki." These failings became described as the perceived crisis of masculinity in Soviet society. Dumančić, *Men Out of Focus*; Zdravomyslova and Temkina, "Crisis of Masculinity."

54. Popov, *Kak mozhno effektivno*, 2, 3.

55. Popov, *Kak mozhno effektivno*, 32.

56. For excellent descriptions of this zeitgeist and its enduring cultural impacts, see Raleigh, *Soviet Baby Boomers*, and Zubok, *Zhivago's Children*.

57. Pomerantsev, "Ob iskrennosti v literature"; Mendel, "Hamlet and Soviet Humanism."

58. The teacher seems to consider Nadia's statement problematic because it alludes to sexuality; she asserts that it is shameful to speak of such issues "in front of boys."

59. Loving kindness gets redeemed at the end of "Air Crew," when this pilot has entered a happy relationship and helps care for his new partner's young child.

60. Zdravomyslova, "Hypocritical Sexuality"; Zdravomyslova and Temkina, "Crisis of Masculinity."

61. Popov, "Planirovanie sem'i na Kamchatke," 53.

62. Popov, 54.

63. Popov, 53.

64. Popov, 53.

65. Popov, 54.

66. Popov's visions to transform the Soviet-era sphere of reproductive health care by rationalizing its modes of operation and newly integrating it with nongovernmental organizations to ensure it addresses clients' interests with flexibility and creativity would be similarly applied to efforts to transform institutions in the cultural sphere, such as museums, festivals, and the like. See Rogers, *The Depths of Russia*.

67. Popov, "Aborty v Rossii," 116.

68. Popov, "Aborty v Rossii," 116.

Chapter 4

1. Kulakov et al., *Rukovodstvo po planirovaniiu sem'i*.
2. Pravitel'stvo Rossiiskoi Federatsii, Rasporiazhenie of 17 January 1992 No. 92, https://rulaws.ru/goverment/Rasporyazhenie-Pravitelstva-RF-ot-17.01.1992-N-92-r.
3. Pravitel'stvo, Rasporiazhenie of 17 January 1992 No. 92-r.
4. Kulakov et al., *Rukovodstvo po planirovaniiu sem'i*, 44.
5. Surveys with physicians in the 1990s revealed that the majority supported contraceptive use as an alternative to abortions. Borisov, Sinelnikov, and Arkhangelsky, "Aborty i planirovanie sem'i v Rossii"; Borisov, Sinelnikov, and Arkhangelsky, "Expert Opinions on Abortions in Russia."
6. Pigg and Adams, "Introduction"; Rivkin-Fish, "Moral Science."
7. Heuvel, "Right-to-Lifers Hit Russia"; Federman, "Seeding Russia's Culture War."
8. Key foci of early feminist activism involved academic discussion and research, mutual aid in the post-Soviet economic crisis, and organizing against domestic violence. Posadskaya, "Tendentsii izmeneniia zakonodatel'stva," 79–88; Posadskaya, *Russia: A New Era*; Sperling, *Organizing Women*; Hemment, *Empowering Women*; Johnson, *Gender Violence in Russia*. To my knowledge, there were no feminist NGOs working on reproductive rights in Russia during the 1990s. With funding from the MacArthur Foundation, a researcher from the Moscow Center for Gender Studies published a book on the topic in Russian. Ballaeva, *Gendernaia ekspertiza zakonodatel'stva RF*.
9. Calculated per one thousand women aged fifteen to forty-nine, excluding miscarriages. Sakevich, Denisov, and Rivkin-Fish, "Neposledovatel'naia politika."
10. According to Minzdrav data, pill use specifically rose from 1.7 percent in 1990 to 6.8 percent in 1997 and to 12 percent in 2010. Denisov, Sakevich, and Jasilioniene, "Divergent Trends in Abortion," 5.
11. Sakevich, Denisov, and Rivkin-Fish, "Neposledovatel'naia politika," 469. Based on Minzdrav data. Among all women aged fifteen to forty-nine, the percentage using IUDs and hormonal contraceptives increased from 18.9 percent in 1990 to 24.6 percent in 1997. Sakevich and Denisov, "Birth Control in Russia," 19.
12. Babasyan, "Freedom or 'Life,'" 5.
13. Babasyan, "Freedom or 'Life,'" 5.
14. Khomasuridze, "Osnovnye rezul'taty," 51.
15. Babin, "Kontratseptivnoe povedenie suprugov."
16. Babin, "Kontratseptivnoe povedenie suprugov," 146; Popov, "Novye napravleniia sanitarnogo," 125.
17. Babin, "Kontratseptivnoe povedenie suprugov."
18. MZ RSFSR prikaz of 15 November 1991 No. 186. "O merakh po dal'neishemu razvitii ginekologicheskoi pomoshchi naseleniiu RSFSR." Document in author's files; Kulakov et al., *Rukovodstvo po planirovaniiu sem'i*, 14–15.
19. Rukovoditeliam organov upravleniia zdravookhraneniem i farmatsiei administrativnykh territorii Rossiiskoi Federatsii July 30, 1992. No. 06–15/7–15 "O sostoianii s abortami v Rossii i organizatsii sluzhby planirovaniia sem'i" Zamestitel' ministra N.N. Vaganov, 5. Document in author's personal files.
20. Popov lauded the end of the state's monopolizing reproductive health policies and

services as a key to dismantling abortion culture and democratizing society. Popov, "Aborty v Rossii."

21. Rivkin-Fish, "Sexuality Education in Russia"; Luehrmann, "Innocence and Demographic Crisis."

22. Heuvel, "Right-to-Lifers Hit Russia."

23. An example of such early Soviet efforts to conceptualize family planning is Achil'dieva, *Vsesoiuznaia nauchno-prakticheskaia konferentsiia 'planirovanie sem'i i natsional'nye traditsii.*

24. Editorial Board, "Rossiiskaia Assotsiatsiia 'Planirovanie Sem'i,' (RAPS)" *Planirovanie sem'i* 1:4–5, 1993.

25. Turbine, "Russian Women's Perceptions"; Turbine, "Locating Women's Human Rights."

26. Editorial Board, "Rossiiskaia Assotsiatsiia."

27. Editorial Board, "Rossiiskaia Assotsiatsiia."

28. See article 57 of the Russian Federation Law "Ob okhrane zdorov'ia grazhdan v Rossiiskoi Federatsii" FZ No. 5487–1 of July 22, 1993, updated in the Law 323-FZ of November 21, 2011, https://minzdrav.gov.ru/documents/7025-federalnyy-zakon-323-fz-ot-21-noyabrya-2011-g; and Konsul'tantPlius nadezhnaia pravovaia podderzhka, Federal'nyi zakon ot 21.11.2011 N 323-F3 (edited 25 December 2023) "Ob osnovakh okhrany zdorov'ia grazhdan v Rossiiskoi Federatsii" (with changes and additions in force from 1 April 2024), https://www.consultant.ru/document/cons_doc_LAW_121895/de4e-541bee5ef8d3679ce919eed8913ea61b3cc6; and Denisov and Sakevich, "Birth Control in Russia," 265.

29. Rivkin-Fish, "Moral Science"; Rivkin-Fish, *Women's Health in Post-Soviet Russia.*

30. Sherwood-Fabre and Bodrova, "Impact of an Integrated Family," 192. In his study of global family planning programs in Egypt, Ali argues that "approaches like the GATHER model that call for 'listening to the patient' are concrete forms through which medical science seeks to make inroads into the private aspects of people's lives," and undermine "the social nature of childbirth and familial relations . . . by focusing on the individual health of the mother." Ali, *Planning the Family in Egypt,* 53, 179. In post-socialist Russia, however, the "social nature" of childbirth and family involved modes of governance imposed on women by the state that ignored women's longings to design personal lives outside of state interests.

31. Rinehart, Rudy, and Drennan, "GATHER Guide to Counseling."

32. Sherwood-Fabre and Bodrova, "Impact of an Integrated Family," 202.

33. Sherwood-Fabre and Bodrova, "Impact of an Integrated Family," 209.

34. Rivkin-Fish, *Women's Health in Post-Soviet Russia.*

35. Rivkin-Fish, *Women's Health in Post-Soviet Russia,* 72–74.

36. Rivkin-Fish, *Women's Health in Post-Soviet Russia.*

37. The foundation spent over $17 million on its initiative in these years. "Grants Approved from 1991–June 1998, Awards amount $17,273,149," Advisory Gp Meeting/FSU Folder, Henry David Files, Countway Library Center for the History of Medicine, Papers, 1965–2008 H MS c319 Accession #2009-038 Box 4; hereafter, David Files.

38. Kennette Benedict, Memorandum to the MacArthur Foundation Board of Directors, May 14, 1993, p.1, box 4, David Files.

39. David and McIntyre, *Reproductive Behavior*; David, "Eastern Europe."

40. Popov, "Family Planning."

41. David, Henry P., Grant GA#93–23451 FSU. Ipas collection—transferred to Rubenstein Library, Duke University; hereafter, Ipas.

42. David, Henry P., "Initiatives in Reproductive Health and Women's Rights in the Former Soviet Union" 3/93, pp.1–4. Box 4, David Files.

43. David, Henry P., Report of Visit to Moscow and St. Petersburg, April 22–May 2, 1993, Box 4, David Files.

44. David, Henry P., Report of Visit to Moscow, p. 3

45. Barroso, C., Memorandum, Moscow Trip Report, May 4, 1993, Box 4, Folder: Barroso, Countway, David Files.

46. Barroso, C., Memorandum, Moscow Trip Report.

47. David, Henry P., "Narrative Report Grant GA #93–23451 FSU," 15 September 1993, p. 8, Ipas.

48. David, Henry P., "Narrative Report Grant GA #93," p. 9, Ipas.

49. Barroso, C. undated handwritten note to HPD, in Box 4, Folder: Barroso, Countway, David Files.

50. Popov, Andrej A., grant proposal to MacArthur Foundation, May 16, 1993. Popov included me (then Michele Miller) in the grant from this award to support my contributions to our planned collaboration.

51. Chervyakov became the director of TFRI after Popov's death, before himself emigrating to the US. Sergei Zakharov oversaw the coordination of Popov's MacArthur grant, and had Borisov and Archangelsky undertake Popov's planned survey of experts' views of abortion. Borisov, Sinelnikov, and Arkhangelsky, "Aborty i planirovanie"; Borisov, Sinelnikov, and Arkhangelsky, "Pravovye i nravstvennye aspekty."

52. Ballaeva, *Gendernaia ekspertiza*; Turbine, "Russian Women's Perceptions."

53. David, "Report of Visit to Moscow and St. Petersburg, April 22–May 2, 1993," TFRI, David Files. Page 6 notes that the association was "under the auspices of then Deputy Minister of Health, Dr. Baranov."

54. A. A. Likhanov, Reshenie prezidiuma No. P 3/3 11 January 1989, "O sozdanii assotsiatsii 'Sem'ia i zdorov'e v ramkakh Sovetskogo detskogo fonda," in *Family Planning and Induced Abortion in the USSR: The Fact Book*, ed. A. Popov, 261–62. Unpublished manuscript.

55. David, "Report of Visit to Moscow," 12. In an interview with me on December 22, 2016, Erofeeva described conflicts between Manuilova and the committee members leading to a breach and organizational dissolution.

56. David, "Report of Visit to Moscow," 6.

57. Editorial Board, "Rossiiskaia Assotsiatsiia 'Planirovanie sem'i,' RAPS)," *Plannirovanie sem'i* 1, no. 4–5 (1993), 5. For an example of a regional clinic in Kaliningrad, see Zhukova, "Spetsial'nyi vypusk 'MG'," 8. Elsewhere, Grebesheva emphasizes that establishing regional branches of the Association and developing their capacities is a priority. Grebesheva, "Russian Family Planning Association," 36.

58. While Soviet society tended to treat adolescents as children, films made during Glasnost such as "Little Vera" provoked enormous debate by depicting teenagers as complex characters who were not only sexually active, but coping with many kinds of adult problems, including their parents' alcoholism. For insights into how the image of the teenager has been an arena for Russian cultural anxieties, see Kaminer, *Haunted Dreams*.

59. David, "Report of Visit to Moscow," 7.

60. David, "Report of Visit to Moscow," 7.

61. David, "Report of Visit to Moscow," 7.
62. The name Yuventa comes from mythology; according to Gurkin, Yuventa was the Roman god of first love. According to the *Encyclopedia of Ancient History*, Juventas was the Roman goddess of men of military age and associated with the Greek goddess of youth. Woodard, "Juventas," 3,671.
63. St. Petersburg state health care institution, "Gorodskoi tsentr okhrany reproduktivnogo zdorov'ia podrostkov," Iuventa, accessed May 28, 2023, https://juventa-spb.info/o-tsentre/istoriya.
64. Miriam Birdwhistell, "Adolescents and the Pill Culture"; Planned Parenthood of New York City, "Family Planning in New York City."
65. Vadim Kuz'mich Iur'ev's doctoral dissertation showed that only one out of ten adolescent girls who needed gynecological services sought it.
66. Staff included ob-gyns, endocrinologists, andrologists, dermatologists-veneralogists, generalists, cosmetologists, psychotherapists, and psychologists; a telephone hotline has existed since the Center opened. In 1996 a specially trained group of mid-level medical personnel began working on the prevention of negative consequences of teenagers' sexual relations. Sankt-Peterburgskoe gosudarstvennoe biudzhetnoe uchrezhdenie zdravookhraneniia, "Gorodskoi tsentr okhrany reproduktivnogo zdorov'ia podrostkov 'Iuventa,'" 'O tsentre,' accessed December 22, 2021. https://juventa-spb.info/o-tsentre/istoriya.
67. Russia's syphilis rates exploded in the early 1990s. See Tichonova et al., "Epidemics of Syphilis."
68. Department for Adolescent Medicine of the Medical Academy of Post-Graduate Education (formerly GIDUV and currently the North-Western University, named for Mechnikov).
69. Sankt-Peterburgskoe gosudarstvennoe biudzhetnoe uchrezhdenie zdravookhraneniia, "Gorodskoi tsentr okhrany reproduktivnogo zdorov'ia podrostkov 'Iuventa,'" 'O tsentre,' accessed December 22, 2021. https://juventa-spb.info/o-tsentre/istoriya.
70. Krotin specifically identified Tver and Ufa as having strong clinics, and noted that the Russian Republic of Bashkortostan had approximately twenty youth reproductive health clinics.
71. Vol'tskaia, "Problema rannei seksual'nosti" *Radio svoboda*, November 3, 2010; Matza, *Shock Therapy*; Price, "Redefining the Pro-Choice Paradigm."
72. Kulakov et al., *Rukovodstvo po planirovaniiu sem'i.*
73. Editorial Board, "Interview: I. I. Grebesheva," 5.
74. Thomas, "Privetstvie mezhdunarodnoi federatsii," 2–3.
75. Thomas, "Privetstvie mezhdunarodnoi federatsii," 3.
76. "Prava klienta," *Planirovanie sem'i* 2, no. 5, inside front cover, not paginated.
77. Turbine, "Russian Women's Perceptions."
78. Editorial Board, "Interview: I. I. Grebesheva," 6.
79. Kulakov et al., *Rukovodstvo*, 32.
80. Kulakov et al., *Rukovodstvo*, 33.
81. Kulakov et al., *Rukovodstvo*, 33.
82. Kulakov et al., *Rukovodstvo*, 43.

83. While I consider Krotin's commitment to family planning, sex education, and less hierarchical forms of clinician power features of his liberalism, it is arguable that his moderate acceptance of women's equality and rigid rejection of LGBTQ rights also characterize key themes of Russia's conservative ideology. See Novitskaya et al., "Unpacking 'Traditional Values.'"
84. Editorial Board, "Interview: I. I. Grebesheva," 3.
85. Editorial Board, "Interview: I. I. Grebesheva," 6.
86. Goldman, *Women, the State and Revolution*; Ilic, *Women Workers*.
87. Rivkin-Fish, "'Change Yourself,'" 289.
88. Pravitel'stvo Rossiiskoi Federatsii, "O sozdanii Rossiiskoi Assotsiatsii 'Planirovanie Sem'i,' osnovnoi deiatel'nost'iu iavliaetsia uluchshenie demograficheskoi situatsii v Rossiiskoi Federatsii, snizhenie urovnia abortov, materinskoi i mladencheskoi smertnosti," January 17, 1992, https://rulaws.ru/goverment/Rasporyazhenie-Pravitelstva-RF-ot-17.01.1992-N-92-r; Timashova, "Mediki vvodiat ogranicheniia," 123–24.
89. Myers, "After Decades, Russia Narrows."
90. Zolotov, "Defending the Unborn."
91. Editorial Board, "Interview: I. I. Grebesheva," 6.
92. Editorial Board, "Rossiiskaia Assotsiatsiia 'Planirovanie Sem'i," 4.
93. Editorial Board, "Interview: I. I. Grebesheva," 7.
94. Editorial Board, "Interview: I. I. Grebesheva," 4.
95. Editorial Board, "Interview: I. I. Grebesheva," 4–5.
96. Notably, Grebesheva added the need to recognize men's parenting rights: "There's another side to this issue, too. The number of divorces is increasing and as a result the children, who should not be betrayed, suffer. And if a divorce occurs, the child has full right to interact with its father, even if they don't live together, and the father, for his part, should have such a right to interact with his own child and provide care for him." Editorial Board, "Interview: I. I. Grebesheva," 7.
97. Rivkin-Fish, "Moral Science."
98. Rivkin-Fish, *Women's Health*; Rivkin-Fish, "Moral Science."
99. Medvedova and Shishova, "Demograficheskaia voina protiv Rossii."
100. Editorial Board, "Rossiiskaia Assotsiatsia 'Planirovanie Sem'i,'" 4.
101. The scholars were involved with the MacArthur consortium of reproductive rights professionals that Henry David organized, and some had received MacArthur funding a few years earlier to study the impact of early sexual experiences on young adults' gender attitudes. Valery V. Chervyakov, "Sexual Behavior Patterns and Gender Relationships Formation among Youth," proposal to the John D. and Catherine T. MacArthur Foundation (undated), Box 4, Chervyakov folder, David Files.
102. Chervyakov, "Report on the Results," 1.
103. Chervyakov, 15, 9.
104. Chervyakov, 12.
105. Chervyakov, 17.
106. Babasyan, "Freedom or 'Life,'" 5.
107. Kon, "Sexual Counter-Revolution in Russia," manuscript written for the *New York Times*, sent by email from Anastasia Posadskaya to Henry David on June 21, 1997, and archived in David's file at Ipas.

108. Authored by Nina Viktorovna Krivel'skaia of the conservative, nationalist Liberal Democratic Party of Russia, led by Vladimir Zhirinovsky. Nina Krivel'skaia, "Planirovanie sem'i —demograficheskaia voina v Rossii," *Federal'noe sobranie —Parliament Rossiiskoi Federatsii Gosudarstvennaia Duma, Analiticheskii vestnik (21) Oborona i bezopasnost'* 14 (Moscow 1997). http://liv.piramidin.com/politica/krivelskaya_plan/krivelskaya_plan.htm.

109. Babasyan, "Freedom or 'Life,'" 5.

110. Babasyan, "Freedom or 'Life,'" 5. Centers for reproductive health continued to be funded by regional budgets, which legitimated their investments by highlighting their contributions to improving maternal health and fertility rates. See Zhukova, "Spetsial'nyi vypusk"; and Leykin and Rivkin-Fish, "Politicized Demography."

111. Babasyan, "Freedom or 'Life,'" 5.

112. Medvedova and Shishova, "Demograficheskaia voina protiv Rossii"; Borenstein, *Plots against Russia.*

113. Nina Krivel'skaia, "Planirovanie sem'i—demograficheskaia voina v Rossii," *Federal'noe sobranie—Parliament Rossiiskoi Federatsii Gosudarstvennaia Duma, Analiticheskii vestnik (21) Oborona i bezopasnost'* 14 (Moscow 1997): 16. http://liv.piramidin.com/politica/krivelskaya_plan/krivelskaya_plan.htm.

114. Kon, "Sexual Counter-Revolution in Russia."

115. *Odin na odin (One on One)* May 4, 1997, https://www.youtube.com/watch?v=yn-m122y9AI8&t=399s. The video clip from the Duma exchange identifies its source as TV-6 "Skandaly nedeli," March 8, 1997.

116. For insights on the talk show in post-Soviet Russia, see Matza, "Moscow's Echo"; and Gradskova, "Personal Is Not Political?"

117. The budget for family planning in 1993 was 1.0 billion rubles (calculated at the ruble rate on January 1, 1993), while the other programs in the Deti Rossii project received substantially more: Disabled Children (Deti-invalidy) received 5.336 billion rubles and Children of Chernobyl (Deti Chernobylia) received 9.042 billion rubles. In 1994, the Russian Federal budget for 1994 (Federal Law of 1 July 1994, No.9-F3 "O federal'nom biudzhete na 1994 god") allotted Disabled Children 54,696.0 million rubles, Orphan Children 443.2 million rubles; Children of Chernobyl 82,317.4 million rubles, and Children and Family Planning 26,644.4 million rubles. Cited in Ukaz Prezidenta RF of 18.08.94 N.1696, "O prezidentskoi programme 'Deti Rossii,'" accessed June 19, 2019, http://www.zakonprost.ru/content/base/part/366840.

118. In accordance with the Russian Federal budget for 1994. Federal Law of 1 July 1994, No.9-F3 "O federal'nom biudzhete na 1994 god"; 1994 Ukaz Prezidenta RF ot 18.08.94 N.1696 "O prezidentskoi programme 'Deti Rossii,'" accessed June 19, 2019, http://www.zakonprost.ru/content/base/part/366840.

119. In their commitment to and confidence in practical solutions to the country's cascading reproductive health crises, family planning proponents' litanies were structured quite differently than the late Soviet conversation rituals Ries elegantly described. Ries, "Russian Talk."

120. Public health surveillance recorded a hundred-fold increase in HIV cases between 1997 and 2005, even as positive cases were assumed to be grossly underreported. Burchell et al., "Characterization of an Emerging Heterosexual," 807. By 2018, Russian

regions with the highest numbers of reported HIV cases included Cheliabinsk (3034.5 per 100,000 population) and Irkutsk (1997.45 per 100,000 population), while the lowest reported cases were in Tuva (55.2) and Dagestan (84.2 per 100,000 population). Poor access to antiretrovirals resulted in high rates of mortality among HIV positive people in Russia. Zlatko, King, and Mossialos, "HIV in the Russian Federation."

121. *Odin na odin*, May 4, 1997. https://www.youtube.com/watch? v=ynm122y9AI8&t=399s. Translation by author.
122. *Odin na odin*, May 4, 1997.
123. Borenstein, "Selling Russia"; Grzebalska and Peto, "Gendered Modus Operandi"; Gal and Kligman, *Politics of Gender*; Kuhar and Paternotte, *Anti-Gender Campaigns in Europe*; Moss, "Russia as the Saviour"; Sperling, *Sex, Politics and Putin*; Zdravomyslova and Temkina, *V poiskakh seksual'nosti*.
124. Azhgikhina, "Chelovek rozhdaetsia dlia togo."
125. Babasyan, "Freedom or 'Life,'" 5.
126. This is not to disagree with scholars who emphasize how family planning initiatives medicalized contraceptives and disciplined women. Larivaara, "'Planned Baby Is a Rarity'"; Temkina, "The Gynaecologist's Gaze."
127. Gorham, *After Newspeak*; Sperling, *Sex, Politics and Putin*; Borenstein, "Selling Russia"; Borenstein, *Overkill*.

Chapter 5

1. While Kamran Asdar Ali showed how family planning in Egypt aimed to create new user selves, I focus here on how this paradigm became an arena for promoting a new form of professional selves. Ali, *Planning the Family in Egypt*.
2. For another example of efforts to train physicians in communication strategies for clinical consultations, see Zueva, "Kruglyi stol."
3. Temkina and Zdravomyslova, "Sexual Scripts and Identity"; Yurchak, "Soviet Hegemony of Form"; Mazzarino, "Entrepreneurial Women"; Lerner and Zbenovich, "Adapting the Therapeutic Discourse"; Lerner, "Changing Meanings"; Salmenniemi and Vorona, "Reading Self-Help Literature."
4. Matza, "Moscow's Echo," 508; Raikhel, *Governing Habits*, 146–47; Lerner and Zbenovich, "Adapting Therapeutic Discourse."
5. Chudakova, *Mixing Medicines*; Leykin, "Rodologia"; Lindquist, *Conjuring Hope;* Raikhel, *Governing Habits*; Salmenniemi and Vorona, "Reading Self-Help Literature"; Zigon, *"HIV Is God's Blessing."*
6. Rivkin-Fish and Samokhvalov, "Seksual'noe obrazovanie."
7. People usually address those older than themselves and those in positions of authority with the formal "you" (*vy*), and use both the first name and patronymic. Viktor's decision to have me forego these signs of respect thus expressed his egalitarian ethos and independent sensibility.
8. Dikke, Iarotskaia, and Erofeeva, "Strategicheskaia otsenka politiki."
9. "Young Pioneers" was shorthand for Vladimir Lenin All Union Pioneer Organization (Vsesoiuznaia pionerskaia organizatsiia imeni V. I. Lenina), the Soviet youth

group for ages nine to fourteen. The tie Viktor wore was part of the required pioneer uniform.

10. Pavlik Morozov was a school boy during the Stalin era who turned in his own father for being disloyal to communism. Soviet leaders celebrated him as a hero and role model for putting class interests ahead of his family.

11. Komsomol was the Communist youth group for adolescents over age fourteen.

12. In 1978 Samokhvalov studied sexology in the first continuing medical education course in Leningrad with Sergei Sergeevich Leibikh.

13. Similarly, the psychotherapists Matza studied described yearning to abandon the Soviet model of "psycho-correcting" patients and to care for patients' development of their "inner freedom." Matza, *Shock Therapy*.

14. Matza, *Shock Therapy*.

15. Matza, *Shock Therapy*, 56.

16. Muckle, *Portrait of a Soviet School*, 58, cited in Matza, *Shock Therapy*, 60. Plotnikov notes how psychological understandings of *lichnost'* came to dominate the notion of the person at this time, marginalizing philosophical, juridical, and other manners of defining individual selfhood. Plotnikov, "Ot individual'nosti k identichnosti," 80.

17. Rivkin-Fish, *Women's Health*. With Samokhvalov's permission, I have dropped the pseudonym used for him in my earlier book.

18. Rivkin-Fish, *Women's Health*, 114.

19. See, for example, Balint, "The Doctor, His Patient, and the Illness."

20. Plotnikov, "Ot individual'nosti k identichnosti," 78.

21. Plotnikov, "Ot individual'nosti k identichnosti," 78. He continues, drawing on Simmel's distinction between "moral individualism," which conceptualized the autonomous person, and "romantic individualism," which constructed the unique person (78n47). Just as Simmel saw the idea of the unique person as an antiliberal reaction to the ideals of freedom and equality of the eighteenth century, Plotnikov views the contemporary Russian concept of *lichnost'*, used to mean "creative individual," as antithetical to the liberal model of equality within market competition now gaining dominance in Russia. Accordingly, he sees *lichnost'* in decline, becoming replaced with the new concept of identity (*identichnost'*), a form of selfhood based on one's consumption choices.

22. Viktor's shift exemplifies Plotnikov's argument that psychological understandings of *lichnost'* were replacing this term's connotation of an exceptionally creative individual. Plotnikov, "Ot individual'nosti k identichnosti," 80.

23. Temkina, "'Childbirth Is Not a Car Rental.'"

24. Rivkin-Fish and Samokhvalov, "Seksual'noe obrazovanie," 41–46.

25. Matza, *Shock Therapy*; Lerner, "Changing Meanings"; Salmenniemi and Vorona, "Reading Self-Help Literature."

26. Psychotherapy is growing in popularity; Matza, *Shock Therapy*; Salmenniemi and Vorona, "Reading Self-Help Literature"; Lerner, "Changing Meanings."

27. A. Kadnikova, "Konservativnaia gendernaiia mobilizatsiia."

28. Borenstein, *Plots against Russia*.

29. Arkadii Mamontov, "Shkola-XXI. Seksprosvet," *Programma Spetsial'nyi Korrespondent* (Russia Channel 1, July 4, 2010). A transcript of the film is in the author's personal files.

30. Mamontov, "Shkola-XXI," transcript, 1. The film is available on several websites,

including https://oum.video/videos/specialnyy-korrespondent-shkola-21-veka and https://www.youtube.com/watch?v=lDvcncWddBc. Russian subtitles are included on the YouTube version.

31. Mamontov, "Shkola-XXI," transcript, 1.
32. Mamontov, 2.
33. Mamontov, 2.
34. Mamontov, 2.
35. Mamontov, 2.
36. Mamontov, 3.
37. Borenstein, *Plots against Russia*, 67–69.
38. Anatolii Atriukh, "Narodnyi sobor podderzhal aktsiiu 'Za nravstvennoe vozrozhdenie Rossii," *Russkaia narodnaia liniia: informatsionno-analiticheskaia sluzhba*, October 16, 2010. www.ruskline.ru/new_rl/2010/10/16/narodnyj_sobor_podderzhival_aktsiiu_ Za_nravstvennoe_vozrozhdenie_Rossii. Conservatives in Russia consider the paradigm of "juvenile justice" to be an unacceptable import from the West that threatens the moral authority of parents in the name of individual rights, further degrading Russian values and society. Morris and Garibyan, "Russian Cultural Conservatism Critiqued."
39. Atriukh, "'Narodnyi sobor' podderzhal."
40. Atriukh, "'Narodnyi sobor' podderzhal."
41. Gurkin, "Deputat Milonov predlagaet."
42. "Deputat Milonov ustroil skandal v meditsinskom tsentre 'Iuventa,'" *MR7.ru*, June 4, 2012, https://mr-7.ru/articles/2012/06/04/ deputat-milonov-ustroil-skandal-v-meditsinskom-tsentre-iuventa.
43. *Questions and Answers about Abortion* (1997), translated with the title *Opposing Abortion with the Bible* ("Biblei dvizheniia protiv aborta").
44. According to its website, "The Orthodox Medical-Enlightenment Center 'Life' was established in the church of the Annunciation to the Most Holy Theotokos in Petrovskii park on April 19, 1993, with the goal of opposing the murder of unborn children and also informing wide strata of society about issues related to family, marriage, and contemporary problems of biomedical ethics." "About Us," The Orthodox Medical and Educational Center "Life," accessed September 8, 2019, http://life.orthomed.ru/about.
45. Support came from a Finnish prolife branch of the American Center for Bioethical Reform, http://www.abortionno.org/about-cbr, which provided posters with images of aborted fetuses and in 2008 undertook a master class on protesting abortions for the Russian organization. Kadnikova, "Konservativnaia gendernaiia," 48–49.
46. Dikke, Iarotskaia, and Erofeeva, "Strategicheskaia otsenka politiki."
47. Dikke, Iarotskaia, and Erofeeva, "Strategicheskaia otsenka politiki."
48. Bloshanskii and Zhukovskii, "Vakuum aspiratsiia soderzhimogo."
49. Teenagers were provided services for free.
50. On the history of Soviet approaches to clinical trials research, see Vasilyev et al., "Clinical Trials of Rhodiola Rosea"; and Geltzer, "Surrogate Epistemology."
51. Organon's strategy of investing in local community needs represents a widespread corporate model for simultaneously entering a market and developing social legitimacy in the neoliberal age. Analyzing the corporate social responsibility campaigns

of Lukoil in the city of Perm, Douglas Rogers demonstrates the new relationships, communities, and identities that were forged when the corporation invested in cultural creativity and entrepreneurship. These initiatives simultaneously address some of the social needs that capitalism generates and expand inequalities in social access and economic assets. Rogers, *The Depths of Russia*, 216–23.

52. David. "Report of Visit to Moscow," 12.
53. For a fascinating analysis of Organon's journal as marketing disguised as science, see Padamsee, "The Pharmaceutical Corporation."
54. Posadskaya, *Russia: A New Era*; Sperling, *Organizing Women*; Hemment, *Empowering Women*.
55. Kulakov et al., *Rukovodstvo po planirovaniiu sem'i*.
56. Ghodsee, "Feminism-by-Design"; Hemment, *Empowering Women*; Rogers, *Depths of Russia*.
57. Petryna, Lakoff, and Kleinman, *Global Pharmaceuticals*; Rajan, *Pharmocracy*.
58. More research is needed on the work of global pharmaceutical firms in the early post-Soviet years.
59. This campaign was led by the All Russian Association of Parents, which claimed to "deal with the undesirable" (*razobrat'sia s neygodnymi*) in society.
60. Gudarenko, "Obshchestvennoi organizatsii."
61. Erofeeva and colleagues were at the center of many key developments in Russian obstetrics and gynecology. See Dikke, Iarotskaia, and Erofeeva, "Vnedrenie sovremennykh metodov."
62. MED-info, "Liubov Erofeeva, V osnove idei planirovaniia sem'i lezhat prava patsienta," webpage, 2014, med-info.ru/content/view/5037.
63. MED-info, "Liubov Erofeeva."
64. Erofeeva, "'Tolerantnost' po gollandskii," 28–29.
65. MED-info, "Liubov Erofeeva."
66. MED-info, "Liubov Erofeeva."
67. Pravitel'stvo Rossiiskoi Federatsii, "Poriadok finansirovaniia predrodovogo."
68. "'Russkii vzgliad'."
69. "'Russkii vzgliad'."
70. "'Russkii vzgliad'."
71. Michelle Murphey explores US feminism as a liberal biopolitics in Murphey, *Seizing the Means of Reproduction*. Interestingly, while advocating for patients' rights and promoting moral education might involve tension, Viktor's concept of *lichnost'* invoked care for the self and self-respect to justify guidance toward "healthy" practices.

Chapter 6

1. This echoes Borenstein's insight that Russians often view the US as "the ultimate 'bad boyfriend.'" Borenstein, "Caught in a Bad Romance."
2. Inna Perheentupa found that the struggle against Russia's culture of violence was a common inspiration. Perheentupa, *Feminist Politics*, 54–56.
3. Baban, "Women's Sexuality."

4. Cassonet, "Romania."

5. Anton, "For the Good of the Nation."

6. Mishtal, *The Politics of Morality*, 70.

7. Mishtal, *The Politics of Morality*, 81, 103.

8. On Russians' long-standing relationships with Western antiabortion organizations, see Federman, *Seeding Russia's Culture War*; Heuvel, "Right-to-Lifers Hit Russia."

9. Draganov, "Proekt, federal'nyi zakon"; Erofeeva, "Christian Values."

10. Kadnikova, "Konservativnaia gendernaiia mobilizatsiia."

11. Hemment, *Empowering Women*; Gapova, "Gender Equality vs. Difference"; Posadskaya, *Russia: A New Era*; Sperling, *Organizing Women*; Johnson and Saarinen, "Twenty-First-Century Feminisms"; Temkina and Zdravomyslova, "Gender's Crooked Path."

12. Johnson and Saarinen, "Twenty-First-Century Feminisms"; Temkina and Zdravomyslova, "Gender's Crooked Path"; Zdravomyslova, "Gendernoe grazhdanstvo."

13. Pravitel'stvo Rossiskoi Federatsii, Rasporiazhenie, no. 12. 1270-r, "Kontseptsiia demograficheskogo razvitiia Rossiiskoi Federatsii na period do 2015 goda," September 24, 2001, reprinted in *Demoscope Weekly*, accessed June 3, 2010, demoscope.ru/weekly/knigi/koncepciya/koncepciya.html; Gudkov, "Bol'she novykh rozhdenii"; Konygina, "Spiker Mironov predlagaet."

14. Pravitel'stvo Rossiskoi Federatsii, Rasporiazhenie, no. 12. 1270-r, "Kontseptsiia demograficheskogo razvitiia"; Konygina, "Spiker Mironov predlagaet"; Rivkin-Fish, "Conceptualizing Feminist Strategies"; Rivkin-Fish, "Pronatalism, Gender Politics"; Rotkirch, Temkina, and Zdravomyslova, "Who Helps the Degraded Housewife."

15. Sperling, *Sex, Politics and Putin*.

16. Novitskaya, Sperling, Sundstrom, and Johnson importantly clarify the distinct degrees of hostility that Russian elites mobilize towards women's rights, on the one hand, and LGBTQ rights, on the other. While the campaign for so-called "traditional values" endorses women increasing their fertility and values mothering, it does not reject other aspects of gender equality, such as women's participation in the public sphere. Much conservative mobilization against LGBTQ people, by contrast, is overtly exclusionary and condones violence. Novitskaya et al., "Unpacking 'Traditional Values,'" 187–92.

17. Tayler, "What Pussy Riot's Punk Prayer Really Said," *Atlantic*, November 8, 2012, https://www.theatlantic.com/international/archive/2012/11/what-pussy-riots-punk-prayer-really-said/264562.

18. "Holy Slight: How Russia Prosecutes for 'Insulting Religious Feelings," Radio Free Europe / Radio Liberty, August 15, 2017, https://www.rferl.org/a/russia-prosecuting-insults-to-religious-feelings/28678284. html; "Stat'ia 148 - Narushenie prava na svobody sovesti i veroispovedanii," Ugolovnyi kodeks RF ot 13. June 1996 No 63-F3 (red. July 1, 2021) UK RF, https://www.consultant.ru/document/cons_doc_LAW_10699/3f061fb01a04145dc7e07fe39a97509bd2da705f; Federal'nyi zakon ot 29.06.2013 No. 135-F3, "O vnesenii izmenenii v stat'iu 5 federal'nogo zakona: O zashchite detei ot informatsii, prichiniaiushchei vred ikh zdorov'iu i razvitiiu i otdel'nye zakonodatel'nye akty Rossiiskoi Federatsii v tseliakh zashchity detei ot informatsii, propagandiruiushchei otritsanie traditsionnykh tsennostei," http://base.garant.ru/12181695.

19. Alexey Yurtaev, "Inside the Fight."
20. *Argumenty Nedeli Peterburg*, "V Peterburg proshel piket." Notably, neither the RAPD nor any other specific organizations were named on the website or in the article, probably as a measure of safety.
21. The bill was authored by Elena Mizulina and Sergei Popov from United Russia, and endorsed by the Russian Orthodox Church. "Mizulina dopuskaet obsuzh-denie popravok o medpomoshchi pri abortakh," *Ria novosti*, May 26, 2015, ria.ru/20150526/1066455412.html.
22. Thompson introduced this concept to illuminate the rationale behind peasant pro-tests in sixteenth-century England. Thompson, "The Moral Economy." Kohli defined it as "the collectively shared basic moral assumptions constituting a system of reciprocal relations." Kohli, "Retirement and the Moral Economy." See also Minkler and Cole, "Political and Moral Economy."
23. "Koalitsiia za reproduktivnyi vybor 'Grozd' riabiny," Rossiiskaia Assotsiatsiia "Narodo-naselenie i Razvitie" (RANiR), 2011. Accessed through the Wayback Machine: https://web.archive.org/web/20111004061543/http://www.za-vybor.ru/ru/2011-07-29-14-46-03, on May 30, 2024.
24. An account of this history can be found in Erofeeva, "Christian Values."
25. Shkel', "Ubitoe detstvo."
26. The bill was accepted as law on November 21, 2011, No. 323-F3: Pravitel'stvo Rossiiskoi Federatsii, "Federal'nyi zakon Ot 21 noiabria 2011 g. No 323-FZ 'Ob osnovakh okhrany zdorov'ya grazhdan v Rossiiskoi Federatsii.'" (Ministry of Health of the Russian Federation, November 21, 2011), https://minzdrav.gov.ru/documents/7025.
27. Specifically, the Budapest office that deals with human rights; the Russian office had already been closed.
28. Ipas is not an acronym but the organization's name.
29. Markelov, Novoselova, and Uzbekova, "K babke ne khodi."
30. In the 1990s, Lakhova proposed a law on gender equality and founded the political party for Women of Russia, yet she later took a conservative turn and was roundly criticized by younger feminists for asserting, for example, that women should give birth between ages twenty-two and twenty-five and those who give birth after thirty are "old mothers" (*starorodok*). Rudina, "Gnev 'starorodok.'"
31. I use pseudonyms here to protect the identity of activists.
32. Anna Politkovskaya was a Russian journalist and human rights activist, murdered October 7, 2006. Natalia Khusainovna Estemirova was a Russian journalist and human rights activist, murdered on July 15, 2009. Sergei Leonidovich Magnitsky, a tax advisor and auditor who exposed Russian state corruption, was arrested and died eleven months later on November 16, 2009, in police custody. Alexander Valterovich Litvinenko was a former FSB officer who accused the Russian regime of ordering murders of political opponents, defected to Britain, and died on November 23, 2006, from poisoning with polonium 210.
33. Pravitel'stvo Rossiiskoi Federatsii, "Federal'nyi zakon ot 08.05.2010 No 83-FZ 'O vnesenii izmenenii v otdel'nye zakonodatel'nye akty Rossiiskoi Federatsii v sviazi s sovershenstvovaniiem pravovogo polozheniia gosudarstvennykh munitsipal'nykh uchrezdenii," Federal'nogo arkhivnogo agenstva, May 8, 2010, archives.gov.ru/documents/fz83.shtml.

34. Feminist scholars of Russia have analyzed the development of women's crisis centers as a key issue propelling local feminism. Sperling, *Organizing Women*; Hemment, *Empowering Women*; Johnson, *Gender Violence*. Creating this infrastructure has been deemed to be one of the Russian feminist movement's greatest achievements. Johnson and Saarinen, "Twenty-First-Century Feminisms."

35. Perheentupa, *Feminist Politics*.

36. Lerner, "Changing Meanings," 349–68.

37. Perheentupa and Salmenniemi, "Treading the Tightrope"; Matza, *Shock Therapy Psychology*.

38. Perheentupa and Salmenniemi, "Treading the Tightrope," 398.

39. Temkina and Zdravomyslova, "Sexual Scripts and Identity."

40. Gradskova, "The Sexual Self in Russian."

41. Perheentupa, *Feminist Politics*; Perheentupa and Salmenniemi incisively analyze these performance strategies. Perheentupa and Salmenniemi, "Treading the Tightrope."

42. A few were by non-Russians, like myself, and two argued against abortion without defending legal access.

43. Hemment, *Youth Politics*.

44. These videos have been posted on a You Tube channel called Pravo na Abort (The right to an abortion); the URL for the channel, with more than a hundred videos, is https://www.youtube.com/@user-js9lj2ou4t. "#Pravonaabort #46," Pravo na Abort, posted Jan. 30, 2015, YouTube video, 0:01–0:53, https://www.youtube.com/watch?v=M9ZGe1q_lkw.

45. "#Pravonaabort #61," Pravo na Abort, posted Feb. 6, 2015, YouTube video, 0:01–0:06, https://www.youtube.com/watch?v=0xnAiPO7IFE.

46. "#Pravonaabort #61," 0:28–0:52.

47. "#Pravonaabort #101," Pravo na Abort, posted Feb 28, 2015, YouTube video, https://www.youtube.com/watch?v=9_47GKnBZ3c.

48. "#Pravonaabort #108," Pravo na Abort, posted Mar. 4, 2015, YouTube video, 1:43–2:06, https://www.youtube.com/watch?v=ScUmoIXPio4.

49. "#Pravonaabort #50," Pravo na Abort, posted Jan. 30, 2015, YouTube video, 0:01-0:10, https://www.youtube.com/watch?v=hbzx19i9Ybc&t=6s.

50. "#Pravonaabort #50," 0:59–1:38.

51. Parsons, *Dying Unneeded*.

52. I have not found evidence of the advocate's statement that the serial killer, A. Chikatilo, was physically abused as a child.

53. "#Pravonaabort #16," Pravo na Abort, posted Jan. 12, 2015, YouTube video, 0:01–1:39, https://www.youtube.com/watch?v=kzVX-NFIOuA.

54. While Gilligan found similar logics in American women's moral deliberations over abortion, the US pro-choice movement has instead emphasized autonomous, individual selfhood. Gilligan, *In a Different Voice*.

55. As the activists in these photos were not identified online, I maintain their anonymity.

56. "We cannot ignore the fact that the conflict in the Ukraine has unambiguous religious overtones," wrote Patriarch Kirill I, Russian Orthodoxy's leader. He described the Ukrainian military as engaged in a religious war to "overpower the canonical Orthodox Church." Higgins, "Evidence Grows of Russian"; Weir, "Is Russia's Intervention."

57. In addition to being an online meme, some Russians placed this image on their cars as a sign of "patriotism." See Vitalii Drobishev, "A mozhem povtorit' . . .?"

58. "Eto iskusstvo ili net"; Gavasheli, "V Peterburge aktivistki."

59. Temkina and Rivkin-Fish, "Creating Health Care Consumers"; Shpakovskaya, "How to Be a Good Mother."

60. Temkina and Zdravomyslova, "Sexual Scripts and Identity."

61. This logic is strikingly similar to the moral reasoning through relationships described among American women. Gilligan, *In a Different Voice.*

62. Russian activists' concerns resemble other contexts where feminist activism developed out of historical commitments to social welfare. Borovoy and Ghodsee, "Decentering Agency in Feminist Theory."

63. Despite the rejection of many socialist symbols and values, ideas that the state should support certain sectors of the population, including veterans, and certain goals, such as childbearing, continue to enjoy legitimacy. Hemment, "Redefining Need"; Hemment, *Youth Politics*; Rotkirch, Temkina, and Zdravomyslova, "Who Helps the Degraded Housewife?"

Conclusion

1. Azhgikhina, "Chelovek rozhdaetsia dlia togo."

2. Wiedlack, Shoshanova, and Godovannaya, *Queer-Feminist Solidarity*; Hartblay, "Good Ramps, Bad Ramps"; Harblay, *I Was Never Alone*; Klepikova, *Navernoe ia durak*; Aronson, *Slozhnye chuvstva.*

3. Ovsyannikova, "How Should We Talk."

4. Chernova and Shpakovskaya, "The Anti-Abortion Agenda." They also rightly note that the Russian state does not pursue forms of pronatalist social policy that enhance well-being, such as providing high-quality, affordable childcare.

5. Contemporary pre-abortion "counseling" in Russia exemplifies the hybridization of Soviet-era tactics and Western anti-abortion techniques. First established as a policy in October 2010, it has evolved and expanded, coopting the psychotherapeutic surveillance of emotions for manipulative, pronatalist purposes. See, for example, Bezrukova, *Psikhologicheskoe konsul'tirovanie zhenshchin.*

6. Chernova and Shpakovskaya, in "The Anti-Abortion Agenda," cite a January 2019 statement by State Duma deputy V. Milonov arguing against using phrases such as "termination of pregnancy," and instead describing the procedure as "the murder of a person in the womb."

7. Russkaia Pravoslavnaia Tserkov', "Soglashenie o sotrudnichestve."

8. Chernova and Shpakovskaya, "The Anti-Abortion Agenda," 8. See the website of the Istoki Foundation's program "Sviatost' materinstva," https://istoki-foundation.org/programs/vserossijskaya-programma-svyatost-materinstva.

9. Kostarnova, "Trudnosti reproduktivnogo vybora."

10. Chernova and Shpakovskaya observe that in 2018 alone, three hundred nominations from sixty regions of the country competed for recognition. "The Antiabortion Agenda", 8.

11. Borozdina and Novkunskaya, "Patient-Centered Care"; Leykin and Rivkin-Fish,

"Politicized Demography"; Temkina and Rivkin-Fish, "Creating Health Care Consumers."

12. Anna Starobinets recounts the cruelty she encountered from Russian physicians when she faced a desired, but unviable, pregnancy. A famous specialist coldly told her that she would either give birth to a child who would suffer and die in a matter of days or could obtain a late term abortion. When Starobinets asked about obtaining the abortion, he responds by implying it is a dirty and despicable act: "My takimi veshchami ne zanimaemsia" (We don't do those things here). Starobinets, *Posmotri na nego*, 41.

13. Snezhina, "Eto khuzhe nasiliia."

14. Gal and Kligman, *The Politics of Gender*; Gal and Kligman, *Reproducing Gender*. For examples of recent policies, see Cursino, "Hungary Decrees Tighter"; Cassonet, "Romania."

15. In addition to the famous case of post-socialist Poland, Czechoslovakian authorities continued to sterilize Roma women without proper consent or through coercive incentives years after the advent of democracy. The liberal, democratic Czech state continued to refuse to recognize this violation of human rights for decades. It was only through the persistent protests of human rights activists against these sterilizations that they became the topic of societal debate over ethics and negative eugenics and the very concept of reproductive freedom became valued. Mishtal, *The Politics of Morality*; Mishtal, "Quietly 'Beating the System'"; Mishtal, "Reproductive Governance"; Marks, "The Romani Minority," 139.

16. This should not surprise, as history provides myriad examples in which contraceptives and sterilization have been used as an instrument of colonial domination, state oppression, and reproductive stratification under liberal democracies. See Hartmann, *Reproductive Rights and Wrongs*; Ginsburg and Rapp, *Conceiving the New World Order*; Roberts, *Killing the Black Body*.

17. Temkina and Rivkin-Fish, "Creating Health Care Consumers"; Temkina, "'Childbirth Is Not a Car Rental.'"

18. West, "From Choice to Reproductive Justice." For a broader argument about the detrimental consequences of policies that prioritize market mechanisms for family support in the United States and the need for a state that ensures opportunities for care, see Eichner, *Free-Market Family*.

19. Lilla, *Once and Future Liberal*. An important text engaging these issues in philosophical and theoretical terms is Fraser and Honneth, *Redistribution or Recognition?*

20. Although some neoliberal corporations and states try to ameliorate broader trends of social malaise related to inequality, their overall impacts have been minimal. See, for example, Rogers, *The Depths of Russia*.

21. Graff and Korolczuk, *Anti-Gender Politics*; Grzebalska and Peto, "The Gendered Modus Operandi"; Kuhar and Paternotte, *Anti-Gender Campaigns*. For a wide-ranging discussion of illiberalism, see Laruelle, "Illiberalism: A Conceptual Introduction."

BIBLIOGRAPHY

Archival Sources

Henry P. David Papers, Center for the History of Medicine, Francis A. Countway Library of Medicine, Harvard Medical School.

Henry David files, Ipas office (2014), transferred to the David M. Rubenstein Rare Book & Manuscript Library, Duke University.

State Archive of the Russian Federation (GARF), Moscow. f. R8009, Ministry of Health, USSR.

Published Primary and Secondary Sources

Achil'dieva, E. F. *Vsesoiuznaia nauchno-prakticheskaia konferentsiia 'planirovanie sem'i i natsional'nye traditsii.* Tblisi: Institut sotsiologii AN SSSR, Muzei druzhby narodov AN GSSR, Vsesoiuznyi nauchnyi-issledovatel'skyi tsentr po okhrane zdorov'ia materi i rebenka Minzdrava SSSR, NII generative. Funktsii cheloveka im. I.F. Zhordania Minzdrava GSSR, 1988.

Ali, Kamran Asdar. *Planning the Family in Egypt: New Bodies, New Selves.* Austin: University of Texas Press, 2002.

American Experience. "Senate Hearings on the Pill." PBS, accessed October 6, 2019. https://www.pbs.org/wgbh/americanexperience/features/pill-senate-holds-hearings-pill-1970.

Andaya, Elise. *Conceiving Cuba: Reproduction, Women, and the State in the Post-Soviet Era.* New Brunswick, NJ: Rutgers University Press, 2014.

Anderson, Barbara A. "The Role of Abortion in Fertility Decisions in the Soviet Union: Results from Analysis of Data from Soviet Emigres." University of Michigan Population Studies Center Research Report No. 91-231. Ann Arbor, MI: University of Michigan, 1991.

Anton, Lorena. "For the Good of the Nation: Pronatalism and Abortion Ban during Ceauşescu's Romania." In *A Fragmented Landscape: Abortion Governance and Protest Logics in Europe*, edited by Silvia Zordo, Joanna Mishtal, and Lorena Anton, 209–25. New York: Berghahn Books, 2017.

———. "On Memory Work in Post-Communist Europe: A Case Study on Romania's Ways of Remembering Its Pronatalist Past." *Anthropological Journal of European Cultures* 18, no. 2 (2009): 106–22.

Antonov, A. I. and V. M. Medkov. *Vtoroi rebenok.* Moscow: Mysl', 1987.

Antonov, A. I., and S. A. Sorokin. *Sud'ba sem'i v Rossii XXI veka. Razmyshleniia o semeinoi politike, o vozmozhnosti protivodeistviia upadku sem'i i depopuliatsii.* Moscow: Izdatel'skii dom "Graal," 2002.

Arbatova, Maria. *Menia zovut zhenshchina.* Moscow: Al'ma mater, 1997.

Argumenty Nedeli Peterburg. "V Peterburge proshel piket za pravo na aborty." June 26, 2011. https://argumenti.ru/society/2011/06/112994.

Aronson, Polina, ed. *Slozhnye chuvstva. Razgovornik novoi real'nosti: ot ab'iuza do toksichnosti*. Moscow: Individuum, 2021.

Arousell, Jonna, Aje Carlbom, Sara Johnsdotter, Elin C. Larsson, and Birgitta Essén. "Unintended Consequences of Gender Equality Promotion in Swedish Multicultural Contraceptive Counseling: A Discourse Analysis," *Qualitative Health Research* 27, no. 10 (2017): 1,518–28.

Atriukh, Anatolii. "Narodnyi sobor podderzhal aktsiiu 'Za nravstvennoe vozrozhdenie Rossii.'" *Russkaia narodnaia liniia: Informatsionno-analiticheskaia sluzhba*, October 16, 2010. https://ruskline.ru/news_rl/2010/10/16/narodnyj_sobor_podderzhal_akciyu_za_nravstvennoe_vozrozhdenie_rossii.

Attwood, Lynne. *The New Soviet Man and Woman: Sex Role Socialization in the USSR*. London: Macmillan / Centre for Russian and East European Studies, 1990.

Avdeev, Alexandre, Alain Blum, and Irina Troitskaya. "The History of Abortion Statistics in Russia and the USSR from 1900 to 1991." *Population* (An English Selection) 7 (1995): 39–66.

Azhgikhina, Nadezhda. "'Chelovek rozhdaetsia dlia togo, shtoby byt' schastlivym.' Rossiiskaia kontseptsiia demograficheskoi politiki ne uchityvaet ni interesov lichnosti, ne interesov sem'i." *Nezavisimaya Gazeta*, March 16, 2001. Reprinted in *Demoscope Weekly*, March 26–April 8, 2001. http://demoscope.ru/weekly/013/strimir21.php.

Baban, Adriana. "Women's Sexuality and Reproductive Behavior in Post-Ceausescu Romania: A Psychological Approach." In *Reproducing Gender: Politics, Publics, and Everyday Life after Socialism*, edited by Susan Gal and Gail Kligman, 225–56. Princeton, NJ: Princeton University Press, 2000.

Babasyan, Natalya. "'Freedom or 'Life': Secular and Russian Orthodox Organizations Unite in a Struggle against Reproductive Freedom for Women." *Izvestiia* 51, no. 12 (1999): 5.

Babin, E. B. "Kontratseptivnoe povedenie suprugov v gorodskikh sem'iakh." In *Detnost' sem'i: Vchera, segodnya, zavtra*, edited by L.L. Rybakovskii et al., 146–56. Moscow: Mysl', 1986.

Bachlakova, Polina. "Talking to My Grandma about Her 12 Abortions." *Vice*, July 6, 2016. https://www.vice.com/en/article/ypaagw/talking-to-my-grandma-about-her-12-abortions.

Balint, Michael. "The Doctor, His Patient, and the Illness." *Lancet* 265, no. 6866 (1955): 683–88.

Ballaeva, E. A. *Gendernaia ekspertiza zakonodatel'stva RF: Reproduktivnye prava zhenshchin v Rossii*. Moscow: Moscow Center for Gender Studies, 1998.

Baranov, Aleksandr. "A Real Threat to the Nation's Future." *Russian Social Science Review* 39, no. 4 (1998): 4–13.

Baranskaya, Natalia. "A Week Like Any Other Week." *Massachusetts Review* 15, no. 3 (1974): 657–703.

Baraulina, Tat'iana. "Moral'noe materinstvo i vosproizvodstvo zhenskogo opyta." In *V poiskakh seksual'nosti*, edited by Elena Zdravomyslova and Anna Temkina, 366–405. St. Petersburg: Dmitrii Bulanin, 2002.

Barker, Adele Marie, and Jehanne M. Gheith, eds. *A History of Women's Writing in Russia*. Cambridge: Cambridge University Press, 2002.

Barry, Andrew, Thomas Osborne, and Nikolas Rose, eds. *Foucault and Political Reason*. London: University College of London Press, 1996.

Bateneva, Tat'iana. "Na sobach'em urovne." *Izvestiia*, April 1, 1997.

———. "Nevezhestvo pod vidom bioetiki." *Izvestiia*, October 13, 1998. https://dlib.eastview.com/browse/doc/3169383

Bednyi, M. S. *Mediko-demograficheskoe izuchenie narodonaseleniia*. Moscow: Statistika, 1979.

Bergman, Jay. *Meeting the Demands of Reason: The Life and Thought of Andrei Sakharov*. Ithaca, NY: Cornell University Press, 2009.

Berlin, Isaiah. *Liberty: Incorporating Four Essays on Liberty*. Edited by Henry Hardy. Oxford: Oxford University Press, 2002.

Bernstein, Anya. *The Future of Immortality: Remaking Life and Death in Contemporary Russia*. Princeton, NJ: Princeton University Press, 2019.

Bernstein, Frances. *The Dictatorship of Sex: Lifestyle Advice for the Soviet Market*. DeKalb: Northern Illinois Press, 2007.

Berry, Ellen, ed. *Postcommunism and the Body Politic*. New York: NYU Press, 1995.

Bezrukova, S. A. *Psikhologicheskoe konsul'tirovanie zhenshchin po voprosam sokhraneniia beremennosti. Metodicheskie rekomendatsii*. Penza: KotOM, 2017.

Bjork-James, Sophie. *The Divine Institution: White Evangelicalism's Politics of the Family*. New Brunswick, NJ: Rutgers University Press, 2021.

Bledsoe, Caroline H. *Contingent Lives: Fertility, Time, and Aging in West Africa*. Chicago, IL: University of Chicago Press, 2002.

Bloshanskii, Iu. M., and Ia. G. Zhukovskii. "Vakuum aspiratsiia soderzhimogo matki pri zaderzhke menstruatsii." *Akusherstvo i ginekologiia* 7 (1985): 55–58.

Blium, Alen. *Rodit'sia, zhit' i umeret' v SSSR*. Translated by E. Kustova and I. Troitskaya. Moscow: Novoe izdatel'stvo, 2005.

Bondarskaia, G. A. *Rozhdaemost' v SSSR (etnodemograficheskii aspekt)*. Moscow: Statistika, 1977.

Borenstein, Elliot. "Caught in a Bad Romance: What American Means to Russia." Russia Today. Part 1. *Public Books*, October 15, 2015. https://www.publicbooks.org/russia-today-part-1/#borenstein.

———. *Overkill: Sex and Violence in Contemporary Russian Culture*. Ithaca, NY: Cornell University Press, 2008.

———. *Plots against Russia: Conspiracy and Fantasy after Socialism*. Ithaca, NY: Cornell University Press, 2019.

———. "Selling Russia: Prostitution, Masculinity, and the Metaphors of Nationalism after Perestroika." In *Gender and National Identity in Russian Culture*, edited by Helena Goscilo and Andrea Lanoux, 174–95. DeKalb: Northern Illinois University Press, 2006.

Borisov, Vladimir A., Alexander Sinelnikov, and Vladimir Arkhangelsky. "Aborty i planirovanie sem'i v Rossii: Pravovye i nravstvennye aspekty (opros ekspertov)." *Voprosy statistiki* 3 (1997): 75–81.

———. "Expert Opinions on Abortions in Russia." *Choices* 26, no. 2 (1997): 23–26.

———. "Pravovye i nravstvennye aspekty iskusstvennogo preryvaniia beremennosti i planirovaniia sem'i v Rossii: Rezul'taty ekspertnogo oprosa, provedennogo v 1996 godu." *Demograficheskoe obozrenie* 8, no. 2 (2021): 51–73.

Borovoy, Amy, and Kristen Ghodsee. "Decentering Agency in Feminist Theory." *Women's Studies International Forum* 35, no. 3 (2012): 153–65.

Borozdina, Ekaterina, and Anastasiia Novkunskaya. "Patient-Centered Care in Russian Maternity Hospitals: Introducing a New Approach through Professionals' Agency." *Health* 26, no. 2 (2020): 200–220.

Bourdieu, Pierre. "Is the Structure of Sentimental Education an Instance of Social Self-Analysis?" In *The Field of Cultural Production: Essays on Art and Literature*, 144–60. New York: Columbia University Press, 1994.

Boym, Svetlana. "'Banality of Evil,' Mimicry, and the Soviet Subject: Varlam Shalamov and Hannah Arendt." *Slavic Review* 67, no. 2 (2008): 342–63.

———. *Common Places: Mythologies of Everyday Life in Russia*. Cambridge, MA: Harvard University Press, 1995.

Bröckling, Ulrich, Susanne Krasmann, and Thomas Lemke. *Governmentality: Current Issues and Future Challenges*. New York: Routledge, 2011.

Brown, Wendy. *In the Ruins of Neoliberalism: The Rise of Antidemocratic Politics in the West*. New York: Columbia University Press, 2019.

Bryant, Amy G., and Erika E. Levi. "Abortion Misinformation from Crisis Pregnancy Centers in North Carolina." *Contraception*, no. 86 (2012): 752–56.

Burawoy, Michael, Pavel Krotov, and Tatyana Lytkina. "Involution and Destitution in Capitalist Russia." *Ethnography* 1, no. 1 (2000): 43–65.

Burchell, Ann, Liviana Calzavara, V. Orekhovsky, and N. Ladnaya. "Characterization of an Emerging Heterosexual HIV Epidemic in Russia." *Sexually Transmitted Diseases* 35, no. 9 (2008): 807–13.

Bystydzienski, Jill M. "Women's Organizations, Neoliberalism, and Feminism in Poland." *Feminist Formations* 33, no. 2 (2021): 106–28.

Caldwell, Melissa L. *Living Faithfully in an Unjust World: Compassionate Care in Russia*. Berkeley: University of California Press, 2017.

———. *Not by Bread Alone: Social Support in the New Russia*. Berkeley: University of California Press, 2004.

Carbaugh, Donal. "Competence as Cultural Pragmatics: Reflections on Some Soviet and American Encounters." In *Intercultural Communication Competence*, edited by Richard L. Wiseman and Jolene Koester, 176–77. London: Sage Publishers, 1993.

———. "'Soul' and 'Self': Soviet and American Cultures in Conversation." *Quarterly Journal of Speech* 79, no. 2 (1993): 182–200.

Cassonet, Florentin. "Romania: Abortion, Mission (Almost) Impossible." *Osservatorio balcani e caucaso transeuropa*, July 4, 2022. https://www.balcanicaucaso.org/eng/Areas/Romania/Romania-abortion-mission-almost-impossible-219108.

Chan, Elaine, Yelena Korotkaya, Vadim Osadchiy, and Aparna Sridhar. "Patient Experiences at California Crisis Pregnancy Centers: A Mixed-Methods Analysis of Online Crowd-Sourced Reviews, 2010–2019." *Southern Medical Journal* 115, no. 2, (2022): 144–51.

Chatterjee, Choi, and Karen Petrone. "Models of Selfhood and Subjectivity: The Soviet Case in Historical Perspective." *Slavic Review* 67, no. 4 (2008): 967–86.

Chen, Junjie. "Globalizing, Reproducing, and Civilizing Rural Subjects: Population Control Policy and Constructions of Rural Identity in China." In *Reproduction, Globalization, and the State: New Theoretical and Ethnographic Perspectives*, edited by Carole H. Browner and Carolyn F. Sargent, 38–52. Durham, NC: Duke University Press, 2011.

Chernetskii, O. E. "Organizatsiia raboty po snizheniiu abortov." *Sovetskoe zdravookhranenie* 20, no. 6 (1961): 20–22.

Chernomazova, Elena. "Rossiiskaia assotsiatsiia 'Planirovanie sem'i.'" *Zhurnal Zhenshchina Plius . . . Sotsial'no-prosvetitel'skoi zhurnal*, no. 3 (1998). http://www.owl.ru/win/womplus/1998/raps.htm.

Chernova, Zhanna V. "Semeinaia politika v sovremennoi Rossii." *Zhenshchina v Rossiiskom obshchestve* 3, no. 60 (2011): 44–51.

Chernova, Zhanna V., and Larisa Shpakovskaya. "Antiabortnaia povestka v konservativnom diskurse sovremennoi Rossii: Ideologicheskie kampanii, pravovye initsiativy i regional'nye praktiki." *Demograficheskoe obozrenie* 8, no. 2 (2021): 27–50.

Chervyakov, Valeriy. "A Report on the Results of a Sociological Survey of Secondary School

Students in Eight Regions of Russia." Edited by Kevin J. Gardner in collaboration with the AESOP Center, Moscow, 1997.

Chudinovskikh, Ol'ga. "Statistika migratsii znaet ne vse." *Demoscope Weekly*, no. 335–336, June 2–15, 2008. http://www.demoscope.ru/weekly/2008/0335/tema02.php.

Collier, Stephen J. *Post-Soviet Social: Neoliberalism, Social Modernity, Biopolitics*. Princeton, NJ: Princeton University Press, 2011.

Connelly, Matthew. *Fatal Misconception: The Struggle to Control World Population*. Cambridge: Belknap Press of Harvard University, 2008.

———. "Population Control Is History: New Perspectives on the International Campaign to Limit Population Growth." *Comparative Studies in Society and History* 45, no. 1 (2003): 122–47.

Cooper, Melinda. *Family Values: Between Neoliberalism and the New Social Conservatism*. New York: Zone Books, 2017.

Cruikshank, Barbara. *The Will to Empower: Democratic Citizens and Other Subjects*. Ithaca, NY: Cornell University Press, 1999.

Cursino, Malu. "Hungary Decrees Tighter Abortion Rules." BBC News, September 13, 2022. https://www.bbc.com/news/world-europe-62892596.

Danilova, Inna, Vladimir Shkolnikov, Evgeny Avdeev, and David Leon. "Changing Relationship between Alcohol and Life Expectancy in Russia, 1965–2017." *Drug and Alcohol Review*, no. 39 (2020): 790–96. https://doi.org/10.1111/dar.13034.

DaVanzo, Julie, ed. *Russia's Demographic "Crisis."* Santa Monica: RAND, 1996.

David, Henry P., Z. Drytrych, Z. Matejcek, and V. Schuller. *Born Unwanted: Developmental Effects of Denied Abortion*. New York: Springer, 1988.

David, Henry P. *Family Planning and Abortion in the Socialist Countries of Central and Eastern Europe*. New York: The Population Council, 1970.

———. "Eastern Europe: Pronatalist Policies and Private Behavior." *Population Bulletin* 36, no. 6 (1982): 1–47

———. "Unwanted, 35 Years Later: The Prague Study." *Reproductive Health Matters* 14, no. 27 (2006a): 181–90.

———. Interview with Deborah McFarlane. Transcript of audio recording, May 3 and 6, 2005. Population and Reproductive Health Oral History Project. Sophia Smith Collection, Smith College, Northampton, MA (2006b).

David, Henry P., ed., with the assistance of Joanna Skilogianis. *From Abortion to Contraception: A Resource to Public Policies and Reproductive Behavior in Central and Eastern Europe from 1917 to the Present*. Westport, CT: Greenwood Press, 1999.

David, Henry P., and Robert J. McIntyre. *Reproductive Behavior: Central and Eastern European Experience*. New York: Spring Publishing, 1981.

Dean, Mitchell. "Liberal Government and Authoritarianism." *Economy and Society* 31, no. 1 (2002): 37–61.

Demko, George J., Grigory Ioffe, and Zhanna Zayonchkovskaya, eds. *Population under Duress: The Geodemography of Post-Soviet Russia*. Boulder, CO: Westview Press, 1999.

Demoscope Weekly. "'Russkii antikrest' ili chto my znaem o lise?" No. 409–410 (February 8—21, 2010). http://demoscope.ru/weekly/2010/0409/lisa01.php.

Denina, L. "'Eti vzroslye podrostki': Razmyshlenii posle fil'ma 'Shkol'nyi Val's." *Sovetskaia kul'tura*, no. 17 (1979): 4.

Denisenko, Mikhail. "Emigratsiia iz Rossii v strany dal'nego zarubezh'ia." *Demoscope Weekly* June 2012: 4–17. https://www.demoscope.ru/weekly/2012/0513/demoscope513.pdf

Denisov, Boris, and Victoria Sakevich. "Birth Control in Russia: A Swaying Population Policy." In *Wenn die Chemie stimmt . . . Geschlechterbeziehungen und Geburtenplanung im Zeitalter der Pille / Gender Relations and Birth Control in the Age of the "Pill"*). Edited by Lutz Niethammer and Silke Satjukow, 245–68. Göttingen: Wallstein Verlag, 2016.

Denisov, B. P., V. I. Sakevich, A. Jasilioniene. "Divergent Trends in Abortion and Birth Control Practices in Belarus, Russia and Ukraine." *PLoS ONE* 7, no. 11 (2012): e49986. https://doi.org/10.1371/journal.pone.0049986.

Deomampo, Daisy. *Transnational Reproduction: Race, Kinship, and Commercial Surrogacy in India*. New York: New York University Press, 2016.

Derzhavina, Olga. "Russia Has 100 Years to Live: The Country Is Experiencing an Unprecedented Crisis." *Current Digest of the Post-Soviet Press* 50, no. 49. Translated and reprinted from *Segodnia* (December 7, 1998): 1–2.

Desfosses, Helen. "Population Policy in the USSR." *Problems of Communism* 22, no. 4 (1973): 41–55.

———. "Pronatalism in Soviet Law and Propaganda." In *Soviet Population Policy: Conflicts and Constraints*, edited by Helen Desfosses, 95–123. New York: Pergamon Press, 1981.

Detwiler, Katheryn, and Ann Snitow. "Gender Trouble in Poland." *Dissent* 63, no. 4 (2016): 57–66. https://doi.org/10.1353/dss.2016.0075.

Dickinson, Edward Ross. "Biopolitics, Fascism, Democracy: Some Reflections on Our Discourse about 'Modernity.'" *Central European History* 37, no. 1 (2004): 1–48.

Dikke, G. B., E. L. Iarotskaia, and Lyubov V. Erofeeva. "Strategicheskaia otsenka politiki, programm, i uslug v sfere neplaniruemoi beremennosti, abortov, i kontratseptsii v Rossiiskoi Federatsii." *Problemy reproduktsii*, no. 3 (2010): 92–107.

———. "Vnedrenie sovremennykh metodov preryvaniia beremennosti v otechestvennuiu praktiku." *Akusherstvo i ginekologiia*, no. 1 (2014): 67–73.

Dobrovol'skaia, A. *Vred aborta*. Moscow: Meditsina, 1964.

Draganov, V. G. "Proekt, federal'nyi zakon 'o vnesenii izmenenii v federal'nyi zakon 'ob osnovnykh garantiiakh prav rebenka v Rossiiskoi Federatsii' i otdel'nye zakonodatel'nye akty Rossiiskoi Federatsii v tseliakh usileniia garantii prava na zhizn," State Duna, Bill no. 556902–5. 2011.

Drezgić, Rada. "Policies and Practices of Fertility Control under the State Socialism." *History of the Family*, no. 15 (2010): 191–205.

Drobishev, Vitalii. "A Mozhem povtorit'. . . ?" *vitalidrobishev* (blog), LiveJournal, May 3, 2019. https://vitalidrobishev.livejournal.com/7207568.html.

Dumančić, Marko. *Men Out of Focus: The Soviet Masculinity Crisis in the Long 1960s*. Toronto: University of Toronto Press, 2020.

Dunn, Elizabeth. *Privatizing Poland: Baby Food, Big Business, and the Remaking of Labor*. Ithaca, NY: Cornell University Press, 2004.

Editorial Board. "Interview: I. I. Grebesheva." *Planirovanie sem'i*, no. 1 (1994): 3–7.

Editorial Board. "Rossiiskaia assotsiatsiia 'Planirovanie sem'i.' (RAPS)." *Planirovanie sem'i*, no. 1 (1993): 4–5.

Eichner, Maxine. *The Free-Market Family: How the Market Crushed the American Dream (and How It Can Be Restored)*. New York: Oxford University Press, 2020.

Ehrlich, Paul R. *The Population Bomb*. New York: Ballantine Books, 1968.

Engelstein, Laura. "Combined Underdevelopment: Development and the Law in Imperial and Soviet Russia." *American Historical Review* 98, no. 2 (1993): 338–53.

Epstein, Mikhail, Alexander Genis, and Slobodanka Vladiv-Glover, *Russian Postmodernism: New Perspectives on Post-Soviet Culture*. Translated by Slobodanka Vladiv-Glover. New York: Berghahn Books.

Erofeeva, Liubov'. "Aborty naprashivaiutsia na zapret." *Gazeta*, 2010. Reprinted in *Demoscope Weekly*, no. 409–410, February 8–21, 2010. http://www.demoscope.ru/weekly/2010/0409/gazeta01.php.

———. "Christian Values and Women's Reproductive Rights in Modern Russia—Is a Consensus Ever Possible?" *American Journal of Public Health*, no. 103 (2013): 1,931–34.

Erofeeva, L. V. "'Tolerantnost' po gollandskii,' oznochaet ne chto inoe, kak samyi nizkii uroven' abortov v mire!" *Planirovanie sem'i*, no. 1–2 (2009): 28–29.

"Eto iskusstvo ili net: Aktsiia—rozhai miaso / feminizm v iskusstve," Kyctto, posted Mar 17, 2019, YouTube video, https://www.youtube.com/watch?v=QlgT9LeFFzg.

Fábián, Katalin. *Contemporary Women's Movements in Hungary: Globalization, Democracy, and Gender Equality*. Washington, DC: Woodrow Wilson Press, 2009.

Feder, E. "Social Hygiene." In *The Reader's Companion to U.S. Women's History*, edited by W. P. Mankiller. Boston, MA: Houghton Mifflin, 1998.

Federman, Adam. "Seeding Russia's Culture War." *The Nation*, January 27, 2014, 17–22.

Fehérváry, Krisztina. "Goods and States: The Political Logic of State-Socialist Material Culture." *Comparative Studies in Society and History* 51, no. 2 (2009): 426–59.

Feshbach, Murray. "A Country on the Verge." *New York Times*, May 31, 2003. https://www.nytimes.com/2003/05/31/opinion/a-country-on-the-verge.html.

———. "Russia's Population Meltdown." *Wilson Quarterly* 25, no. 1 (2001): 15–2.

———. *The Soviet Population Policy Debate: Actors and Issues*. Santa Monica, CA: RAND, 1986.

Field, Deborah. *Private Life and Communist Morality in Khrushchev's Russia*. New York: Peter Lang, 2007.

Food and Drug Administration. "Certain Combined Oral Contraceptives for Use as Postcoital Emergency Contraception." *Federal Register* 62, no. 37 (February 25, 1997): 8,610–12.

Foucault, Michel. *The History of Sexuality*. New York: Pantheon Books, 1978.

Foucault, Michel, Michel Senellart, and Graham Burchell. *The Birth of Biopolitics: Lectures at the Collège de France, 1978–79*. Basingstoke, UK: Palgrave Macmillan, 2008.

Fraser, Nancy. "Feminism, Capitalism and the Cunning of History." *New Left Review*, no. 56 (2009): 97–117.

Fraser, Nancy, and Axel Honneth. *Redistribution or Recognition?: A Political-Philosophical Exchange*. Translated by Joel Golb, James Ingram, and Christiane Wilke. London: Verso, 2003.

Frejka, Tomas, and Sergei Zakharov. "The Apparent Failure of Russia's Pronatalist Family Policies." *Population and Development Review* 39, no. 4 (2013): 635–47.

Fruehan, Shana. "Reproductive Technologies in Japan." *Anthropology News*, January 2005, 15–18.

Funk, Nanette. "Contra Fraser on Feminism and Neoliberalism." *Hypatia* 28, no. 1 (2013): 179–96.

———. "Feminist Critiques of Liberalism: Can They Travel East? Their Relevance in Eastern and Central Europe and the Former Soviet Union." *Signs* 29, no. 3 (2004): 695–726.

Funk, Nanette, and Magda Mueller, eds. *Gender Politics and Post-Communism: Reflections from Eastern Europe and the Former Soviet Union*. New York: Routledge, 1993.

Gal, Susan. "Feminism in Civil Society." In *Transitions, Environments, Translations: Feminisms in International Politics*, edited by Joan W. Scott, Cora Kaplan, and Debra Keates, 30–45. New York: Routledge, 1994.

———. "Gender in the Post-Socialist Transition: The Abortion Debate in Hungary." *East European Politics and Societies* 8, no. 2 (1994): 256–86.

Gal, Susan, and Gail Kligman. *The Politics of Gender after Socialism*. Princeton, NJ: Princeton University Press, 2000.

Gal, Susan, and Gail Kligman, eds. *Reproducing Gender: Politics, Publics, and Everyday Life after Socialism*. Princeton, NJ: Princeton University Press, 2000.

Gammeltoft, Tine. *Haunting Images: A Cultural Account of Selective Reproduction in Vietnam*. Berkeley: University of California Press, 2014.

Gapova, Elena. "Gender Equality vs. Difference and What Post-Socialism Can Teach Us." *Women's Studies International Forum*, no. 59 (2016): 9–16.

Gavasheli, Mayya. "V Peterburge aktivistki proveli aktsiiu 'Rozhai miaso' protiv sluzhby v armii." *TJournal*, February 23, 2019, https://tjournal.ru/news/88753-v-peterburge-aktivistki-proveli-akciyu-rozhay-myaso-protiv-sluzhby-v-armii.

Geltzer, Anna. "Surrogate Epistemology: The Transition from Soviet to Russian Biomedicine." PhD diss., Cornell University, 2012.

Gessen, Masha. *Dead Again: The Intelligentsia after Communism*. New York: Verso, 1997.

———. *The Future Is History: How Totalitarianism Reclaimed Russia*. New York: Riverhead Books, 2017.

Ghodsee, Kristen. "Feminism-by-Design: Emerging Capitalisms Cultural Feminism, and Women's Nongovernmental Organizations in Postsocialist Eastern Europe." *Signs* 29, no. 3 (2004): 727–53.

———. "Why Women Had Better Sex under Socialism." *New York Times*, August 12, 2017. https://www.nytimes.com/2017/08/12/opinion/why-women-had-better-sex-under-socialism.html.

———. *Why Women Have Better Sex under Socialism (and Other Arguments for Economic Independence*. New York: Bold Type Books, 2018.

Gilligan, Carol. *In a Different Voice: Psychological Theory and Women's Development*. Cambridge, MA: Harvard University Press, 1982.

Ginsburg, Faye. "America's Souls: Operation Rescue's Crusade against Abortion." In *Fundamentalisms and the State: Remaking Politics, Economies, and Militance*, edited by Martin E. Marty and R. Scott Appleby, 557–88. Chicago: University of Chicago Press, 1993.

Ginsburg, Faye D. *Contested Lives: The Abortion Debate in an American Community*. Berkeley: University of California Press, 1989.

Ginsburg, Faye D., and Rayna Rapp. *Conceiving the New World Order: The Global Politics of Reproduction*. Berkeley: University of California Press, 1995.

Goldman, Wendy Z. *Women, the State and Revolution: Soviet Family Policy and Social Life, 1917–1936*. Cambridge: Cambridge University Press, 1993.

Gorbachova, Ada. "Demographic Twilight." *Current Digest of the Post-Soviet Press* 52, no. 30 (2000): 7–8. Translated and reprinted from *Nezavisimaya gazeta*, July 6, 2000: 9.

Gordon, Linda. *The Moral Property of Women: A History of Birth Control Politics in America*. Urbana: University of Illinois Press, 2007.

Gorham, Michael. *After Newspeak: Language Culture and Politics in Russia from Gorbachev to Putin*. Ithaca, NY: Cornell University Press, 2014.

Goscilo, Helena. *Dehexing Sex: Russian Womanhood During and After Glasnost*. Ann Arbor: University of Michigan Press, 1996.

———. "Perestroika and Soviet Prose: From Dazzle to Dispersal." In *A History of Women's Writing in Russia*, edited by Adele Barker and Jehanne Gheith, 297–312. Cambridge: Cambridge University Press, 2002.

Goscilo, Helena, and Beth Holmgren, eds. *Russia—Women—Culture*. Bloomington: Indiana University Press, 1996.

Goscilo, Helena, and Andrea Lanoux, eds. *Gender and National Identity in Russian Culture*. DeKalb: Northern Illinois University Press, 2006.

Gradskova, Yulia. "The Sexual Self in Russian Talk Shows of the 1990s." *Sexuality and Culture*, no. 24 (2020): 389–407.

Gradskova, Yulia, and Ildikó Asztalos Morell, eds. *Gendering Postsocialism: Old Legacies and New Hierarchies*. New York: Routledge, 2018.

Graff, Agnieszka, and Elżbieta Korolczuk. *Anti-Gender Politics in the Populist Movement*. New York: Routledge, 2022.

Granat, N. E., and V. F. Volgina. "Ispol'zovanie khudozhestvennoi literatury v protivabortnoi propagande." *Fel'dsher i akusherka* 12, no. 1 (1991): 29–33.

Grebesheva, Inga. "Russian Family Planning Association." *Planned Parenthood in Europe* 23, no. 2 (1994): 35–36.

Greenhalgh, Susan, and Edwin Winkler. *Governing China's Population: From Leninist to Neoliberal Biopolitics*. Redwood City, CA: Stanford University Press, 2005.

Grzebalska, Weronika, and Andrea Peto. "The Gendered Modus Operandi of the Illiberal Transformation in Hungary and Poland." *Women's Studies International Forum* 68 (2018): 164–72. https://doi.org/10.1016/j.wsif.2017.12.001.

Gudarenko, R.F. "Obshchestvennoi organizatsii 'Otvetstvennoe roditel'stvo' (Stavropol'skii krai) v sodeistvii i ukreplenii prestizha semi'i v obshchestve." *Planirovanie sem'i* 1, no. 2 (2009): 12–14.

Gudkov, Andrei. "Bol'she novykh rozhdenii." *Vedomosti*, January 16, 2008. Reprinted in *Demoscope Weekly*, Jan. 21–Feb. 3, 2008. http://www.demoscope.ru/weekly/2008/0317/gazeta09.php.

Gurkin, Sergei. "Deputat Milonov predlagaet zakryt' tsentr 'Iuventa,' gde podrostkam delaiut aborty." *Delovoi Peterburg*, DP.Ru, April 19, 2012. https://dp.ru/a/2012/04/19/Deputat_Milonov_predlagae.

Haavio-Mannila, Elina, and Osmo Kontula. "Single and Double Sexual Standards in Finland, Estonia, and St. Petersburg." *Journal of Sex Research* 40, no. 1 (2003): 36–49. https://doi.org/10.1080/00224490309552165.

Halfin, Igal. *Terror in My Soul: Communist Autobiographies on Trial*. Cambridge, MA: Harvard University Press, 2003.

Halkias, Alexandra. *The Empty Cradle of Democracy: Sex, Abortion and Nationalism in Modern Greece*. Durham, NC: Duke University Press, 2004.

Hall, Bogumila. "Resistance to Right-Wing Populism: Black Protest and a New Wave of Feminist Activism in Poland?" *American Behavioral Scientist* 63, no. 10 (2019): 1,497–515.

Hamilton, Matt. "Two Antiabortion Activists behind Undercover Planned Parenthood Videos Charged with 15 Felonies." *Los Angeles Times*, Mar. 28, 2017. https://www.latimes.com/local/lanow/la-me-ln-planned-parenthood-charges-activists-20170328-story.html.

Handler, Richard, and Daniel Segal. *Jane Austen and the Fiction of Culture: An Essay on the Narration of Social Realities*. Lanham, MD: Rowman and Littlefield, 1999.

Hartblay, Cassandra. "Good Ramps, Bad Ramps: Centralized Design Standards and Disability Access in Urban Russian Infrastructure." *American Ethnologist* 44, no. 1 (2017): 9–22.

_____. *I Was Never Alone, or, Oporniki: An Ethnographic Play on Disability in Russia*. Toronto: University of Toronto Press, 2020.

Hartmann, Betsy. *Reproductive Rights and Wrongs: The Global Politics of Population Control and Contraceptive Choice*. New York: Harper Collins, 1987.

Haugeberg, Karissa. *Women against Abortion: Inside the Largest Moral Reform Movement of the Twentieth Century*. Urbana: University of Illinois Press, 2017.

Heer, David M. "Contraception and Population Policy in the Soviet Union." *Demography*, no. 2 (1965): 531–39.

Hemment, Julie Dawn. *Empowering Women in Russia: Activism, Aid, and NGOs*. Bloomington: Indiana University Press, 2007.

⸻. "Nashi, Youth Voluntarism, and Potemkin NGOs: Making Sense of Civil Society in Post-Soviet Russia." *Slavic Review* 71, no. 2 (Summer 2012): 234–60.

⸻. "Redefining Need, Reconfiguring Expectations: The Rise of State-Run Youth Voluntarism." *Anthropological Quarterly* 85, no. 2 (2012): 519–54.

⸻. *Youth Politics in Putin's Russia: Producing Patriots and Entrepreneurs*. Bloomington: Indiana University Press, 2015.

Hemment, Julie, and Valentina Uspenskaya. "'The 1990s Wasn't Just a Time of Bandits; We Feminists Were also Making Mischief!' Celebrating Twenty Years of Feminist Enlightenment Projects in Tver.'" *Aspasia*, no. 14 (2020): 20–36. https://doi.org/10.3167/asp.2020.140104.

Heuvel, Vanden Katrina. "Right-to-Lifers Hit Russia." *The Nation*, November 1, 1993, 489–92.

Higgins, Andrew. "Evidence Grows of Russian Orthodox Clergy's Aiding Ukraine Rebels." *New York Times*, September 7, 2014. https://nytimes.com/2014/09/07/world/europe/evidence-grows-of-russian-orthodox-clergys-aiding-ukraine-rebels.html.

Hilevych, Yuliya. "Abortion and Gender Relationships in Ukraine, 1955–1970." *History of the Family* 20, no. 1 (2015): 86–105. https://doi.org/10.1080/1081602X.2014.996913.

Hilevych, Yuliya, and Chizu Sato. "Popular Medical Discourses on Birth Control in the Soviet Union during the Cold War: Shifting Responsibilities and Relational Values." In *Children by Choice?: Changing Values, Reproduction, and Family Planning in the 20th Century*, edited by Ann-Katrin Gembries, Theresia Theuke, and Isabel Heinemann, 99–122. Berlin: De Gruyter, 2018.

Hinterhuber, Eva Maria and Gesine Fuchs. "Neoliberal Intervention: Analyzing the Draculić-Funk-Ghodsee Debates." In *The Routledge Handbook of Gender in Central-Eastern Europe and Eurasia*, edited by Katalan Fábián, Janet Elise Johnson, Mara Lazda, 28–40. New York: Routledge, 2022.

Hockstader, Lee. "Antiabortion Activists Backed by Americans Launch Drive in Russia." *Washington Post*, May 19, 1994, A38.

Hodgson, Dennis, and Susan Cotts Watkins. "Feminists and Neo-Malthusians: Past and Present Alliances." *Population and Development Review* 23, no. 3 (1997): 469–523.

Hoffmann, David L. "Mothers in the Motherland: Stalinist Pronatalism in Its Pan-European Context." *Journal of Social History* 34, no. 1 (2000): 35–54.

Höjdestrand, Tova. *Needed by Nobody: Homelessness and Humanness in Postsocialist Russia*. Ithaca, NY: Cornell University Press, 2009.

Holmgren, Beth. "Bug Inspectors and Beauty Queens: The Problems of Translating Feminism into Russian." In *Postcommunism and the Body Politic*, edited by Ellen Berry, 15–31. New York: New York University Press, 1995.

Hubbs, Joanna. *Mother Russia: The Feminine Myth in Russian Culture*. Bloomington: Indiana University Press, 1988.

Humphrey, Caroline. *The Unmaking of Soviet Life: Everyday Economies after Socialism*. Ithaca, NY: Cornell University Press, 2002.

Ignaciuk, Agata. "No Man's Land?: Gendering Contraception in Family Planning Advice Literature in State Socialist Poland, 1950s–1980s." *Social History of Medicine* 33, no. 4 (2020): 1327–49. https://doi.org/10.1093/shm/hkz007.

⸻. "Reproductive Policies and Women's Birth Control: Practices in State-Socialist Poland (1960s–1980s)." In *"Wenn die Chemie stimmt . . ." Geschlechterbeziehungenvund Geburtenkontrolle im Zeitalter der "Pille,"* edited by Lutz Niethammer and Silke Satjukow, 305–28. Göttingen: Wallstein, 2016.

Ilic, Melanie. *Women Workers in the Soviet Interwar Economy: From 'Protection' to 'Equality.'* New York: St. Martin's Press, 1999.

Illouz, Eva. *Intimacies: The Making of Emotional Capitalism.* New York: Polity, 2007.

Inhorn, Marcia. *Cosmopolitan Conceptions: IVF Sojourns in Global Dubai.* Durham, NC: Duke University Press, 2015.

———. *Mating Gaps: Why American Women Are Freezing Their Eggs.* New York: New York University Press, 2023.

Ipas. *The Evidence Speaks for Itself: Ten Facts about Abortion.* Chapel Hill, NC: Ipas, 2010.

Ivanova, Elena I., and Anna R. Mikheeva, "Unwed Motherhood in Russia," *Russian Social Science Review* 42, no. 3 (2001): 32–40.

Johnson, Janet. *Gender Violence in Russia: The Politics of Feminist Intervention.* Bloomington: Indiana University Press, 2009.

Johnson, Janet Elise, and Aino Saarinen. "Twenty-First-Century Feminisms under Repression: Gender Regime Changes and the Women's Crisis Centre Movement in Russia." *Signs* 38, no. 3 (2013): 543–67.

Johnson-Hanks, Jennifer. "Demographic Transitions and Modernity." *Annual Review of Anthropology*, no. 37 (2008): 301–15.

Kadnikova, A. "Konservativnaia gendernaia mobilizatsiia v sovremennoi Rossii: Sluchai antiabortnoi aktivistskoi organizatsii 'Mezhdunarodnoe dvizhenie prolaiferov voiny zhizni.'" Master's thesis, European University of St. Petersburg, 2013.

Kaminer, Jenny. *Women with a Thirst for Destruction: The Bad Mother in Russian Culture.* Evanston, IL: Northwestern University Press, 2014.

———. *Haunted Dreams: Fantasies of Adolescence in Post-Soviet Culture.* Ithaca, NY: Cornell University Press, 2022.

Katkova, I. P. *Rozhdaemost' v molodykh sem'iakh.* Moscow: Meditsina, 1971.

Kelly, Catriona. *A History of Russian Women's Writing 1820–1992.* New York: Oxford University Press, 1994.

Kelly, Kimberly. "In the Name of the Mother: Renegotiating Conservative Women's Authority in the Crisis Pregnancy Center Movement." *Signs* 38, no. 1 (2012): 203–30.

Kharkhordin, Oleg. *The Collective and the Individual in Russia: A Study of Practices.* Berkeley: University of California Press, 1999.

Kharkhordin, Oleg, ed. *Mishel' Fuko i Rossiia.* Sbornik statei. St. Petersburg: European University of St Petersburg, 2001.

Khodakov, N. M. *Molodym suprugam.* 3rd ed. Moscow: Meditsina, 1979.

Kholin, Igor'. *Izbrannoe: Stikhi i poemy.* Moscow: Novoe literaturnoe obozrenie, 1999.

Khomasuridze, A. G. "Osnovnye rezul'taty i puti razvitiia gormonal'noi kontratseptsii." In *Mediko-sotsiologicheskie aspektie rozhdaemosti: Sbornik nauchnykh trudov*, edited by A. G. Khomasuridze et al., 50–61 (Tblisi: NIIGFCh, 1985).

Khorev, Boris. "Rynok: Podi pri nem rodi . . ." *Pravda*, March 30, 1995.

———. "'V chem ostrota demograficheskoi problemy v Rossii?' Rossiia i Mir (Informatsionnyi ekspress biulleten' dlia deputatov Gosudarstvennoi Dumy)."*Communist Party of the Russian Federation*, June 1997, 1–45.

Kideckel, David A. *Getting By in Post-Soviet Romania: Labor, the Body, and Working Class Culture.* Bloomington: Indiana University Press, 2008.

Kishkovsky, Sophia. "Russia Enacts Laws Opposing Abortion." *New York Times*, July 15, 2011. https://www.nytimes.com/2011/07/15/world/europe/15iht-russia15.html.

Klepikova, Anna. *Navernoe, ia durak: Antropologicheskii roman.* St. Petersburg: European University in St. Petersburg, 2019.

Kligman, Gail. *The Politics of Duplicity: Controlling Reproduction in Ceausescu's Romania.* Berkeley: University of California Press, 1998.

Koch, Erin. *Free Market Tuberculosis: Managing Epidemics in Post-Soviet Georgia.* Nashville, TN: Vanderbilt University Press, 2013.

Kohli, M. "Retirement and the Moral Economy: An Historical Interpretation of the German Case." *Journal of Aging Studies* 1, no. 2 (1987): 125–44.

Kon, Igor Semenovich. *The Sexual Revolution in Russia: From the Age of Czars to Today.* New York: The Free Press, 1995.

———. "Personal Website of I.S. Kon." Sexology, accessed on 3/7/2017. https://sexology.in-carne.net/about.html.

Kondakov, Alexander Sasha, and Evgeny Shtorn. "Sex, Alcohol, and Soul: Violent Reactions to Coming Out after the 'Gay Propaganda' Law in Russia." *Russian Review* 80, no. 1 (2021): 37–55. https://https://doi-org.libproxy.lib.unc.edu/10.1111/russ.12297.

Kondrashkova, Kristina. "Postavki budut, no kogda i po kakoi tsene?" *Russian Demographix* (blog), March 4, 2022. https://russiandemographix.blogspot.com/2022/03/eeriness.html.

Konovalova, Aleksandra Andreevna. "Istoriia razrabotki gormonal'noi kontratseptsii v SSSR v ramkakh politiki pronatalizma (1960–1980)-e g." Department of History, Higher School of Economics, Moscow, 2021.

Konovalova, Alexandra, Michele Rivkin-Fish, and Pavel Vasil'ev. "Exploring the Material and Symbolic Powers of Oral Contraceptives." Paper presented at Gender and Materiality in the 20th Century, Institut d'études politiques de Paris conference, Paris, 2021.

Konygina, Natal'ia. "Spiker Mironov predlagaet podelit'sia s novorozhdennymi." *Izvestiia*, October 6, 2005. Reprinted in *Demoscope Weekly*, October 10–23, 2005. http://www.demoscope.ru/weekly/2005/0217/gazeta01.php.

Koopman, Colin, and Tomas Matza. "Putting Foucault to Work: Analytic and Concept in Foucaultian Inquiry." *Critical Inquiry* 39, no. 4 (2013): 817–40.

Korostelev, G. M., and A. A. Petrakov. "Izuchenie praktiki planirovaniia sem'i." *Sovetskoe zdravookhranenie* 8 (1967): 30–33.

Kościańska, Agnieszka. *Gender, Pleasure, and Violence: The Construction of Expert Knowledge of Sexuality in Poland.* Bloomington: Indiana University Press, 2020.

Kostarnova, Natal'ia. "Trudnosti reproduktivnogo vybora." *Kommersant'*, May 2, 2023. Reprinted in *Demoscope Weekly*, May 16-29, 2023. https://www.demoscope.ru/weekly/2023/0987/gazeta010.php.

Kostyuk, Yelena. "Contracts for Babies Might Save the Nation." *Current Digest of the Post-Soviet Press* 52 no. 40 (2000):17–18. Translated and reprinted from *Vremya MN*, September 2000, 1–5.

Kotkin, Stephen. *Magnetic Mountain: Stalinism as Civilization.* Berkeley: University of California Press, 1997.

Kowalski, Julia. *Counseling Women: Kinship against Violence in India.* Philadelphia: University of Pennsylvania Press, 2022.

Krastev, Ivan, and Stephen Holmes. *The Light That Failed: Why the West Is Losing the Fight for Democracy.* New York: Pegasus Books, 2020.

Krause, Elizabeth. "'Empty Cradles' and the Quiet Revolution: Demographic Discourse and Cultural Struggles of Gender, Race, and Class in Italy." *Cultural Anthropology* 16, no. 4 (2001): 576–611.

Krause, Elizabeth, and Silvia DeZordo. "Introduction: Ethnography and Biopolitics: Tracing 'Rationalities' of Reproduction across the North–South Divide." *Anthropology and Medicine* 19, no. 2 (2012): 137–51.

Krause, Elizabeth L., and Milena Marchesi. "Fertility Politics as 'Social Viagra': Reproducing Boundaries, Social Cohesion, and Modernity in Italy." *American Anthropologist* 109, no. 2 (2007): 350–62.

Kravel-Tovi, Michal. "Specter of Dwindling Numbers: Population Quantity and Jewish Biopolitics in the United States." *Comparative Studies in Society and History* 62, no. 1 (2020): 35–67.

Krylova, Anna. "In Their Own Words?: Soviet Women Writers and the Search for Self." In *A History of Women's Writing in Russia*, edited by Adele Barker and Jehanne Gheith, 243–76. Cambridge: Cambridge University Press, 2002.

———. "The Tenacious Liberal Subject in Soviet Studies." *Kritika* 1, no. 1 (2000): 119–46. https://doi.org/10.1353/kri.2008.0092.

Kuehnast, Kathleen, and Carol Nechemias, eds. *Post-Soviet Women Encountering Transition: Nation-Building, Economic Survival, Civic Activism*. Washington, DC: Woodrow Wilson Press, 2004.

Kuhar, Roman, and David Paternotte, eds. *Anti-Gender Campaigns in Europe: Mobilizing against Equality*. New York: Rowman & Littlefield, 2017.

Kulakov, V. I., V. N. Serov, N. N. Vaganov, V. N. Prilepskaia, O. G. Frolova, B. L. Gurtova, L. V. Gravrilova, and E. E. Zaporoshets. *Rukovodstvo po planirovaniiu sem'i*. Moscow: RUSFAR-MAMED, 1997.

Kumar, Anuradha. "Disgust, Stigma, and the Politics of Abortion." *Feminism & Psychology* 28, no. 4 (2018): 1–9.

Kuźma-Markowska, Sylwia, and Agata Ignaciuk. "Family Planning Advice in State-Socialist Poland, 1950s–80s: Local and Transnational Exchanges." *Medical History* 64, no. 2 (2020): 240–66.

Kuznetsova, Larisa. "Glazami zhenshchiny." *Novoe vremia* 10 (1989): 33–35.

Kvasha, A. I. *Demograficheskaia politika v SSSR*. Moscow: Finansy i statistika, 1981.

Lansing, J. Stephen. "The Cognitive Machinery of Power: Reflections on Valeri's *The Forest of Taboos*." *American Ethnologist* 30, no. 3 (2003): 372–80.

Laruelle, Marlene. "Illiberalism: A Conceptual Introduction." *East European Politics* 38, no. 2 (2022): 303–27. https://doi.org/10.1080/21599165.2022.2037079.

Latikhina, Kira. "Demografiia s pliusom." *Rossiiskaia gazeta*, January 19, 2010. Reprinted in *Demoscope Weekly*, Jan. 25–Feb. 7, 2010. http://www.demoscope.ru/weekly/2010/0407/gazeta02.php.

Larivaara, Meri M. "'A Planned Baby Is a Rarity': Monitoring and Planning Pregnancy in Russia." *Health Care for Women International* 32 no. 6 (2011): 515–37.

Lemke, Thomas. *Biopolitics: An Advanced Introduction*. New York: New York University Press, 2011.

Leon, David A., Laurent Chenet, Vladimir Shkolnikov, Sergei Zakharov, Judith Shapiro, Galina Rakhmanova, Sergei Vassin, and Martin McKee. "Huge Variation in Russian Mortality Rates 1984–94: Alcohol, Artefact, or What?" *Lancet* 350, no. 9075 (1997): 383–88.

Lerner, Julia. "Changing Meanings of Russian Love: Emotional Socialism and Therapeutic Culture on the Post-Soviet Screen." *Sexuality & Culture* 19, no. 2 (2015): 349–68.

Lerner, Julia, and Claudia Zbenovich. "Adapting the Therapeutic Discourse to Post-Soviet Media Culture: The Case of Modnyi Prigovor." *Slavic Review* 72, no. 4 (2013): 828–49.

Leykin, Inna. *Caring Like a State: The Politics of Russia's Demographic Crisis*. Bloomington: Indiana University Press, 2025.

———. "Uneasy Translations: Vernacularizing Demography for Post-Soviet Statecraft." *Journal of the Royal Anthropological Institute (N.S.)*, no. 26 (2019): 86–104.

———. "Rodologia: Genealogy as Therapy in Post-Soviet Russia." *Ethos* 43, no. 2 (2015): 135–64.

Leykin, Inna, and Michele Rivkin-Fish. "Politicized Demography and Biomedical Authority in Post-Soviet Russia." *Medical Anthropology* 41, no. 6-7 (2021): 702–17. https://doi.org/10.1080/01459740.2021.1987897.

Lilla, Mark. *The Once and Future Liberal: After Identity Politics*. New York: Harper Collins, 2017.

Lindquist, Galina. *Conjuring Hope: Magic and Healing in Contemporary Russia*. New York: Berghahn Books, 2006.

Lipovetsky, Mark. "Clarifying Positions." *Ab Imperio* 1 (2013): 208–19.

———. "The Poetics of ITR Discourse: In the 1960s and Today." *Ab Imperio* 1 (2013): 109–31.

Loseff, Lev. *On the Beneficence of Censorship: Aesopian Language in Modern Russian Literature*. Munich: Verlag Otto Sanger in Kommission, 1984.

Luehrmann, Sonja. "Innocence and Demographic Crisis: Transposing Post-Abortion Syndrome into a Russian Orthodox Key." In *A Fragmented Landscape: Abortion Governance and Protest Logics in Europe*, edited by Silvia Zordo, Joanna Mishtal, and Lorena Anton, 103–22. Oxford: Berghahn, 2017.

Luna, Zakiya, and Kristin Luker. "Reproductive Justice." *Annual Review of Law and Social Science* 9 (2013): 327–52.

MacNamara, Trent. *Birth Control and American Modernity: A History of Popular Ideas*. New York: Cambridge University Press, 2018.

Magun, Artem. "They Were Genuinely Liberal: Liberals of the Right," *Ab Imperio* 1 (2013): 183–88.

Makarova, Elena. "Na sokhranenie." In *Otkrytyi final*. Moscow: Sovetskii pisatel', 1989.

———. "Ulitka v kosmose," unpublished ms., 1983.

Makarychev, Andrey, and Sergei Medvedev. "Biopolitics and Power in Putin's Russia." *Problems of Post-Communism* 62, no. 1 (2015): 45–54.

Makarychev, Andrey, and Alexandra Yatsyk. *Critical Biopolitics of the Post-Soviet: From Populations to Nations*. Lanham, MD: Lexington Books, 2020.

Malinova, O. Iu. "Konstruirovanie 'liberalizma' v postsovetskoi Rossii: Nasledie 1990-kh v ideologicheskikh bitvakh 2000-kh." *Politiia* 1, no. 84 (2017): 1–28.

Mamontov, Arkadii. "Shkola-XXI: Seksprosvet." Programma Spetsial'nyi Korrespondent. Russia Channel 1, July 4, 2010. Patriot Belverus, posted Jan. 30, 2013, YouTube video. https://www.youtube.com/watch?v=lDvcncWddBc.

Manuilova, I. A., N. S. Trutko, S. I. Sleptsova, and V. F. Volgina. *Metody preduprezhdeniia beremennosti: Metodicheskie Rekomendatsii*. Moscow: Minzdrav SSSR, Glavnoe upravleniie lechebnno-profilakticheskoi pomoshchi detiam i materiam, 1983.

Marchesi, Milena. "Reproducing Italians: Contested Biopolitics in the Age of 'Replacement Anxiety.'" *Anthropology and Medicine* 19, no. 2 (2012): 171–88.

Markelov, Roman, and Alena Uzbekova. "K babke ne khodi- zdorov'e." *Rossiiskaia gazeta*, Nov. 26, 2013. Reprinted in *Demoscope Weekly*, December 2–15, 2013. http://www.demoscope.ru/weekly/2013/0577/gazeta04.php.

Marks, Lara V. *Sexual Chemistry: A History of the Contraceptive Pill*. New Haven, CT: Yale University Press, 2001.

Marks, Sarah. "The Romani Minority, Coercive Sterilization, and Languages of Denial in the Czech Lands." *History Workshop Journal*, no. 84 (2017): 128–48.

Matza, Tomas. "Moscow's Echo: Technologies of the Self, Publics and Politics on the Russian Talk Show," *Cultural Anthropology* 24, no. 3 (2009): 489–522.

———. *Shock Therapy: Psychology, Precarity, and Well-Being in Postsocialist Russia*. Durham, NC: Duke University Press, 2018.

Maxwell, Carol J. C. *Pro-Life Activists in America: Meaning, Motivation, and Direct Action*. New York: Cambridge University Press, 2002.

Mazzarino, Andrea. "Entrepreneurial Women and the Business of Self-Development in Global Russia." *Signs* 38, no. 3 (2013): 623–45.

McGowan, John. *Pragmatist Politics: Making the Case for Liberal Democracy.* Minneapolis: University of Minnesota Press, 2012.

MED-info. "Lyubov Erofeeva: 'V osnove idei planirovaniia sem'i lezhat prava patsienta.'" MED-info, March 10, 2014. https://med-info.ru/content/view/5037.

Medvedev, Sergei. *The Return of the Russian Leviathan.* New York: Polity, 2020.

Medvedova, Irina, and Tat'iana Shishova. "Demograficheskaia voina protiv Rossii." *Nash sovremennik*, no. 1 (2000).

Mendel, Arthur P. "Hamlet and Soviet Humanism." *Slavic Review* 30, no. 4 (1971): 733–47.

Michaels, Paula A. *Curative Powers: Medicine and Empire in Stalin's Central Asia.* Pittsburgh, PA: University of Pittsburgh Press, 2003.

———. *Lamaze: An International History.* Oxford: Oxford University Press, 2014.

Minzdrav (Ministerstvo Zdravookhraneniia) RSFSR. "Opredelenie potrebnosti v protivozachatochnykh sredstvakh, metodologicheskie rekomendatsii." Edited by N. A. Shneiderman, Andrej A. Popov, and N. S. Trutko. Moscow: Respublikanskaia nauchno-issledovatel'skaia laboratoriia meditsinskoi demografii, i vsesoiuznyi nauchno-issledovatel'skii tsentr okhrany zdorov'ia materi i rebenka, 1983.

Minzdrav (Ministerstvo Zdravookhraneniia) SSSR. "Informatsionnoe pis'mo: O pobochnom deistvii i oslozhneniiakh pri primenenii oral'nykh kontratseptivov." In *Vsesoiuznyi tsentr po izucheniiu pobochnogo deistviia lekarstvennykh sredstv*, edited by E. A. Babaian, A. S. Lopatin, and I. G. Lavretskii. Moscow: Vsesoiuznyi tsentr po izucheniiu pobochnogo deitstviia lekarstvennykh sredstv, 1974.

———. Prikaz No. 620-DSP. "O sostoianii i merakh po snizheniiu abortov v strane." GARF f. R-8009 o. 50, d. 7697, l. 103–12. Moscow: Minzdrav SSSR, 1979.

———. Prikaz no. 377. "O merakh po usileniiu bor'by s abortami." August 2, 1962. Gosudarstvennaya Tsentral'naya Meditsinskaia biblioteka 0-68467, https://rusmed.rucml.ru.

Minkler, Meredith, and T. Cole. "Political and Moral Economy: Getting to Know One Another." In *Critical Gerontology: Perspectives from Political and Moral Economy*, edited by Meredith Minkler and Carroll L. Estes, 37–53. Amityville, NY: Baywood Publishing, 1999.

Mishle, Nadezhda Aleksandrovna. *Iuridicheskii spravochnik: Zhenshchiny i deti: Semeinoe pravo, trudovoe pravo, sotsial'nye l'goty.* Moscow: Filin', 1998.

Mishtal, Joanna. "Irrational Non-Reproduction?: The 'Dying Nation' and the Postsocialist Logics of Declining Motherhood in Poland." *Anthropology and Medicine* 19, no. 2 (2012):153–69.

———."Quietly 'Beating the System': The Logics of Protest and Resistance under the Polish Abortion Ban." In *A Fragmented Landscape: Abortion Governance and Protest Logics in Europe*, edited by Silvia Zordo, Joanna Mishtal, and Lorena Anton, 226–44. New York: Berghahn Books, 2017.

———. "Reproductive Governance and the (Re)Definition of Human Rights in Poland." *Medical Anthropology* 38, no. 2 (2019): 182–94. https://doi.org/DOI:10.1080/01459740.2018.1472090.

———. *The Politics of Morality: The Church, the State, and Reproductive Rights in Postsocialist Poland.* Athens: Ohio State University Press, 2015.

Molodtsova, Viktoria. "Sex: Perversion Instead of Education." *CDPSP* 51, no. 45 (1999): 18. Translated and reprinted from *Rossiiskaia gazeta*, no. 24 (June 10, 1999).

Morgan, Lynn M. "Afterword: Reproductive Governance Meets European Abortion Politics: The Challenge of Getting the Gaze Right." In *A Fragmented Landscape: Abortion*

Governance and Protest Logics in Europe, edited by Silvia Zordo, Joanna Mishtal, and Lorena Anton, 266–82. Oxford: Berghahn, 2017.

Morgan, Lynn M., and Elizabeth F. S. Roberts. "Reproductive Governance in Latin America." *Anthropology and Medicine* 19, no. 2 (2012): 241–54.

Morris, Jeremy. *Everyday Postsocialism: Working Class Communities in the Russian Margins*. London: Palgrave Macmillan, 2016.

Morris, Jeremy, and Masha Garibyan. "Russian Cultural Conservatism Critiqued: Translating the Tropes of 'Gayropa' and 'Juvenile Justice' in Everyday Life." *Europe-Asia Studies* 73, no. 8 (2021): 1,487–507. https://doi.org/10.1080/09668136.2021.1887088.

Moss, Kevin. "Russia as the Saviour of European Civilization: Gender and the Geopolitics of Traditional Values." In *Anti-Gender Campaigns in Europe: Mobilizing against Equality*, edited by David Paternotte and Roman Kuhar, 195–214. New York: Rowman & Littlefield, 2017.

Murphey, Michelle. *Seizing the Means of Reproduction: Entanglements of Feminism, Health, and Technoscience*. Durham, NC: Duke University Press, 2012.

Myers, Steven Lee. "After Decades, Russia Narrows Grounds for Abortions." *New York Times*, August 24, 2003.

Nakachi, Mie. "Liberation without Contraception?" In *Reproductive States: Global Perspectives on the Invention and Implementation of Population Policy*, edited by Rickie Solinger and Mie Nakachi, 290–319. New York: Oxford University Press, 2016.

———. *Replacing the Dead: The Politics of Reproduction in the Postwar Soviet Union*. New York: Oxford University Press, 2021.

Narayan, Kirin. *Alive in the Writing: Crafting Ethnography in the Company of Chekov*. Chicago: University of Chicago Press, 2012.

———. "Ethnography and Fiction: Where Is the Border?" *Anthropology and Humanism* 24, no. 2 (1999): 134–47.

Nasir, Muhammad Ali. "Biopolitics, Thanatopolitics, and the Right to Life." *Theory, Culture and Society* 34, no. 1 (2017): 75–95.

Nathans, Benjamin. "Coming to Terms with Late Soviet Liberalism." *Ab Imperio* 1 (2013): 175–82.

Nikonchik, O. K. "Problema kontratseptsii i organizatsiia bor'by s abortami v SSSR." *Akusherstvo i ginekologiia* 6 (1959).

Novitskaya, Alexandra, Valerie Sperling, Lisa McIntosh Sundstrom, and Janet Elise Johnson. "Unpacking 'Traditional Values' in Russia's Conservative Turn: Gender, Sexuality and the Soviet Legacy." *Europe-Asia Studies* 76, no. 2 (2023): 173–97. https://doi.org/10.1080/09668136.2023.2215484.

Odin na odin. Television episode, May 4, 1997. https://www.youtube.com/watch?v=ynm122y9AI8&t=529s.

Oosthuizen, Kobus. "Similarities and Differences between the Fertility Decline in Europe and the Emerging Fertility Decline in Sub-Saharan Africa." In *International Union for the Scientific Study of Population (IUSSP). International Population Conference*, vol. 3. Beijing: IUSSP, 1997.

Otkroi glaza, Rossiia, "Fraza 'U nas v SSSR net seksa' spetsial'no izvrashchena." Open Eyes Russia, Dec. 1, 2011. http://open-eyes-russia.com/russia/428-we-have-a-phrase-in-the-ussr-there-is-no-specific-sex-perverted.html.

Oushakine, Serguei. "In the State of Post-Soviet Aphasia: Symbolic Development in Contemporary Russia." *Europe-Asia Studies* 52, no. 6 (2000): 991–1,016.

———. "Pol'ze fiktivnogo rodstva: Zametki o 'propushchennykh imenakh.'" *Novoe literaturnoe obozrenie* 1 (2008): 201–2.

———. *The Patriotism of Despair: Nation, War, and Loss in Russia*. Ithaca, NY: Cornell University Press, 2016.

Ovsyannikova, Anastasiya. "How Should We Talk About Abortion in Russia?" *Open Democracy Russia*, October 3, 2016. https://www.opendemocracy.net/en/odr/how-should-we-talk-about-abortion-in-russia.

Padamsee, Tasleem Juana. "The Pharmaceutical Corporation and the 'Good Work' of Managing Women's Bodies." *Social Science and Medicine*, no. 72 (2011): 1,342–50.

Palei, Marina. "Losers' Division." In *Ward of Lost Souls*. Moscow: Moskovskii rabochii, 1991.

Parsons, Michelle A. *Dying Unneeded: The Cultural Context of the Russian Mortality Context*. Nashville, TN: Vanderbilt University Press, 2014.

Patico, Jennifer. *Consumption and Change in a Post-Soviet Middle Class*. Washington, DC: Woodrow Wilson Center Press Stanford University Press, 2008.

Paxson, Heather. *Making Modern Mothers: Ethics and Family Planning in Urban Greece*. Berkeley: University of California Press, 2004.

PBS. "Senate Hearings on the Pill." *American Experience*, 2003. https://www.pbs.org/wgbh/americanexperience/features/pill-senate-holds-hearings-pill-1970.

Perevedentsev, Viktor. "Neobkhodimo stimulirovat' rost naseleniia v nashei strane." *Voprosy filosofii*, no. 11 (1974): 88–92.

Perheentupa, Inna. *Feminist Politics in Neoconservative Russia: An Ethnography of Resistance and Resources*. Bristol, UK: Bristol University Press, 2022.

Perheentupa, Inna, and Suvi Salmenniemi. "Treading the Tightrope of Femininity: Transforming Gendered Subjectivity into a Therapeutic Community." *European Journal of Women's Studies* 26, no. 4 (2019): 390–404.

Persianinov, L. S., and I. A. Manuilova. "O rasshirennoi programme VOZ po reproduktsii cheloveka." *Akusherstvo i ginekologiia* 6 (1975): 1–3.

———. "O sostoianii nauchnykh issledovanii v oblasti razrabotki sovremennykh metodov reguliatsii rozhdaemosti (po dannym rasshirennoi programmy VOZ po reproduktsii cheloveka za 1977 g)." *Akusherstvo i ginekologiia* 2 (1979): 3–5.

Pesman, Dale. *Russia and Soul: An Exploration*. Ithaca, NY: Cornell University Press, 2000.

Petchesky, Rosalind. *Global Prescriptions: Gendering Health and Human Rights*. New York: Palgrave, 2003.

Peterburgskii, F. E., V. I. Babukhadiia, E. D. Polinskaia, S. I. Bogdan, E. I. Obodianik, V. I. Khilobok, and I. V. Latyk. "Opyt organizatsii bor'by s abortami." In *Trudy V s"ezda akusherov-ginekologov Ukrainskoi SSR. Kiev. 18–20 November 1971*, edited by H. S. Baksheev, 148–51. Kiev: Zdorov'ia, 1972.

Petit, Véronique, Kaveri Qureshi, Yves Charbit, Philip Kreager, eds. *The Anthropological Demography of Health*. Oxford: Oxford Academic, 2020. https://academic.oup.com/book/33505.

Petrushevskaia, Liudmila. "Bednoe serdtse Pani." In *Svoi krug*, 32–34. Moscow: Pravda, 1990.

Petryna, Adriana, Andrew Lakoff, and Arthur Kleinman. *Global Pharmaceuticals: Ethics, Markets, Practices*. Durham, NC: Duke University Press, 2006.

Phillips, Sarah. *Disability and Mobile Citizenship in Postsocialist Ukraine*. Bloomington: Indiana University Press, 2010.

———. *Women's Social Activism in the New Ukraine: Development and the Politics of Differentiation*. Bloomington: Indiana University Press, 2008.

Pigg, Stacy Leigh, and Vincanne Adams. "Introduction: The Moral Object of Sex." In *Sex in Development: Science, Sexuality, and Morality in Global Perspective*, edited by Vincanne Adams and Stacy Leigh Pigg, 1–38. Durham, NC: Duke University Press, 2005.

Piskunov, V. P., and V. C. Steshenko. "O demograficheskoi politike sotsialisticheskogo ob-shchetsva." In *Demograficheskaia politika*, edited by V. C. Steshenko and V. P. Piskunov, 15–27. Moscow: Statistika, 1974.

Plamper, Jan. "Foucault's Gulag." *Kritika: Explorations in Russian and Eurasian History* 3, no. 2 (2002): 255–80.

"Planirovanie Nebytiia." *Novaia gazeta* 32, no. 555 (1999): 1–13.

Platonov, Andrei. *Chevengur*. Moscow: Khudozhestvennaia literatura, 1988.

Plotnikov, Nikolai. "Ot individual'nosti k identichnosti." *Novoe literaturnoe obozrenie* 3 (2008): 64–83.

Polchanova, S. L. "Analiz metodicheskikh oshibok protivoabortnoi propagandy." In *Trudy tsentral'nogo nauchno-issledovatel'skogo instituta sanitranogo prosveshcheniia*, vol. 4, ed-ited by D. N. Loranskii, 36–41. Moscow: Ministerstvo zdravookhraneniia SSSR, 1973.

Polesskii, V. A. "Sanitarnoe prosveshchenie: Problemy i perspektivy." *Zdravookhranenie Ros-siiskoi Federatsii* 1 (1995): 30–31.

Pomerantsev, V. M. "Ob iskrennosti v literature." *Novyi Mir* 8 (1953): 218–45.

Popov, Andrej A. "Novye napravleniia sanitarnogo prosveshcheniia po profilaktike iskusst-vennykh abortov." In *Aktual'nye voprosy gigienicheskogo vospitaniia naseleniia v svete reshenii XXYI s"ezda KPSS. Tezisy konferentsii*, edited by D. N. Loranskii, 126–28. Moscow: Ministerstvo Zdravookhraneniia SSSR, Glavnoe sanitarno-epidemiologicheskoe uprav-lenie, Tsentral'nyi NII sanitarnogo prosveshcheniia, 1982.

———. "O chastote i prichinakh vnebol'nichnykh abortov (Obzor literatury)." *Zdravookhranenie Rossiskoi Federatsii* 6 (1982): 27–30.

———. "Regulirovanie rozhdeniia v sovremennykh sem'iakh." In *Sem'ia zdorov'ie obsh-chestvo*, edited by M. S. Bednyi, 181–207. Moscow: Mysl', 1986.

———. "Aborty v Rossii." *Chelovek* 1 (1995): 113–18.

———. "Demograficheskii aspekt regulirovaniia rozhdenii." In *Vzaimodeistvie mezhdu preo-brazovaniiami okruzhaiushchei sredy i adaptivnoi demograficheskoi i geneticheskoi struk-turoi narodonaseleniia*, 75–77. May 15–19, 1984.

———. "Family Planning and Induced Abortion in the USSR: The Fact Book," unpublished manuscript, 1992

———. *Kak mozhno effektivno, udobno i bez vreda dlia vashego zdorov'ia predupredit' beremen-nost'*. Moscow: Natsional'nyi biotekhnologicheskii tsentr "Biopolis," 1990.

———. "Planirovanie sem'i na Kamchatke." *Vek XX i Mir* 12 (1991): 52–54.

———. "Family Planning and Induced Abortion in the USSR: Basic Health and Demo-graphic Characteristics." *Studies in Family Planning* 22, no. 6 (1991): 368–77.

Popov, Andrej A., and Henry P. David. "Russian Federation and USSR Successor States." In *From Abortion to Contraception: A Resource to Public Policies and Reproductive Behavior in Central and Eastern Europe from 1917 to the Present*, edited by Henry P. David, 240–45. Westport, CT: Greenwood Press, 1999.

Popov, Andrej A., and V. A. Lukina. "Planirovanie sem'i i iskussvennye aborty v Rossii." *Zdravookhranenie Rossiiskoi Federatsii* 1, no. 1 (1995): 25–30.

Popov, Andrej A., Adriaan Ph. Visser, and Evert Ketting. "Contraceptive Knowledge, Attitudes and Practice in Russia during the 1980s." *Studies in Family Planning* 24, no. 4 (1993): 227–35.

Popovskii, Mark. *Tretii Lishnii: On, ona i Sovetskii rezhim*. London: Overseas Publications Interchange, 1985.

Posadskaya, Anastasia. *Russia: A New Era in Russian Feminism*. Translated by Kate Clark. London: Verso, 1994.

Posadskaya, A. I. "Tendentsii izmeneniia zakonodatel'stva v oblasti sotsial'noi zashchity materinstva." In *Zhenshchiny i sotsial'naia politika: Gendernyi aspekt*, edited by Z. A. Khotkina, 79–88. Moscow: Institut sotsial'no-ekonomicheskikh problem narodonaseleniia, 1992.

Pravitel'stvo Rossiiskoi Federatsii. "Poriadok finansirovaniia predrodovogo i poslerodovogo patronazha." *Rossiiskaia gazeta*, October 1, 2007.

Pravitel'stvo Rossiiskoi Federatsii. Federal'nyi zakon ot 08.05.2010 No. 83-FZ. "O vnesenii izmenenii v otdel'nye zakonodatel'nye akty Rossiiskoi Federatsii v sviazi s sovershenstvovaniem pravovogo polozheniia gosudarstvennykh (munitsipal'nykh) uchrezhdenii." GARANT.

———. Federal'nyi zakon ot 29.06.2013 No. 135-F3. "O zashchite detei ot informatsii, prichinikhiushchei vred ikh zdorov'iu i razvitiiu." GARANT.

———. Federal'nyi zakon ot 21 noiabria 2011 g. No 323-FZ. "Ob osnovakh okhrany zdorov'ia grazhdan v Rossiiskoi Federatsii." GARANT. https://base.garant.ru/12191967.

———. "Kontseptsiia demograficheskogo razvitiia Rossiiskoi Federatsii na period do 2015 goda Ot 24 September 2001 No.1270-R." *Demoscope Weekly*, Chital'nyi zal. http://www.demoscope.ru/weekly/knigi/koncepciya/koncepciya.html.

———. Postanovlenie 11 Avgusta 2003g. No. 485. "O perechne sotsial'nykh pokazanii dlia iskussvennogo preryvaniia beremennosti." Reprinted in *Demoscope Weekly*, Aug. 25–Sept. 7, 2003. http://www.demoscope.ru/weekly/2003/0123/tema03.php.

———. Ugolovnyi kodeks Rossiiskoi Federatsii ot 13 iiunia 1996 g. No. 63-FZ. GARANT.

Prezidium Verkhovnogo Soveta SSSR. Ukaz ot 23 noiabria 1955 g., "Ob otmene zapreshcheniia abortov." *Vedomosti Verkhovnogo Soveta SSSR* 1955, No. 22.

Price, Kimala. "Redefining the Pro-Choice Paradigm." *Meridians* 10, no. 2 (2010): 42–65.

———. "What Is Reproductive Justice?: How Women of Color Activists Are Redefining the Pro-Choice Paradigm." *Meridians* 10, no. 2 (2010): 42–65.

Programma Spetsial'nyi korrespondent. "Shkola-XXI. Seksprosvet." Transcript of TV broadcast. July 4, 2010, 23:15–0:15. 1st Channel, "Russia." https://www.speckor.ru.

Prozorov, Sergei. "Foucault and Soviet Biopolitics." *History of the Human Sciences* 27, no. 5 (2014): 6–25.

———. *The Biopolitics of Stalinism: Ideology and Life in Soviet Socialism*. Edinburgh: Edinburgh University Press, 2016.

Putin, Vladimir "Poslanie federal'nomu sobraniiu Rossiiskoi Federatsii." Moscow, May 10, 2006.

———. "The Kind of Russia We Are Building: Annual Message from the President of the Russian Federation to the Federal Assembly of the Russian Federation, July 8, 2000, Moscow," *Current Digest of the Post-Soviet Press* 28, no. 52 (August 9, 2000): 5.

Raikhel, Eugene. *Governing Habits: Treating Alcoholism in the Post-Soviet Clinic*. Ithaca, NY: Cornell University Press, 2016.

Raleigh, Donald J. *Soviet Baby Boomers: An Oral History*. New York: Oxford University Press, 2011.

Randall, Amy. "'Abortion Will Deprive You of Happiness!': Soviet Reproductive Politics in the Post-Stalin Era." *Journal of Women's History* 23, no. 3 (2011): 13–38.

Ransell, David L. "A Single Research Community: Not Yet." *Slavic Review* 60, no. 3 (2001): 550–57.

Remennick, L. I. "Epidemiology and Determinants of Induced Abortion in the USSR." *Social Science and Medicine* 33, no. 7 (1991): 841–48.

————. "Patterns of Birth Control." In *Sex and Russian Society*, edited by J. Riordan and J. Kon, 45–63. Bloomington: Indiana University Press, 1993.

Renne, Tanya. "Disparaging Digressions: Sisterhood in East-Central Europe." In *Ana's Land: Sisterhood in Eastern Europe*, edited by Tanya Renne, 1–11. Boulder, CO: Westview Press, 1997.

Ria Novosti. "Mizulina dopuskaet obsuzhdenie popravok o medpomoshchi pri abortakh." *Ria novosti*, May 26, 2015. https://ria.ru/20150526/1066455412.html.

Ries, Nancy. *Russian Talk: Culture and Conversation during Perestroika*. Ithaca, NY: Cornell University Press, 1997.

Rinehart, W., S. Rudy, and M. Drennan. "GATHER Guide to Counseling." *Population Reports, Series J, Family Planning Programs*, no. 48 (1998): 1–31.

Rivkin-Fish, Michele. "Anthropologies of Reproduction, Abortion, and Biopolitics." In *The Cambridge Handbook of the Anthropology of Gender and Sexuality*, edited by Cecilia Mc-Callum, Silvia Posocco, and Martin Fotta, 395–424. Cambridge: Cambridge University Press, 2023.

————. "Anthropology, Demography, and the Search for a Critical Analysis of Fertility: Insights from Russia." *American Anthropologist* 105, no. 2 (June 2003): 289–301.

————. "'Change Yourself and the Whole World Will Become Kinder': Russian Activists for Reproductive Health and the Limits of Claims Making for Women." *Medical Anthropology Quarterly* 18, no. 3 (2004): 281–304.

————. "Conceptualizing Feminist Strategies for Russian Reproductive Politics: Abortion, Surrogate Motherhood, and Family Support after Socialism." *Signs* 38, no. 3 (2013): 569–93.

————. "From 'Demographic Crisis' to a 'Dying Nation': The Politics of Language and Reproduction in Russia." In *Gender and National Identity in Twentieth-Century Russian Culture*, edited by Helena Goscilo and Andrea Lanoux, 151–73. DeKalb: University of Northern Illinois Press, 2006.

————. "Moral Science and the Management of Sexual Revolution in Russia." In *Sex in Development: Science, Sexuality, and Morality in Global Perspective*, edited by Vincanne Adams and Stacy Leigh Pigg, 71–94. Durham, NC: Duke University Press, 2005.

————. "Pronatalism, Gender Politics, and the Renewal of Family Support in Russia: Towards a Feminist Anthropology of 'Maternity Capital.'" *Slavic Review* 69, no. 3 (2010): 701–24.

————. "Sexuality Education in Russia: Defining Pleasure and Danger for a Fledgling Democratic Society." *Social Science and Medicine* 49 (1999): 801–14.

————. *Women's Health in Post-Soviet Russia: The Politics of Intervention*. Bloomington, IN: Indiana University Press, 2005.

Rivkin-Fish, Michele, and Viktor Samokhvalov. "Seksual'noe obrazovanie i razvitie lichnosti: Pereosmyslenie professional'noi vlasti." In *Doverie i zdorov'e: Gendernyi podkhod k reproduktivnoi meditsine*, edited by Elena Zdravomyslova and Anna Temkina, translated by Irina Tartakovskaia, 21–50. St. Petersburg: European University of St. Petersburg, 2009.

Roberts, Dorothy. *Killing the Black Body: Race, Reproduction and the Meaning of Liberty*. New York: Vintage Books, 1999.

Rogers, Douglas. *The Depths of Russia: Oil, Power, and Culture after Socialism*. Ithaca, NY: Cornell University Press, 2015.

Rose, Nikolas. *The Politics of Life Itself: Biomedicine, Power, and Subjectivity in the Twenty-First Century*. Princeton, NJ: Princeton University Press, 2009.

Rosefielde, Steven, and Stefan Hedlund. *Russia since 1980: Wrestling with Westernization*. Cambridge: Cambridge University Press, 2009.

Ross, Loretta and Rickie Solinger. *Reproductive Justice: An Introduction*. Oakland: University of California Press, 2017.

Rotkirch, Anna, Anna Temkina, and Elena Zdravomyslova. "Who Helps the Degraded Housewife?: Comments on Vladimir Putin's Demographic Speech." *European Journal of Women's Studies* 14, no. 4 (2007): 349–57.

Roudakova, Natalia. *Losing Pravda: Ethics and the Press in Post-Truth Russia*. Cambridge: Cambridge University Press, 2017.

Rudina, Asia. "Gnev 'starorodok': Zhenshchin vozmutilo ukazanie rozhat' do 30." *Radio Svoboda*, June 8, 2020. https://www.svoboda.org/a/30657753.html.

Russell, Andrew, Elisa Sobo, and Mary Thompson, eds. *Contraception across Cultures: Technologies, Choices, Constraints*. Oxford: Berg, 2000.

"'Russkii Vzgliad'—Planirovanie sem'i." Foma.ru, January 1, 2008. http://foma.ru/russkiy-vzglyad-planirovanie-semi-html.

Sadvokasova, E. A. *Sotsial'no-gigienicheskie aspekty regulirovaniia razmerov sem'i*. Moscow: Meditsina, 1969.

Sakevich, Viktoria. "Abort ili planirovanie sem'i?" *Demoscope Weekly*, March 5, 2007. http://www.demoscope.ru/weekly/2007/0279/tema05.php.

———. "Novye ogranicheniia prava na abort v Rossii." *Demoscope Weekly*, February 20, 2012. http: //www.demoscope.ru/weekly/2012/0499/repr.

———. "Ot Aborta k kontratseptsii." *Demoscope Weekly*, May 23, 2016. http://www.demoscope.ru/weekly/2016/0687/demoscope687.pdf.

Sakevich, Viktoria, Boris Denisov, and Michele Rivkin-Fish. "Neposledovatel'naia politika v oblasti kontrolia rozhdaemosti i dinamika urovnia abortov v Rossii." *Journal of Social Policy Studies* 14, no. 4 (2016): 461–78.

Sakevich, Viktoria I., and Boris P. Denisov. "Birth Control in Russia: Overcoming the State System Resistance." *Basic Research Program Working Papers Series: Sociology WP BRP 42/SOC*. Moscow: National Research University Higher School of Economics, 2014.

Salmenniemi, Suvi, and Mariya Vorona. "Reading Self-Help Literature in Russia: Governmentality, Psychology and Subjectivity." *British Journal of Sociology* 65, no. 1 (2014): 43–62.

Savitskii, Nikolai. "Tvoia otvetstvennost': Kino." *Pravda* no. 95 (April 5, 1979): 6.

Schneider, Jane C., and Peter T. Schneider. *Festival of the Poor: Fertility Decline and the Ideology of Class*. Tucson: University of Arizona Press, 1996.

Seaman, Barbara. *The Doctor's Case against the Pill*. Garden City, NJ: Doubleday Books, 1969.

Sherwood-Fabre, Howard Goldberg, and Valentina Bodrova. "Impact of an Integrated Family Planning Program in Russia." *Evaluation Review* 26, no. 2 (2002): 190–212.

Shevchenko, Olga. *Crisis and the Everyday in Postsocialist Moscow*. Bloomington: Indiana University Press, 2009.

Shkel', Tamara. "Ubitoe detstvo." *Rossiiskaia gazeta*, June 3, 2011.

Shkolnikov, Vladimir, Martin McKee, and David Leon. "Changes in Life Expectancy in Russia in the Mid-1990s." *Lancet* 357, no. 9260 (2001): 917–21.

Shlapentokh, Vladimir. *Strakh i druzhba v nashem totalitarnom proshlom*. St. Petersburg: Zvezda, 2003.

Shneiderman, N. A., and Andrej A. Popov. "Mediko-Demograficheskoe izuchenie potrebnosti naseleniia v protivozachatochnykh sredstvakh." In *Mediko-Demograficheskie Issledovaniia (Sbornik nauchnykh rabot)*. Moscow: Moskovskii nauchno-issledovatel'skii institut epidemiologii i mikrobiologii im. G.N. Gabrichevskogo, Ministerstvo Zdravookhraneniia RSFSR, 1982.

Sholokhov, Mikhail. *Quiet Flows the Don*. Edited by Brian Murphy. Translated by Robert Daglish. New York: Carroll & Graf, 1996.

Shpakovskaya, Larisa. "How to Be a Good Mother: The Case of Middle Class Mothering in Russia." *Europe-Asia Studies* 67, no. 10 (2015): 1,571–86.

Shumilin, Vadim. "Russians Are Leaving the Volga: Change in Ethnic Balance Is an Extremely Painful Process." *Nezavisimaya gazeta* 52, no. 36 (September 5, 2000): 9,11. Translated and re-printed in *Current Digest of the Russian Press* 52, no. 36 (October 4, 2000): 13.

Siegl, Veronika. *Intimate Strangers: Commercial Surrogacy in Russia and Ukraine and the Making of Truth.* Ithaca, NY: Cornell University Press, 2023.

Sinel'nikov, A.B. "Sotsial'nyi i emotsional'no-psikhologicheskii aspekty i potrebnosti individa v sem'e i detiakh." In *Planirovanie sem'i i natsional'nye traditsii*, edited by A. I. Antonov, Sh. Kh. Kadyrov, and Giorgi Tsuladze, 47–51. Moscow: Institut Sotsiologii AN SSSR, 1988.

Sister Song; Women of Color Reproductive Justice Collective. "Reproductive Justice." Sister Song, accessed May 15, 2023. https://www.sistersong.net/reproductive-justice.

Snezhina, Anna. "'Eto khuzhe nasiliia': Kakie novye prepiatstviia zhdut zhenshchin, reshivshikh sdelat' abort." Novye izvestiia, January 26, 2024. Reprinted in *Demoscope Weekly*, February 13–6, 2024. https://www.demoscope.ru/weekly/2024/01019/gazeta04.php.

Snitow, Ann. "All Were Rebels: The Founding of the Network of East-West Women." *Dissent* 67, no. 1 (2020): 145–56. https://doi.org/10.1353/dss.2020.0019.

———. *The Feminism of Uncertainty: A Gender Diary.* Durham, NC: Duke University Press, 2015.

Sobotka, Tomáš. "The Stealthy Sexual Revolution? Birth Control, Reproduction, and Family under State Socialism in Central and Eastern Europe" In *Wenn die Chemie stimmt . . . Geschlechterbeziehungen und Geburtenplanung im Zeitalter der 'Pille'/ Gender Relations and Birth Control in the Age of the 'Pill'*, edited by Lutz Niethammer and Silke Satjukow, 121–50. Göttingen: Wallstein Verlag, 2016.

Sokolová Vera. "Planned Parenthood behind the Curtain: Population Policy and Sterilization of Romani Women in Communist Czechoslovakia, 1972–1989." *Anthropology of East Europe Review* 23, no. 1 (2015): 79–98.

Solinger, Rickie, and Mie Nakachi, eds. *Reproductive States: Global Perspectives on the Invention and Implementation of Population Policy.* Oxford: Oxford University Press, 2016.

Solomon, Susan Gross. "Social Hygiene and Soviet Public Health, 1921–1930." In Solomon and Hutchinson, *Health and Society in Revolutionary Russia*, 175–99.

———. "Social Hygiene in Soviet Medical Education, 1922–1930." *Journal of the History of Medicine and Allied Sciences*, no. 45 (1990): 607–43.

———. "The Demographic Argument in Soviet Debates over the Legalization of Abortion in the 1920s." *Cahiers du Monde Russe et Soviétique* 33, no. 1 (1992): 59–82.

Solomon, Susan Gross, and John Hutchinson, eds. Introduction to *Health and Society in Revolutionary Russia.* Bloomington: Indiana University Press, 1990.

Sopronenko, Igor, dir. *Feminism: Twenty Years Forward* (film). Written and produced by Beth Holmgren. Durham, NC: Duke University, Signature Media Production, 2009.

Sperling, Valerie. *Organizing Women in Contemporary Russia: Engendering Transition.* New York: Cambridge University Press, 1999.

———. *Sex, Politics and Putin: Political Legitimacy in Russia.* Oxford: Oxford University Press, 2014.

Starks, Tricia. *The Body Soviet: Propaganda, Hygiene, and the Revolutionary State.* Madison: University of Wisconsin Press, 2008.

Starobinets, Anna. *Posmotri na nego.* Moscow: ACT—Corpus, 2017

Stawkowski, Magdalena. "'I Am a Radioactive Mutant': Emergent Biological Subjectivities at Kazakhstan's Semipalatinsk Nuclear Test Site." *American Ethnologist* 43, no. 1 (2016): 144–57.

Stepanov, L. G. "Organizatsionnye voprosy problem kontraktseptsii." *Akusherstvo i ginekologiia* 35, no. 6 (1959): 6.

Stoliarenko, Liudmila. "Roddoma Rossii vypolniaiut plan!" *Novaia gazeta*, November 2000, 23–26.

Sunder Rajan, Kaushik. *Pharmocracy: Value, Politics, and Knowledge in Global Biomedicine*. Durham, NC: Duke University Press, 2017.

Sutcliffe, Benjamin M. *Prose of Life: Russian Women Writers from Khrushchev to Putin*. Madison: University of Wisconsin Press, 2009.

Szacki, Jerry. *Liberalism after Communism*. Budapest: Central European University Press, 1995.

Tayler, Jeffrey. "What Pussy Riot's 'Punk Prayer' Really Said." *The Atlantic*, November 8, 2012.

Teitelbaum, Michael, and Jay Winter. *A Question of Numbers: High Migration, Low Fertility and the Politics of National Identity*. New York: Hill and Wang, 1998.

Temkina, Anna. "Childbearing and Work-Family Balance among Contemporary Russian Women." *Finnish Yearbook of Population Research*, no. 45 (2010): 83–101.

———. "'Childbirth Is Not a Car Rental': Mothers and Obstetricians Negotiating Customer Service in Russian Commercial Maternity Care." *Critical Public Health* 30, no. 5 (2020): 521–32.

———. "The Gynaecologist's Gaze: The Inconsistent Medicalisation of Contraception in Contemporary Russia." *Europe-Asia Studies* 67, no. 10 (2015): 1,527–46.

Temkina, Anna, and Michele Rivkin-Fish. "Creating Health Care Consumers: The Negotiation of Un/Official Payments, Power and Trust in Russian Maternity Care." *Social Theory and Health* 18, no. 1 (2019): 340–57.

Temkina, Anna, and Elena Zdravomyslova. "Gender's Crooked Path: Feminism Confronts Russian Patriarchy." *Current Sociology* 62, no. 2 (January 7, 2014): 253–70.

———. "The Sexual Scripts and Identity of Middle-Class Russian Women." *Sexuality and Culture* 19, no. 2 (2015): 297–320.

Thomas, Lyn [*sic*]. "Privetstvie mezhdunarodnoi federatsii planirovaniia sem'i (IPPF)." *Zhurnal planirovaniia sem'i* 1 (1993): 2–3.

Thompson, E. P. "The Moral Economy of the English Crowd in the Eighteenth Century." *Past & Present* 50 (1971): 76–136.

Timashova, Natal'ia. "Mediki vvodiat ogranicheniia na pozdnie aborty v nadezhde povysit' rozhdaemost'." *Novye izvestiia*, August 19, 2003, 123–24. Reprinted in *Demoscope Weekly*, Aug. 25–Sept. 7, 2003. http://www.demoscope.ru/weekly/2003/0123/gazeta01.php.

Tol'ts, M. S. "Kharakteristika nekotorykh komponentov rozhdaemosti v bol'shom gorode." In *Demograficheskii analiz rozhdaemosti*, edited by D. I. Valentei, 45–55. Moscow: Statistika, 1974.

Turbine, Vikki. "Locating Women's Human Rights in Post-Soviet Provincial Russia." *Europe-Asia Studies* 64, no. 10 (2012): 1,847–69.

———. "Russian Women's Perceptions of Human Rights and Rights-Based Approaches in Everyday Life." In *Gender, Equality and Difference during and after State Socialism*, edited by R. Kay, 167–87. Basingstoke: Palgrave Macmillan, 2007.

Turbine, Vikki, and Kathleen Riach. "The Right to Choose or Choosing What's Right?: Women's Conceptualisations of Work and Life Choices in Contemporary Russia." *Gender, Work and Organization* 19, no. 2 (2012): 165–87.

Ulitskaya, Ludmila. *Kazus Kukotskogo*. Moscow: Eskmo, 2006.

———. *The Kukotsky Enigma*. Translated by Diane Nemec Ignashev. Evanston, IL: Northwestern University Press, 2016.

———. "The Orlov-Sokolovs." Translated by Arch Tait. *New Yorker*, April 18, 2005, 174–80, 184.

Urlanis, B. T. *Problemy Dinamiki Naseleniia SSSR*. Moscow: Nauka, 1974.

Utrata, Jennifer. *Women without Men: Single Mothers and Family Change in the New Russia*. Ithaca, NY: Cornell University Press, 2015.

Vail', Petr, and Aleksandr Genis. *60-ye: Mir sovetskogo cheloveka*. Ann Arbor: Ardis, 1988.

Vald'shtein, Maksim. "O liberal'nom meinstrime' i kul'turnom konservatizme." *Ab Imperio* 1 (2013): 141–58.

Valentei, D., and G. Kiseleva. "Vzroslie i deti." *Literaturnaia gazeta*, March 17, 1971.

Varley, Emma. "Islamic Logics, Reproductive Rationalities: Family Planning in Northern Pakistan." *Anthropology and Medicine* 19, no. 2 (2012): 189–206.

Varsa, Eszter. "'Respect Girls as Future Mothers': Sex Education as Family Life Education in State Socialist Hungary, 1950s–1980s." In *Children by Choice?: Changing Values, Reproduction, and Family Planning in the 20th Century*, edited by Ann-Katrin Gembries, Theresia Theuke, and Isabel Heinemann, 77–98. Oldenbourg: De Gruyter, 2018.

Varsa, Eszter, and Dorottya Szikra. "'New Eugenics,' Gender and Sexuality: A Global Perspective on Reproductive Politics and Sex Education in Cold War Europe." *History of the Family* 25, no. 4 (2020): 527–49. https://doi.org/10.1080/1081602X.2020.1807385.

Vasilenko, Svetlana. *Shamara and Other Stories*. Translated by Helena Goscilo. Evanston, IL: Northwestern University Press, 2000.

Vasilyev, P. A., O. I. Zvonareva, and N. A. Petrenko. "Clinical Trials of Rhodiola Rosea in Tomsk in the Late Soviet Period: Vestnik of Saint Petersburg University." *History* 65, no. 3 (2020): 814–25.

Verbenko, A. A., S. E. Il'in, V. N. Chusova, and T. N. Al'shevskaia. *Aborty i protivozachatochnye sredstva*. Moscow: Meditsina, 1968.

———. "Effektivnost' protivozachatochnykh sredstv i metodika ee rascheta," *Akusherstvo i ginekologiia*, no. 3 (May–June 1965), 40–45.

Verdery, Katherine. *What Was Socialism, and What Comes Next?* Princeton, NJ: Princeton University Press, 1996.

Vishnevsky, A. G. "Byli li 90-e demograficheskoi katastrofoi dlia Rossii?" The Question. Ru, Reprinted in *Demoscope Weekly*, October 5–18, 2015. http://www.demoscope.ru/weekly/2015/0657/gazeta06.php

———. "Demografiia stalinskoi epokhi," *Demoscope Weekly*, March 3–16, 2003. http://www.demoscope.ru/weekly/2003/0103/tema02.php.

———. "Demograficheskaia revoliutsiia." *Voprosy filosofii* 2 (1973): 53–64.

———. "Demograficheskie protsessy v SSSR." *Voprosy filosofii* 9 (1973): 115–27.

———. "Ideologizirovannaia demografiia." *Vestnik akademii Nauk SSSR* 10 (1991): 3–18.

———. "Konservativnaia revoliutsiia v SSSR." *Mir Rossii* 5, no. 4 (1996): 3–66.

———. "Russkii krest." *Novye izvestiia*, February 1998.

_____. *Serp i rubl': Konservativnaia modernizatsiia v SSSR*. Moscow: OGI, 1998.

———. "The Demographic Situation." *Studies on Russian Economic Development* 6, no. 1 (1995): 35–45.

Vishnevsky, A. G., ed. *Demograficheskaia modernizatsiia Rossii: 1900–2000*. Moscow: Novoe izdatel'stvo, 2006.

Vishnevsky, A. G., Boris Denisov, and Viktoria Sakevich. "The Contraceptive Revolution in Russia." *Demograficheskoe obozrenie* 4, no. 5 (2017): 86–108.

———. "Zapret aborta: Osvezhite vashu pamiat." *Demoscope Weekly*, Nov. 28–Dec. 11, 2016. http://www.demoscope.ru/weekly/2016/0707/demoscope707.pdf.

Vishnevsky, A. G., and Sergei Golod. "Krylatyi eros vchera." *Komsomol'skaia pravda* (1976). Reprinted in *Demoscope Weekly*, February 21, 2013, http://www.demoscope.ru/weekly/2013/0539/old_gazeta01. php.

Vishnevsky, A. G., and Sergei V. Zakharov. "Demograficheskie trevogi Rossii." *Vestnik akademii nauk SSR* 8 (1990): 16–33.

Volgina, V. F. "Sotsial'no-gigienicheskaia kharakteristika zhenshchin, prervavshikh vpervye nastupivshuiu beremennost'." In *Aktual'nye voprosy okhrany zdorov'ia zhenshchiny, materi i novorozhdennogo*, 12–13. Alma-Ata: Alma-Atinskii gosudarstvennyi meditsinskii institute, 1984.

Volkov, Andrei Gavrilovich. *Sem'ia —ob"ekt demografii*. Moscow: Mysl', 1986.

Voznesenskaya, Julia. *The Women's Decameron*. Translated by W. B. Linton. New York: Atlantic Monthly Press, 1985.

Wallace, Daniel L. "Father Aleksandr Men' and the Struggle to Recover Russia's Heritage." *Demokratizatsiya* 17, no. 1 (2009): 73–91.

Watson, Peggy. "Civil Society and the Politics of Difference in Eastern Europe." In *Transitions, Environments, Translations: Feminisms in International Politics*, edited by Joan W. Scott, Cora Kaplan, and Debra Keates, 21–29. New York: Routledge, 1997.

———. "Explaining Rising Mortality among Men in Eastern Europe." *Social Science and Medicine* 41, no. 7 (1995): 923–34.

Weir, Fred. "Is Russia's Intervention in Syria a 'Holy War'?: Russian Orthodox Church 'Yes.'" *Christian Science Monitor*, November 23, 2015. https://csmonitor.com/World/ Europe/2015/1123/Is-Russia-s-intervention-in-Syria-a-holy-war-Russian-Orthodox-Church-yes.

West, Robin. "From Choice to Reproductive Justice: De-Constitutionalizing Abortion Rights." In *Search of Common Ground on Abortion : From Culture War to Reproductive Justice*, edited by Robin West, Justin Murray, Meredith Esser and Martha Fineman, 19–51. Burlington, VT: Ashgate, 2014.

Westoff, Charles F., and Norman B. Ryder. *The Contraceptive Revolution*. Princeton, NJ: Princeton University Press, 1977.

Wiedlack, Katharina, Saltanat Shoshanova, Masha Godovannaya, eds. *Queer-Feminist Solidarity and the East-West Divide*. New York: Peter Lang, 2020.

Woodard, Roger D. "Juventas." In *The Encyclopedia of Ancient History*. Edited by Roger S. Bagnall, Kai Brodersen, Craige B. Champion, Andrew Erskine, and Sabine R. Huebner, 3671. Oxford, UK: Blackwell Publishing, 2013.

Yurchak, Alexei. *Everything Was Forever, until It Was No More: The Last Soviet Generation*. Princeton, NJ: Princeton University Press, 2006.

———. "Soviet Hegemony of Form: Everything Was Forever, until It Was No More." *Comparative Studies in Society and History* 45, no. 3 (2003): 480–510.

Yurtaev, Alexey. "Inside the Fight over Russia's Domestic Violence Law." *OpenDemocracy*, February 17, 2020. https://www.opendemocracy.net/en/odr/russia-domestic-violence-law.

Zakharov, Sergei V. "Fertility, Nuptiality, and Family Planning in Russia: Problems and Prospects." In *Population under Duress: The Geodemography of Post-Soviet Russia*, edited by George J. Demko, Grigory Ioffe, and Zhanna Zayonchkovskaya, 41–57. Boulder, CO: Westview Press, 1999.

———. "Rozhdaemost' v Rossii: Pervyi i vtoroi demograficheskii perekhod." *Demoscope Weekly*, May 7, 2010. http://www.demoscope.ru/weekly/knigi/konfer/konfer_08.html.

_____. "Russian Federation: From the First to the Second Demographic Transition." *Demographic Research* 19 (2008): 907–72. DOI: 10.4054/DemRes.2008.19.24

_____. "Vozrastnaia model' braka v Rossii." *Otechestvennye zapiski* 4 (2006): 271–300.

Zakharov, Sergei V., ed. "Naselenie Rossii 2014. Dvadtsat' tretii ezhegodnyi demograficheskii doklad." Moscow: Izdatelskii dom Vysshei shkoly ekonomiki, 2016.

———. "Naselenie Rossii 2015. Dvadtsat' tretii ezhegodnyi demograficheskii doklad." Moscow: Izdatelskii dom Vysshei shkoly ekonomiki, 2017.

———. "Naselenie Rossii 2018: Dvadtsat' shestoi ezhegodnyi demografisheskii doklad." Moscow: Izdatelskii dom Vysshei shkoly ekonomiki, 2020.

Zakharov, Sergei V., and Elena I. Ivanova. "Fertility Decline and Recent Changes in Russia: On the Threshold of the Second Demographic Transition." In *Russia's Demographic "Crisis,"* edited by Julie DaVanzo, 36–82. Santa Monica: RAND, 1996.

———. "Regional Fertility Differentiation in Russia: 1959–199." *Studies on Russian Economic Development* 7 (1995): 354–68.

Zakharov, S. V., and V. I. Sakevich. "Osobennosti planirovaniia sem'i i rozhdaemost' v Rossii: kontratseptivnaia revoliutsiia—svershivshiisia fakt?" In *Roditeli i deti, muzhchiny i zhenshchiny v sem'e i obshchestve*, vol. 1, edited by T. M. Maleva and O. V. Siniavskaia. Moscow: Independent Institute for Social Politics, 2007.

———. "Rozhdaemost' i planirovanie sem'i." In *Naselenie Rossii 2015*, edited by S. V. Zakharov, 169–70. Moscow: Higher School of Economics, 2017.

Zavisca, Jane R. *Housing the New Russia.* Ithaca, NY: Cornell University Press, 2012.

Zdravomyslova, Elena. "Gendernoe grazhdanstvo i abortnaia kul'tura." In *Zdorov'e i doverie: Gendernyi podkhod k reproduktivnoi meditsine*, edited by Elena Zdravomyslova and Anna Temkina, 108–35. St. Petersburg: European University of St. Petersburg Press, 2009.

———. "Hypocritical Sexuality of the Late Soviet Period: Sexual Knowledge and Sexual Ignorance." In *Education and Civic Culture in Post-Communist Countries*, edited by S. Webber and I. Liikanen. London: Palgrave, 2001.

Zdravomyslova, Elena, and Anna Temkina, eds. *V poiskakh seksual'nosti: Sbornik statei.* St. Petersburg: Dmitrii Bulanin, 2002.

Zdravomyslova, Elena, and Anna Temkina. "The Crisis of Masculinity in Late Soviet Discourse." *Russian Studies in History* 51, no. 2 (2012): 13–34.

Zhivov, Viktor. "Chto delat' s Fuko, zanimaias' Russkoi istoriei?" *Novoe literaturnoe obozrenie* 3 (2001): 85–87.

Zhukova, Alena. "Spetsial'nyi vypusk 'MG': Kaliningradskaia oblast'. Sem'iu planirovat' mozhno i nuzhno." *Meditsinskaia Gazeta*, July 29, 2005. http://dlib.eastview.com/sourses/article.jsp?id+8054177

Zhurzhenko, Tatiana. *Sotsial'noe vosproizvodstvo i gendernaia politika v Ukraine.* Kharkiv: Folio, 2001.

Zigon, Jarrett. *"HIV Is God's Blessing": Rehabilitating Morality in Neoliberal Russia.* Berkeley: University of California Press, 2010.

Zlatko, N., E. King, E. Mossialos. "HIV in the Russian Federation: Mortality, Prevalence, Risk Factors, and Current Understanding of Sexual Transmission." *AIDS* 37, no. 4 (2023): 637–45.

Zolotov, Andrei, Jr. "Defending the Unborn." *Moscow Times*, July 10, 1999. https://www.themoscowtimes.com/archive/defending-the-unborn.

Zubok, Vladislav. "Technologies of Bringing a 'True' Freedom to One-Sixth of the World: On Soviet Modernity, Progressivism, and Beyond (Discussing Mark Lipovetsky's 'The Poetics of ITR Discourse')." *Ab Imperio*, no. 1 (2013).

———. *Zhivago's Children: The Last Russian Intelligentsia.* Cambridge, MA: Belknap Press of Harvard University, 2011.

Zhukhov, Boris. "Neizbezhnost'. Men'she narodu—bol'she kislorodu." *Itogi*, March 16, 1999, N11. https://dlib.eastview.com/browse/doc/3030918.

Zueva, Valentina. "Kruglyi stol: Razgovor na delikatnuiu temu." *Meditsinskaia gazeta*, October 28, 2005.

INDEX

Page numbers in *italics* refer to figures; page numbers in **bold** refer to tables

www.ingramcontent.com/pod-product-compliance
Lightning Source LLC
Chambersburg PA
CBHW021118270326
41929CB00009B/936